THE INSIDERS' GUIDE TO

North Carolina's OUTER BANKS

THE INSIDERS' GUIDE TO

North Carolina's OUTER BANKS

by
Dave Poyer
and
Mary Marcoux

Insiders' Guides, Inc.

Published and Distributed by:
The Insiders' Guides, Inc.
P.O. Box 2057 • Highway 64
Manteo, NC 27954
(919) 473-6100

🍂

THIRTEENTH EDITION
1st printing

🍂

Copyright ©1992
by David Poyer and
The Insiders' Guides, Inc.

🍂

Printed in the United States of
America

🍂

🍂

ISBN 0-912367-33-4

The Insiders' Guides, Inc.

Publisher/Managing Editor
Beth P Storie

President/General Manager
Michael McOwen

Manager/Creative Services
David Haynes

Advertising Sales Manager
Georgia Beach

Manager/Distribution
Giles Bissonnette

Fulfillment Coordination
Gina Twiford

Controller
Claudette Forney

Preface

*T*his year The Insiders' Guide to the Outer Banks continues its long tradition of bringing to the reader an extensive history of the barrier islands, thoughtful commentaries and interviews. In addition there are updated descriptions of the attractions, restaurants, accommodations and opportunities for recreation and shopping. The Insiders' Guide includes important information on medical services, camping, real estate and vacation rentals, annual events, places of worship, fishing and ferry schedules.

There are maps to assist the reader in a visual journey to the many towns and villages, from north to south, of the Outer Banks. There are references to National Park Service and Outer Banks' visitor centers. The ongoing interpretive exhibits and programs offered at these locations will further enhance your journey to the Outer Banks. Bring your binoculars, your camera and your adventurous enthusiasm to explore the island habitats.

Whether you're an arm-chair traveler or on location, the Insiders' Guide will serve as a handy reference for all aspects of life on the Outer Banks. For many years the wide, desolate beaches were in themselves an adventure. Even as growth continues, from the off-road areas north of Corolla to the rustic island village of Ocracoke, ways of exploring the Banks

are brought to your attention in this Guide. There's no doubt you'll uncover some interesting places and facts on a trip of your own, as we've done each time we explore the beaches and villages. You'll meet up with warm, friendly people (more than the usual number of descendants of islanders of long ago), and an environment beyond the ordinary.

If you're looking for big fish or to try your wings in flight -- in the air or across wind-swept waters -- you'll find exciting adventures. If you're looking for peace and quiet on the beach or a chance to explore history -- welcome to the Outer Banks.

This thirteenth edition of the Insiders' Guide to the Outer Banks reflects the sights, sounds and feelings of this year's new writer, Mary Marcoux; and the interviews, historical narratives and other words of wisdom written by the well-established writer, Dave Poyer, whose idea was the beginning of this book in 1979. His novels and stories of life on the Outer Banks are listed in the back. And, we're delighted to say that some are being adapted for the screen.

The success of a serious guidebook is measured not by its first reception, but by its service, dependability and acceptance by the travelling public over a period of years. Since we will see over 160,000 books in print with this edition, we feel justifiably proud that our readers continue to find this book helpful, and obviously encourage others to use it, too.

From the beginning, we designed the book not to sit on a shelf, or in a glove compartment, but to be used, steadily, every day and often every hour. We designed it for the visitor and resident alike. Even a glance will show you the time and effort that have gone into it.

Some people down the years have told us we didn't need to be so thorough. We could reprint press releases instead of doing our own research, or update less often. That we didn't have to improve and expand every year.

We didn't agree. We have an old-fashioned mind set: that painstaking research and careful writing, that solid value rather than glossy paper and bathing beauties would pay off in repeat sales. And time has proven us right.

Not that we, as authors, deserve too much credit. We have to thank our publisher for riding herd on our enthusiasms, or prodding us where necessary; to Banks residents, who are the first to inform us when we've fallen short; and to our readers, who have never failed to write when they don't find in our pages what they needed to know. Thanks to you all!

The Banks have changed immensely since our first edition. Miles of open beach have become populated areas; empty dunes, shopping centers; the islands themselves have moved noticeably before the sea. The north-

ern Banks have been opened to widespread settlement. Ocracoke has condominiums and is well on its way to popularity rather than seclusion. Avon is booming, and the Buxton area is being heavily marketed. The central Banks, Nags Head, Kitty Hawk, and Kill Devil Hills, are as busy as they've ever been, with new shops, restaurants and cottages appearing regularly. And Manteo continues its face lift downtown, with power lines going underground and roads being resurfaced, and continuing its growth as a service area to the beach.

But some things haven't changed. The Outer Banks is still a vacationer's paradise. It's still home for the old residents and hundreds of new ones. It's still a daughter of the sea, tumultuous with storm in February and placid and glittering in July. It's still dunes and wild ponies, sea oats and yaupon. It's still raucous amusement at Dowdy's and quieter times touring the Elizabethan Gardens. We have had many happy times here, and hope you will too.

Thank you for your support over the years. We've done everything we can to make your time on the Banks a happy time. That was our goal from the beginning. We promise you it will continue to be, for years to come.

Dave and Mary

About the Authors

Dave Poyer is a novelist, naval Reserve officer, diver and sailor. His contributions to this book represent thousands of hours and thousands of miles over seventeen years of researching and appreciating the Outer Banks and their people.

Along with his work on this book, almost two million copies of his novels are in print. Poyer has published *White Continent, The Shiloh Project, Star Seed, The Return of Philo T. McGiffin, The Dead of Winter, Stepfather Bank* and *The Med. The Gulf* was a bestseller in 1990 and 1991, and his newest, *The Circle*, published in June, 1992, has already reached that status. He writes the Tiller Galloway series of novels, set in the Banks, including *Hatteras Blue* (1989) and *Bahamas Blue* (1991). *The Return of Philo T. McGiffin* will soon be a major motion picture from Universal Studios, and Columbia Pictures will soon begin work on two movies based on *Hatteras Blue* and *Bahamas Blue*.

Dave and his wife, Lenore Hart, also a published author, recently became parents of Naia Elizabeth, a collaborative effort of which they both are proud.

Mary Marcoux is a native of Winston-Salem and lived in Chapel Hill and Charlotte before moving to suburban Maryland. For 28 years she first raised a family of five sons, then embarked on another career in the business world. As a travel agent, she traveled to the northwestern US, Alaska and to countries of central Europe before joining a Bethesda-based real estate developer in the late 1970s. Realizing a long time dream to live at the beach, she "discovered" the Outer Banks in 1987 and moved to Southern Shores in 1988.

She is a freelance journalist and writer of numerous articles for Outer Banks' newspapers. She has edited a Hatteras monthly tabloid, taught creative writing and is a member of the Dare County Arts Council Writers' Group. Her interests in people, lifestyles and social issues reflect an intense desire for personal change and concern for the way people live in the world.

During the past four years her discovery of the many communities that make up the Outer Banks is reflected with freshness as she writes about the geography, the communities and their shops, restaurants and accommodations from Corolla to Ocracoke.

Table of Contents

Photography in this issue of the Insiders' Guide was supplied by:
Phil Ruckle; Michael Halminski; J. Foster Scott; The National Geographic
Society; The National Park Service; D. Westner; The Dare County Tourist
Bureau; and The Lost Colony.
Line drawings courtesy of Jerry Miller, Raleigh, NC.

Photo: DCTB

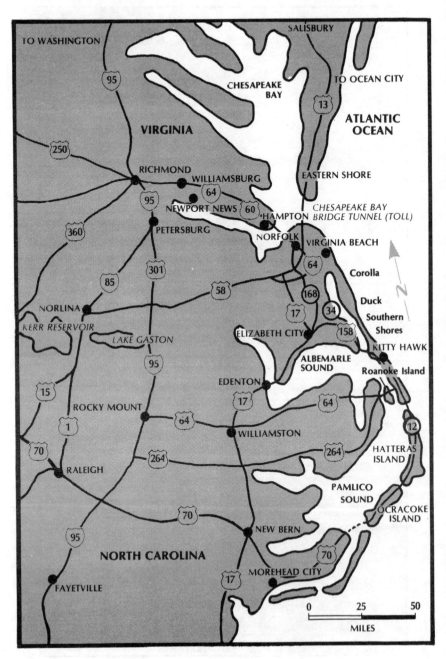

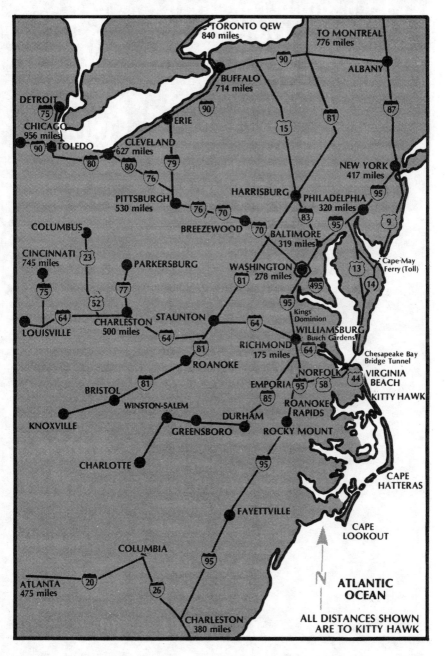

ALL DISTANCES SHOWN
ARE TO KITTY HAWK

Inside
The Outer Banks

*A*lthough it is well known through recounting the lives of the Native Americans and the early English colonists in plays, books and historical sites, the geological interpretation of these islands warrants some reflection from earlier times.

"Barrier island" is the term used to describe a land form made up entirely of sand and without the keel of rock that normally anchors most islands to the earth. This fascinating phenomenon of a constantly changing land form is not so difficult to understand once it is realized that such a land mass is subjected to the process of change by the wind and the sea.

The level of the ocean has changed as a result of water released or stored in great polar icecaps. When, during the ice ages, great amounts of water are not circulated, the consequence of a lowering sea and extended sandy coastline are illustrated in these island lands. As the last great ice age ended, approximately 20,000 years ago, the seas began to fill. Slowly, the sea has risen some 400 feet. North Carolina's Outer Banks, authorities agree, were formed in this process. The Banks were a mixture of maritime forests and sparsely vegetated sand

dunes. Perhaps, silt from inland rivers contributed to the build up of sand as well as the wash of the ocean. Shifting sandbars, raging winds and lofty breezes somewhat artistically formed high and low areas of land separated by water. Thus the string of islands.

In times of wild, wind-driven storms, sections or small islands were over-washed by the oceans. This created what we refer to as sounds. Differing from bays, the waters of the sound are trapped waters, not essentially bodies of water created by rivers emptying into them, which correctly describes the Chesapeake Bay, for example. Sounds in this eastern region of North Carolina -- Roanoke, Currituck, Pamlico and Albemarle sounds -- were formed by such an over-wash of land mass. Some areas became completely covered by water, thus creating inlets where sand again accumulates and often closes an inlet to navigation. These islands today are separated by inlets and sounds, and in more recent times the waters have been spanned by bridges or connected by ferry service.

Prior to recent times, however, ships at sea were subjected to shifting sand and the variations of the North

American Continental Shelf. More than 500 shipwrecks attest to the difficulty of navigation around these shores. Once a ship navigated the coast, inlets or sounds and arrived in an open harbor, there were no assurances that the same passage would be open on recurring journeys to these barrier islands. The history of Sir Walter Raleigh's arrival on these shores from England is filled with agonizing tales of hardship in sea-faring exploits, as well as those about establishing land settlements. Since his journey, others have documented the perils of the sea in search of safe harbor.

The change in the shorelines and land masses of the Outer Banks has occurred over hundreds of years, so don't cancel your reservations yet. It will be thousands of years before these barrier islands rejoin the North Carolina mainland. But it's fascinating to understand how dynamic, moving, living these Banks are.

Today we observe this string of barrier islands, measuring from about 7-12 feet above sea level and stretching from a few hundred feet to several miles across, in a fascinating shift or movement. For example, as you cross Oregon Inlet, your drive on the Herbert Bonner Bridge will expose a view across an expanse of low, flat land under the northern piers of the bridge. A marshland area of numerous waterfowl and wildlife, it was not there when the bridge was built in 1964. This indicates the islands are moving south since sand and vegetation are accumulating here.

Oyster and water-snail shells found on the beach in the areas of Nags Head, Coquina Beach or on Hatteras Island and some large chunks of peat formed in freshwater bogs are indications of how the sand-islands have changed. These shells have been washed from interior regions or shellfish beds towards the ocean, perhaps

during high winds from the west which push water in an easterly flow. Ancient tree stumps protruding from the ocean at various places along the Outer Banks reveal the existence of maritime forests along the once-extended coastline. The islands are moving west.

The movement occurs slowly and for those who inhabited the islands years ago, the history of Kinnakeet on Hatteras Island reveals large forested areas and wild grapes which grew in abundance. Ships left for points north loaded with lumber from large oak trees which grew in these forests. In more recent times, the Outer Banks terrain exposes wide expanses of open, flat beach with some maritime forests farther inland on the west side of the islands.

Bridges and roads have been built and subsequently maintained at great costs to keep the islands connected. During the fall storms of 1990, a section of the Bonner Bridge was knocked out by a major storm which drove a barge into the pilings. Prior to this, constant wind-blown sand created the necessity of building a portion of the highway farther to the west on a narrow stretch of Hatteras Island in Rodanthe.

During the Halloween Storms of 1991, portions of the National Sea-shore highway south of the Bonner Bridge experienced ocean over-wash. Huge sandbags are being used to build a "wall" against the surge of the ocean. During storms or exceptionally high, full-moon tides, water continues to wash over the road. Salt water intrusion into the marshlands poses a threat to waterfowl and wildlife. The water tables or aquifer providing drinking water are threatened by salt-water intrusion, which in turn threatens the habitability of the land. While we are focusing on a very small area of the Outer Banks by comparison, this natural occurrence of ocean over-wash is of some concern.

However, the events or results of storms have been separated by time in such a manner that continuing development of the Outer Banks has been possible. The wildlife existing on the islands is abundant and in some areas even increasing. The soundside of the Outer Banks is home to thousands of birds, deer, fox and rabbits. The oceanside habitat reveals a large variety of marine animals, such as ghost crabs, clams and skates. The present-day Outer Banks offers extraordinary adventure and exploration.

It was the same to explorers over 400 years ago. To go back in history, it is possible that Italian

Insiders like:
Crabbing in the Sound with their families.

Insiders' Tip

Giovanni Verrazano sailed and mapped these coasts as early as 1524. Others may have learned to use Cape Hatteras as a navigable area or a shortcut from the West Indies back to Spain.

If these lands were discovered in sea-faring days of Spanish and Italian explorers, it wasn't until English seamen, determined to establish colonies on the new land, discovered and settled on the islands off the coast of North America and later the area that was to become the coast of North Carolina. The first recorded community was on Roanoke Island, near the current site of Fort Raleigh National Historic Site. This community failed, but the English kept trying, and a few years later John Smith succeeded at Jamestown where John White had failed on Roanoke Island.

In many ways, residents of the Banks still look north to Virginia as their homes. This may reflect their ancestry, for the Banks were permanently settled by second-generation English who trickled down from Jamestown, Williamsburg and Norfolk, leavened by fugitives from the King's justice and shipwrecked mariners. These early settlers were the direct ancestors of today's numerous Midgetts, Austins, Baums, Grays, Ethridges, Burruses, Tilletts, Manns, Twifords and other old and famous families of the Banks. They settled at the islands' widest points -- Kitty Hawk, parts of Hatteras and Ocracoke, as well as Roanoke and Colington Islands -- where forests offered shel-

ter and the land mass provided the opportunity to raise cattle and crops to sustain life. It was not an easy existence, but it was a free one, and doubtless healthier than the cramped and plague-haunted cities of Olde England.

There was one part of the Banks that did flourish in those early days, and that was Ocracoke. The inlet, deeper then, was an important place of entry for oceangoing vessels. But Ocracoke was also attractive to another sort of seagoing entrepreneur: the pirate, especially the infamous "Blackbeard." The story of Captain Edward Teach's (as was his real name) "war" with the law-abiding citizens of these shores is told in the Ocracoke Island section of this book.

Another war, this one the War between the States, left its mark along the Outer Banks with battles at Hatteras Inlet (August, 1861), Chicamacomico (October, 1861) and Roanoke Island (February, 1862). The Federalists won victories in early skirmishes and established control of an area which geographically would seem to have been influenced by "southern causes." At that time, however, the inhabitants were not strongly attached to that point of view as few owned slaves. Many took an oath of allegiance to the United States.

As if to reward them, the post-war era saw a steady flow of Federal dollars to the Banks, and they were spared Reconstruction. Navigational improvements had become unavoidable, and three fine lighthouses, at

Photo: Michael Halminski

Once a threatened species, the brown pelican has made a tremendous comeback and is a frequent sight on the Outer Banks.

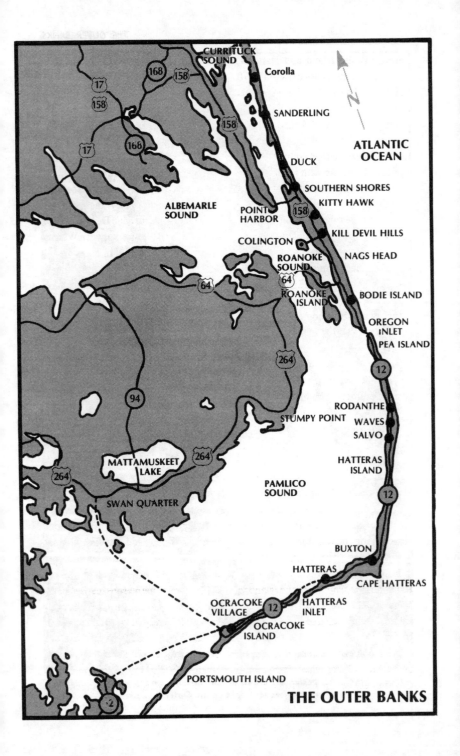

Corolla, Bodie Island and Hatteras, were built in the years between 1870 and 1875. The U.S. Lifesaving Service -- the forerunner to the Coast Guard -- was also established and lifesaving stations were built along the Banks. These stations and the service provided residents with jobs, and the accompanying cash that employment brought.

Changes were taking place in the Banks' internal economy as well. Nags Head was becoming the area's first and finest summer resort. Commercial fishing and wildfowl hunting were replacing wrecking and whale oil as sources of income.

The twentieth century, destined finally to end the fabled isolation of these low, remote islands, began with a symbolic event: the arrival of the Wright brothers. The history of their failures and their final success is probably the best-known story of the Outer Banks, though the Lost Colony must run a close second.

The boom years began in 1930-31. The rest of the country was in a depression, true, but these years marked the completion of the first road accesses to the 'beach,' the Wright Memorial Bridge across Currituck Sound to Kitty Hawk and the Washington Baum Bridge from Roanoke Island to Nags Head. Paved roads down the islands followed, and development began.

Another milestone was passed in the late 1930s, when the Federal Government set up six camps for its Civilian Conservation Corps and millions of dollars were spent erecting sand fences and planting vegetation along 115 miles of shoreline -- all designed to "save" the Outer Banks. Manmade dunes as high as 14 feet in many areas were built. The Cape Hatteras National Seashore was officially established in 1953. The major section of land controlled by the National Park Service arm of the Department of the Interior is the area between Whalebone Junction (at South Nags Head) and Ocracoke Inlet. There are villages established in exempted portions, such as Waves, Rodanthe, Salvo, Avon, Buxton, Frisco, Hatteras Village and Ocracoke Village. Fort Raleigh on Roanoke Island and the Wright Memorial in Kill Devil Hills are also maintained by the National Park Service.

Surprising to more recent residents and visitors, many World War II confrontations at sea took place on the coastline of North Carolina. In 1942, Hitler's U-boats struck at American merchant ships. A look at a National Geographic map of shipwrecks and battles reveals a number of these confrontations. In fact, the first U-Boat sunk by Americans lies a few miles off the beach of Bodie Island.

One of the reasons that the northern beach communities were not developed as early as those farther south in the Nags Head area is the close proximity to the military bases in Norfolk, Virginia. Lifelong residents of the tiny village of Duck recall the days when bombing tests were conducted along the shores north of the village.

The permanent population of the area has grown from approximately 7,000 in 1970 to approximately 25,000 today. Many derive their income from businesses which provide services to visitors. Commercial fishing is alive in the villages of Hatteras, Wanchese and Colington. Real estate has provided employment opportunities for many since the early 1980s.

As more people discover the unpolluted environment and the more casual lifestyle (in spite of certain hardships which come with island living), communities have grown and the permanent residents are called on to support adequate services, schools, medical facilities, churches and other community needs. Mayors, planners, civic groups and others are giving careful attention to growth. There is a need for better access and egress to the communities and resorts of the Outer Banks. Roads are being widened and bridges are planned. A new two-lane bridge will be built parallel to the present Wright Memorial Bridge which connects Point Harbor, NC (on the mainland) with Kitty Hawk and other villages of the Outer Banks. Another bridge connecting the mainland to the northern beaches of the Outer Banks has been widely supported recently. Termed "The Bridge," it will connect Currituck County with its own Outer Banks beach community, Corolla. Local government officials have been working with a lobbying group to request federal funding for this span. If successful, the northern Outer Banks could see a new bridge early in the next century.

Regardless of the changes taking place, the way of life is extraordinary in many ways. The residents know they're onto something precious: a land of beginnings not to be taken lightly. All its treasures -- the waters, maritime forests, beaches and small, quaint towns -- are worth exploring, whether as a one-time visitor or as a lifelong lover of the Outer Banks.

Photo: D. Westner

The Light Keeper's house at Currituck Beach Lighthouse casts interesting shadows with its turn-of-the-century architecture.

The Outer Banks
Getting Here, Getting Around

*A*rrival on the Banks is an adventure in itself. Most will come by car, though many choose to arrive by light plane, boat or even bicycle. It depends on how much of a hurry you are to get here --and how fit you are -- which method you choose.

The popularily of the Outer Banks has no limit for those in the northeastern regions of the country. Major highways are traveled for most of the journey by car. North of Richmond you'll take I-295 towards Norfolk and Williamsburg and then I-64 eastbound to the Norfolk-Hampton Roads area. I-64 is a major highway around Norfolk in the Tidewater area of Virginia. You'll want to exit at Chesapeake onto Route 168. The exits of I-64 have recently been re-numbered, so Exit 290 is the one you'll take. Pay close attention to the southbound exit 290-B, onto route 168. Continue on this route through Chesapeake and on towards Nags Head and Manteo. The highway becomes Route 158 about 30 miles from the beach. Stay on Route 158 and when you cross the Wright Memorial Bridge you're on the Outer Banks.

If you're a resident of North Carolina you'll more than likely arrive via Route 64 onto Roanoke Island and then to the beaches of the Outer Banks. Visitors from other southern routes can travel the same route, or perhaps arrive by toll ferry from Swan Quarter and Cedar Island onto Ocracoke Island where NC 12 actually begins. Of course, another ferry ride, this one free, from Ocracoke to Hatteras Island is in store for you on such a journey.

The ferry rides are fun and we recommend one in the early morning if you're here during the summer months. The departures are frequent -- every 15 minutes during the busy time of day during high season -- from Hatteras to Ocracoke, but the lines are often long during the middle of the day. A complete ferry schedule is listed in the Ferry section.

Air service to the Outer Banks is available via Southeast Airlines' scheduled flights from Norfolk International Airport or through charters with Outer Banks Airways. Arrival at

Dare County Regional Airport in Manteo or First Flight Airstrip in Kill Devil Hills by private plane is also an option (information on the airport is found in the Roanoke Island section and in the Kill Devil Hills section for the airstrip). Car rentals are listed in the Service & Information Directory.

Once you're here, you'll definitely need a car. There is no public transportation here, though there are several dependable cap companies. Also, a caveat: The Dare County police force is quite large (per capita) in order to handle the load that thousands of summer visitors create. This means that in the off season, there are six cops per driver (an exaggeration, but it sure *seems* that way). They also are extra watchful for drunk drivers, which we applaud. So, consider yourself warned.

The islands are strung out for over 100 miles and it's an impossible walk...though we know by saying that, we'll probably hear from some of you who have proved us wrong! Some villages and towns are conducive to "pleasure" walking, however, Ocracoke and Manteo being two.

Biking is popular along Route 158 where bike lanes are well-marked. A stretch of NC 12 north of Southern Shores also has bike lanes. Other towns also have marked bike paths. There are plenty of places in the area to rent bicycles if you don't want to lug yours along.

It's possible to visit the Outer Banks and just enjoy the beach where you're staying. But there's so much to see that we recommend a car tour or a combination of car, bike and walking. You know your preferences and capabilities; you're in charge of how you get around to see everything, we're in charge of bringing them to your attention!

As you can see from the map at the beginning of this section, the barrier islands don't leave much room to roam from east to west. But, those areas included in a north to south exploration, from Corolla to Ocracoke, will provide many adventures. Enjoy!

PUBLIC ACCESS AREAS

Public access on the northern beaches from Southern Shores to Corolla is not allowed except when you are renting a cottage -- in other words, there's no parking and only those who own property or lease through a property management company have access to the beach. (The 4-wheel drive or off road areas north of Corolla are open to bathing and fishing within the limits of posted regulations at the beach access ramp north of Corolla.)

Public access to the beach is marked along Route 158 and the Beach Road from Kitty Hawk to Nags Head. Along the highway you'll notice large green signs with white lettering noting the distance to Public Access and Parking. As you travel the Beach Road, the signs are orange and blue. Some access points have parking lots, others are walking paths to the beach. Many public access parking lots were covered with several feet of sand and debris during last winter's storms and a few are still being cleared. As we go to press, Kill Devil Hills and Nags Head have completed their clearing operations and the beach is waiting for you! Kitty Hawk, reeling from winter storms and clean up delays, has very limited public access paths or parking lots at the present time.

Along the Cape Hatteras National Seashore, parking lots have been cleared and provide ample parking for visitors who want to get out beyond the dunes and explore the uninhabited beaches of the south shores. (Shell picking is different here, so if that's a hobby, you might not want to miss an afternoon walk in this area.) Some folks like to run off the side of the road, park their cars and hike over the dunes. We don't recommend it. If you're unaccustomed to driving on soft shoulders, and if you don't happen to be driving a 4-wheel drive vehicle, you could encounter some difficulty -- "sandy shoulders are softer than soft." And, once you're stuck, you probably won't get "unstuck" until you're pulled out, either by a good samaritan for free, or by a tow service...not for free. Besides, walking over the dunes creates breaks in the vegetation and promotes erosion during winter storms, heavy rains and winds. The National Park Service

maintains many public parking areas and the walkways to the beach are easier to "navigate" for walkers of all ages.

We're not encouraging additional driving for visitors who come here on a vacation, but most visitors are unable to check into their cottage or motel until around 4 o'clock. The traffic is heaviest during the hours around noon and it can sometimes be exasperating to try to just drive around and kill time. So, if you want to come early in the day and have no place to go, hit the beach. It's here -- just beyond the public access areas -- and there are small public bathhouses along the Beach Road in Kitty Hawk, Kill Devil Hills and Nags Head so you can conveniently shower before putting back on your "street clothes." It's just an idea! I know a family that traveled at night and arrived on the Outer Banks at day-break. Their check-in time was 4 p.m. but with a little early planning for getting to those chairs and towels, they drove to a public parking area and hit the beach in time to see the sunrise! They grabbed some extra beach time and less time in traffic. After a light lunch and some leg-stretching through a grocery store, they were ready to check into their cottage at 4 p.m. and were rested, happy and already ahead on their tans! ﹌

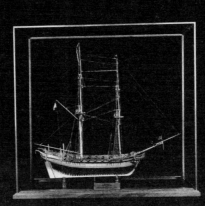

Inside
The Northern Banks

*T*he northern Outer Banks has become a destination all its own. The area refers to the beaches along NC 12 north of Kitty Hawk and includes Southern Shores, Duck, Sanderling, Ocean Sands, Whalehead Beach, Corolla and the off-road beaches of Ocean Hill, Seagull and Carova.

The town of Southern Shores is one of the delightful surprises for the first-time visitor to the northern beaches. Older fishing cottages of another era are becoming extinct as newer large beach homes are being built along the oceanfront, visible from the main road north. Although some homes are sitting right out there where the winds and salt air slash and pound during winter storms, others are almost hidden from view in the edges of the maritime forest which gives Southern Shores two environments. If you prefer the wide open skies over your part of the beach, the oceanside and dunes area promises a grand vacation. If you'd rather live in the woods year round or on vacation, try Southern Shores woods. The homes along the quiet waters of Currituck Sound offer a vastly different beach environment.

There is no commercial development in the town and its permanent residents work hard to maintain its unique lifestyle.

Southern Shores was first developed by Frank Stick, the well-known outdoorsman and artist. He purchased 2600 acres of ocean-to-sound property for a reported $25,000 in the late 1940s. As an environmentalist before his time, he envisioned careful development which is evident from many angles in this town.

Traveling north on NC 12, you next come to the popular village of Duck, nestled along the sound on the curves of a shopping mecca. The wide dune area to the east of Duck Road is dotted with fine oceanside homes. The center of the village has been developed as an area of wonderful shops with a few good restaurants. Water sports such as windsurfing, sailing and jet-skiing are popular and have easy access.

A lifelong resident of Duck, Blanche Utz, reminisced to me one day about the bombing ranges located north of Duck Village back during the war years. The residents were given ample time to get off the island during drills and head up to Norfolk. When it was over, they all returned. There were no paved roads then. A sand road wound around the edge of the sound through what is now Southern Shores all the way to Duck. From Duck the road went north closer to the ocean.

The area north of the village, around Carolina Dunes, is typical of the wide open spaces and high dunes along this portion of the Outer Banks. But the road now winds through some areas of woods and low-growing shrubs such as Sound Sea Village and on into Sanderling.

The community of Sanderling is partially hidden by the heavy growth of live oaks and pines. Here, as with their more southern neighbors, the development has been carefully planned to respect and care for the environment. The resort, Sanderling Inn, captures the remoteness of the area in a natural setting. (A detailed description of Sanderling Inn Resort is included in the section on northern Outer Banks accommodations.)

After you enter Currituck County, just north of Sanderling, you'll drive through the Pine Island Audubon Sanctuary then on to Ocean Sands, one of the largest developments on the northern Outer Banks. Ocean Sands is a subdivision of beach homes, very popular with year round residents as well as investors. Rental cottages book up early in this area.

Further north, Whalehead Beach now boasts a full-service shopping center and the oceanside homes

situated in this flat open area of beach allow for great vacations. The beaches are some of the widest on the Outer Banks.

Farther north still along Ocean Trail (NC 12), Monteray Shores stands out with its unusual architecture. This development boasts luxury homes of unique design and a grand club house for entertaining, as well as pool and tennis courts.

Probably the best all round resort is Corolla Light located almost at the end of the paved road. Richard A. Brindley, the developer, has created a multi-faceted year round resort on the northern Outer Banks. His concept that everyone deserves a piece of the beach is reflected in the way oceanfront and oceanside homes are situated along the dunes and back a few rows but separated by a huge oceanfront complex, accessible to all who own property or vacation here. The clubhouse, swimming pools, tennis courts, indoor sport center and soundfront activity center make Corolla Light Resort very popular for owners and vacationers.

The old village of Corolla is tucked in between the resort, Currituck Beach Lighthouse and the end of the paved road. There is one stop shopping at a Wink's grocery, complete with a few gas pumps, before you discover the end of the paved road. From the ramp, you'll need a 4-wheel drive vehicle. Pay strict attention to the rules of the road, posted on the dune.

NORTHERN BANKS

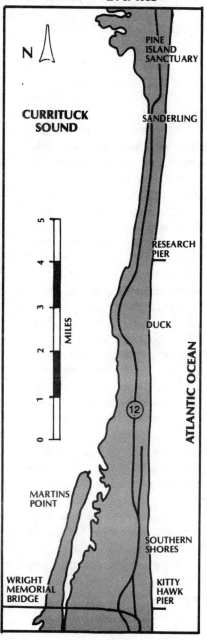

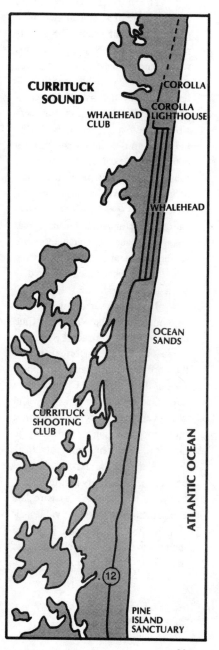

The northern Outer Banks beaches have experienced incredible growth in recent years. The area is remote and is fronted by gorgeous white sandy beaches. Local families gather on these wide beaches for volleyball games that last all day, complete with picnic, awnings for an occasional shady spot, especially for the kids, and an overall attitude that encourages a relaxed lifestyle not often found at beaches along the east coast of our country. Adults and children are welcomed to spend their "dream-vacation" here and that means a real change of pace. Although there are some shops and restaurants, getting into life at the beach is emphasized — it's a grand experience.

History is a surprising source of enjoyment here. The Whalehead Club and the Currituck Beach Lighthouse are just two of the historical sites of the northern Outer Banks. In recent months the Whalehead Club has been purchased by Currituck County and will eventually become a wildlife museum, preserving the history of the area as a popular hunting ground.

Although the real estate market has declined in activity during the past two years, northern beaches real estate companies are experts on values, financing and construction if you're inclined to capture your own piece of the beach.

Southern Shores, Duck, Sanderling and Corolla

ATTRACTIONS

Pine Island Sanctuary

Situated on both sides of Ocean Trail, or NC 12, as you head north past Sanderling, this 7,000-acre wildlife sanctuary is home to ducks, geese, sanderlings and many other species of the bird population along with deer, rabbits, foxes and other animals who inhabit the wilderness. This area has a distinct attraction due to its low-growing live oaks, bayberry, ink-berry, pine, yaupon, holly and many varieties of sea grass. It looks primitive and weather- beaten and holds our attention for this reason. There are very few places like this in the world. If you're a member of the Audubon Society tours are available; if not, then there's no trespassing. The drive is enjoyable and during the off season, the quietness of the area is intense.

A portion of the oceanside property is being carefully developed; however, the western portion bordered by marsh grass and wetlands will remain a sanctuary.

Currituck Wild Horse Sanctuary

The wild horses of Corolla have become famous during the past few years. These Spanish mustang ponies are descendants of early animals and were here long before the Outer Banks became a popular place to hunt, fish or

Photo: D. Westner

A wild Corolla Stallion stands sentinel over his herd.

vacation on the wide beaches.

There are many homes and many vacationers on the northern beaches now and there have been incredible efforts to protect these last remaining ponies from extinction. Their numbers have dwindled since 1987 due to their tendency to inhabit areas of development which contain lush vegetation, rather than remain in the remote off-road areas of the northern Outer Banks where food is not as plentiful. With their migration to "civilization," they encounter automobiles. Motorists are cautioned by a number of signs, but it is impossible to predict the movement of these ponies who graze alongside the road and are prone to walk right out into the path of oncoming vehicles.

Nevertheless, if you see the ponies, you're watching animals whose history dates back to 1584 on this side of the Atlantic. It is reasoned that the ponies were brought here with other livestock for Sir Walter Raleigh's colonization of Roanoke Island. Indians took many of the ponies on their westward migrations.

The ponies are being provided a fenced area north of Corolla and hay is trucked in to this designated area. It remains a challenge to keep the ponies in "captivity" for their own protec-

tion. It goes without saying that if you see these animals beware of the fact that they are wild. In appearance they're not as large as some horses, but they're not to be petted or fed. Approaching them for snapshots is not recommended either.

Donations for the preservation of these animals may be made to the Corolla Wild Horse Fund, P.O. Box 361, Corolla, NC 27927.

Kill Devil Hills Lifesaving Station
Corolla

This lifesaving station built in 1878 is now the property of Twiddy Realty in Corolla, NC. Lifesaving stations were built along the Outer Banks for the purpose of resue operations when powerful storms hit the coastal areas. This is the lifesaving station once located in Kill Devil Hills from which assistance was given to the Wright brothers during the years of experiments in flying their gliders and planes.

It was moved to Corolla in 1986 and became a realty office after considerable restoration. It is open for interested viewers and there is a collection of memorabilia used by the Lifesaving service and the Wrights.

You'll spot this unique build-

Insiders' Tip

Insiders like:
Walking the beach and looking for "sea glass." If you find a piece of blue sea glass it means good fortune.

ing on the west side of Ocean Trail in the village of Corolla.

Whalehead Club
Corolla

New plans for this grand old hunting mansion are being considered. Once the restored focal point of a resort development, it is now the property of Currituck County and plans for a wildlife museum are underway. Until then, however, the Whalehead Club remains closed, though partially renovated by its most recent former owners. There's a lot of history attached to the club which dates back to 1874.

Back then, hunting clubs were a popular gathering place for sportsmen from New York. These men formed a club known as the Lighthouse Club of Currituck Sound. The first building was situated on 2,800 acres of the best duck hunting area on the east coast. Up to 300 birds a day were being brought down by expert marksmen, including President Teddy Roosevelt, as indicated by old record books.

One who came to hunt, a Mr. Edward Collins Knight, wanted to bring his wife. Mrs. Knight, of French descent and an excellent markswoman, was discouraged from coming to the all-male Lighthouse Club hunting parties. So, Mr. Knight bought some of

the land and built this grand mansion for themselves and their friends. The mansion was built in 1922 for approximately $380,000. Construction is said to have taken three years. The walls are 18 inches thick and those five chimneys and its copper-clad roof have been its most distinguishing characteristics. On the inside, Tiffany light fixtures and fine home furnishings gave the mansion a sense of splendor. The Knights called their mansion, the "Castle." The house has a basement - which is unusual so near sea level — containing 16 rooms for storage, wine cellars, food cellars, offices and the like.

The Knights passed away within months of each other in 1936 and the mansion was subsequently purchased in 1940 by Mr. & Mrs. Ray Adams of Washington, DC. The Adamses named it the Whalehead Club. Mr. Adams was a wholesale meat broker in Washington and used the mansion to entertain business associates and friends. It was Adams who leased the property to the U.S. Coast Guard during WWII. There were many other buildings then put up hurriedly and scattered throughout what is now Corolla Light, Monteray Shores and Whalehead Beach.

The mansion next became the property of George T. McLean and W.I. Witt of the Virginia Beach and Portsmouth areas. Under their ownership it was once use as a boys school, Corolla Academy.

Through the years, the once grand mansion suffered from lack of maintenance and use. Vandals removed many of its furnishings and fixtures. The proposed development of the late 1980s failed to give it a proper place in

a resort community and during the fall of 1991 negotiations got underway for its restoration and eventual use as a wildlife museum.

Currituck Beach Lighthouse and Keeper's House, Corolla Village

The northernmost lighthouse on the Outer Banks is this red-brick Currituck Beach Light which was built and lighted in 1875. It is still an active lighthouse with 50,000 candlepower.

The Lightkeeper's house which is located adjacent to it has recently been restored by a local historical architect, John Wilson, IV. He and others concerned that the house would fall to ruin worked hard to get the house a historical designation and then began restoring it.

You'll notice the lighthouse when you arrive on the northern Outer Banks. The approach is along Ocean Trail (NC 12) through Corolla Light Resort and into Corolla Village. Actually, when you pass the famous Whalehead Club, the sandy lane to the left is the one leading to the parking area of the lighthouse grounds. The Currituck Beach Lighthouse is open for a walk up the 214 steps which have a landing every 25 steps. Check your own mobility before getting underway on this climb.

From March 25 hours are 3-6 p.m.; April and May, 1-6 p.m.; June thru September, 10-6p.m.; October thru November, 1-6 p.m. It is closed on Sunday. Admission is $3/person applied to preserve the lighthouse, or donate $10/person or $25/family per year and visit as often as you like.⁂

Photo: Michael Halminski

Photo: Phillip Ruckle

Soundside on the northern banks offers calm waters and consistant breezes for great sailing.

Southern Shores, Duck, Sanderling and Corolla

RECREATION

The Northern Outer Banks beaches, stretching from Southern Shores to Corolla, offer a wide range of recreational possibilities and accompanying sports facilities. When the beach itself isn't enough and you're anxious to get out on the sound for sailing or windsurfing, play tennis or miniature golf, a number of places come to mind. Let's take a look at what's available.

Southern Shores

Southern Shores has some of the most private beaches along the coast. There are several parking lots for access to the beaches for use by property owners or renters, but these may not be used by the public in general. In addition, the streets which run perpendicular to the ocean are off limits for public parking. In other words, if you live in Southern Shores, whether you are a property owner or temporary guest renting a cottage, you have beach access (by permit) to park in marked areas. If not, then no access is permitted. This appeals to many who are truly getting away from it all! Therefore, there is no public recreation, per se. (Refer to the section on real estate/ rentals for property management companies that have rental housing and handle sales in this area.)

Duck

Next, as you head into Duck Village, along Duck Road or NC Hwy. 12, you'll see **Waterworks, Too Sailing**, 261-7245. The wide open waters of the Currituck Sound await your pleasure. Take off on your sailboard or sailboat or rent jet skis. Parasailing has also been added for the '92 season. They're open from 9:00 a.m. til 6:00 p.m. and rental equipment of several kinds is available.

Kitty Hawk Sports, 261-8770, is a water sports legend on the Outer Banks. The challenge is all yours if you have your sights set on some lessons here or in Nags Head. Kayacking, windsurfing and sailing are offered and equipment rentals and sales, clothing and a lots of accessories are featured in this location in Wee Winks Square, soundside in Duck Village. They're open March through January.

Before you leave Duck Village heading north on Duck Road is **Barrier Island Sailing Center**, 261-7100. A large facility, many windsocks and flags attract your attention. It is operated by Bill Miles, a sailing and windsurfing enthusiast for many years. There's a wide range of water activities here, and if it's a sailboard, catamaran or smaller monohull you want to sail, rent one here, sign up for lessons and spend the day. You'll enjoy hanging out at the gazebo, which offers a nice vantage point for waiting your turn, or for the right conditions or for talking with the experts and novices.

Farther north on Duck Road, you'll find the Nor'Banks Sailing Center, 261-2900. It is located on the sound a short distance past the Duck Fire Department. It's the oldest sailing school on the north beaches and offers instruction in sailing and windsurfing. Jon Britt really loves teaching and regardless of age, he has something for everyone. For family water recreation, there are all kinds and sizes of boards and sails. He has small motor boats built in Wanchese, a classic sailboat - - a Flying Scot, as well as Waverunners and the big fun boards. You won't find clothes here -- just watersports! Well, he does sell some t-shirts. They're open from 9:00 a.m. til dusk.

Duck Water Sports, is located on Currituck Sound at Sound Sea Village near Sanderling. This new venture (there was no phone listing as we went to press) is the former site of Outer Banks Cruising and features Waverunners, small boats and a pontoon cruising boat. Private boats are allowed to launch here as well.

Pine Island

North of Sanderling

Once you're in Currituck County north of Sanderling, Duck Road becomes Ocean Trail (NC 12). You'll discover the **Pine Island Indoor Racquet Club**, 441-5888, approximately 3 miles north of the county line. It is open to the public and has three tennis courts, one squash court, one racquetball court and an outdoor plat-form tennis court.

Corolla

You'll drive into Corolla along Ocean Trail and into Corolla Light Resort Village. If you're a guest you'll have access to many tennis courts and the new **Sports Center at Corolla Light**, 453-4565, which opened in 1991. This facility has indoor tennis, racquetball, indoor swimming and a spa. It is one of the finest sports centers on the east coast.

Soundside sailing, windsurfing and hang gliding are available in Corolla, too. **Corolla Flight**, 261-6166, sets you free to fly over the Currituck beaches. Owner Greg DeWolf recommends reservations by phone or at the beach office — the tailgate of their Toyota 4x4 — for tandem hang gliding from the northern Currituck beaches. Flights are $59 for individuals or $49 for groups of 8 or more. Weather variations dictate actual flying, but every perfect day from June til August is fly-time with Corolla Flight. It's possible to get picked up from your place on the beach when you're ready to fly. Fly-time April, May, September and October is on request.

If you have your own board and sail, take off from the **Bell Tower Station** (near the Sport Center) launch area for a day on the beautiful waters of Currituck Sound. Or, take the family for a challenge on **The Grass Course and Garden Golf**, also a part of Corolla Light Resort Village. These two miniature golf courses are open to the public and offer something different for those who love golf. For more information, call Bell Tower Station, 261-4650.

Off Road Beaches

North of Corolla, 4-WD Access

Recreation of a different style awaits those who have a 4-wheel drive vehicle. At the end of the paved road, just north of Corolla, is a point of access. The "rules of the road" are posted and if you'll stop and take time to read, it'll save you a lot of trouble. The speed limit and where to drive on the beach are probably two of the most important things to observe in this area. 4-Wheeling is not a sport, but a different way to enjoy fishing, volleyball, family picnics and swimming in the ocean. The beaches are wide, flat

and a careful attitude will suffice for this area. It's 14 miles to the Virginia state line. A drive north at low tide is recommended for the beauty you'll see, but a return is necessary, because there is no outlet into Virginia.

But this area of beach is not for racing or recklessly cruising along. During summer months, families use the beach for sunbathing, the kids run into the water the same as on other beaches and the surf-fishing is some of the best on the Outer Banks so there are lots of fisher-folks to look out for. Caution is the word so everyone can enjoy the wide open beaches. There's room for volleyball and launching your sailboard or boat. Spending an entire day "off the road" in this northern paradise sure clears the cobwebs.🪶

Southern Shores, Duck, Sanderling and Corolla

SHOPPING

The shops along the 20 mile stretch of the Outer Banks known as the northern beaches begin with the Marketplace in Southern Shores and end at Corolla. Most beach shops are open for extended hours during the summer months, but during the off-season some have early closings, some are open only on weekends until Thanksgiving and some close during the winter and reopen in March. For this reason, telephone numbers are provided. Shopping on the northern beaches is a pleasant experience whether you're looking for the ordinary or the unusual.

Southern Shores

Your search for a special place to shop in Southern Shores is easily discovered on the wide stretch of highway (158 Bypass) carrying traffic on to or off of the beach. The **Marketplace Shopping Center** is situated adjacent to the west side of Southern Shores and the edge of Kitty Hawk.

The **Food Lion** is where you stop for the week's groceries, but there are other shops here as well. **Daniels**, 261-8200, a locally-owned department store, offers quality and affordable clothing for the family, home furnishings, shoes and gifts. The **Mule Shed**, 261-4703, features a top line women's wear, sportswear and lingerie. **Radio Shack**, 261-6334, is the place to buy the latest tapes, CDs, batteries and electronic games and equipment.

One of my favorite places is **Paige's**, 261-1777. A couple of years ago, Paige Harrell left The Galleon in Nags Head and set out on her own to make women's dressing an event. That she has achieved in her shop of one-of-

a-kind garments. You'll be delightfully surprised to discover **Robin's Jewelry**, right there, to pick up for a finishing touch.

The Marketplace also provides the only drug store on the northern beaches. **Revco**, 261-5777, is a general store of sorts, but a full time pharmacist can assist with prescriptions while you're at the beach.

Across the road in Kitty Hawk, the folks at **Carawan Fish Co.**, 261-2120, are ready and willing to provide you with the fish you didn't catch for dinner, or for that special feast at the beach. Take time to consider their selections of wines, spices and sauces to create a new taste. They will gladly pack your fish on ice for travel.

Duck

When Duck was discovered in the early 80s by families on vacation, the Wee Winks general store, Duck Blind Art Gallery and Bob's Bait and Tackle joined the Duck Methodist Church as places to see other folks at the beach. All that has changed and if you're inclined to shop-til-you-drop, you won't be disappointed. Duck Village has a distinction of its own, as a tour of the many shops will show.

As you drive into Duck Village, do stop in at Duck Blind Limited Art Gallery, 261-2009, on the right. This unique collection of fine art, crafts, jewelry and carvings is one of the best on the beach. You'll learn about local artists during their special exhibits and shows throughout the year.

Across the road on the sound, you'll discover the treasures of the sea in **The Sea Shell Shop**, 261-7828, fine women's apparel, unique jewelry and accessories at **La Rive Boutique**, 261-

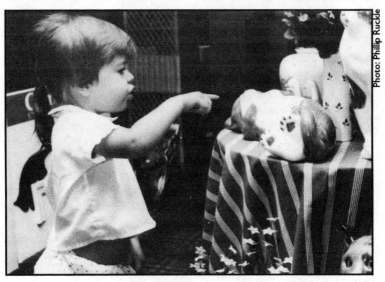

Photo: Phillip Ruckle

7197, and everything for a country home at **The Farmer's Daughter**, 261-4828. If you're looking for advice on where to catch that "big one," stop in at **Bob's Bait & Tackle**, 261-8589. This store is an original building from the old days when a soundside dock out back served as a port to ship fresh fish from the ocean to points north and west.

Scarborough Faire, one of the most carefully developed shopping centers in this area, offers a variety of shops featuring everything from art to videos. On a visit to this collection of shops, you'll discover **Morales Art Gallery**, 261-7190, which features a varied selection of art by Outer Banks artists and, in 1991, opened an upstairs loft gallery featuring alternating artists-in-residence. **The Flag Stand**, 261-2837, **Elegance-of-the-Sea**, 261-7872, and **Bizarre Duck**, 261-8116, offer some of the best of the Duck shops. Bizarre Duck is more than a shop, it's a fine arts and crafts gallery with art work from all over the world.

Being at the beach is a time for fun and you'll discover some great toys and ice cream at **Floats, Flippers & Flyers, and Grannys**, 261-3939. Owners Cheryl and Woody West also collect antiques. Among the wonderful stuffed bears and toys you'll see an old sled, tools and other things. **Gourmet Kitchen Emporium**, 261-8174, features every kitchen gadget imaginable, gift baskets and condiments.

Motifs, 261-6335, is a great place for women's apparel and finely crafted jewelry by Sara De Spain. **Kids Kloset**, 261-4845, carries an assortment of clothes for the little ones who like to have something new at the beach too! **Island Bookstore**, 261-8981, is one of the best bookstores on the Outer Banks. Owner Martha Monroe keeps adding to her collection of unusual books and, of course, the best sellers are all there. **Ocean Annie's**, 261-3290, an Outer Banks tradition in pottery, jewelry and fine wood carvings, tempts you with a special piece to take home from the beach or to give a loved one. **Trappings**, 261-8113, is a quaint shop of exquisite one-of-a-kind accessories and gifts for your home. A new shop opened in 1991, **Lion's Paw**, 261-5575, is a unique ladies apparel shop featuring linen and silk clothing. **Smash Hit**, 261-1138, is a great place to shop for women's and men's tennis and golf clothing, shoes, equipment and gifts. Owner Sally Dowdy, who keeps her shop open year round, has some of the nicest selections on the east coast. If you've been to the Outer Banks through the years, you'll have come to know the Gray family department stores. There's a **Gray's**, 261-3514, here at Scarborough Faire with their complete selection of clothing for the whole family. You'll be happy to find their famous Ducks looking at you as you come in the door!

Osprey Landing is a small shopping area overlooking the Sound as you continue north through the village. **Carolina Moon**, 261-7199, is the place to go if you're looking for the unusual.

The collection of crystals, jewelry, cards and gifts is interestingly displayed, and the music they play while you shop is usually too melodic to pass up (featured tapes are always available for sale). **Birthday Suits**, 261-7297, carries a variety of beachwear and clothing for men and women. They have one of the best collection of bathing suits around, and are great at helping you find one that actually fits. **Osprey Gourmet**, 261-7133, is a delightful cafe for take-out or eating on the waterfront deck.

Schooner Plaza, featuring an extraordinary perennial garden, is where you'll find **Confetti**, 261-5444, one of the newest shops in Duck Village that sells clothing and theme costumes (see their write up under Monteray Shores, below). Farther along Duck Road you'll find **Loblolly Pines Shopping** which features **Lady Victorian**, 261-8622, a boutique of fine clothing for children and women.

The **Duck Duck Shop and Post Office**, 261-8555, features every wood-carved duck imaginable and **Yesterday's Jewels**, 261-4869, carries an interesting collection of old but fashionable jewelry. **The Phoenix**, 261-8900, has a collection of eclectic clothing and jewelry and is a popular place. **TW's Bait & Tackle Shop**, 261- 8300, is probably the first door open every morning in Duck to provide all those necessary fishing supplies, and **Just For the Beach**, 261-7831, comes close to being a general store for beach stuff and casual clothing.

Along the narrow winding road into the heart of Duck Village you'll find **Wee Winks Square**. **Kitty Hawk Sports**, 261-8770, has enough color to invite you in for clothing selections in name brands such as Raisens and Quicksilver, along with their full selection of boogie boards, accessories and sunglasses. **Kitty Hawk Kites**, 261-4450,

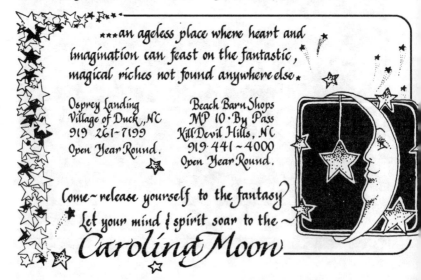

is next door and ready to supply you with everything from roller blades to kites, unusual games and wind socks. **The Lucky Duck,** 261-7800, offers a wide selection of accessories for the home, cards, toys and games. This store started out in a smaller location several years ago and became so popular that they had to find a much bigger space to accommodate the demand...a good clue to how appealing their merchandise is. Clothes are the pitch for several other shops in Wee Winks Square. If you're looking for good quality casual wear for women with fuller figures, you'll find it at **Real Women,** 261-1282. **Lady Victorian,** 261-1654, and **Beach Essentials,** 261-1250, carry everything in swim wear, sportswear, exquisite lingerie, potions, lotions and accessories. For the best fresh seafood, **Dockside 'n Duck,** 261-8687, has it. They also carry steamers, condiments and sauces, and the finishing touches for the gourmet chef on

vacation. **Wee Winks,** 261-2937, has been remodeled — including new gas pumps — and getting in and out for those last minute food purchases or grabbing a newspaper is easier than ever. **Green Acres Produce** stand is open in season and their fresh-from-the-farm vegetables and fruits are the best in the Village.

Tommy's Market, 261-8990, is a place to pick up delicious fresh baked goods in the early morning and a full range of groceries from early morning til late at night.

Next to Tommy's, the **Duck Waterfront Shops** provide a variety of beach wear, soaps, gourmet sauces, books and gifts. Stop in at **Duck's General Store,** 261-5164, which moved over next to Blue Point this year, where you'll find products such as cards, books, jewelry and t-shirts manufactured by companies that donate part of their proceeds from your purchases to environmental

causes...help yourself and the earth at the same time! There's also **L'Oceans**, 261-5174, where the sensual in you is sure to come out amidst their offerings of bath and body products, lotions and custom scentings, none of which have been tested on animals. They also feature discounted prices on famous name brand lingerie. **Barr-EE-Station Catalog Store** and **Barr-EE For Kids**, 261-1650, feature some unbelievably low prices on name brand clothing and they're always well-stocked. One of the best-dressed people we know buys most of her clothes here, at a fraction of the cost she'd typically pay for the brands elsewhere...who says you need big city shopping! **Donna's Designs**, 261-6868, has clothing and t's for kids and adults in artistically-designed fish-printed designs, all crafted by Donna. She also has a location in the Kitty Hawk Connection shops in Nags Head. **North Beach Sailing**, 261-6262, offers the latest in sailing gear, equipment and accessories.

Not a shop in the real sense but a fine craft gallery, is the unusual **Marine Model Gallery**, 261-5977, also located in the Waterfront Shops. Owners Jim and Debbie Millis have created an exquisite nautical ambience

with high-polished woods and brass to display some fascinating fine crafts. Models of ships created by artists from around the country reflect an exacting art form and history of the high seas. Models are for sale but the emphasis of this gallery is to bring the artists' work to a realistic setting, a place along the waters of the Currituck Sound in Duck, which long ago was a fishing port-village. Children are not encouraged to visit the gallery for obvious reasons. But those who appreciate the fine work on display and the history behind the ships will enjoy a visit to talk with Jim and select from the collection of one-of-a-kind creations.

MONTERAY PLAZA
10 miles north of Duck

Out there in the wide open spaces of Whalehead Beach and about 10 miles north of Duck, a new convenience awaits those who come to this area of the northern Outer Banks.

Monteray Plaza, which opened in 1991, brought a major supermarket within easy reach of families vacationing on the northern Currituck Beaches, the **Food Lion**. Other businesses opened as well to make Monteray Plaza a nice place to shop. There's a **Gray's Department Store**, 453-4711, continuing their Outer Banks clothing tradition, with quality and name brands of clothes for men and women. Gray's has a nice assortment of gift items, too. Debbie Pelley and Howard Goldstein opened two women's boutiques in

1991, one here and the other in Duck. **Confetti**, 453-8888, features a varied line of beach wear and clothing for other occasions for adults and kids. They also have fun things, like dress-up fashions that are a little girl's dream -- feather boas, sequined shoes, tiaras, magic wands, fairy dresses -- and theme costumes, like Peter Pan, Beauty and the Beast, Madonna and Cinderella. **Ocean Annie's**, 453-4102, is another fine shop with attractive displays of handcrafted pottery, jewelry, fine gifts and gourmet coffees. **Kitty Hawk Kites**, 453-8845, opened another colorful shop of unique games and an assortment of kites —just the thing for those wide open skies of the northern beaches.

And, one of the most exciting wine selections can be discovered at **Bacchus**, 453-4333. If you know what you want, you'll find it and if you're uncertain about wines, the experts at Bacchus will recommend one. Owners Holly and Glen Branham and Gordon Hoy know wines and carry the wine connoisseur's "bible," *The Wine Spectator*, for reference. This wine and cheese deli features an incredible assortment of gourmet condiments and foods. One popular line is the Busha Browne Jamaican jams, jellies and sauces. **Elegance-of-the-Sea**, 453-4644, offers one of the most attractive selection of shells, baskets, flowers, soaps and candles on the beach. You'll know the touch and selections of owner Gail James when you enter this attractive shop. She has another shop in

Duck Village. And, you'll find **Pink Flamingo's**, 453-8747, a convenient place to drop in for delicious frozen yogurt. Owner Jim Grabinski has those wonderful Ottis Spunkmeyer cookies and homemade candies, and he plans to start selling ice cream in the 1992 season.

Corolla

Driving north on Ocean Trail and into Corolla Light Resort Village, you'll find the soundside shops of the **Bell Tower Station**, 453-3987 or 261-4650. Nestled among the trees and overlooking Currituck Sound the resort wear shop, **Corolla Collectibles**, 453-4731, features casual attire for women and children. **Sweet Endings** is a place to cure your sweet-tooth with an array of pastries and ice cream.

Corolla Light Village Shops have been open for several years. Some have changed ownership, but a variety of goods and services is available at **Ocean Threads**, 453-8967, **Sidney's**, 453-8918 and Ocean Atlantic Rentals, 453-2440. You can call **Ocean Atlantic Rentals** 1-800-635-9559 to reserve something for your vacation that you'd rather not haul in the car. The **Silk Gardenia**, 453-8863, offers fresh and lovely silk flowers and wreaths for every occasion. Ed and Ruby Cox, the owners, have been in business since the Corolla Light Village Shops opened and even before that at a shop in Nags Head.

The small **Winks** store with a

LINGERIE
•
BATH & BODY PRODUCTS
•
CUSTOM SCENTING
•
FOR MEN & WOMEN

!!We've Moved down the deck next to the Blue Point !!   The Lingerie, Bath & Body Shop is Now L'Oceans

DUCK VILLAGE WATERFRONT SHOPS • (919)261-5579

few gas pumps and the **Corolla Post Office** occupy a small strip north of the Currituck Beach Lighthouse. For many years, it was the center of activity and the only place to buy groceries in Corolla. Winks, 453-8166, is a general store and with an adjacent shop and office is often referred to as "the mall" by those who live and work there.

Things have changed in Corolla and just north of the Winks store is a new row of shops and businesses. Known as **Whalehead Landing Station**, you'll find several shops and offices. **Kitty Hawk Sports**, 453-4999, one of the Outer Banks' most prolific surf wear and rental shops, **Tackle 'n Tours**, 453-4266, which has everything for the fisherman, **John de la Vega Gallery**, 261-4964, showing fine art work by local artists and featuring oils, pastels and photographs by Mr. de la Vega himself, and **North Beach Videos**, 453-4733 are within walking distance for vacationers in Corolla Village.

Again, we've provided telephone numbers and suggest you call before you go for off-season shopping. Merchants open early for business in season, but in the fall and early spring, some have irregular hours during the week or open only on weekends.

Happy Shopping!

Photo: D. Westner

The head keeper's house stands close to the Currituck Beach Light.

A Life on the Northern Banks:
Maggie Mae Twiford

*T*he late November sunlight glints off the Nags Head dunes outside the window, and glints again off Maggie Twiford's snow-white hair. It is cut short and pinned up with a brown barrette. Her tiny hands lie softly together in the colorful afghan that covers her lap, except when they twist at the plastic band at her wrist. Outside in the corridor there is the hiss of wheelchairs on tile, the chatter of nurses.

"It was all dirt roads in them days. All such as that. And I remember a lot about it. My mother and my father have been dead for years, and my sisters and my brothers too. And I've got three relatives here, and all my other kinfolks are dead. I've got children — three, two boys and a girl. And today's my youngest son's birthday, he's 62 years old today.

"I was born in 1900. Our closest doctor was at Poplar Branch, Doctor Griggs. Had to go by water to get him, wa'n't no bridges, you see. Sometimes you died fore the doctor got there. My mother had a doctor, Doctor Newburn. He lived at Jarvisburg. And both of them was with my mother when I was born.

"Most all my people were Ser-vice people. My father was in the Coast Guard — it was the Lifesaving Service, years ago. He was a surfman. I heard him say that his mother died when he was thirteen years old, and he couldn't go to school. He had to go out and work to take care of his mother; his daddy was dead. He had it pretty hard. I never heard him say what he did when he was a boy. I imagine he fished. T'weren't nothing else much to do here. He didn't have no educa-tion, that was the reason he couldn't get rated, couldn't get up. Well, he was a big stout man, and he had a red complexion. Oh, he was a wonderful father. And he didn't live too long after he was retired. But he was in the Service 37 years. I heard him say that when he went in the service it was at Number Nine station. That was Poyner's Hill. Then he was transferred to Paul Gamiels. Don't imagine there's anything left there now, they've had so many storms.

"My people come from Kitty Hawk. My people were Beals. B-E-A-L. Some B-E-A-L-E. We call ours B-E-A-L-S. Now my father I don't know where really he come from. Up in the hills...seems to me I've heard him say that his mother was from Columbia or somewhere over that way. Uh huh. My mother's family name is Perry. She was a Kitty Hawk Perry. They have a lot of Perrys in Kitty Hawk. Used to. There's a few still living but not as many as there was years ago. And my mother's mother, she was a Fisher. I think there were four of them, Fisher girls. My grandmother Betty, and Thanny, Amy, and Lebarcia. I didn't know them, that was before I was born. I didn't have no grandparents when I was small.

"My mother died having my sister, when I wasn't quite three years old. I don't remember what she looked like. I wish I had some faint remembrance of her but I don't. She's buried in Kitty Hawk. All my people are buried in Austin's Cemetery there.

"But my little sister lived to be grown and married. And she died the same way my mother died. And she had typhoid fever along with it, and of course the baby didn't live. There wasn't time for it to be borned. And my sister Martha, she died about the same way my mother died. In childbirth. And then my oldest sister died in 1919 of the flu, when it was raging, you know, so bad? She didn't live but one week from the time she was taken, went into pneumonia and died.

"My daddy was a hard workin' man. And he raised a big family. I had three sisters, and I had one, two, three — four brothers. There was eight of we children to raise up, and he in the service. He had to have a housekeeper

to take care of us. No, not colored, elderly white women mostly. And I'm telling you he had a hard time of it.

"But he was a good father. Didn't make much money, but there was a lot of people didn't make as much as he did. We had something to eat and a place to stay in. He always worshipped we four girls.

"I was a little barefooted girl. In the summer I went barefoot. We had a little one-room schoolhouse in Duck. You wouldn't believe it to go up there now. There's a art gallery there now. And it was history, geography, arithmetic, things like that.

"We had ball games. We had a game we called fifty-oh. And ring around the roses. And a game we called sheepie. You'd be surprised at the silly things we had them days. How do you play fifty-oh? Some would go off and hide, and we'd try to find them. And if you found them and could make the home run before they did we'd win the game. Yes, hide and seek was what it was, and they called it fifty-oh then. We played cat, sure did. It's been so long ago I nearly forgot. And we had a croquet set, young people used to come to our lawn and play.

"And on Sunday afternoon we'd go to this big hill north of Duck. It wasn't as big as Jockey's Ridge, but it didn't lack much. And we'd run up and down it and play until we were so tired we couldn't hardly get back.

"We had one teacher that rang a bell — it was a hand bell. The teacher would stand in the door and ring, ring, when we children would be playing, for us to come in. And we had to stay in at recess a lot, we'd misbehave and done something we shouldn't. Whisperin' in school, or laughing. There was a lot of laughing. And certain ones had to stay and sweep the schoolroom and put things in order for next day. Went to school in the summertime, hot weather, barefoot — we didn't have to wear shoes, no.

"The Wright brothers? They flew in 1903. I was born in 1900. Oh, yes, they came back in 1908. I remember that. But there was always something going on that I didn't know about. I didn't really live that close to Kill Devil. I saw them flying around. It looked different from planes they have now. We thought it was something scary, flying around up there.

"My daddy had a horse that he used at the station, and then on his liberty at home. He'd bring the horse home. He didn't have but one day liberty a week, one day and one night. He come home at twelve and left next day at eleven to get back to the station. It was about a hour's ride on the horse because it was sand, it took longer to go. He had to be on time, they were strict them days. The horse was named Fanny. That horse ran away with him. I think he was on patrol and the horse got frightened, something happened that he just ran. And throwed him out of the cart and hurt him pretty bad. Throwed him out on his head. Doctor had to tend him.

"Sometimes he patrolled with the horse, but most times he walked. He had what they call a lay-house on each end. Between the two stations, you know. And most times he had to walk the night. He had a north patrol, sometimes he had a south patrol. If it was a stormy night he'd patrol twice a night. And again he'd just have one patrol a night. He'd walk up and down the beach — that ocean had to be watched for ships, y'know. And I can remember all the ships come ashore when he was in there and I used to worry when I was a kid when I'd hear talk — we'd get word from the station there was a shipwreck on the beach, and I knew my daddy had to go. I remember how I used to worry about it, thought maybe he wouldn't make it back. Because then they said go, you didn't have to come back. It was the rule. If it was possible to get to the ship, to get the men off, they had to go. And sometimes you didn't come back. You got drowned. I remember seein' em come ashore. Ships from different countries. Some men got lost, some got saved. Some ships was torn to pieces. I've seen men washed ashore on the beach drowned. That's when I was a little girl.

"There wasn't very much. The houses weren't very well kept up. There weren't very many big homes. There were some hunting lodges, one or two. The people who weren't in the service depended on fishing.

"I'm telling you we had a rough time of it, but them were the happy days. Happier than they are in this day and time. We didn't have a lot, but what we had we enjoyed. And we didn't look for a whole lot. If I got a rag doll at Christmas, and a stocking full of nuts and candy and all that, I was happy with it. Now little children gets everything and in no time it's tore up and gone. We took care of our little things that we got.

"But we were happy people them days. It was almost like one big family. Some of them was poorer than others. And them that had a little bit more they'd always divide. I know my daddy did.

"My daddy never had much money but he always raised a lot of stuff to eat around him. Even guineas. And hogs. He had a lot of hogs. We didn't have to buy no meat, no lard. The hogs went free till the new law, the fence law come in, and he had to get rid of them. The woods used to be full of hogs and cattle. Always had a plenty to eat on Christmas. Wasn't like it is now — all beefsteak. We raised chickens and raised geese and ducks, we had fowls of all kinds. And then gunnin', you know, you killed wild ducks and geese. No problem 'bout eating. We had a garden and grew beans, and collards, and cabbage, sweet potatoes and horse potatoes, cucumbers, tomatoes, most every kind of vegetable you could raise around here. It wasn't the kind of food people eats this day and time. It was good food, it sure was.

"No, you wouldn't hardly believe how people lived them days. We only went to the city once a year. Elizabeth City, that was the closest city. That wasn't very big but to us it was a big one. It was like goin' to New York. Nobody got nowhere much — I think I did go to Norfolk once or twice when I was growin' up. Went on a steamboat. The , I think.

"I moved to Chesapeake in 1918. We didn't have no high school. I went there to take a business course. It was in Norfolk, on Main Street. Mr. Wresler's college. He died, and Mr. Keyes took it over.

"No, I didn't get a job then. I married William Twiford, in 1918, and he wouldn't let me go to work. He was from Princess Anne, there's where his people was from. He lived down Corolla. But we lived in Norfolk for right many years. My oldest son was born in South Norfolk, and my daughter was born in South Norfolk.

"Then we moved from Norfolk to Church's Island. He was a guide, for two lodges. White's, and for Hampton. Duck hunting lodges. Oh, yes, I know that's a unpleasant job — he complained about it. I think we were there a couple, three year he worked for the lodge. From there he put in for the Coast Guard. He decided he'd better when he was younger go in the service.

"And we were stationed in Dam Neck. And we lived there I think two year. From there we moved from one station to the other. And finally settled down in Duck, where I was born. And he was in Caffey's Inlet, and then in Kitty Hawk. And I think in Nags Head too. He was all over. And he went to Florida too, was there a whole winter. But I didn't go, the children was small. And he got transferred back. We were in Wash Woods I think six years. That's up above Corolla. And Caffeys Inlet. I think he retired out of Kitty Hawk. He's been dead — buried him close to twenty year.

"I remember the worst hurricane up there was in 1933. You can't imagine what a hurricane sounds like. It's terrible — Whoooo. The water came up and flooded us out of our house. Everybody had to leave their home. First we went to the garage, on a hill, and there was lots of women and children in there. The ocean was between us and the station, and the surf had bursted their lifeboat all to pieces. So the men couldn't come and help us. We were helpless. And the water was rising. There was this old lady who had a big house, and she would take people in. The children wanted to go there. So to please the children I left the garage and was trying to get to it. Wading. But the water was too deep, and it was coming in, and I had to try to get up to the top of a hill. And it was sand, and I had the children by both my hands, trying to get up to the top of that sand hill. And I couldn't do it, and the water was rising. But just then the eye of the storm came and we was able to get to safety at the house.

"Some of the houses was took away — the ocean just took them away. I was lucky. The sand was hilled up as high as the eaves of my house. The wind was so strong it blew the winter lights and the curtains and the shades and the glass out, and blew some of the roof off. And the sea had eat under my kitchen. But I had my house. That's the reason I don't think much of the beach. I just look on that water and walk away. And I think that was why when I was growing up, my father kept us so far from the shore.

"Oh, yes, I really feel lucky to have my children. I got five or six grandchildren. There's more than grandchildren, of great ones. I don't know how many I got, haven't counted them up lately. And I love the great ones just as good as I do the grandchildren.

"I've been in here for two years now. I'm not getting much better, but my mind seems to be clearer. But I'm a lot better than some of them in here. I'll tell you, this is a pitiful place. You go around and see the sufferin' and the sick people. I'm not bodily sick, but I broke my hip a couple of year ago and something happened that the leg got twisted. They did try to straighten it out, but I think they waited too long. It can't never be back right. And this wheelchair...I'm still not well. And I don't think I've got enough time for this hip to ever heal.

"This is a wonderful place to be. They have helicopters here, they take you to hospitals, to the doctors. I haven't been on them. We have everything here that's needed for this kind of home. And my children take care of me pretty good, they do all they can for me. But I'll be glad if I can get out.

"I've had a lot of trouble in my life, yes I have. I think the unhappiest time was when the children left home. I had two in the war. Clyde was in Germany, right in the midst of the battle there. He got his feet froze there. He still has trouble with his legs. And Tom was in the Navy, on the high seas the times when ships were getting sunk down here. You never knew when word was coming that he was drowned. I had a lot of worry on to me. You're bound to worry about them when they're facing danger every minute of their life. And Tom got rheumatic fever in England, and it still bothers him.

"The happiest time was when I was young—getting married, I reckon.

"The best way I'm happiest is when I know the Lord's going to take care of me. I know I've got to die. But while I'm living I feel like if I live the right life, which I try my best, then he'll take care of me. Although I'm suffering, that'll be over after a while. I want to be prepared to not have none of these aches and things. No, I'm not afraid, not a bit. I want to live as long as the Lord sees fit for me to live, then when it's time I got no dread. No worry about my soul. I know the Bible tells us a lot, but I still think we got to die and go on to find out really what it's all about. Maybe I'm wrong, but if I am it's ignorance, the Lord will forgive me."

Maggie Twiford sits facing the window, immobile in the waning sunlight, watching as the wind ruffles the beach grass at the top of a dune. If you were eight years old, barefoot, you could scramble to the top in a minute. And see for a long, long ways

Photo: DCTB

Even at the height of the season, a visitor can enjoy the solitude of a sunrise over the Atlantic Ocean.

Inside
Kitty Hawk

*I*f you arrive in Kitty Hawk from the north you'll cross the bridge over Currituck Sound. Travelers from the southern United States or western North Carolina will arrive in Kitty Hawk from the other end of the Outer Banks, probably through Manteo, Nags Head and Kill Devil Hills. For the purpose of this guidebook and a visual trip of Kitty Hawk, we'll begin as though you're arriving from the north end. Regardless, it's a time to slow down; remember you're on a mission to unwind and get accustomed to doing things differently. Even the highway takes some getting used to. It's wide and looks like a place to drive fast, but wait! The outside lane has many access and egress points and the inside lane serves as an exit to the turn lane which runs down the middle so be safe and drive with care.

The use of milepost markers will give travelers a hint of where they are, as most cottage rentals, shops, restaurants and resorts located north, south, east and west of this bridge will be noted by milepost indicators along the roads running parallel to the beach. The first milepost marker is located in Kitty Hawk, or Southern Shores, whichever side of the road you're on - - Southern Shores was a part of Kitty Hawk for many years!

The maritime forests of the west side surprise the first-time visitor. After all the beach is flat and forests belong on higher ground. Not so, here on the Outer Banks.

Two roads run parallel through the easterly portions of Kitty Hawk. The old two-lane Beach Road, a.k.a. NC 12, and the newer dual lane route 158 reflect their own uses. If you're looking for a string of older beach cottages, ravaged by wind and tides through the years, a trip along the Beach Road will definitely give you some idea of how the harshness of life by the sea eventually takes it toll.

The winter storms of 1991 hit the beaches of Kitty Hawk with a vengeance in some areas. Clean up and restoration are underway. Sad but true, life along this stretch of beach has changed drastically. Kitty Hawk was one of the first popular beach settlements on the Outer Banks, but the deep erosion along this portion of the Outer Banks has given way to a narrower, unprotected beach.

Businesses and homes adjacent

to the highway are newer and on higher ground. The views from some Kitty Hawk cottages, especially along the golf course, are great.

Many houses and rental cottages located between the Beach Road and the bypass are getting a fresh look after the winter storms. Otherwise, more protected, year round homes of Kitty Hawk are discovered on the west side, along the sound.

A new post office was opened in Kitty Hawk this year and its conveniently located between the highways, at milepost 4.

Regional Medical Center located next to the Aycock Brown Welcome Center opened a year ago and is convenient and well-staffed, at MP 1-1/2.

The Bypass was widened three years ago but the name Bypass doesn't fit. The highway doesn't by-pass anything except the beach. Another reason to travel within the speed limits (or under the posted speed limit) is the threat of suddenly finding yourself right behind a car whose occupants have discovered it's time to turn. Ah, yes, you're on the Outer Banks, where often the ordinary is elusive...things are done differently.

The first families of Kitty Hawk were named Twiford, Baum, Etheridge, Perry and Hill. Many descendants of these first families live

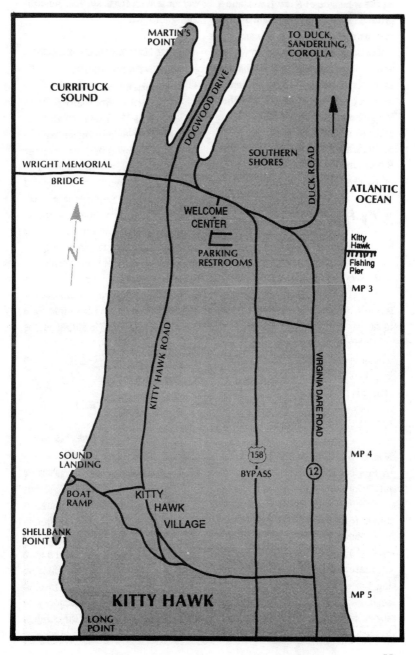

on the west side of Kitty Hawk and a drive on Kitty Hawk Road will lead you to other roads with such names as Elijah Baum Road, Herbert Perry Road and Moore Shore Road. Along the latter is a monument which designates the spot where Orville and Wilbur Wright assembled their plane before their historic flight a few miles away in 1903. More on this part of Outer Banks History is found in the section on Kill Devil Hills.

Kitty Hawk

ATTRACTIONS

THE AYCOCK BROWN WELCOME CENTER
Route 158 Bypass, MP 1-1/2 (919) 261-4644

It's just what it says it is -- a welcome center -- and you'll enjoy a stop here. Information on the Outer Banks is in abundance. Free community newspapers offer good reading and a flavor of what constitutes important news in this part of the world. Maps, flyers, motel and hotel information, cottage rental books, community events and information about the prospects of good fishing can be obtained from the friendly people who work here. The Welcome Center is open from 8:30 a.m. till 5 during the off season, with extended hours during the spring, summer and fall to accommodate visitors. The building is accessible for the handicapped and has restrooms. A picnic area will be a welcome sight for those who've been riding for a while.

KITTY HAWK PUBLIC BEACH & BATH HOUSE
Beach Road, MP 4-1/2

Located across the road from the ocean, a bathhouse and small parking area offers visitors a place to go on the beach as soon as they arrive on the Outer Banks. If you want to drive on to the Outer Banks early in the day and have rented a cottage for late afternoon arrival, it is possible to come on to the beach and get your feet in the sand here. During the winter of 1991, some big waves of the Halloween storm filled the parking lot with sand, but it's all been shoved back towards the beach and the bathhouse is accessible for a short visit or a day's outing at the public beach.

Kitty Hawk

RECREATION

WATERFALL GREENS
Kitty Hawk, MP 1/4
West side of Route 158   261-3844

Located near the bridge, this forested area on Currituck Sound is home to wildlife as well as family recreation. An 18-hole miniature golf course and a separate putting green are open from 9 a.m. until midnight from Easter through Thanksgiving. In addition to golf, there's an arcade with pinball and video games for children and adults. An ice cream and hot dog stand as well as public restrooms (with baby-changing table) make this a great place for families.

DUCK WOODS COUNTRY CLUB
Southern Shores, MP 1   (919) 261-2744

Located just over the bridge in Southern Shores which is an incorporated town and eastern part of Kitty Hawk, Duck Woods is a private club with golf, tennis and swimming. Contact the membership chairman through the club number for fees and dues. It's the only private club on the beach and has the usual food services and pro shop merchandise.

COLONY HOUSE CINEMA
Southern Shores Marketplace, MP 1
(919) 261-7949

Twin theaters are housed in the shopping center and offer first run movies. You'll notice this shopping center just past Duck Woods Club. The movies are open here year round and offer attractive matinee prices.

KITTY HAWK FISHING PIER
Beach Road, MP 1   (919) 261-2772

Once you cross the bridge, count the traffic lights and at the 3rd light, turn east towards the beach road. You'll see the Kitty Hawk Fishing Pier straight ahead. Built in the mid-fifties, it is privately owned and operated by friendly experts. It is 714 feet out into the ocean, has a nice bait and tackle shop and a good restaurant. Fishing is good for all the inshore species normally caught. Some record-holding catches have been landed here and it is a very popular, easy to reach pier when the blues are blitzin'. Kitty Hawk pier is open April 1 - Thanksgiving. Daily admission is: Adult $5.00, Children $3.00. A weekly pass is $25 and season passes are $125. Handicapped and blind persons are admitted free.

SEA SCAPE GOLF CLUB
Route 158 MP 2-1/2   (919) 261-2158

After you pass the Aycock Brown Welcome Center, you'll see the fairways of Sea Scape golf course to the west. This is a Scottish-type golf course without trees or water hazards, but the sand traps are as big a challenge as anywhere. The course boasts top notch greens -- as smooth as any in the state. There are 18 holes on the par 72, 6200-yards long course.

Cart rental is required; a bar and grill at the 19th hole is available. Sea Scape is open from 7:00 a.m. till dark every day of the year. Bring mosquito repellant for use during the summer,

Insiders like:
Watching sunsets from the deck at Papagayo's on the beach road. Remember to keep an eye out for whales.

Insiders' Tip

especially after a rain. Some light spraying is underway to control those irritating little things.

COLONY HOUSE CINEMAS
Route 158, MP 4-1/2   (919) 261-7949

Kitty Hawk Center on the west side of the highway offers twin theaters for family entertainment. The phone number above carries a recorded announcement for all theaters and movies on the Outer Banks.

Kitty Hawk

SHOPPING

Surf shops and a couple of department stores join the usual run of banks, hardware stores, lumber yards, fishing tackle and grocery stores which serve most year round communities. For those wanting to pick up household supplies or art supplies, the kind folks at **Virginia Dare Hardware**, 261-2660, on the Beach Road, (MP 2-1/2) will have what you need. When one surf shop opens, it's never enough. A year or so ago, **Whalebone Surf Shop**, 261-8737, left the confines of a shopping center and built its own establishment at MP 2-1/2 on the bypass and the first thing you know, **Wave Riding Vehicles**, 261-7952, at MP 2-3/4 had enlarged their shop and **Bert's Surf Shop**, 261-7584, famous in Nags Head, built a new establishment in Kitty Hawk at MP 3-1/2 on the bypass. All these stores have great clothes in addition to what they're in business

for -- surfing and surf boards!. And, luckily, the chase for the perfect wave often ends right here in the Outer Banks' surf!

Gray's department store, 261-1776, an Outer Banks legend opened in Kitty Hawk a few years ago at MP 4. You'll find top name brands and friendly service for a casual beach shopping trip.

Right next door is the **Ben Franklin** department store. While that's a good, overall description of the items you'll expect to find here, their clothing is especially stylish and more what you'd expect to find in more specialized stores. They also have anything you could possibly need to have fun on the beach.

Just about every store on the Outer Banks carries fishing gear, but you really can't beat **TW's Bait & Tackle**, 261-7848, next to the 7-11 at MP 4. For the best gear and info on what's biting stop in. Owner, Terry "T.W." Stewart has been in business for about ten years and can sell you what you need, including ice and live bait.

A couple of supermarkets added to the first Kitty Hawk grocery store will have all the food you need for your vacation. The Marketplace Shopping Center (see the description under Northern Beaches Shopping), MP 1, has a **Food Lion** supermarket for big shopping trips; the same for the Food-A-Rama in Kitty Hawk, MP 4. A more authentic beach grocery store is also Kitty Hawk's center of community conversation. The **Winks Grocery** is on the Beach Road at MP 2-1/2. Miles Davis, Margaret, Jeanette and all the others will welcome you to the beach. Shopping here is what it is supposed to be like at a beach store, with their sometimes-sandy floors and laid-back atmosphere. You'll find all the reality-soaked newspapers you thought you'd left behind for your trip to the beach and everything else you need, food-wise. The radio and speakers hanging inside the door on the wall grabbed my attention one day with some good beach music, not often found while shopping. Get to know the folks at Wink's.

Photo: Michael Helminski

The Wright Brothers Memorial in Kill Devil Hills honors those who made powered flight possible.

Inside
Kill Devil Hills

*T*he Town of Kill Devil Hills, situated in the middle of the barrier islands, has some unique characteristics which set it apart from other beach communities. Nearly all Dare County community services such as the public library, the adult service center, the Chamber of Commerce, as well as the Kill Devil Hills offices are located here, centrally located for residents of all beach communities.

Kill Devil Hills boasts some newer condos scattered along the oceanfront and homes between the highways and on the sound but for the most part the town remains an older Outer Banks community whose numerous fishing cottages and vacation homes were built 30-40 years ago.

One or more explanations for the origin of the town's name bear repeating here. Some say the name originated when a shipment of New England 'Kill Devil' rum arrived on shore and others prefer the possible connection to the name of a once-common shore bird, the 'killdee' or 'killdeer.' Other stories emerge about the legends of bargains with the devil. At the turn of the century, however, a sandy hill west of the ocean captured the drama of man's first flight and an awesome place in history. This story has been told many times as well. We're not sure when Kill Devil Hill added the "s" to become Kill Devil Hills.

The Wright Brothers from Ohio first built bicycles, then gliders and airplanes. They began to track weather conditions to determine the best place to test their "heavier than air machine." Ideal conditions were located in Kitty Hawk, North Carolina. Constant winds and soft hills of sand met their requirements. Responding to their inquiry, Capt. Bill Tate of the Kitty Hawk Weather Station wrote to the Wright brothers encouraging them to come here and try their machine. He promised to do everything possible to assure a successful venture in a convenient location, among friendly people.

Wilbur Wright arrived on September 13, 1900, after a dismal two-week schooner trip from Elizabeth City. He set up camp near Capt. Tate's home, in Kitty Hawk Village about four miles north of Kill Devil Hills. Orville Wright arrived two weeks later, and they began assembling their first glider. They first experimented with tie-lines as though they were flying a kite. Later, they carried it four miles to a 90-foot high sand hill and made about a dozen glides, taking turns piloting it. Their total time aloft was about 15 seconds.

The gliding season for 1900 was over and although their time in the air had been short, they made some important observations. The lifting power of the wings was less than they had expected, but the wing warping system they had invented to enable them to turn the machine worked well. They left for Dayton, Ohio, resolving to return the following year.

By the summer of 1901, they had completed a second glider. This model had wings 22 feet wide and 7-foot chord, with increased curvature to conform to Otto Lilienthal's aerodynamic theories. They arrived at Kill Devil Hill with this new glider on July 10, and put in a few days building a large shed and drilling a well. Between July 27 and August 20 they made several dozen flights. These flights proved Lilienthal's figures inaccurate. They decided a vertical surface was needed at the tail. But in spite of that, they succeeded in gliding farther and more skillfully than anyone had before.

They returned to Dayton that winter and continued in the bicycle business. They also built the first scientifically accurate wind tunnel to carry out their own calculations of wing curvature and lift. By September 19, 1902, they were back on the Outer Banks, in Kill Devil Hill. They brought a new glider with a tail and designed with new knowledge of aerodynamic principles and theories.

During September and October that year, tests proved they were very near the 'secret' of flying. The glider soared, remaining aloft for more than a minute and going over 600 feet. When they added a movable rudder to the vertical tail, the basic idea of the airplane was complete.

Back in Dayton to obtain an engine yet unavailable, they built their own. A four-cylinder, aluminum block gasoline engine that delivered between 9 and 12 horsepower was completed to the Wright's demanding specifications.

Then they built a complete new plane. No one had ever built propellers, so they designed and built one for their new plane.

The final result produced all the elements of today's aircraft, if not in appearance, in theory. A 40-foot span of double wings with aileron control interacting with a movable rudder pro-

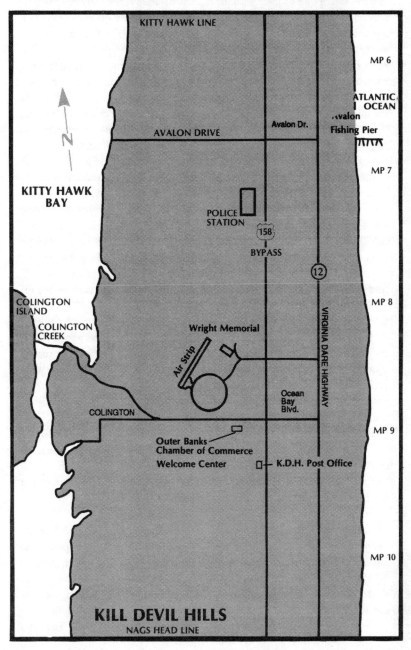

KITTY HAWK LINE

MP 6

ATLANTIC
OCEAN

Avalon
Fishing Pier

AVALON DRIVE   Avalon Dr.

MP 7

KITTY HAWK
BAY

POLICE
STATION

(158)

BYPASS

(12)

MP 8

COLINGTON
ISLAND

COLINGTON
CREEK

Wright Memorial

Air Strip

VIRGINIA DARE HIGHWAY

COLINGTON

Ocean
Bay
Blvd.

MP 9

Outer Banks
Chamber of Commerce
Welcome Center

K.D.H. Post Office

MP 10

KILL DEVIL HILLS
NAGS HEAD LINE

vides a description of their machine, which also had a gasoline engine placed alongside the prone pilot on the lower wing, driving two counter-rotating pusher props. The launching system consisted of a rail down which the plane could roll on a dolly before dropping off.

Their fourth trip to Kill Devil Hill came in September 1903. They stayed busy building another shed, repaired a number of breakdowns and ground-tested the machine. The Wright brothers' work had aroused the interest of the press and this time, Wilbur and Orville had to ignore the distractions caused by such interest.

By December 14 they were ready to fly. Men from the lifesaving station were signalled to come and help. The launch rail was set up near the top of the hill. Wilbur won the toss, the engine was warmed up and the flying-machine slid down the rail. Wilbur enthusiastically brought the nose up too fast, stalled the plane and dropped it into the sand at the foot of the hill.

Repairs were made and on December 17 with cold 27-mph winds blowing, the brothers pulled out the machine again and called the men from the lifesaving station for help. With such strong winds they decided to fly from a level track and set up the launching apparatus near the sheds. At 10:35, Orville climbed aboard and started the engine. The propellers began to turn.

Facing a 27-mph wind, the machine started very slowly when Orville released the hold-down wire. Wilbur ran alongside. The flier, in Orville's words later:

...lifted from the track just as it was entering on the fourth rail. Mr. Daniels took a picture just as it left the tracks. I found the control of the front rudder quite difficult on account of its being balanced too near the center and thus had a tendency to turn itself when started so that the rudder was turned too far on one side and then too far on the other. As a result the machine would rise suddenly to about 10 feet and then as suddenly, on turning the rudder, tip towards the ground. A sudden drop, when out about 100 feet from the end of the tracks, ended the flight....

He had been in the air only 12 seconds. Other attempts went like this:

At 11:20 a.m. on the second flight, Wilbur piloted. The wind dropped for a time and the machine flew faster, going 175 feet in 12 seconds.

At 11:40 a.m. on the third flight, Orville piloted the plane for a distance of 200 feet in 15 seconds.

At 12 noon a fourth and last flight with Wilbur flying went 852 feet in 59 seconds.

The brothers planned to go for distance on the next flight, perhaps as far as the lifesaving station in Kitty Hawk, but a few minutes later, as the flier was sitting on the sand, a gust of wind struck. The machine rolled over and over, destroying itself. The 1903 flying season was at an end.

That afternoon, after eating lunch and washing their dishes, the Wright brothers walked to the Kitty Hawk weather station which had a telegraph connection. Orville wrote the famous message:

Success Four Flights Thursday Morning All Against Twenty-One Mile Wind Started From Level With Engine Power Alone Average Speed Through Air Thirty-One Miles Longest 50 Seconds Inform Press Home Christmas. Orville Wright.

In 1904, the Wrights shifted their experiments to a field near Dayton, extending their flights to twenty-four miles in 38 minutes by the end of 1905. Incredibly, they attracted very little attention, even in Dayton. In 1908, they returned to Kill Devil Hill to test new aircraft, engines, and control arrangements. The press discovered them around this time and history was recorded.

Kill Devil Hills' population grew with the construction of bridges spanning Roanoke and Currituck sounds between 1920 and 1930. The famous hill had been stabilized with grass in 1928 and was capped with the Wright Brothers Memorial, a granite monument in 1932.

In 1938 a post office opened in Kill Devil Hills and in 1953 the town became incorporated. Today, the area is a demographic mixture of new and old, residential and commercial pockets, often without boundaries and spanning the area from the ocean to the sound.

It is a mostly a family beach; surfing and fishing are as popular here as anywhere on the Outer Banks. Avalon Pier has been refurbished in recent years providing the town with its own centrally located fishing pier.

Flying tours are offered from the Wright Brothers Monument grounds, bathing and swimming are enjoyed on the beaches of Kill Devil Hills, so there's plenty to see and do here.

Big Colington Island on the western perimeter of Kill Devil Hills offers some history of its own. The island is known for it rugged maritime forest and marshlands and is home to abundant wildlife, plants and trees draped with Spanish moss. Back in the mid-1600s, Sir John Colleton, an English gentleman, was granted this small island in Roanoke Sound. Original inhabitants of this island lived a hard existence farming and raising livestock. In more recent years Colington was home to large numbers of families who lived on the water. Some older areas of Colington Island are still inhabited by sea-faring families. There are small restaurants and seafood businesses lining the narrow curving road on Colington Island. During the month of May when soft-crabs are plentiful, a drive down this road in the wee hours of the morning or late at night will reveal people at work in the shedding troughs along the water. Newer communities are being developed in this attractive island setting, beyond the

WRIGHT BROTHERS NATIONAL MEMORIAL

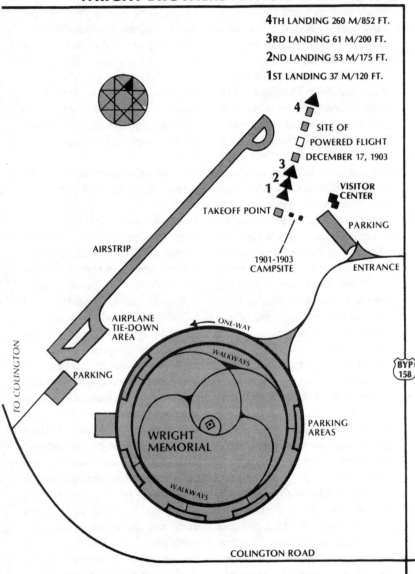

4TH LANDING 260 M/852 FT.
3RD LANDING 61 M/200 FT.
2ND LANDING 53 M/175 FT.
1ST LANDING 37 M/120 FT.

4

SITE OF
POWERED FLIGHT
DECEMBER 17, 1903

3
2
1

VISITOR
CENTER

TAKEOFF POINT

PARKING

AIRSTRIP

1901-1903
CAMPSITE

ENTRANCE

AIRPLANE
TIE-DOWN
AREA

ONE-WAY

WALKWAYS

TO COLINGTON

PARKING

BYP
158

WRIGHT
MEMORIAL

PARKING
AREAS

WALKWAYS

COLINGTON ROAD

small bridges spanning creeks and waterways, where the evening sun quietly melts into Roanoke Sound. Take time to drive out Colington Road and experience something of a bygone era.

New schools for children on the Outer Banks are centrally located in Kill Devil Hills. The Dare County Reverse Osmosis Water Treatment Plant (tours are conducted every day), new public library and the Thomas A. Baum Center (for senior adult activities) are located in this mid-beach town. Outer Banks Chamber of Commerce offices and welcome center, Dare County satellite offices and the newest shopping center, the Dare Center, are located in Kill Devil Hills as well. Regardless of the trend towards bigger and better resort homes and amenities elsewhere on the Outer Banks, Kill Devil Hills remains attached to its place in history as a family-oriented, low-key beach for visitors and a centrally located town of moderately-priced housing for the permanent population. Fishing, crabbing, kite flying, wind-surfing, sunbathing, air tours, shopping, restaurants, motels and close proximity to Kitty Hawk's Regional Medical Center or Nags Head's Medical Center, churches, libraries and schools make this town a choice for many.

Kill Devil Hills

ATTRACTIONS

WRIGHT BROTHERS MEMORIAL
Route 158, Bypass, MP 8   (919) 441-7430

The monument to Orville and Wilbur Wright sits majestically on a high grassy dune to the west of the bypass. This high dune was the site of the first flight in December 1903. The granite monument was established in 1932, and when seen during evening hours presents an imposing silhouette against a fading sunset or a softly lit reminder of the creativity and innovation of two men from Ohio.

The low, domed building on the right of the main drive provides interpretive exhibits of man's first flight and of those which came later. These explanations of the Wright brothers' struggle to fly include parts of their planes, engines and notes. Reproductions of their gliders are located here.

From the exhibit center a short walk outside will reveal the reconstructed wooden sheds of the Wrights' 1903 camp. These sheds are furnished with tools and equipment like those used by Orville and Wilbur Wright.

The walking distance to the memorial itself is a true test of stamina and fitness -- though it's all flat, it's a bit of a distance from the Visitor's Center to the Memorial itself. Parking is available closer to the base of the hill and away from the exhibit center. Paved walkways are for walking, yet a number of things discourage walking:

rain-water doesn't run off quickly in the low-lying areas at the base of the dune and there are pesky little sand spurs and cactus hiding in the grass awaiting an errant bare-foot! In fact, one *real* insiders' tip is to be sure you're wearing shoes - not flip flops - when you visit since these sticky beasts are everywhere.

The Exhibit Center is open for summer programs and kite flying demonstrations. The grounds are open 9:00 a.m. till 7:00 p.m during summer, 5:00 p.m. at other times, to vehicles, but you can walk the grounds any time.

KITTY HAWK AERO TOURS
Wright Memorial   441-4460

To experience the thrill of flying over the Outer Banks take a 1/2 hour tour from the flight booth a short distance from the parking lot at the west side of the memorial. The first time I came to the Outer Banks, I went flying. A flight from here will take you out over the water, beyond the pines and roof tops to a new adventure. Believe me, it's a thrill! This author took a flying lesson or two long ago, and a "fly" over the Outer Banks in one of the small aircraft at the Wright Memorial is an exciting experience! Pilots know the history of the area and the location of sunken ships in the ocean. The views are breath taking and evoke a sense of wonder about who we are and how we live. Rates are: $19/person for a party of 3 and $24/person for a party of 2. Starting around Easter the booth is open daily

and flights are scheduled everyday except when weather conditions aren't favorable. To make a reservation, call ahead.

COLINGTON ISLAND
Colington Road, MP 8-1/2
West of Bypass

This winding road takes you away from today's world to that of the commercial fisherman. There are campgrounds, seafood packers, bait & tackle stores, small cafes and restaurants and the almost-world-famous Billy's Seafood which doubles as the island's general store. While you're driving, look beyond the mobile homes with additions or small bungalows to the magnificent marshlands and maritime forests. Huge live oaks draped in Spanish moss, flowering dogwoods, and a multitude of ferns, holly and pine grow in this environment. Bring your camera, and if you plan to go crabbing or be near the marshgrass along the road or waterways, don't forget the insect repellant!

OUTER BANKS CHAMBER OF COMMERCE
WELCOME CENTER
Colington Road & Mustian Street
West of Route 158, Bypass, MP 8
441-8144

A new building houses the Chamber's welcome center in Kill Devil Hills. This center has tons of information for the visitor or resident of the area. It's a nice place to stop in, if you've passed up the Aycock Brown Welcome Center in Kitty Hawk. The Center is a clearing-house for written or telephone inquiries and the friendly staff can assist in relating information about activities, accommodations and the like. Mailing address: P.O. Box 1757, Kill Devil Hills, NC 27948. The Center is open from 9 to 5, Monday through Friday.

DARE COUNTY LIBRARY
KILL DEVIL HILLS BRANCH
Mustian Street & St. Clair St. west of Bypass (Route 158) MP 8   441-4331

The new library holds somewhere between 10,000 and 20,000 books, tapes and videos and offers meeting rooms for small groups. If you have books you'd like to donate, they're much appreciated. The hours are Monday through Friday, 9:30 to 6:30, Saturday, 10 to 4 and closed Sundays.

NAGS HEAD WOODS
ECOLOGICAL PRESERVE
**Ocean Acres Drive, MP 9-1/2
west of Route 158, Bypass   441-2525**

Nags Head Woods Ecological Preserve is a very special place. If you've had a little too much sun, or if you'd just like to spend time observing a part of the unique environment of the Outer Banks, you'll find it here. The Nature Conservancy, a privately-funded organization dedicated to preserving a barrier island ecosystem, oversees the land making up this Outer

Banks maritime forest. It is private property, not a park, but open to visitors Tuesday, Thursday and Saturday 10 till 3. Two loop trails begin at the Center and wind through forest, dune, swamp and pond habitats. Organized groups may arrange further use of the Center by calling the staff.

No camping, loitering, firearms, alcoholic beverages, picnicking, or pets are allowed. The maritime forest itself is well-hidden on the west side of the Outer Banks and many wonders of nature are hidden within the forest. There is a small exhibit center and a staff member can provide information on how to join the Friends of Nags Head Woods. Mailing address: 701 W. Ocean Acres Drive, Kill Devil Hills, NC 27948. Levels of membership are $15 individual and $25 family; these fees go towards the support of the Preserve's environmental education and research programs.

Kill Devil Hills
RECREATION

AVALON FISHING PIER
**Beach Road, off Route 158 at MP 6
441-7494**

Avalon Pier was built in 1960 and is 705 feet long. The pier was refurbished in 1990-91, has lights for night fishing, a restaurant, bait & tackle shop, ice, and rental fishing gear. A popular place in season, the pier is closed December 1 to March 1. Admission prices: $4.95 for adults and

$2.75 children under 12. Weekly pass: $28, weekend pass: $13.00, season pass: $100. Handicapped in wheelchairs are admitted without charge.

SEA RANCH TENNIS CENTER
Beach Road, off Route 158 at MP 7
441-7126

A large indoor tennis center across from the oceanfront hotel of the same name, the Sea Ranch is open year round from 9:00 a.m. until 9:00 p.m. (with extended hours in summer). There are two courts and an observation lounge. Tennis racquets and balls are available for purchase. A selection of clothing is available as well. The pro gives lessons by appointment only. Reserve court time in advance.

NAUTILUS ATHLETIC CLUB
Beach Road, off Route 158 at MP
7441-7001

This athletic center is located on the lower level of Sea Ranch II and has a full complement of exercise and fitness equipment. Nancy and Stu Golliday are in charge to assist you in developing a program suited to your needs. Jacuzzi, saunas and exercise bikes are available, but there are no aerobics classes. Open year round, Monday through Friday 7:30 a.m. to 9:00 p.m. and Saturday, 10:00 a.m. to 7:00 p.m. Memberships are available and there are daily fees for nonmembers.

Other forms of recreation are available in Kill Devil Hills. Miniature golf is a popular pastime for visi-

tors. There's a new **Grass Course Miniature Golf** layout under construction on Rt. 158 Bypass, at MP 5 1/2, near the Kill Devil Hills/Kitty Hawk town line. It's the second such course for developer Rick Willis. His popular Grass Course in Corolla Light Resort Village prompted this one. **Frontier Golf**, located on the Bypass near MP 7, is a longtime favorite with visitors and locals alike.

Kill Devil Hills

SHOPPING

Shopping is something to look forward to in the shops along Route 158 Bypass and the Beach Road. When you've had too much sun or you're just in the mood for leisurely shopping, Seagate North, located at MP 6 on the Bypass has a variety of stores and shops. **T.J.'s Hobbies and Sports Cards**, 441-3667, has collectibles, jewelry and Fenton glass. They have metal detectors, too. **Sea Birds**, 441-5223, has religious cards and gifts. **Mom's Sweet Shop**, 441-2829, has everything for your sweet tooth, delicious ice creams and yogurts. **Time After Time**, 480-0008, has antiques and vintage clothing of quality and some consignment items. **Movies, Movies**, 441-2377, has more videos than you can imagine! The same for the selection of shirts and prints at **T-Shirt Whirl**, 441-1414. **Surfside Books**, 441-1484, has a good collection of paperback mysteries for beach "consumption" as well as classic literary works and of-

The Outer Banks
with Ken Mann

6:00 PM and 11:30 PM nightly
News, Events, Sports,
Fishing & Features
TV Channel 12 - Vacation Channel

fers a friendly place to browse and get in out of the heat. **The Wooden Feather**, 480-3066, is an art gallery featuring wood carvings of waterfowl. **Pearl Factory**, 441-7722, moved from the Beach Road, has jewelry, accessories and a repair shop.

The **Dare Center** is the Outer Banks' newest shopping center and is located on the west side of the Bypass at MP 7. **Belk, Rose's** and a **Food Lion** are the anchors here with a nice array of smaller shops. For good eats, try **Lil' Caesar's Pizza**, 480-1354, **NY Bagels**, 480-0990, and Petrozza Deli, 441-1642. **Petrozza's** features fresh Italian breads, great entrees and super sandwiches. Freshly made pasta and sauces are expertly created in this popular store which specializes in buffet platters and is open all the time!

Clothing Liquidators has gobs of neat clothes at very reasonable prices. On the other end of the shopping center is **MoYo**, a full-menu yogurt shop specializing in healthy foods: **Book Scents, Subway Sandwiches** and **Harrell's Too** home furnishings are the other stores here.

Shops located at the Sea Ranch on the Beach Road at MP 7 include a full-service hair salon, **Shear Genius**, 441-3571. The salon, under the ownership of Linda Porter, offers natural shampoos, perms and super hair cuts. Color and highlighting are a specialty and they also offer full body massages. **Alice's Looking Glass,** 441-7126, is a fine apparel shop for women. Their sweater collection for any sea-

son is probably the best on the beach. Friendly people to serve you, as well.

North Carolina Books is located at MP 7-1/2 in the Times Printing building. Thousands of second hand paperback books are stocked. Some reduced hardcover books have been added. There is a bring-in-old-books and apply-credit-to-new-books policy in effect here. **Jim's Camera House**, 441-6528, is a popular place on the Outer Banks. Jim and Hattie Lee have a full service store on the ByPass at MP 9. If you have a question, have film to be developed, need to purchase film or any camera equipment, this is the place to stop. Jim likes to talk about lighting, subjects and his interesting adventures all over the world on the sight-side of a camera. Family vacation portraits, weddings, you name it -- call Jim Lee for experienced photography and helpful advice.

Farther down the Bypass, around MP 9-1/2 is **Roanoke Press** and **Croatan Bookery**, 480-1890, owned by the same folks who own the *Coastland Times* newspaper and **North Carolina Books.** This store offers still more second hand books, primarily on North Carolina. They've opened recently and some good browsing is available here as well as good reading. It is an interesting addition to the beach this year.

Sea Holly Square at MP 9-1/2 on the Beach Road is a popular shopping center. **Beach Boys & Girls Surf and Volley**, 441-7176, has Guatemalan clothing, accessories and gifts. **Sea Holly Hooked Rugs**, 441-8961, has supplies and fine crafts, kits and patterns. **Miss Charlotte's**, 441-7890, is a southern boutique with great clothing and accessories. The ever-popular **Tar Heel Trading Company**, 441-5278, is filled with quality American crafts, many of which are Carolina crafted. If you're looking for a special collection of serving pieces, accessories and the like, Mary Ames' shop will have it.

Sea Isle Gifts and Lamp Shop, 441-7206, has been on the Beach Road, MP 9-1/2, for a long time. They carry lamps, repair kits, shells galore, jewelry and an assortment of small gift items. **Frames At Large** and **Dip 'n Deli** are convenient for folks staying at the oceanfront hotels and guest cottages at this point on the beach.

The Beach Barn Shops, located in the red barn on the Bypass at MP 10, are a nice change of pace. **Carolina Moon**, 441-4000, is a favorite place for unusual gifts, pottery, cards, tapes and jewelry. The shop has a "new age" ambience and a fine collection of esoteric gifts. Across the hall of the barn, **Birthday Suits**, 441-5338, is loaded with men's and women's clothing for young adults and older. It's a boutique of California fashions that you don't find in every shop, which makes it all the more fun to take something home from a beach shopping spree. Both **Carolina Moon** and **Birthday Suits** have shops in Duck Village.

Food stores are well-spaced up and down the Bypass from Kitty Hawk to Nags Head. Smaller grocery stores fill in on the Beach Road. **The Trading Post** on the Beach Road in Kill Devil Hills also has a branch post office. This general store carries everything. The **Argyle Bake Shop**, 441-7710, MP 9-1/2 on the Beach Road has fresh baked breads, cakes, pastries and is open 7:30 a.m. til 5:00 p.m. during the season. Their off-season hours are adjusted occasionally, but essentially they are a year round business.

Fresh seafood is available along the Bypass, too. **Billy's** has a location in Kitty Hawk (open only in summer) and a larger store in Colington. Then there's **Jerry's** near MP 8-1/2. Watch for specials and talk about where the fish came from and when it was caught. You want good fish, fresh fish and then fish stories!

Jockey's Ridge (now a state park) is the tallest sand dune on the East Coast.

Inside
Nags Head

*N*ags Head is the destination for many who come to the Outer Banks. In early times it carried the legend of how the inhabitants tied lanterns around horses' necks and led the animals up and down the beach signalling merchant ships at sea that perhaps these lights meant other ships were safely in the harbor. The legend further promotes the idea that when these ships ran aground, the natives salvaged the cargo to supplement their own needs.

Other strange goings-on are recorded from the early 1800s. There were tales of ships missing at sea and of a twenty-nine year old woman named Theodosia Burr Alison, the daughter of adventurer, duelist and former vice-president Aaron Burr, who was lost at sea when her New York-bound ship, the *Patriot*, disappeared in late 1812. Later on, a portrait bearing a startling resemblance to Theodosia was discovered in a cottage in Nags Head by its owner, who said that it had been taken from aboard a deserted schooner around 1813. Other stories capture the confessions of former pirates during their final hours; their tales of murder-ing all hands on ocean-going vessels and seizing the goods for their own use or for trading..

Nevertheless, Nags Head was becoming a summer resort even during the mid-1850s. Only the wealthy could manage the trip here aboard ships crossing the waters separating the Outer Banks from the mainland to the west and north. Summer cottages began to appear and the first hotel was built in 1838. A grand structure, the Nags Head Hotel, attracted many who enjoyed a vacation here in early times. Fishing, sea-bathing, dancing, gambling in the hotel's casino and bowling occupied the visitors while the natives kept mostly to themselves in the soundside village in Nags Head Woods. In 1851, the hotel was enlarged and a half-mile of mule-drawn railway was laid to make the journey to the ocean less troublesome. During the Civil War the Nags Head Hotel was burned by retreating Confederates and later rebuilt in the early 1870s.

During this time, the area was not only vulnerable to pirate ships and war, but the rugged coastline also became a burial ground for ships and crews during massive storms.

One of the worst disasters in Outer Banks history happened in Nags Head in 1877, when the 541-ton barkentine-rigged steamer, USS *Huron*, went aground in a November storm. Due to Congressional cut-backs, Nags Head Lifesaving Station No. 7, located only two miles away, was unmanned at the time. Local fishermen helped those who made it to shore. The remains of the *Huron* lie on the bottom of the Atlantic Ocean, straight out between mile-markers 11 and 12 and almost even with the end of the Nags Head Fishing Pier. Diving enthusiasts continue to recover artifacts from the wreckage.

Nags Head-style architecture refers to the simple cottage design first built here by a Dr. Pool of Elizabeth City in the early 1880s. The cottage was set on pilings to allow the stormy ocean to flow under it. Most of the timber used to build his and other cottages came from wood washed ashore after shipwrecks. The homes included two or three rooms with lots of windows, all of which were closed in winter months by heavy wooden shutters. Large porches adorned the homes, which were left unpainted.

In the period after World War I, a local builder S.J. Twine modified the design into what today is recognized as a classic architectural form. Many older cottages have been renovated;

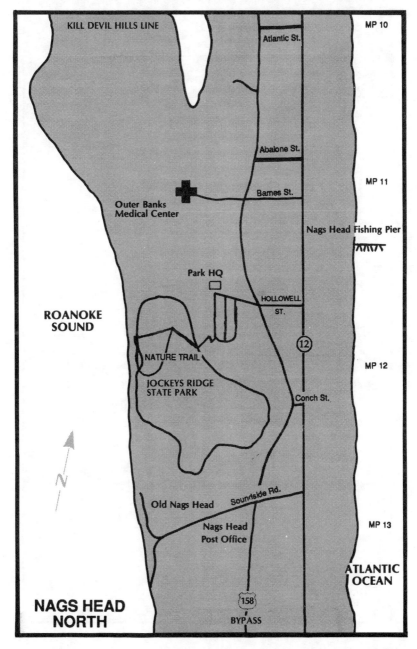

KILL DEVIL HILLS LINE

Atlantic St.

MP 10

Abalone St.

Barnes St.

MP 11

Outer Banks
Medical Center

Nags Head Fishing Pier

Park HQ

HOLLOWELL
ST.

ROANOKE
SOUND

(12)

MP 12

NATURE TRAIL

JOCKEYS RIDGE
STATE PARK

Conch St.

N

Old Nags Head

Soundside Rd.

Nags Head
Post Office

MP 13

ATLANTIC
OCEAN

NAGS HEAD
NORTH

158
BYPASS

Photo: Michael Helminski

A skimmer skims for morsels in the sound.

other much larger homes are built of similar style and are today's most popularly-designed beach homes.

In the early 30s, the Outer Banks began to attract many more visitors to its peaceful atmosphere. It became the summer place of the wealthy of the Albemarle region of the state (the mainland area across the waters of Albemarle Sound and inclusive of towns like Elizabeth City and Edenton). Leroy's Seaside Inn was built on the oceanfront, slightly north of Jockey's Ridge to accommodate large numbers of these guests. Today, that old hotel, moved off the oceanfront and completely refurbished as a bed and breakfast, has become the First Colony Inn, a romantic spot where the sweeping roof and wide porches hold a certain charm for visitors to the area. (Further description of First Colony Inn is noted in the section on Accommodations.)

Newman's Shell Shop, noted in the section on Attractions, was the first store on the beach. Sam & Omie's, noted in the section on Restaurants, located at Whalebone Junction, was opened around the same time. Both are over 50 years old.

Nags Head became an incorporated town in 1961 and by this time it also became a well-known fishing and vacation destination for people from the state and well beyond. Whether folks came to stay at places in Nags Head or Kitty Hawk, the phrase, "we're going to Nags Head" often referred to any town or village on the Outer Banks -- and still does. Hotels, motels, fishing piers, restaurants, kite-flying (and now hang gliding), dancing, artistry and many other forms of recreation became popular here.

Businesses opened, small communities were built and folks who were once just loyal visitors began to come here to live year round. Native families were generally engaged in fishing as a livelihood, later opening restaurants and other seafood businesses. As commercial development continued, the Outer Banks was connected to the mainland by bridges across Roanoke and Currituck sounds, providing easier access thus making necessary the development and construction that have transformed the area into the popular destination it is today. The Village of Nags Head, with its magnificent golf course, is the most recently developed resort community. The golf course opened in 1988 and hundreds of homes have been built. Most of the homes, as you will see, are variations of the Nags Head style, mentioned earlier.

The primary reason the Outer Banks has retained its low-rise development is that most folks want to keep it as close to the way it was as is possible. There are no high-rise buildings on the oceanfront to block out the sun or restrict the view. Changes are managed, ever so slightly, here and there, to reflect its growth as a resort, enjoyed by families from all over the east coast. Yet the fragile ecology of the barrier islands, the threat of hurricanes and nor'easters keep a sense of natural order about development here. So, while growth occurs, it stops (or, at least, has so far) before the somewhat primitive, private feeling of Nags Head that has attracted so many over the years, is lost.

Nags Head

ATTRACTIONS

JOCKEY'S RIDGE STATE PARK
Route 158, Bypass, MP 12   441-7132

Jockey's Ridge has been a tourist attraction since 1851 and was established as a state park in 1965. There is a legend that "...the lady who may accompany you to its summit if not already a wife will shortly become yours." Whether or not the legend is believable becomes a moot question. Questions about how this 410-acre hill was formed or about its unique ecosystem of shifting sand ridges, dense shrub thickets, temporary pools and soundside habitats come to mind.

It is a mile long, up to 12,000 feet wide and rises to 140 above sea level. The Ridge forms the tallest "medano" (the geological word for a large isolated hill of sand, also called a "transverse dune") on the east coast. Once thought to be caused by the early colonists destroying the natural cover of the banks with logging and stock grazing, it now seems certain that these huge bare sand hills have been here for thousands of years. Actually, there are two great dunes, one lower on the east and a higher one beyond.

From the top of the ridge, you can see both ocean and sound. The homes along the beach appear as tiny huts of a fishing village. Kite-flying and hang-gliding enthusiasts hike to the top of the dunes to catch the breezes which flow constantly, shifting the sands in all directions. The desert-like appearance of the sand dunes reveals strange but artistic patterns of those winds and of the footprints made by people who climb the hills. The climb is a test of stamina on hot sunny days, however it's more manageable after a stabilizing rainfall.

The park headquarters is located near the northern end of a parking lot to the west of the main highway. You'll notice an entrance sign at MP 12, Carolista Drive in Nags Head. Maps are available from the park ranger which will indicate walking areas. There are natural history programs and sheltered picnic areas for a leisurely lunch. Call 441-7132 for program schedules. A self-guided 1-1/2 mile nature trail was dedicated in 1989. It starts from the southwest corner of the parking lot and proceeds towards Roanoke Sound. The trail is marked by plant identification -- persimmon, bayberry, Virginia creeper, wild grapes and black cherry. Animal tracks are identified as well, among them fox, raccoon, white-tailed deer, racerunner lizard, antlions, opossums and hognosed snakes. It takes about 1-1/2 hours to walk at a leisurely pace. Wear shoes, as there are sand spurs. There's a special 360-foot boardwalk if mobil-

Glenn Eure

cordially invites you to experience his
Ghost Fleet ART GALLERY
where tradition and the avant garde converge.

This versatile artist expresses his unique sense of artistic adventure in collographs, etchings, woodblocks, oils, sculptural canvases, drawings and carvings on a variety of themes. The gallery also features one person shows and special exhibitions, an art lecture series and museum quality custom framing.

From nautical . . .

to the abstract . . .

ity is impaired. For the visually handicapped, there are audio guides at the park office. Pick up a brochure at the visitor center to explain and illustrate the tracks.

A traffic light was installed by the Dept. of Transportation at the crosswalk on the highway, farther south. The colorful flags and kites of Kitty Hawk Connection attract visitors; however, it is recommended that a walk on the dunes begins at the park visitor center.

NEWMAN'S SHELL SHOP
Beach Road, MP 13-1/2   441-5791

Newman's Shell Shop is an Outer Banks attraction as well as shop. The bright pink establishment qualifies as an Outer Banks Museum. This was the first store on the beach and it opened in 1939. It has remained a family-owned shop through the years and carries shells from all over the world. Owner Susie Stoutenberg's shop contains a labeled shell collection which displays shells from places such as India and Peru -- those faraway beaches which most of us can only imagine. A large variety of gifts and accessories spill from attractive displays. Sea shells are hanging all over the place in an assortment of mobiles and wind-chimes. Newman's is an important stop on the tour, not just a place to browse or make a purchase. Woodcrafted birds and fish hang from the ceiling; accessories from napkins, cards, and placemats to mugs, crystals, Christmas ornaments and

millions of shells are for sale. An enormous variety of shell jewelry, jewelry made from stones and various metals from far away places and handmade locally will surely amaze you.

There's even a collection of antique guns, pistols and swords on display which have been in the family for many years. The building is 54-years old and we can only imagine the stories that have been traded here as well as the millions of people who have visited and made a purchase. Susie notes that many of their shell crafts are make on site and visitors can observe this activity. Fresh flower arrangements are also made here in the summer. And, of course, hermit crabs are a most popular item with the younger set. There's even a Hermit Crab Race, held on the last Saturday in July.

On another side of Susie's busy life is her involvement in the establishment of a Youth Center on the Beach. She chairs a committee of nine and has been working for the past three years to see this much-needed facility for the permanent residents of the beach become a reality. The Outer Banks Youth Center, Inc. has established its non-profit status, largely through her efforts and if any of our readers would like to make a donation, stop in and see her, or mail a donation to OBYC, Inc., P.O. Box 249, Nags Head, NC 27959.

OLD NAGS HEAD
Route 158, MP 12

Most of the villages on the Outer Banks began as small community on the soundside. Just south of Jockey's Ridge you'll notice a narrow road leading towards the sound. Here are some of the original, old-style Outer Banks' homes. Others were built on the ocean side of the highway. In the soundside area, some properties have been lost due to the shifting sands of Jockey's Ridge. It is a most interesting area of the Outer Banks.

On the oceanfront, older houses reflect their age in the dark brown color of shake-siding and wooden shutters propped open with poles during the summer and closed during the winter. Some are built low as though tucked behind the dunes for protection and now sit vulnerable and open to storms which have caused erosion of the dunes. Nevertheless, these older homes lend significant character to determining the harshness of life.

OUTER BANKS MEDICAL CENTER
W. Barnes, west of Route 158, MP 11
441-7111

Not necessarily an attraction but worth mentioning here, the Outer Banks Medical Center is a family and emergency medical center. It is a nonprofit branch of Chesapeake General Hospital of Virginia. Appointments can be made between 9 and 5 Monday through Friday, and 9 to 12 on Saturday. Emergency care is available 24 hours a day, and Dare County Emergency Services has a helicopter pad for transportation to nearby hospitals. Laboratory services and x-ray facilities are available as well. Hospital signs are noted on the Bypass.

GALLERY ROW
Driftwood Street, MP 10-1/2

The Outer Banks is home to many artists and the galleries located on this street and along Gallery Row were established some years ago. We've included a complete list of the art galleries at the end of the Service Directory section of this book for easy reference, but some of the first galleries bear mentioning here.

Glenn Eure's Ghost Fleet Gallery, 441-6584, is open all year and is one of the most popular galleries, displaying local art. Each year in February, the Frank Stick Memorial Art Show is held here. It is a juried exhibit and a popular cultural addition to life on the Outer Banks. The literary artists also hold readings of original work as a part of the Frank Stick show and poetry readings held in the gallery are quite popular during the off season.

Glenn is at home here with his own artistic creations. You might find him sketching or carving an ice sculpture in the parking lot. He's an interesting person of many adventures in

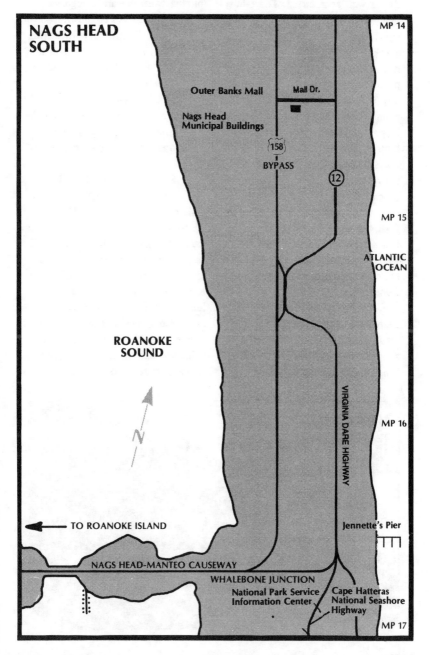

NAGS HEAD SOUTH

Outer Banks Mall — Mall Dr.

Nags Head Municipal Buildings

(158) BYPASS

(12)

MP 14

MP 15

ATLANTIC OCEAN

ROANOKE SOUND

N

MP 16

VIRGINIA DARE HIGHWAY

← TO ROANOKE ISLAND

Jennette's Pier

NAGS HEAD-MANTEO CAUSEWAY

WHALEBONE JUNCTION

National Park Service Information Center

Cape Hatteras National Seashore Highway

MP 17

life as well as an artist. **The Ghost Fleet Gallery** comes alive in its own structure of planks and boards. Glenn and Pat, his wife, who works magic with framing and matting artwork and photography, support the art community with numerous exhibits in the main gallery, and they are often there to provide interesting commentary. Stop by and meet them. Off season hours are posted, but most of the time, between 10 a.m. and 5 p.m. it's open for casual viewing and conversation.

Across the street, **Jewelry by Gail**, 441-5387, is an interesting place. Gail Kowalski is a designer-goldsmith who has won national recognition for her creations in precious metals and stones.

An unusual amethyst crystal chandelier created by Pennsylvania artist Michael Fornadley is hung in the shop and is definitely worth a look. Most of the jewelry created here falls into the "wearable art" category.

Next door is **Terra Cotta**, 480-2323. It's a delightful shop filled with art made by artists from all over the country. Owners John and Lisanne List have a broad selection of leather and stained glass jewelry, unusual pottery (raku, for example) salt-marsh pottery, handmade paper and fiber art. The shop is open all year except January.

A walk down Gallery Row to the south takes you to the **Morales Gallery**, 441-6484. Owners Mitch and Christine Lively feature collections of local art in oils and watercolors as well as photographs, some by nationally known photographers. Along Gallery Row, you'll also see **Ipso Facto Gallery**, 480-2793, where antiques, books and Oriental rugs are displayed along with visual artistry. It's a great place to browse, ohh and ahh and, of course, find a treasure to take home.

Down the Beach Road to MP 10-1/2, you'll discover Anna Gartrell's **Gallery By the Sea**, 480-0578. Anna's artistry is discovered in an exceptional display of watercolors and photography.

Nags Head

RECREATION

HANG GLIDING

This sport has become increasingly popular through the years and if you're into flying like the gulls you can sign up for lessons. Hang gliding has its roots back beyond the Wright brothers flight. Lilienthall was killed flying a glide and kite flying has been popular for years. The more modern hang gliding devices are an improvement on the devices used in the American space program. Francis M. Rogallo, a retired NASA engineer now living in Southern Shores, developed the flexible Rogallo Wing in order to bring down space capsules. Though the parachute finally won out for this endeavor, the light, mylar and aluminum gliders began to appear in the hands of sport fliers about 20 years ago and now the sport has caught on in a big way, especially here on the Outer Banks.

John Harris, president of Kitty Hawk Kites, says, "It's as close as you can get to flying as the birds do." The novice hang glider begins with basic instruction to glide from a high elevation to a lower one. Gradually you learn to make use of the same thermals and ridge lift air currents that birds use in order to extend their powerless flights.

The Rogallo Foundation to benefit low-speed flight has been established in Kitty Hawk. The goal of the foundation is to support education, research and literary pursuit of aerodonetics, the science of gliding and soaring flight. The Board of Directors includes people from Virginia, Maryland and Florida. A museum of interpretive exhibits is planned in the future to assist the public in understanding the contributions aerodenetics and low-speed aerodynamics have made to society. Rogallo, now 80, and his wife serve on the board of the foundation. Tax deductible donations can be sent to: Rogallo Foundation, P.O. Box 1839, Nags Head, NC 27959.

For those of you who like to read up on a sport before asking your body to do it, a brief description of hang gliding follows. The flier is attached at the waist to the center of gravity of the wing. In front of the flyer is a triangular metal control bar. After a good run downhill against the wind to gather speed, the glider will begin to lift and leave the ground. From here on, altitude and direction are controlled by the pilot. Shifting body weight will turn the glider right or left. Moving the control bar forward or back with the hands causes the center of gravity to move the kite's nose to pitch up or down. When the pilot runs out of hill or wind, a soft landing is managed by pushing the control bar out, causing the glider to stall. Several practice landings are the norm for soft, ideal landings.

It's a fairly safe sport but lessons are definitely suggested. Sign up at Kitty Hawk Kites, located across the road from Jockey's Ridge. Crash helmets are highly recommended. Accidents have resulted in some minor injuries, however, the most common injury is a broken arm. Over all the years of gliding, only one fatality has been recorded on Jockey's Ridge as a result of the sport.

During the past few years other locations on the Outer Banks have proven popular for hang gliding.

Truck-towing along the open beach areas north of Corolla has become the way to lift off, since the dunes of that area are not high enough for an unassisted launch. A glider and pilot are tethered to the back of a pickup truck and a hydraulic winch permits the glider to ascend to proper height and catch the wind, after a fast start.

Most hang gliding enthusiasts are in good physical condition, have above average intelligence and are extroverts! Participants prefer this sport almost year round, but are most frequently airborne during warm days.

KITTY HAWK CONNECTION
Route 158 Bypass, MP 13

The attractive, 2-story wooden structure across the road from Jockey's Ridge is called Kitty Hawk Connection. It is a conglomeration of shops virtually centered around hang gliding and kite flying. Kitty Hawk Kites and Kitty Hawk Sports are waiting to show you how to enjoy the latest Outer Banks' sports. From the towering observation deck you can see for miles. When you're on the ground, if hang gliding is your desire, the instructors at **Kitty Hawk Kites** will put you through the drills and lessons so vital to learning about hang gliding. Most equipment used for visitors is rented, however, Kitty Hawk Kites handles gliders from major manufacturers and prices run from a few hundred dollars for used gliders to several thousand dollars for new.

Lessons require a 3-hour commitment and then five flights, all skillfully monitored by the experts at Kitty Hawk Kites. Reservations are required. Call 441-4124, for times and rates.

If it's kite flying or hobby crafts, Kitty Hawk Kites has some of the most beautiful and unusual kites, toys and games found anywhere in the world.

If water sports are more your thing, **Kitty Hawk Sports** is the place to be. Surfboards, sails, Boogie boards, rafts and catamarans are featured here. Kayacking is new this year and the sport is seeing increased popularity for those who find choppy seas a thrilling adventure. In addition to their excellent equipment and all the accessories that go along with them, they also feature a great collection of sports clothes for men and women.

Pro Dive Center of Nags Head is also located here at the Kitty Hawk Connection. Although there is no water for these activities on site, you will be directed to the soundside center near Windmill Point, MP 16. In season Kitty Hawk Kites is open from 7:30 a.m. till 10:30 p.m. Kitty Hawk Sports is open at 8:30 a.m. and closes about 10:30 p.m. Other shops in the complex follow similar hours.

NAGS HEAD GOLF LINKS
Route 158, Bypass, MP 15
Village at Nags Head   441-8073

The Outer Banks' newest golf course, Nags Head Golf Links, is an 18-hole course, resembling those of Scotland with few trees but with wind-blown, open fairways and well-tended greens. A par 71 course of overall length of 6,126 yards, it was voted in the top 50 for the southeastern region by *GolfWeek* magazine. Call for green fees, cart information and starting times. It's open to the public all year, 7:30 a.m. till 6:00 p.m. There's also a beautiful clubhouse with a restaurant, The Links Room, serving snacks or full meals, with a full bar.

VILLAGE AT NAGS HEAD BEACH CLUB
On the Atlantic Ocean, MP 15
480-2222

This beautiful, oceanfront facility is part of the Village at Nags Head development and, as such, is *basically* private. We say basically, because it *is* available -- happily -- to the public for rent for special events such as wedding receptions, corporate outings and private parties. Catering is even available through the Village's catering service. Call for information or reservations.

NAGS HEAD FISHING PIER
On the Atlantic Ocean, MP 12
441-5141

This is one of the most popular fishing piers on the Outer Banks. It is 750 feet long and has its own bait and tackle shop. There is night fishing, game tables for the kids and a restaurant which features fresh seafood and wonderful views of the ocean. The pier is open year round and from April 1 till November 1 it never closes. Admission is $5/day for adults, $12/3-day pass and $30/8-day pass. Season rates are $135/$225 for singles and couples. Kids are always half price.

JENNETTE'S PIER
On the Atlantic Ocean
at Whalebone Junction
441-6116

This popular fishing pier is undergoing restoration and, when finished, will be the largest on the Outer Banks. It's also the oldest, having been originally built in 1932, then knocked down in the Ash Wednesday Storm, then rebuilt in 1962. About 250 feet of brand new decking opened for fishing around Easter weekend of '92, and construction continues on the other 500 feet, with completion expected in the fall. The current rates are $2.75/day, but they will probably change when all the construction is finished. This pier is usually crawling with people who fish (we're told that the activity here is not putting a damper on the fish being caught) and the location is in the heart of Whalebone Junction -- along the hot-bed of big catches and tall stories. As we write, it's crawling with people who have a talent with hammer and nails. Rest assured, the pier, a very popular place at anytime, will be even more so by late spring and summer.

OUTER BANKS FISHING PIER
On the Atlantic Ocean in South
Nags Head, MP 18-1/2
441-5740

This 650'-long pier was originally built in 1959 and rebuilt in 1962 after the Ash Wednesday storm. Owner Garry Oliver has all you need in the bait and tackle shop for a day of fishing along this somewhat remote stretch of beach. The pier closes during the winter and reopens in late March. Rates are $5/day, $12.50/week, $90-$150/season. While there is no specific rate for children, it's generally half price.

NATIONAL PARK SERVICE
INFORMATION CENTER

Whalebone Junction   441-6644

This information stop is located on the west side of NC Hwy. 12 as you head south on the Cape Hatteras National Seashore. Hours are 9:00 a.m. till 6:00 p.m. in season, Memorial Day through Labor Day.

KITTY HAWK SPORTS
SAILING CENTER
Route 158, Bypass, MP 16
at the Windmill
441-6800, 441-2756

Kitty Hawk Sports operates this waterfront recreation center. From April through October, 9:00 a.m. till 6:00 p.m., those who enjoy water sports will find a haven here. Instruction is offered in windsurfing, sailing and kayacking. Equipment is available for sale and rent. This is an inter-

nationally recognized high wind test center for Mistral and North High Wind windsurfing products. Plenty of colorful activity goes on here, especially when the spring regattas get underway drawing windsurfers from all over the country.

SOUNDSIDE WATERSPORTS
Route 158, Bypass, MP 16   441-4270

Soundside Watersports provides all kinds of rental equipments for a day on the water. Waverunners, JetSkis, Hobie Cats, canoes, windsurfing gear and lessons are available. If you would like to rent a small boat for the week, they'll deliver it to your cottage. Hours are 9 a.m. to 6 p.m. daily.

WATERWORKS
Route 158, Bypass, MP 16-1/2
441-8875

The two-story soundside building is the place to buy or rent equip-

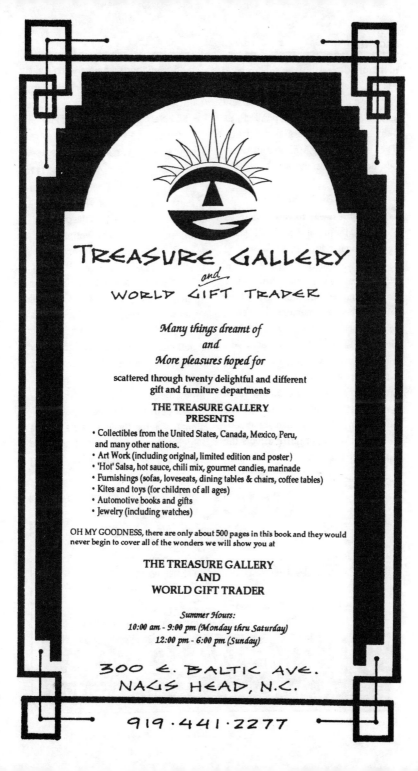

TREASURE GALLERY
and
WORLD GIFT TRADER

Many things dreamt of
and
More pleasures hoped for

scattered through twenty delightful and different
gift and furniture departments

THE TREASURE GALLERY
PRESENTS

- Collectibles from the United States, Canada, Mexico, Peru,
  and many other nations.
- Art Work (including original, limited edition and poster)
- 'Hot' Salsa, hot sauce, chili mix, gourmet candies, marinade
- Furnishings (sofas, loveseats, dining tables & chairs, coffee tables)
- Kites and toys (for children of all ages)
- Automotive books and gifts
- Jewelry (including watches)

OH MY GOODNESS, there are only about 500 pages in this book and they would
never begin to cover all of the wonders we will show you at

THE TREASURE GALLERY
AND
WORLD GIFT TRADER

Summer Hours:
10:00 am - 9:00 pm (Monday thru Saturday)
12:00 pm - 6:00 pm (Sunday)

300 E. BALTIC AVE.
NAGS HEAD, N.C.

919·441·2277

ment for a day on the water. They have t-shirts, wet suits and other accessories. You can buy or rent boards and sails. Waterworks has expanded this year and now offers parasailing. They're open mid-April to mid-October, depending on the weather.

AIR BOAT RIDES
On the Causeway towards Manteo

Beginning a couple of years ago, air-boat rides became an option to other ways of getting out on the water. They will appeal to older adults or children accompanied by adults who aren't able to manage other forms of windsurfing, sailing, etc. Our experience with the ride was that it was thrilling, cooling (you do usually get wet), interesting in terms of the marsh areas you're able to see, but *loud*. Even with the cotton in our ears, it was bothersome. There is also some concern as to how that noise affects the marine life in the marshes. Still, it is a

fun 45-minute trip and could be right up your alley.

SUNSET TEEN CLUB at THE VILLAGE BEACH CLUB
5805 S. Virginia Dare Trail, MP 15
Nags Head 480-2222

The Village Beach Club is a private club and its activities are centered around the needs of the membership. But, there's an exception which is worth noting, especially for those in the 12-17 year old age group.

The "Sunset Teen Club" was started in the spring of '92, for all teens here, not just Beach Club members. The idea is to get young people together for dancing as well as other activities. During the summer, the Sunset Teen Club meets on Monday nights beginning mid-June and continues until late August. The admission is $5 for the evening's events which begin at 7 p.m. and continue until 11 p.m. In addition to dancing

and dance contests with a DJ, there are other activities around and in the ocean-front pool. Lifeguards are on duty. There's also a game room and snack bar available. Local businesses, such as Hardee's, Kitty Hawk Sports and Little Caesar's Pizza, are supporting the Sunset Teen Club with donation of prizes to the winners of the dance contests.

There is a requirement that you come and stay for the evening. No leaving and returning is allowed. The activities are supervised or monitored by adult chaperons and from time to time members of the Nags Head police force have dropped in unnoticed.

We think the concept is great and offer Tom Hall and his co-workers our thanks. We hope families with young people coming to the beach will join the fun on Monday nights at the Village Beach Club.

OTHER THINGS TO DO...

Nags Head is the activity center of the Outer Banks when it comes to variety. While some other towns and villages feature plenty of water sports, Nags Head has other things to do, as well.

The **Beach Bowling Center**, 441-7077, is located at MP 10, on the west side of Route 158 Bypass. **Surf Slide** is an outdoor adventure on the west side of Route 158 Bypass at MP 11, open summers only 10 a.m. till midnight. **Colony House Cinema's** new location in Nags Head on the east side of Route 158 Bypass at MP 10-1/

2 is convenient for vacationers and locals who live more on the south end of the beach. The land available for full-sized golf courses on the Outer Banks is scarce, but there are a number of miniature golf courses in the Nags Head area and they provide recreation for everyone. **Deep Africa Mini Golf** has 36 lighted holes with an African jungle motif. Located at MP 11-1/2 on the Beach Road, open summers from 10 a.m. till midnight. **Forbes Candy and Miniature Golf** is also a favorite gathering place for family activity on the Beach Road. **Soundside Golf** is located on the west side of Route 158 Bypass.

Nags Head

SHOPPING

Nags Head claims the bulk of Outer Banks shopping from small boutiques along the Beach Road and Route 158 Bypass to large shopping centers. You'll definitely need to drive along the Bypass and the Beach Road to discover a whole array of shopping options here in Nags Head. You can't miss the surf shops and **Whalebone Surf Shop**, 441-6747, at MP 10, is a new place to shop for neat clothes and of course surf-wear and gear. Art work and fine crafts are available along Driftwood Street and Gallery Row, as we mentioned in Attractions.

At MP 10-1/2 **The Christmas Mouse**, 441-8111, is open all year and is a delightful store. **Nags Head Hammocks**, 441-6115, has two locations, one on the Beach Road at 10-1/2 MP and another on Route 158 Bypass at MP 9-1/2. They not only feature the famous hammocks made right here in Nags Head, but they also have beautifully landscaped, award-winning grounds, vastly different from the Outer Banks au naturale-style. **Gray's Department Store**, 441-5143, on the Beach Road at MP 10-1/2 opened 40 years ago and is a favorite place to shop. **The Treasure Gallery**, 441-2277, is the newest creation of George Crocker, the genius behind the heyday of the Galleon Esplanade. The inventory here ranges from antiques to selections from world bazaars. Once inside the white concrete building, which once housed his Rearview Mirror Car Museum, you'll see a variety of smaller shops featuring collectibles and fine gifts from all over the world. We think browsing here is one of the best rainy-day activities you could find on the Outer Banks, and even if you don't

have any grey days while you're here, you shouldn't miss this gallery. It's located between the Route 158 Bypass and the Beach Road at MP 11.

Seaside Art Gallery, 441-5410, is located around MP 11 on the Beach Road and features sculpture, paintings, drawings, Indian pottery, and animation art. **Yellowhouse Gallery** and **Annex**, 441-6928 at MP 11-1/2, is a treasure-house of old prints, books and more. "Uncle Jack" Sandberg has a large collection of posters and prints and does custom framing. There's a large collection of cats here as well. You can have one free with your purchase. A visit to this unusual place and the family of cats is a story worth hearing and seeing. The **Secret Spot Surf Shop**, 441-4030, MP 11-1/2 on Route 158, is one of the most interesting places on the beach. Owner Steve Hess has been in business since 1977 and is unusually helpful to the youngsters who aspire to be surfers. This is

a good place for beginners and long-time enthusiasts.

Twila Zone, 480-0399, is located across from the Nags Head Fishing Pier at MP 11 on the Beach Rd. It is a wonderful shop of vintage clothing for women, children and men. Owner Jo Ruth Patterson has a nice selection of hats, accessories and costume jewelry as well as dolls, dollhouses and other fine quality vintage furnishings.

Pirate's Quay, a shopping center located at MP 11-1/2 on Route 158 Bypass, is home to several nice shops and larger stores. **Island Magic**, 441-5692, features contemporary fashions and wood crafts from Bali. You'll enjoy these creations, especially the colorful wood masks. **Chef's Corner**, 441-6042, is under new management but still caters to those who love freshly baked breads and pastries, as well as salads and made-to-order sandwiches. **Cloud Nine**, 441-2992, is an adventure in clothing, accessories and other discoveries from around the world. Plan on spending some time here. **Rainbow Harvest**, 441-0453, is a new shop with hand-crafted usable items from all over the country. Several other shops here at Pirate's Quay feature original crafts, jewelry and clothing.

Across from Jockey's Ridge at MP 12-1/2, **Kitty Hawk Kites** and **Kitty Hawk Sports** are located at opposite ends of the complex known as Kitty Hawk Connection, also described in our Attractions section of this chapter. There's a big play area for the kids and that makes shopping more fun. You'll enjoy a stop at the ice cream and candy shops as well as a shopping spree in **Donna Designs**. It's a store of one-of-a-kind sportswear with air-brush designs. There's everything from children's shoes and shirts to adult sportswear. All have been designed and painted with soft subtle colors of the beach, fish and birds, by the artist.

A stop at MP 13 will be justified. **Surfside Plaza** has numerous shops featuring everything from fishing tackle to contemporary clothing and crafts. **Surfside Casuals**, 441-7449, has more swimsuits than in any store on the beach. **Beach Peddler**, 441-5408, "peddles" everything you'd need at the beach and then some. **Darnell's Gifts**, 441-5687, and **Fishing Hook**, 441-6661, for fishing and camping supplies are just a few of the other nice shops.

The **Outer Banks Mall** is located at MP 15 on Route 158. Shops spread out between **Seamark Foods** and **Roses**. There is a pet shop, dry cleaners, an optician and several other service stores. **The Mule Shed**, 441-4115, is a popular clothing store for local women. They carry quality brand clothing and stay open most all year. **Ocean Annie's**, 441-4500, offers a large assortment of gifts from all over the country, with strong emphasis on pottery and jewelry. They also sell gourmet, ground-to-order coffees. **Lady Dare**, 441-7461, is a clothing

store for fuller figured women. They carry a very nice selection of fashions and accessories. Their styles appeal to women of all ages and the sales staff is especially helpful in selecting and coordinating outfits. **Soundfeet Shoes**, 441-8954, specializes in shoes for sports and comfort. They carry name brands such as Reebok, Nike, and Bass for the entire family. **Video Andy**, 441-2666, has a mind-boggling selection of videos for rent and does offer weekly memberships for visitors. A new store on the scene is **The Sesame Seed**, 441-5030, carrying healthful snacks and sodas, vitamins and herbs, low-salt, low-fat and sugar-free products, body building supplements and body care products. Yes, you *can* eat healthy food while you're on vacation! The owner, Dena Radley, also runs a pet and house sitting service.

The Farmer's Daughter, 441-3977, is located at MP 16 on the Bypass. It's a delightful place to browse and find a special gift or hand-crafted accessory for your own home -- this is country craft and folk art heaven. The owners, John and Julie Boyd, have another location in the heart of Duck. The **Chalet Gift Shop**, 441-6402, is located at MP 15-1/2 on the Beach Road. It's one of the nicest stores on the beach and features exquisite gifts and collectibles. Lladro and other porcelains, dolls and jewelry are things you'd expect to find in fine gift shops, but they're here too. Just to balance things out, there is another side to the store, one where you can find just

about anything and everything for the beach. **Sea Shore Stuff**, 441-8446, is located behind The Chalet on Route 158. They have things to keep the kids occupied while you shop and they carry everything from suntan lotions and t-shirts to sea shell jewlery and note cards.

Greenleaf Gallery, 480-3555, is a new art gallery located on the Bypass near MP 16. Rick Tupper, a local artist and owner, has work by renowned artists (his own also falling that category), fine jewelry and handcrafted furniture of superior quality.

At MP 16 on the Beach Road, you'll see **Souvenir City**, 441-7452. They probably have the largest collection of souvenirs on the beach. You'll want to take something home from here and the kids will almost certainly push for a hermit crab -- they're for sale and the folks here will instruct you on how to care for it. There's also a great collection of miniature lighthouses and miles of t-shirts. The **Dare Shops**, 441-1112, at MP 16-1/2 on the Beach Road has been in business for 35 years. It's a store that carries a nice selection of men's and women's sportswear, sweaters and other items as well as beautiful gold and silver jewelry.

Soundings Factory Stores, 441-7395, is a discount outlet mall with numerous shops carrying all sorts of things from clothes to dishes. It's located at MP 16-1/2 on Route 158. Some of our favorites here are

Westport and **Westport Woman**, 441-1568, for stylish and affordable clothing and accessories; a **Pfaltzgraff Collector's Center**, 441-1800; a **London Fog** outlet, 441-6409, with a vast selection of coats; and a **Rack Room Shoes**, 441-9288, carrying all the styles you expect with the kind of prices you can afford.

If you're looking for grocery stores in Nags Head, **Food Lion** is located at MP 10 on the Bypass. **Seamark Foods**, located at the Outer Banks Mall, is a great choice for food shoppers on the Outer Banks. It is one of the cleanest stores around and the aisles are wide to maneuver even on crowded days.

Cahoon's on the Beach Road is a large variety store and it's located at MP 16-1/2. Dorothy and Ray Cahoon bought their store shortly before the Ash Wednesday Storm of 1962 and, despite what must have been a rather wild start, have had great success for the past 30 years. Everything you need for your visit to the beach is here, plus good meats which butcher Rob Cahoon cuts to perfection. They're convenient to Jennette's Pier and nearby motels and cottages. You'll find this family-owned store a nice change of pace from the large city-size supermarkets.

There are several seafood stores in Nags Head. **Austin Fish Co.**, 441-7412, is located at MP 12-1/2 near Jockey's Ridge. They've been here for years and it has the look of a gas station, which it also is. Watch the signs. **Whalebone Seafood**, is run by the Daniels family at MP 16-1/2. The fish is always fresh and they'll know how to cook every fish they sell.

If you follow Route 158 to its end, you'll see the highway signs designating Hwy. 64 to Manteo. You're still in Nags Head as you cross the causeway and a few stores are worth mentioning here. **Blackbeard's Treasure Chest**, 441-5772, is one of those places the whole family will enjoy. There's a 10-foot tall yellow octopus out in front, so you won't miss it. Farther along this road is **Shipwreck**, 441-5739, which you won't want to miss. It has driftwood, nets, shells and other nautical treasures piled everywhere.

Another store along the causeway will delight all who love fresh steamed crabs. **Daniels Crab House**, 441-5027, is the place to go. There's a picking room in the back and large steamers, so you get the drift on steamed crabs here.

Photo: DCTB

The Elizabeth II, sails set, leaves Manteo for an historical voyage inland.

Open
All Year

Plenty of
Parking

Since 1967

Every Season There Are New Things To Discover

In a pleasant setting of tall pines and gardens, you'll find five rambling buildings where room after room is filled with shopping treasures... Spring, summer, winter and fall!

the Outer Banks' Original

christmas shop

IS IN MANTEO

The

island gallery

Representing over 100 local and regional artists... watercolors, oils, decoys, jewelry, pottery, sculpture and more.

at The Christmas Shop in Manteo • 473-2838

Inside
Roanoke Island

*B*efore we get into the history of Roanoke Island, the town of Manteo deserves a brief review. Manteo is the county seat of Dare County which includes most of the Outer Banks, except for Ocracoke Island and the very northern beaches.

As you drive into Manteo from Nags Head or from the western village of Manns Harbor, you'll notice the abundance of trees. Tall pines and live oaks reach for the sky here, and in summer the crepe myrtles bloom profusely along the streets. If it's a breezy day, pull off the road into a parking lot and stand there and listen for a few minutes; the melody played by the wind in the trees is worth a quite moment or two. The area just beyond the fringes of the business section is the best place for listening -- near the Elizabethan Gardens and Fort Raleigh Historic Site.

A sense of history abounds in this small, comfortable town. You have to stretch your imagination to consider the hardships of discovery four hundred years ago, since this island is the site of the first attempt at permanent settlement by the English in the 1500s -- more about that in a minute.

Everything appears to be in place, comfortable and easy-going.

The almost-new reconstruction of the Waterfront provides a place to ponder the days of the first landing and the immense beauty of the water just beyond the shores of Roanoke Island. Geographically, the island seems protected from the ocean by other land -- across the sound is Nags Head -- a slim strip of protection in times of angry storms. And, the picturesque, open waterfront and the tall pines of Main Hwy. evoke a slower pace, a relaxed feeling.

Part of the business area is scattered along Main Hwy. Everything from car dealerships, marinas, flower shops, eateries, gas stations, the library, an auto body shop, a tire shop, schools, motels and restaurants, to the Art Deco Ace Hardware store, optician, seafood shop and drug stores dredges up memories of those times when all the businesses necessary for day-to-day comfort were within walking distance in many towns all over the country. There are a few cattle grazing along the roadside not far from the ABC Store -- funny juxtaposition -- but representative of the interesting diversity and range of sites offered to visitors of all ages by this gem of a small town.

Roanoke Island is steeped in the history of exploration and discovery. In the late 1500s the English colonization of America began. Spain ruled the oceans in those days and had made historical discoveries of treasure in the New World nearly one hundred years earlier. Their plundering of South American Indian empires had left that area devastated. Other than a small settlement at St. Augustine, Florida, North America was left untouched. Then, the French explored the southeastern part of North America and Canada. It was inevitable that England's growing naval expeditions would reach these shores. They were looking for an advanced base of operations against the Spanish and for new land for permanent settlement.

Sir Walter Raleigh's expedition to the new land in 1584 followed that of Humphrey Gilbert in 1583, during which Gilbert himself was lost. Raleigh caught the "fever" of colonization of America and he was determined that the English would be the first to settle the area.

On July fourth — a date later to be commemorated throughout the land, but for different reasons — Captains Arthur Barlowe and Philip Amadas arrived off the Banks and began their explorations. They landed north of Kitty Hawk to take formal possession, and were astounded at the profusion of cedar, deer, wildfowl and wild grapes

(see 'Mother Vineyard'). They met the local Indians, who had a village on the northwest end of Roanoke Island, and found them friendly. They left after a month, taking along two Indians named Manteo and Wanchese, and their reports caused a stir in England. In fact, by the very next spring Raleigh had outfitted seven ships and 600 men, getting them to sea in April. Again, Raleigh himself could not go; Elizabeth wanted him in England in case of Spanish attack. Sir Richard Grenville was placed in charge of the fleet, with Ralph Lane as Lieutenant Governor.

Grenville had a little trouble at Ocracoke Inlet — his flagship *Tiger* went aground and was almost lost — but he freed and floated her and pushed on, into the sound.

He took a week to explore the mainland within the sounds. The English visited several Indian village, and were well received at most. After a visit to one named Aquascococke, however, Grenville found himself missing a silver cup (it is possible there was a misunderstanding about an exchange of gifts). Unable to regain it, he had his men burn the town, then proceeded on his explorations.

At last he pushed on up the sound, to Roanoke, and after some time decided that this would be the site for the first settlement.

Why did Grenville and Lane choose Roanoke? There were better sites for a colony already known — the Chesapeake Bay area, farther north,

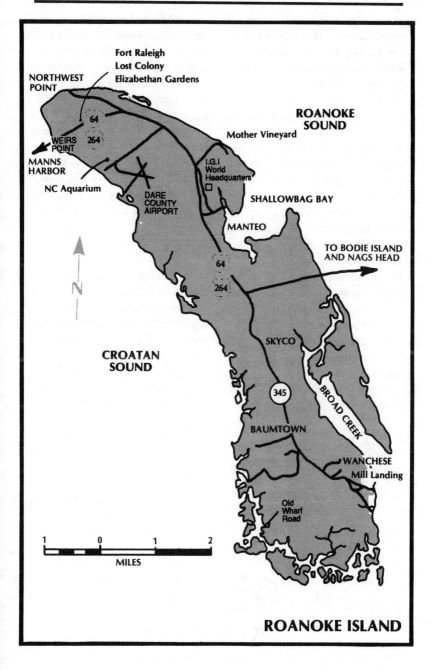

ROANOKE ISLAND

had much better soil, deep rivers and better harbours. They may have chosen Roanoke because it was inaccessible to large ships — Spanish ships. Or it may have been a simple miscalculation.

The six hundred men spent the summer building a small earthwork fort, Fort Raleigh, and a few houses. In August Grenville sailed with his ships, leaving Governor Lane in charge of 107 men.

The winter was not easy, but more ominous than the weather was the worsening of relations with the Indians. Lane and some of his men explored up the rivers of the Albemarle, following rumors of cities of gold, but their methods of obtaining food and information quickly turned the inhabitants against them. When he returned, the Governor, alleging conspiracy, then led an attack on the village of the Roanoke weroance (king), Wingina, killing the chief and his advisors. Af-

terward he tried to set up Manteo, who remained pro-English to the end, as the new king, but it was evident that English and Indian were beginning to regard each other as enemies.

Perhaps that was why, when Grenville was late in returning, Lane decided to pull out when Sir Francis Drake stopped by in the spring. Grenville's relief fleet arrived just a few weeks later and he was surprised to find the island deserted. Unwilling to abandon the fort, he left fifteen soldiers there to winter over before sailing again for home.

High dreams were dreamed that winter of 1586-7 in England, for Raleigh was pulling together, at long last, his colonizing expedition. Led by John White, three ships left Plymouth, carrying 120 men, women and children.

The first mystery met them when they landed. The 15 men Grenville had left were gone; only one skeleton

was found, moldering beside the demolished fort.

The new colonists shook their heads, doubtless prayed, but pitched in to clear land and build homes, guarding always against the hostile and shadowy figures in the forest. On August 18 a child was born, Virginia Dare, the first English child born in the New World (though let us not forget that the Spanish had been around, farther south, for almost a century). Governor White, her grandfather, left with the autumn for England to organize more supplies and colonists.

But war intervened, war with Spain, and, with Philip's Armada menacing England, Elizabeth had no ships to spare for Raleigh's dream colonies. It was not until 1590 that White was able to return, and when at last he landed again on Roanoke, the village had been evacuated, and the colonists had gone — where? On trees nearby were carved the words: CROATOAN; CRO. But on Croatan Island no traces have ever been found.

What happened to the "Lost Colony"?

Paul Green, in the last scene of his historical drama of the same name, suggests that they abandoned Roanoke because of a Spanish threat, hoping to stay with friendly Indians of Manteo's tribe. As to what happened after that, many theories have been advanced over the years. One, widely believed early in this century but now largely discredited, was that the main body found friendly Indians at Croatan Island (now part of Hatteras), intermarried with them as they wandered about North Carolina, and survived until modern times in the English surnames and blue eyes of the Lumbee Indians of Robeson County. Today most scholars believe that the main body went north rather than south, arriving safely at the southern coast of the Chesapeake Bay. They lived with the Indians there peacefully, but were massacred by Powhatan when the Jamestown expedition arrived in 1607. No one will ever know for sure.

Roanoke was left to the Indians for a long time after, but eventually, circa 1655, the press of whites southward out of Tidewater Virginia reached the Northern Banks, and families still seen today on the island — names like Gallop, Baum, Meekins, Tillet, Daniels and Midgett — settled down to stay. The small population was supported by stock raising and small-scale farming through the 17th and 18th centuries.

The Civil War began the process of the island's awakening with a cannonade. At 10:30 a.m., February 7, 1862, a gigantic shallow-draft Federal fleet, with 12,000 troops aboard, began a bombardment of Confederate shore batteries on the northern end of the island (an overlook at Northwest Point today commemorates this battle). That evening 7500 Federals disembarked at Ashby's Landing (now Skyco). The next morning they moved north, opposed bitterly every step of the way up the island, till a final charge routed the Rebels, who surrendered. The War was marked also by the quartering, on the northern end of the island (west of where the Elizabethan Motel now stands) of some three thousand newly freed slaves, most of whom were relocated off the island when the war ended.

As population increased after 1865, homes clustered around the two harbors at Shallowbag Bay and at Mill Landing. These were referred to respectively as the 'Upper End' and 'Lower End' of the island. Around 1886 the 'Lower Enders' grew understandably tired of being called that and chose the name of Wanchese for their town; Manteo followed suit, incorporating in 1899, shortly after being named seat of newly formed Dare County. Since then both towns have grown slowly but steadily.

In 1902, Reginald Fessenden, a pioneer in the development of radio, transmitted signals from an apparatus on Roanoke Island to one on Hatteras.

In 1900-1903, the brothers Wright took a ship from Roanoke for Kitty Hawk.

In 1928, a privately-constructed bridge first connected the Island with the Beach at Nags Head, opening the outer islands to development.

In 1937, The Lost Colony was performed for the first time.

After World War II, the stabilization of the Banks and the construction of roads and bridges, along with the creation of the National Park, brought modern tourism and real-estate development to the Island.

Today Roanoke Island has two characters. For much of the year it is a quiet, low-key area where most of the permanent residents know one another by name or at least by face, and the principal commercial activities are fishing at Mill Landing and service-related businesses. All this begins to change round about May, when the golden tide of tourists begins; and the months of summer are full of activity, especially at Fort Raleigh, The Lost Colony, *Elizabeth II* and in the shops and stores of downtown Manteo and along Route 64/264. Still, though activity is brisk, Roanokers have not yet succumbed to full-scale commercialism. Most of the island is still wild, with forests and marshes covering the land outside the town. The people are still friendly, and beauty still lies on the land during the long humming evenings of summer. As Amadas and Barlowe found in 1584, this might still be said to be "...the goodliest land under the cope of heaven."

Roanoke Island

ATTRACTIONS

THE ELIZABETHAN GARDENS

Manteo   **473-3234**

Located in Manteo off Main Hwy. (Route 64) on the north end of Roanoke Island, The Elizabethan Gardens are open all year from 9:00 a.m.

to 5:00 p.m. except Saturday and Sunday during the months of December and January. They are adjacent to Ft. Raleigh and the Waterside Theatre, where The Lost Colony is performed. When The Lost Colony is playing during the summer months, the Gardens are open later, however all guests are asked to leave by 8:00 p.m. so that the grounds may be cleared. There is a small admission ($2.50 per adult). Children under age twelve are free if accompanied by an adult.

These magnificent gardens were created by the Garden Club of North Carolina, Inc. in 1951 and are maintained with the cooperation of the State of North Carolina. The Gardens are a most delightful environment where the visitor enters at the Great Gate into formal gardens containing trees, flowers and statuary amidst curving walkways of brick and sand. Horticulturists, nature lovers, history buffs and culturists will find these classical gardens a sensual escape from the anxiety of twentieth century living.

There is a great deal more than meets the casual eye in these Gardens. The bricks used throughout are handmade from the Silas Lucas Kiln, in operation during the 1890s in Wilson, North Carolina. The famous Virginia Dare statue located here was conceived after an Indian legend that said Virginia grew up in their midst and became a beautiful woman. The statue was sculpted by Maria Louisa Lander in Italy in 1859, affirming the Graeco-Roman influence of its appearance.

Prior to being situated in these gardens, the statue was reportedly lost at sea for some years, recovered, then displayed in the North Carolina State House before being given to Paul Green to take back to Roanoke Island. (Paul Green wrote the historical drama, "The Lost Colony," previewed later in this section.)

Spring in the Gardens is breath taking. Azalea, dogwood, pansies, wisteria and tulips are in full bloom. During May, rhododendron, roses, lacecap and hydrangea appear. Summer brings fragrant gardenias, colorful annuals and perennials, magnolia, crepe myrtle, oriental lilies and herbs. Autumn begins its show with chrysanthemums and the changing colors of trees. Camellias bloom from late fall through the winter.

Herbs, bedding plants, vines, ivy and other plants are for sale in the gift shop.

FORT RALEIGH

Manteo   **473-5772**

Located on the north end of Roanoke Island (Route 64) in Manteo, the center of history on the Outer Banks begins here. Fort Raleigh was designated as a National Historic Site in 1941. Its 144-acre expanse of woods and beach includes the location of the settlement sites by English colonies of 1585 and 1587, a Visitor Center, a restored fort and nature trail. The Elizabethan Gardens, the Waterside Theatre and National Park Service Headquarters for the Outer Banks are also

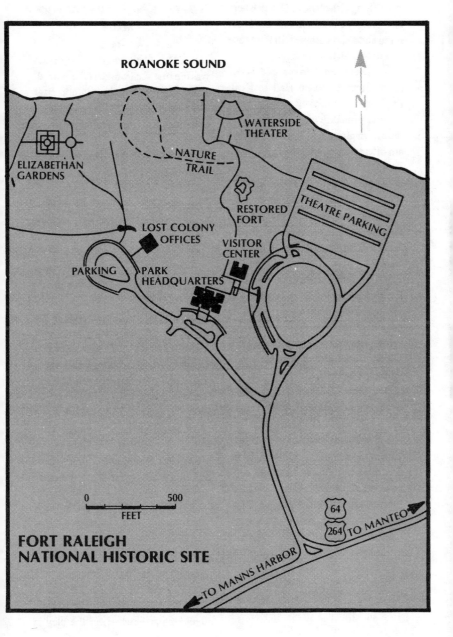

ROANOKE SOUND

N

WATERSIDE
THEATER

NATURE
TRAIL

ELIZABETHAN
GARDENS

RESTORED
FORT

THEATRE PARKING

LOST COLONY
OFFICES

VISITOR
CENTER

PARKING

PARK
HEADQUARTERS

0   500
FEET

64
264 TO MANTEO

FORT RALEIGH
NATIONAL HISTORIC SITE

TO MANNS HARBOR

located here.

Stop at the Visitor Center where interpretive exhibits in the small museum and a short movie will introduce you to this historic place.

There is a 400-year old Tudor room from Heronden Hall in Kent, England. The furnishings, carved mantelpiece, panelling, stone fireplace and the blown glass in the leaded windows are interesting to note.

Self-guided tours or tours led by the Park Service are optional. Interpretive exhibits and living history programs are an important part of Fort Raleigh's attraction. The program varies depending on the time of day and year.

The Thomas Hariot Nature Trail is a short self-guided trail whose soft pine-needle paths lead to the sandy shores of Roanoke Sound, near the spot where it is thought that Sir Richard Grenville first stepped ashore on Roanoke Island.

Before you leave the area, drop by the Lost Colony Craft Shop.

The Fort Raleigh National Historic Site is open mid-June till late August: 9:00 a.m. till 8:00 p.m. Monday through Saturday; Sunday, 9:00 a.m. till 6:00 p.m. And, September through mid-June it's open from 9:00 a.m. till 5:00 p.m. seven days a week. Closed Christmas Day.

THE LOST COLONY
Near Fort Raleigh, in the Waterside Theatre
473-3414

This historical outdoor drama was the first such work ever produced. Pulitzer Prize-winning author Paul Green brought the history of English colonization to this outdoor theatre in 1937.

It is a wonderful experience to learn the story of The Lost Colony, that first English settlement on Roanoke Island, through drama. The choir, costumes and re-enactments are exciting and well-performed by the Lost Colony troupe.

The play is presented in two acts. Act I opens with a prologue by the Choir and the Historian, a sort of narrator who provides for unity in the drama. Subsequent scenes are set in an Indian village on Roanoke, 1584; in England, in the court of Elizabeth; again, on Roanoke, a year later; and on a street in Plymouth, England, as the colonists embark, filled with fear and hope. Act II is set, for the most part, in the 'Cittie of Raleigh' on Roanoke — which was somewhere within a quarter-mile of where the Waterside Theatre now stands — and follows the web of circumstance that led to the final tragedy: the disappearance of the colonists, into...legend.

It's great entertainment, but it's more. The ending is powerful, and sad. You may find yourself weeping.

The Waterside Theatre is the semicircular bowl where the play is presented. It's just north of Fort Raleigh; bear to the right as you enter from Route 64 to reach the large parking area. As you walk in you can see the waters of the sound over the backdrop.

Things to be aware of at the Waterside are: the wooden seats are uncomfortable so bring stadium cushions for comfort! Pillows can also be rented at the Theatre. It gets cold in the evenings, when the wind blows off the sound, so bring sweaters along even in July and August. Finally, mosquitoes can be vicious, especially when it has rained recently. The woods nearby are sprayed, but this is only partially effective; bring repellent. There are special accommodations available for the handicapped in the uppermost row at the entrance and in the first row.

And with all the creature comforts taken care of, settle back and enjoy a thoroughly professional, well-rehearsed, technically outstanding show. The leads are played by professional actors, and most of the backstage personnel are pros too; and it shows. Supporting actors are often local people, and some island residents pass from part to part as they grow up. The colorful costumes, the choir, the tension inherent in the play itself make it a combination of delights that you won't soon forget.

Now: tickets. All shows start at 8:30 p.m. The show season runs from mid-June to late August and is presented nightly, except Sunday. Adult tickets are $10.00, children 12 and

under $5.00, active military, senior citizens $9.00. Accompanied children are free on Monday night performances. Groups of 15 or more can call for a discount.

This is probably the most popular event on the Banks in the summer, and we recommend you make reservations, though you can try your luck at the door if you care to. You can make paid mail reservations by writing The Lost Colony, Box 40, Manteo, NC 27954; or make phone reservations starting in early June by calling (919) 473-3414. These reservations will be held at the box office for pickup until 7:30 p.m.

NORTH CAROLINA AQUARIUM ON ROANOKE ISLAND
Rt. 116 (Airport Road)   473-3493

Tucked away northwest of Manteo on route 64, by Manteo Airport, is a surprising place called the North Carolina Aquarium. It's one of the 'sleepers' of the Banks, a place you won't want to miss if you have the slightest interest in the sea, the Banks, or the life that thrives in this unique chain of barrier islands.

The Aquarium contains labs for the use of marine scientists and a reference library on marine-related topics. But these aren't what attracts visitor. The display section and aquarium—that's what you'll want to see.

Once in the door, you'll walk among changing displays on such topics as underwater archaeology and marine ecosystems. Children love the "shallow observation tank" with live marine creatures you can feel. The aquarium is surprisingly beautiful. Set like jewels in a long, darkened corridor, the lighted tanks display sea turtles, longnosed gar, ugly burrfish and sea robin, lobster and octopi. The aquaria start out with fresh water species, shading through brackish to salt water. The biggest is 3000 gallons, holding salt water. And there's still more. A special room exhibits information on sharks -- kids marvel at the open shark jaws showing rows and rows of pointy teeth. Feature films on marine and biological topics are shown at different times. There's a schedule of daytime programs for all age groups, including field trips, bird walks through Pea Island, and more; check at the desk for a current schedule. The Aquarium caters to groups of any kind, and can even supply meeting facilities in its conference room, seminar room, or 240-seat auditorium. There's also a great gift shop with marine-related gifts, books and t-shirts.

To reach it, drive north from Manteo on route 64. Turn left on Rt. 116, following signs to airport; the Aquarium will be on your right. It's open from 9 a.m. to 5 p.m. Monday through Saturday, 1 p.m. to 5 p.m. Sundays. Admission is free but donations to support their important work, and make it available to the public, are gratefully accepted.

WEIRS POINT AND FORT HUGER
N. end of Roanoke Island

Weirs Point, at the northwest corner of the island, where the Route 64/264 bridge arrives from Manns Harbor, is an interesting place to visit. Empty shoreline as recently as fall of '83, it is now a pretty, easily accessible public beach. Parking is available at the first turnoff after the bridge.

About three hundred yards out (the island has migrated quite a bit in a hundred and twenty years), in six feet of water, lie the remains of Fort Huger, the largest Confederate fort on the island during the Union invasion of 1862.

A few years later, from a hut on this beach, one of the unsung geniuses of the electrical age began investigating what was then called "wireless telegraphy." Reginald Fessenden held hundreds of patents on radiotelephony and electronics, but died without credit for many of them.

For most people, though, swimming and fishing in the sound will take precedence over vanished forts and disappointed inventors. The beach is sandy and shallow, and shoals very gradually, except under the bridge, where currents scour a bit deeper. If you approach in a boat, watch carefully for stumps and old pilings. Picnic benches, a Dare County information kiosk and restrooms are also available at Weirs.

DARE COUNTY REGIONAL AIRPORT
Rt. 116 (Airport Road), next to the N.C. Aquarium
473-2600

Dare County (formerly Manteo) is the major airfield serving the Outer Banks, and the only one with fuel and services (the others, at Kitty Hawk, Hatteras and Ocracoke, are paved strips only). Manteo has two runways, both asphalt-surfaced. Runways 16-34 measure 3290, and runways 4-22 measure 3300, with 500-foot stopways. (Runways 10-28 were closed permanently in 1986.) Fuel: 100 octane low-lead and jet "A" fuel available. Equipment: VOR and DME, NDB, VASI, REILS, Unicom U-1 122.8. For runway lights key 122.8 five times in five seconds.

Dare County is the point of arrival of most of those who come to the Banks by air, including some VIPs, and it has the services to match. There are rental cars by B & R, a local company; a limo service; hot sandwiches and drinks from machines; and restrooms. There are also taxi services (see the Service Directory for information on car rentals, limos and taxis).

Dare County Airport is operated by the Dare County Airport Authority. It provides light aircraft rentals, flight instruction, sightseeing tours and charter services out of Dare County. Call the number above to make arrangements.

Dare County Airport provides service and minor maintenance from 8 a.m. until 7:30 p.m. during the summer and from 8 a.m. until 6 p.m. during the off season.

Southeast Airlines, 473-3222, has regularly scheduled flights to and from Norfolk International Airport as well as to and from Raleigh-Durham and other airports on the east coast.

Outer Banks Airways provides daily on-demand charter flights to Norfolk International from Dare County. It also charters "anywhere." Call 441-7677 for reservations and information.

Kitty Hawk Air Tours provides air tours and aircraft maintenance. Call 473-3014 for additional information.

Wright Brothers Air Tours provides air tours from here as well. Call 441-5909 for additional information.

MOTHER VINEYARD
Manteo

Mother Vineyard Scuppernong, the Original American Wine, is still produced by a company in Petersburg, Virginia. Old-timers in town say the wine once produced in Manteo was far superior, but the Petersburg product did not taste bad when we sampled a couple of bottles. It is a pink wine, quite sweet. If you like white port or Mogen David you will take to scuppernong wine. You can find it in many of the Banks groceries.

All this is a roundabout way of getting to the fact that the oldest grapevine in the U.S. is in Manteo.

That's right: the oldest. You see, when the first settlers arrived here, the Banks were covered with wild grapes. Arthur Barlowe wrote to Sir Walter Raleigh in 1584:

"...being where we first landed very sandy and low toward the water side, but so full of grapes as the very beating and surge of the sea overflowed them, of which we found such plenty, as well there as in all places else, both on the sand and on the green soil, on the hills as in the plains, as well on every little shrub, as also climbing toward the tops of high cedars, that I think in all the world the like abundance is not to be found."

The Mother Vine is one of those ancient grapevines, so old that it may have been planted even before whites arrived in the New World. Certainly it was already old in the 1750s, as records attest, and scuppernong grape vines do not grow swiftly. Another story is that this vine was transplanted to Roanoke Island by some among the Fort Raleigh settlers. Whichever story is true, whoever planted the Mother Vine, it is ancient — over four hundred years old, most likely. And still producing fine fat tasty grapes.

In fact, for many years a small winery, owned by the Etheridge family, cultivated the vine on Baum's Point, making the original Mother Vineyard wine until the late 50s.

Despite all its history, the Mother Vine doesn't offer much to the eye, nor is it easy to find. To try, drive north out of Manteo on Route 64. About 3/4 mile past the city limits, turn right on Mother Vineyard road.

Go about half a mile, to where the road makes a sharp turn to the right at the bay. The patient old vine crouches beneath a canopy of leaves, twisted and gnarled, ancient and enduring, about three hundred feet on the left past the turn. It's private property — so please stay on the road.

DARE COUNTY LIBRARY
Manteo   **473-2372**

Sometimes there's nothing for it but to curl up with a good book. From a location on Highway 64, about half a mile north of downtown Manteo, Librarian Amelia Frazer runs a 37,000-volume library with recordings, video tapes, slides, books-on-tape, meeting facilities, and a local history room that's invaluable for probing more deeply into the lore of the Banks. Hours: Monday, 8:30 AM to 7 PM; Tuesday through Friday, 8:30 AM to 5:30 PM; Saturday, 10 AM to 4 PM; closed Sunday. See the Service Directory for Kill Devil Hills and Hatteras branch information.

DARE COUNTY TOURIST BUREAU
Manteo   **473-2138**

Got a question? The Dare County Tourist Bureau is set up to help, with a large collection of brochures, maps and the latest data on hand and available to the visitor. They're located at the corner of Virginia Dare Road (Route 64/264) and Budleigh Street, in a low white stucco building. Parking is available in back;

the information desk is through the right-hand door, fronting on Budleigh. Open year round Monday through Friday, 8:30 a.m. to 5 p.m., and open Saturdays and holidays as well during the summer season, 10 a.m. to 3 p.m.

In case you want to write ahead for specific information and a detailed and beautiful Vacation Guide, Dare County's mailing address is P.O. Box 399, Manteo, N.C. 27954.

THE ISLAND GALLERY AND CHRISTMAS SHOP

Manteo   473-2838

There is only one word for the Christmas Shop and Island Gallery: fascinating. From hundreds of miles away people travel to the Banks for the (nearly) sole purpose of visiting Edward Greene's burgeoning world of fantasy, which opened its doors on June 1, 1967.

Basically, you might say that this establishment is a store...because

things are sold here. There, all resemblance to conventional stores ends. There are seven rambling, multilevel buildings in the Shop, but there's not a single counter, display rack, or glass case. Instead there are rooms, room after room, furnished with antique furniture (not for sale), and each is filled with wonder.

"We stock a minimum of about 50,000 different items, from 200 companies, 150 artists and craftspeople, and 35 countries," says Greene, formerly an actor in New York City. "And there isn't a thing in the building anybody *needs* to have. So we have to let each product tell us how it wants to be displayed."

The result is mind-boggling...like a child's dream of everything you ever wanted in the world rolled into one. Whole walls are filled with toys, pottery, handcrafts. Whole rooms of porcelain eggs, others filled with baskets, with carvings, with min-

iatures, with handmade jewelry, with ornaments, with seashells, art, Christmas cards. 125 switches light innumerable atmosphere lights that give everything a magic glow. Imagine, added to all this, scores of decorated Christmas trees. It sounds like quite a production...and it is. You'll have to see it before you realize what a fantastic place this is. Bring plenty of money or your credit cards, because, believe us, you won't be able to resist purchases.

The Shop and Gallery also contains an old-fashioned candy store, a card and stationery shop, a basket shop, candles, suncatchers and fun things for kids.

The shop and Gallery is located about half a mile south of Manteo, on the sea (east) side of Route 64/264. Hours: Memorial Day through mid-October, daily 9:30 a.m. to 9 p.m., Sundays 9:30 a.m. to 6:00 p.m.; mid-October through mid-June, 9:30 a.m. to 6:00 p.m., Sundays 9:30 a.m. to 5:30 p.m. Closed Christmas and New Year's Day.

THE WEEPING RADISH BREWERY

Manteo   **473-1157**

Did you know that the first beer brewed in America was right here on Roanoke Island? True. History tells us that when Lane's exploratory colony was here in 1585, they made a batch — to befriend the Indians or maybe to keep their nerves calm while waiting for the next encounter with the "new world" they had come upon. In any event, Roanoke Island again is the home of its own brewery at the Weeping Radish. A brewmaster makes both light and dark lager beers to be sipped on-site at the restaurant of the same name. But five-liter minikegs are sold to take home.

Curious beer lovers can actually see the brew being made — there are daily tours — and, afterwards, sit and have a mug or two. We found it to be especially tasty — richer than the six-pack variety.

Annual SpringFest, Autumnfest and OktoberFest events are held at the Weeping Radish, complete with oompah bands and German folk dancers. Easter Weekend is SpringFest; OktoberFest is the weekend after Labor Day; AutumnFest is the second weekend of November; the festivities can be watched from the comfortable outdoor beer garden.

Locals find this a favorite evening spot in the off season, when the draw -- other than, of course, the beer -- is special movie nights, darts and seeing all your friends. Visitors will feel at home, too, if they happen upon it on a chilly autumn night.

ANDREW CARTWRIGHT PARK
Manteo

This small state park commemorates the Outer Banks' black community. Born in northeastern North Carolina in 1835, Andrew Cartwright devoted his life to spreading the Gospel among his brethren.

After organizing 12 A.M.E. Zion churches on or near Roanoke Island after the Civil War, he founded the first Zion Church in Liberia and worked on in Africa until his death in 1903. Plaques recount the history of the Freedman's Colony on Roanoke Island, the Pea Island Crew, and the African Methodist Episcopal Zion Church. To reach it turn west off Highway 64 at Sir Walter Raleigh Street and go three-tenths of a mile. The park is on the right.

WANCHESE AND MILL LANDING
Wanchese

Don't look for downtown Wanchese — you won't find it anywhere. This quintessential small town is miles of winding country roads, lined with white-clapboard 1920s-style homes, each with a boat in either the front or the back yard. Girls riding bareback on horses clop along the roads, and the people (almost all year round residents — Wanchese is no summer community) are North Carolina at its best, honest and hard working and friendly. Small shops selling shells, curio and handicrafts are open in the summer, and if you're after sand-cast pewter, decoy carvings, patchwork tablecloths, rusty old trawler anchors or handmade shell goods, you can easily spend a day just wandering, looking and buying.

At the very end of Route 345 (Mill Landing Road), you'll find one of the most picturesque, and also most overlooked, parts of the entire Outer Banks — Mill Landing. Painters, photographers, those who love the sea and just plain tourists shouldn't miss it.

Mill Landing is a quarter-mile of crowded soundfront that is home port for a small but highly productive fleet of oceangoing fishing trawlers. These sea-battered ships spend most of their lives off Cape May and Hatteras, fifty miles out at sea, bringing in the seafood that appears in a day or two in restaurants all along the East Coast. Mill Landing is fish companies: Wanchese Fish Co., Etheridge's, Jaws Seafood, Quality Seafood and Moon Tillet's. In the middle of it all, perched above the booms and nets, is the Fisherman's Wharf Restaurant. Mill Landing is hardly a "touristy" place, but it has its appeal. It's a real work-intensive fishing village and if you want to lay in a stock of fresh fish, shrimp or scallops, stop at the Wanchese Fish Company, or Etheridge's Retail. Fisherman's Wharf is the tall wooden building with the stairway. Just past it is a free boat ramp, and beyond that, if you like to sketch or photograph half-sunken trawlers and minesweepers, you're in for a treat.

Out beyond the inlet, you'll see the concrete bulkhead built by the State of North Carolina as part of their effort to develop the fishing industry. It was designed to bring the really big companies in to pack fish right here in Wanchese. The current difficulty is the shoaling that Oregon Inlet (under the bridge to Hatteras Island) is experiencing; several trawlers have gone aground there, and many are avoiding it by using other, but less convenient, means of getting to the open sea. Large-scale dredging is necessary, and even this might not work. It has the local trawler operators worried (see "Oregon Inlet"). Meanwhile, though, the visitor can enjoy the photo and painting opportunities. An especially interesting facility is a four-hundred-ton marine railway at Wanchese Shiplift, Inc. It's an interesting sight even if you don't have a hole in your hull! Wanchese Marina (473-3247) hosts trawlers and drop-netters with fuel and a small, homey store. Farther south from Mill Landing, Davis Yachts has been building large fiberglass Sportfishermen since 1984. They turn out over 20 beautiful boats a year. Plant tours are given on 24-hours notice (473-1111), contact Jim Polatty.

On the east side of Wanchese Harbor, things get less picturesque and more productive. Here the Wanchese Industrial Park hosts the Marine Maintenance Center, Coastal Engine and Propeller, Fisherman's Seafood, Harbor Welding, Wanchese Trawl and Supply and Carolina Boats. Owned by the State of North Carolina, it leases property for use of seafood or marine-related industries. Nina Green, the administrator, says visitors are welcome to drive in to watch a boat being hauled or a skiff being built, but if you'll be here for a while (to paint, for example) check in at the Administration building (or call 473-5867).

The Park hosts the annual Wanchese Seafood Festival the last Saturday in June.

The residents of Wanchese generally welcome visitors, but there are a few common-sense things to keep in mind. The trawlers are working boats, and the fishermen are not enthusiastic about having uninvited visitors aboard. The fish processors and boatyards are also industrial enterprises, as well as presenting special hazards to the unwary, so don't go bumbling around; sketch and photograph as much as you like, but please don't interfere with work.

PIRATE'S COVE
Manteo-Nags Head Causeway
473-1451   1-800-762-0245
Marina
473-3906   1-800-367-4728

There have been a lot of changes over the past couple of years at Pirate's Cove, and more are on the way. The marina now has 119 wet slips for 25-foot outboards to 75-foot yachts, with plans for more. A quickly-growing number of charter boats run Gulf Stream fishing trips out of here to where the big ones roam; full day trips cost about $775 for six people, half day, $350. Other types of charters, both inshore and sound, can be arranged individually. Allen Foreman's perennially popular head boat, *Crystal Dawn*, operates out of here. Allen now books cruises from the Ships Store, or you can call 473-5577. June through August he runs two trips a day, plus an enjoyable evening cruise, six days a week; and he takes a break on Sundays. During the off-season he runs one trip a day.

The marina has a Ships Store, serving almost any nautical need with a full line of marina supplies, groceries and clothes. 1992 is the ninth year for the popular Annual Bill Fish Tournament, run here in mid-August; other fishing contests exercise anglers of red drum, blues and king mackerel. Tournaments run from May to September. Write P.O. Box 1997, or call 473-3906 for details. Pirate's Cove Restaurant and Raw Bar serves fresh seafood and great steamers, and is located on the second floor above the Ships Store. Perhaps the biggest news is Pirate's Cove's growing, residential-marina-resort community. Of the 600-odd acres on the north side of the causeway, 500 are being left as untouched marsh preserves, and the remaining 100 acres turned into 627 residential units over the next three years—single-family townhomes and condominiums and individual homes. All have deep-water dockage. A clubhouse, pool, tennis courts and boardwalk surrounding the entire development are amenities that make this an attractive place.

Downtown Manteo

Despite its indirect "Cittie of Ralegh" antecedents, Manteo, as a town, is not all that old. There were only a few houses on Shallowbag Bay, on the eastern coast of the island, when Dare County was formed in 1870 and the town designated as the county seat. ("Manteo" was one of the two Roanoke Indians who accompanied the explorers back to England after the first expedition.) Today, though, after over a century of slow growth, Manteo is the largest town on the Banks, and a year round, comfortable, diversified community.

The downtown area, fronting directly on the bay, has undergone intensive redevelopment in the last few years. "The Waterfront," a pleasingly styled shopping and residential project, and Tranquil House, a 28-room inn built after the style of an inn of the same name that stood nearby early in the century, both projects of Renaissance Development Corporation, are the main attractions of this new look to Manteo. Within the three-story, courtyard design of the Waterfront, specialty shops, condominiums and several good restaurants are located. With the breezeways and water views and the exceptional landscaping that surrounds the Waterfront, it provides a relaxing, cool alternative to the busier shopping available in the beach area. More information on The Tranquil House can be found in Manteo Accommodations. There are also 53 modern docks with 110 and 220 hook-ups and a comfort station with restrooms, showers, washers and dryers. Sales for the condominiums are handled by Hudgins Real Estate.

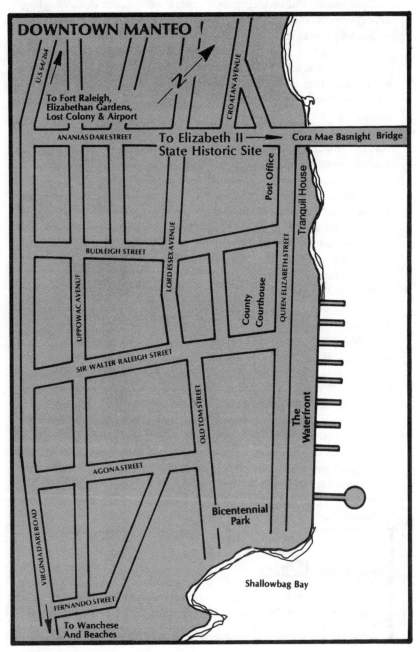

DOWNTOWN MANTEO

U.S 64/264

To Fort Raleigh,
Elizabethan Gardens,
Lost Colony & Airport

CROATAN AVENUE

ANANIAS DARE STREET

To Elizabeth II →
State Historic Site

Cora Mae Basnight Bridge

Post Office

Tranquil House

LORD ESSEX AVENUE

BUDLEIGH STREET

UPPOWAC AVENUE

QUEEN ELIZABETH STREET

County
Courthouse

SIR WALTER RALEIGH STREET

OLD TOM STREET

The Waterfront

AGONA STREET

VIRGINIA DARE ROAD

Bicentennial
Park

Shallowbag Bay

FERNANDO STREET

To Wanchese
And Beaches

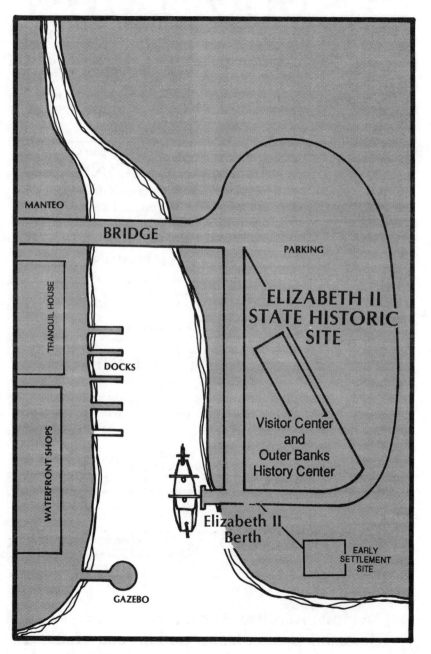

MANTEO

BRIDGE

PARKING

TRANQUIL HOUSE

ELIZABETH II
STATE HISTORIC
SITE

DOCKS

WATERFRONT SHOPS

Visitor Center
and
Outer Banks
History Center

Elizabeth II
Berth

EARLY
SETTLEMENT
SITE

GAZEBO

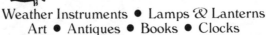

TOWN MANTEO

Across the street from the Waterfront, in the center of the downtown area, are other shops well worth your visit. Establishments such as Fearing's, the Green Dolphin pub, Manteo Booksellers, the Duchess of Dare Restaurant, the Pioneer Theatre, Philo's and almost forty other small-to-medium-sized businesses are packed into a four-square-block area, just like the center of every small town used to be before Henry Ford came up with his infernal carriage. (There's plenty of parking, though, across the street from Manteo Booksellers.)

There's more to do than shop and eat. Around the southeast point of the waterfront stands the town's American Bicentennial Park. Read the inscription under the cross...and shudder at its relevance today. There are picnic benches and comfortable places nearby for you to sit and enjoy the view.

Turning north, you will find the docking of the waterfront a pleasant place to stroll, sit on weathered benches and take pictures. The Four Hundredth anniversary of the Roanoke Voyages brought the *Elizabeth II* to her mooring across Dough's Creek; more about her in a moment. A bit farther north is the municipal parking lot, a public boat ramp and the Manteo post office.

Many visitors find that a walk or bike ride around town is relaxing, and provides a chance to see some of the nice, older homes and talk with the locals (see Manteo Walking Tour in this section). Bikes are provided for

guests of the Tranquil House Inn or the Roanoke Inn, and there's a good chance that Butch's Hotdogs, 473-3663, located in downtown Manteo, will be renting them during the '92 season. (Butch's is also the spot to get a great "dog," fixed up just the way you like it.)

The relaxed, small-town atmosphere typical of Manteo in the years we have known it picked up during Dare County's four-year-long commemoration of the Roanoke voyages (see "Roanoke Island"). During these celebration years visitors to the island, and to the town, found a lot of new construction and a lot of things to do, and the pace has never really slowed down since. Several downtown streets were resurfaced with river rock. A boat construction way was built at the end of Sir Walter Street, and the *Elizabeth II*, a full-size reproduction of a 16-century English sailing ship, was launched there in 1983; it is moored at The Elizabeth II State Historic Site (see "Elizabeth II"). Be sure and head across the bridge and take in the Visitor's Center, History Center and beach there. The latest project is a new $4.5 million sewage treatment plant that will remove the unsightly old tank from the waterfront.

If, as most visitors do, you reach the Banks via Route 158, you can find Manteo by continuing south till you reach Whalebone Junction. Turn right there on Route 64/264. Continue across both bridges and the causeway and turn right again at the T at its end. Turn

Photo: DCTB

Chief Manteo and Chief Wanchese as portrayed by members of
The Lost Colony cast.

right at either of the town's first two stoplights to go downtown.

We think you'll like Manteo, and make friends there. We certainly have.

THE WATERFRONT

Manteo Docks   **473-2188**

The Waterfront is a 34-unit condominium and marketplace at the head of downtown Manteo overlooking Shallowbag Bay. The four story architectural style is Old World, and its scale complements the small town feel of Manteo. With its festive shops, opening onto a breezy courtyard, it is one of the cornerstones of the revitalized downtown area.

The first level of the development is reserved for private parking. Level two contains some 20,000 square feet of retail space. The third and fourth levels are entirely residential. Residents get to keep their "yachts" at the backdoor docks on the Manteo harbor. A ship's store, shower facilities and washer and dryers are available for boaters' use. The north and south channels and Shallowbag Bay were dredged in 1989.

Visitors can enjoy the public areas of The Waterfront which include a dockside walkway, two restaurants and a variety of shops, including a clothing store for men and women, a boutique, a hair salon, an art gallery, a gift shop and a jewelry store. (See the Roanoke Island shopping section for more details.)

THE ELIZABETH II

Elizabeth II State Historic Site
473-1144

The centerpiece of the quadricentennial, moored in the harbor of downtown Manteo, is one of the most characteristic artifacts of English preindustrial civilization — a wooden sailing ship.

And a beautiful one it is. Unexpectedly colorful in bright blue, red and yellow, her hull of nut-brown, gradually weathering wood, she lifts her foremast, mainmast and lateen mizzen sharply toward the sky. Her rigging is a hempen web of tackle, so complex as to confuse the eye. Her high-sided hull and sloped stern and foredeck lend her the awkward grace of a newly hatched duckling.

Elizabeth II's story properly begins in 1584, when Thomas Cavendish mortgaged his estates to build the *Elizabeth* for the second expedition to Roanoke Island. With six other vessels, she took the first colonizing expedition to the New World.

Four hundred years later, galvanized by the approaching quadricentennial of that faraway beginning, private and governmental entities in North Carolina began planning for an ambitious commemorative project: an authentic reproduction of an Elizabethan ship, a living and sailing link to the past.

After thorough research of available plans and histories, the American Quadricentennial Corporation, the organization funding and directing the construction, concluded that there wasn't enough information today to faithfully reconstruct one of Sir Walter's original vessels. But there was, fortunately, some data available for one of the ships in Sir Richard Grenville's 1585 expedition. With this as guidance, William Avery Baker and Stanley Potter, probably America's foremost experts on Elizabethan-era sailing ships, designed the *Elizabeth II*.

The construction contract was let in 1982 to O. Lie-Nielsen, a ship-builder in Rockland, Maine, and construction began at a for-the-purpose boatyard on the Manteo waterfront. The completed fifty-foot, twin-decked ship — all seventy feet of her — slid smoothly down hand-greased ways into Manteo Harbor in late 1983. She is as authentic as love and research could make her. Built largely by hand, her frames, keel, planking and decks are fastened with seven thousand trunnels (pegs) of locust wood. Every baulk and spar, every block and lift, are as close as achievable to the original, with only two exceptions: a wider upper-deck hatch, for easier visitor access, and a vertical hatch in the afterdeck to make steering easier for the helmsman.

In July 1984, the official opening of the quadricentennial, *Elizabeth II* was turned over to the state of North Carolina for berthing and display at a brand-new visitor's center and dock, across a bridge east of downtown Manteo. Currently, she leaves the is-land in spring and fall for trips to nearby towns, making her the only traveling historic site in the state.

To reach the ship, you can park in downtown Manteo and walk across, or drive over the arched bridge and park on the island (on the whole, we recommend the latter). Once there, you'll find the Visitor's Center and the Outer Banks History Center.

The Visitor's Center is built after the style of the classic old Nags Head cottages, with cedar shake roofing and wide porches. Inside, you'll find an exhibit area, a gift shop, auditorium and restrooms. Behind the Center a raked path leads to the ship and to another summer event, the Early Settlement Site. *Elizabeth II* is to the right and the settlement to the left. The site is an eternally frozen August 17, 1585, with soldier's tents, a general's tent and living history demonstrations of woodworking, ninepins and cooking.

Admission is $3.00 for adults; $2.00 for senior citizens; $1.50 for students; free for children under 6. Group of 10 or more receive 50 cents off the admission price. The price of admission includes the twenty-minute presentation, held every half hour in the auditorium, a tour of the ship, and settlement site. Costumed sailors and soldiers explain how the ships of Elizabethan England were built and sailed (in authentic Elizabethan dialect). Hours of operation: November 1 through March 31, 10 to 4 Tuesday through Sunday; closed Mondays. April 1 through October 31, 10 to 6 daily. (The costume presentation is Tuesday through Saturday in the summer only, from early June through August.) Note: the last tickets are sold at 3 p.m. from Nov. 1 through March 31, and at 5 p.m. from April 1 through Oct. 31, to allow time for a complete tour.

OUTER BANKS HISTORY CENTER
Ice Plant Island   473-2655

As you cross the bridge onto Ice Plant Island from the Waterfront of Manteo, the Outer Banks History Center is located in the building on the right. Adjoining it is the Elizabeth II Exhibit Center. There is plenty of parking for a day of exploring history. You'll find here a large collection of National Park Service interpretive work, personal estate collections of North Carolina families and many books by North Carolina authors.

The Outer Banks History Center was opened in 1988. Natives of the state can take time to explore a bit of their own history here. Visitors might find traces of their ancestors and other interesting facts. The collection of North Carolina history found here is second only to that located at the University of North Carolina in Chapel Hill.

The History Center, a repository of writings, maps, photographs, books and pamphlets, houses the enormous collection of well-known author David Stick. Due in large part to his dedication and hard work, the History Center is an important facility for the area.

Mr. Stick, local historian and author of many books on the Outer Banks, had collected these works during his years of research and writing. Untold hours were spent categorizing and cataloguing this collection. He continues to write narratives to accompany photographs and other documents, which will make the collection one of the most extensive and accurately detailed found anywhere.

It was after some inquiries about what he planned to do with his papers, maps and documents, that Mr. Stick saw the importance of keeping all of it in one place, rather than dispatching parts to one interested group or another.

In 1984 he began working with the North Carolina Division of Archives and History to establish a private library. He requested two conditions for his sizeable collection: one was that the library be maintained as a research facility and secondly, that it have proper security.

When assured of this, David Stick worked with others to obtain the necessary funding for the facility. Although many people supported the David Stick Library as a name for the facility, he preferred it to be known as the Outer Banks History Center. He credits strong interest and support from many, including local resident and television actor Andy Griffith and State Senator Marc Basnight, as especially helpful in seeing the project become a reality.

The Elizabethan Gardens near Manteo are designed to reflect English Gardens as they were around the time of Sir Walter Raleigh's American expeditions to the New World

Curator Wynne Dough and his staff work year round receiving and organizing historical works into the research center.

In addition to the research library where journalists, history professors, graduate and high school students come for information, an exhibit gallery is located here. Among the primary exhibits, which change from time to time, is the artistry of Frank Stick, David's father.

The Frank Stick Collection consists of over 325 paintings of fish and wildlife and lends an important dimension to the written documents of Outer Banks and North Carolina history.

While the art exhibits change from time to time, historical flats, documentary pieces and other interesting works are displayed.

Featured recently was an exhibit entitled "An Artist's Catch," a collection of watercolor fish paintings by Frank Stick.

Dough notes the reading room is open 9:00 a.m. till 5:00 p.m. Monday through Friday and 10:00 a.m. till 3:00 p.m. Saturday all year.

Gallery hours are 10:00 a.m. to 4:00 p.m. Monday through Friday, and 10:00 a.m. to 3:00 p.m. on Saturday all year.

THE MANTEO WALKING TOUR

For a leisurely-paced introduction to the town of Manteo, there's no better mutual friend than a walking tour. "The Manteo Walking Tour,"

available at gift shops and bookstores throughout the Banks, is a chapbook of vintage photos and reminiscences of the town as it was in 1900, 1923 and 1938. The pictures and stories are woven into a two-hour walking tour. The mile-and-a-half circuit starts at the foot of the Basnight Bridge, and proceeds around town by way of 34 stops, tales and photos back to the waterfront. It's a relaxing and serene way to pass an afternoon.

Roanoke Island

RECREATION

FISHING CHARTERS

Half-day and all day trips are available for fishing and for scenic cruises. Take your pick: trolling for blues, Spanish mackerel, king mackerel, speckled trout, red fish, or bottom fishing for flounder, spot and trout. Also, off-shore fishing for tuna, dolphin, blue marlin, sail fish and more is available.

For booking information:

Pirate's Cove Yacht Club: Reservations for offshore and inshore charters can be made by calling the Pirate's Cove Booking Desk, 473-3906 or 1-800-367-4728. Headboat information, 473-5577. MC, VISA are accepted at Pirate's Cove.

Additional reservations:

From Wanchese: Capt. Vernon Barrington at P.O. Box 270, Manteo, NC 27954 or call 473-6242 between 8:00 a.m. and 9:00 p.m.

From Manteo Waterfront: Capt. Sandy Griffin. Call before 9:00 p.m. 441-1816 or 473-3236

From Pirate's Cove Marina: Capt. Hank Beasley. Call 473-5618

Camping

CYPRESS COVE CAMPGROUND
Main Hwy.

Manteo   **473-5231**

An intown campground, Cypress Cove has conveniently shaded sites bordering the town of Manteo. Rates begin at $16 for 1 or 2 occupants of RV/Campers and $13 for 1 or 2 in tents. Pets are allowed provided they are quiet and on a leash. Call for reservations and other details of Cypress Cove.

Fitness

NAUTICS HALL HEALTH AND
FITNESS COMPLEX
Main Hwy. at The Elizabethan Inn
473-1191

Nautics Hall provides the facilities all year long from 6:30 a.m. to 9:30 p.m., 7 days a week for exercise, fitness, aerobics, yoga, swimming, racquetball and weight training by the year, month or day.

Indoor and outdoor pools, sun deck, tanning bed, aerobicycle, Nautilus and Paramount equipment, dressing/shower/locker rooms, and whirlpool and sauna are all offered.

Roanoke Island

SHOPPING
Manteo

Shopping on Roanoke Island runs the gamut from small shopping centers and businesses along Main Highway (Route 64) to a collection of shops on and near the waterfront.

We covered the **Island Art Gallery and Christmas Shop** in the section on Attractions -- you'll notice the lovely flower beds along Main Hwy. There's plenty of parking in lots on both sides of the road. Plan enough time to enjoy the array of fine art and crafts.

The **Chesley Mall** has several stores including **Ben Franklin**, 473-2378, which has name-brand items: accessories, clothing and housewares. The **Davis Clothing Store**, 473-2951, carries clothes for the whole family. There's a **Revco Drug Store**, 473-5056, to fill your needs for prescription drugs and sundries. **Viti's Italian Cafe** is also located here -- scrumptious food to eat in or carry out. **Qwik Shot**, 473-5598, can provide fast turnaround for your vacation film; and next door, **The Video Store**, 473-3278 rents to visitors and they have huge array of 1st rate movies.

Across the street is **The Card Shed**, 473-3459. This is a sports fanatic's dream. They have collectible sports cards -- football, baseball, basketball, hockey, golf -- along with hat with sports logos and pennants. They also carry Marvel cards and have a big selection of those great old comic books you loved as a kid. Next door to them is **Crockett's Seafood Market**, 473-2912, selling right-off-the-boat fresh seafood and all the accompaniments.

There's an abundance of clothing and other household items at **Second Time Around**, 473-3127, located on Main Hwy. past the Dare County Public Library. This is a fund-raising shop for the benefit of the Outer Banks Hotline, and the inventory includes good used furniture.

Fearings, 473-2149, on Budleigh Street, has been a downtown Manteo institution for 60 years. From time to time the merchandise changes, but it's this change that keeps it interesting. Children's clothing is featured and the **Pig and Phoenix** soda fountain in the back serves sandwiches, old-fashioned thick milkshakes and the best freshly-made orangeade on the Outer Banks.

Located near the waterfront on Sir Walter Raleigh Street are the Essex Square Shops. **Philo Farnsworth & Daughters, Ltd**, 473-2886, is a new shop for the '92 season. Bonnie Farnsworth, owner of this interesting spot, offers gourmet and international foods, imported beers and wines, exotic gifts and gift baskets, which are delivered locally or shipped UPS. She also has developed a series of international cookery kits, her first being "The Thai Experience," which are marketed under A Universal Foods Odyssey, and marketed at Philos as well.

Next door is the finest bookstore on the Outer Banks and quite possibly in the region (and we'd even say the country, but we haven't been to *every* bookstore out there to compare). **Manteo Booksellers**, 473-1221, has several rooms just packed with books covering everything from the literary classics to delightful childrens' books. Plan on giving yourself a *long* time to browse. If you don't know what you want, manager Steve Brumfield or his sister, Chris Kidder, a well-known Outer Banks writer, will assist you. The bookstore features evenings of story-telling and readings by authors of books and poetry.

Across the way are **The Waterfront Shops** which were also mentioned briefly in the section about Attractions. **Shallowbags**, 473-3078, is a quality women's boutique. Contemporary fine clothing, accessories and gifts are offered and the attentive help by the staff is professional and appropriate. **Donetta Donetta**, 473-5323, is a full-service beauty salon for men and women situated on the waterfront side of this shopping arcade. They can pamper you from head to toe and have a sun tanning bed if you feel you need to augment your summer color.

Island Trading Company, 473-3365, features antiques, original art, greeting cards and finewares. Owners Jack and Marilyn Hughes also own **Island Nautical**, 473-1411, where you'll find an interesting array of gifts and accessories. These are two of our favorite shops for Christmas present buying on the whole Outer Banks. Ken Kelly and Eileen Alexanian are the owners of a new jewelry shop, **Diamonds and Dunes**, 473-1002. This new shop features fine, hand-crafted designs. With over 19 years' experience in the jewelry business in the New York market, this is a great shop to come to for professional work - everything from setting a stone or sizing a ring to creating a one-of-a-kind keepsake. **Darwin's Cafe**, 473-1660, is a small natural foods cafe on the waterfront side with a large menu and daily specials worth fighting over they're so good. You can also get deli sandwiches. They also carry natural cosmetic products and vegetarian foods. **Clara's Seafood Grill** is also located here, serving wonderfully-prepared lunches and dinner, and featuring a steam bar in the '92 season. Both these restaurants are described in more detail in the Restaurants section.

Venture out onto Main Hwy. again and head northeast to Etheridge Road. Turn left and visit **The Cloth Barn**, 473-2795. Linda and Harry Bridges keep their store packed with everything you need to sew -- lots of fabrics, motions and patterns.

Wanchese

After your trip across Roanoke Sound on the Nags Head-Manteo Causeway Bridge, the left turn at the intersection will take you to the village of Wanchese. Large areas of marshland and tall stands of pine trees create a beautiful scene as you drive along this road. You'll discover **Added Touch**, 473-2972, a craft shop opened 10 years ago by Maxine Daniels, a friendly local resident. She makes a lot of things and sells items made by other local craftspeople.

At the end of the road, you'll come to a conglomeration of seafood businesses and a restaurant which we've covered in the section on Roanoke Island Restaurants. After coming this far, it's easy to see that the seafood industry has put Wanchese on the map!

After you've turned around at the end of the road, return to Old Wharf Road and go left for an excursion off the beaten path. **Nick-E**, 473-5036, is a stained glass wonderland, with original creations by Ellinor and Robert Nick. These two have been married for 34 years and "live their work" here in this shop and studio. They teach classes through the College of the Albemarle curriculum and give private instructions as well. They've had people come from as far away as Pennsylvania to learn the art of stained glass and ceramics. In addition to the fine crafts on display, they sell supplies and tools. The Nicks will explain the process of their work to create stained glass sun-catchers and ceramics. Only their own professional work is sold here. Students' work is neither displayed nor sold.

Queen Anne's Lace, 473-5466,

is a gift shop of local crafts and art. It is situated on the grounds of Queen Anne's Revenge, noted in the section on restaurants. The gifts here are displayed in a renovated house which originally sat on Jigsaw Road in Nags Head, near Jockey's Ridge. During the Ash Wednesday Storm of 1962 it was washed off its pilings and sat in disrepair for years before Wayne Gray had it moved here to Wanchese. The shop features pottery by Wanchese potter Bonnie Morrill, and Jan Mann of Kitty Hawk. The shop caters to those who come for dinner at the restaurant and like to browse for a gift or a purchase of local crafts to take home. It's open from 6 until 10 p.m. all year.

Photo: Phillip Ruckle

The Manteo waterfront, including the Elizabeth II.

Photo: DCTB

A statue of Virginia Dare, the first English child born in America, greets visitors to the Elizabethan Gardens in Manteo.

Photo: DCTB

The Manteo waterfront.

I May Become A Cultivated Man

Nicholas Longworth Meekins: A life In Manteo

*T*he house is small, neat, one of dozens just like it in the tract in western Manteo. Inside it, wrapped in a vanilla-scented cloud of Captain Black that fills the living room, Nicholas Meekins is sitting back, repacking a curved briar pipe. He is a tall man with a pepper and salt moustache. He's still not entirely gray, but he finds it difficult to get up from his easy chair.

"When I was born? July twentieth, nineteen oh five.

"My father's name was Theodore Meekins. They have a plaque down there right where Pea Island Station was located. It mentions the fact that my father was on patrol that particular night when this *E. S. Newman* run aground. And he sounded the alarm and rushed to the station, and the crew got ready to go out and rescue the passengers.

"Now, I might be a little biased, but a neutral report, if it was given, would say that not only did my father sound the alarm, but—they have what they called a Lyle gun. They shoot this line across the bow of a ship. And they

attach the breeches buoy and bring them ashore. Well, the Lyle gun wouldn't work that night, the powder or something was wet. They had no way of gettin' the line across. But my father — don't mind my sayin' so — was the best swimmer in the outfit. He weighed two hundred and thirty-five, forty pounds. I'm not that small but my mother weighed a hundred and twenty. You see why I'm not big.

"But anyway, they had to tie a rope around his body. And he swam out there in that ragin' surf to the ship. And they pulled him aboard so they could get the lines. And they brought the women and children safely across on shore. They didn't lose a single passenger. Now, as a memento for that they gave my father the name plate off'n the side. A board about six seven feet long. *E.S. Newman*. And he had a storage place down in the yard and he had that tacked across there. That was one of the most eventful or historic things that happened on the coast there, at the Pea Island Station.

"That was before I was born. It was eighteen something. I guess it was ten or fifteen years before I was born.

"It was after I was born and grew up to be 'bout eleven years old, my father used to have me to come down with the man who was coming back on liberty, coming back the day before my father was due to come on liberty. I'd go down and spend the night with my father. And once I went on the south patrol with him when he was on duty there. Well, I didn't walk that patrol. They had big horses that used to haul the surfboats around. And so he took me in a buckboard. So he carried a clock with him that they would punch. Your key was down at the end of the patrol. You strike that clock, then at the keeper's station the next morning he could tell exactly when you hit that clock. Well, I went in the Coast Guard myself in World War Two and I was glad to go, for I wanted to follow in the same footsteps he had gone. And I had the same duty up in Long Island. It was a similar patrol to the one he was on when he sighted the *Newman* on shore, in a storm, on that particular night.

"I'd give anything if I had my father's picture. He was, you might say, quite a specimen of a man. One of the tests that some of the men found difficult to do he found easy. He had to dive down in six feet of water and bring up a fifty-pound weight. My father had eight gold stripes on his arm. That was for good conduct and unbroken service.

"My mother's name was White. Her father was Rowan White, her mother was Sarah White. She had about four, five sisters, and three brothers. They all grew up here. But they moved after they were grown. I had a uncle once lived in New Bern the rest of his life, and some of them went up to Hampton, Virginia; but they didn't go too far away.

"I really don't know how my people happened to come here. My father's father was John Meekins. Now a lot of the people who came here, they came from Hyde County, but most from Tyrrell County. Most of the people I knew were from Tyrrell and Washington County. I taught school in Washington County and I met quite a few people who knew people I knew when I was growing up. The short migration was from Hyde and Tyrrell. I think most of those who came to Roanoke Island came when they were freed, after the war. Maybe it was somewhat of a haven. There was a place they used to call Burnside, after General Burnside, in the Civil War. Burnside used to belong mostly to Negroes. And the fellow who owned the best land up there was Ben and Hannah Golden, which was my wife's grandfather.

"I grew up here until I was thirteen. And I was here off and on then. 'Cause I went to high school in Elizabeth City. I was there for about six years. I was here off and on and during the summer. After I finished high school I was here more infrequently, but I never stayed away more than two years at a time.

"The first thing I remember in growing up? At an early age — I suppose I must have been about seven, eight years old — when my father, I was the youngest, he took me when he was on vacation once and we went to see my oldest brother and sister, who were living in Phoebus. That was you might say the most eventful trip in that it was the first one I had leavin' the island. They had the steamboat to Elizabeth City, then we'd take the train, the Norfolk & Southern, to Norfolk. First they had a gas boat, the *Hattie Creef*, then they had the steamer *Trenton*. The *Trenton* was the main boat I took going back and forth from Elizabeth City there.

"I went to the Roanoke Academy here in Manteo until I was thirteen. It was a frame two-story building. We had hygiene, history, geography. We had the Riverside Literature and the regular Milne Arithmetic. I haven't thought of that book in years. It wasn't as standardized as it might have been. But I wasn't too far behind, when I went to Elizabeth City. They put you back a grade anyway. It has its advantages and disadvantages. You do a little bit of repeating, but some things stick better going over them a second time.

"We didn't teach the Bible as such in school. The last principal we had here was the Reverend Dickens. He was a minister, but he didn't dwell on anything too religious. Maybe, more, morality. (Laughs.) Growing up here I went to Haven Creek Baptist Church. Our ministers were just way above par. They had been to seminaries and they were well versed in the Scriptures. I tell you frankly — well, I go to church now and I really find that some of the sermons I heard then were more educational, more revealing, and better prepared than many of the sermons I hear now.

"My mother took me to church. We had the morning service, then we had Sunday School. Then the evening service. So I went to church three times a day on Sunday. I still remember some of the texts that I learned when I was 14, 15 years old. I recall two ministers in particular. Reverend Sharp, from Edenton. And one of the best sermons I ever heard, he gave from the Eighth Psalm. I memorized it afterward:

Oh Lord our Lord, how excellent is thy name in all the earth! who hast set thy glory above the heavens.

Out of the mouth of babes and sucklings hast thou ordained strength because of thine enemies, that thou mightest still the enemy and the avenger.

When I consider thy heavens, the work of thy fingers, the moon and the stars, which thou hast ordained;

What is man, that thou art mindful of him?

" — And so on, I won't go on with the rest of it. That was one of the best sermons. But I gave you the wrong man. Reverend Sharp preached a sermon wonderful like that, but this was Reverend Delanie, from Washington County. But we had on our baccalaureate sermon, Reverend John Moore, and that was one of the best I ever heard. And he took his text which I remember from Jeremiah, 48th chapter, 11th verse. "Moab hath been at ease from his youth." I won't quote that. But all the worthwhile sermons — well, maybe all of them are worthwhile — but the best, they were in my earliest childhood here.

"The only game I played mostly was we played a little sandlot baseball. We usually had a homemade ball, but once in a while we had a little league baseball. But we only had one, so if you knocked it over in the bushes that stopped the game until you found it. They had a lot up here about where you see the community building out here. There weren't any houses being built up there then. We had almost two acres of playing ground. No, we never played with the white boys while I was here. They played cross town.

"When we had quite a influential speaker here we would reserve seats for part of the white congregation. One of the old gentlemen was quite a close friend of mine. Mister Acie Evans. My aunt used to cook for them. I don't know why he took a liking to me. He ran the Tranquil House downtown. That was the main hotel here then. His son Charlie was the postmaster here for a while. I knew old Charlie and his father very well. In fact Mister Evans thought so much of me he used to have me around in the flower yard as a companion for him. When grown men were gettin' a dollar a day for work, he'd pay me a dollar just for helpin' him set out flowers. Let's see, I was eleven or twelve then.

"In those days a dollar would go quite a distance. When you only had to pay a penny for a postcard and two cent for a stamp letter a dollar would go pretty good. It was like in Depression days. When I first went to New York in '29, down in Delancey Street on the East Side, you could go to a stand and get a kosher, strictly beef hot dog and a mug of root beer for five cent. The hot dog was full dressed with onions and sauerkraut. So you could buy a whole lot for a dollar.

"The first time I tasted liquor? Well, when my father came home from the Coast Guard station on his liberty he might have a bottle of gin. He didn't ever give me any, but I might have sneaked a little bit. Not enough to be noticed, or for it to go to my head. But he would make apple cider. We had a lot of fruit trees. See, my father had two months vacation — they would come home first of June and stay till the first of August. Unless they had a wreck or a storm, then they had to go back. But during that time my father would have us to farm. We raised everything we need. Chickens, and hogs, and all kind of crops. But he would grind up apples and make a 55-gallon drum of apple cider. Um hum. Now we could drink all that cider we wanted till he put sugar in it. Then he'd put lock and key on it. See, after you put the sugar in it ferments, and it gets as strong as your average liquor. He would save that for his company. He might let you have just a little sampling of it. But it wasn't free like it was before he made it hard. It was very delicious, but it'll slip up on you. You can become intoxicated before you realize it.

"Our farm was down there near where the Hardee's place is — that takes in part of it. It was all strictly along the highway, over a quarter mile long. Twenty-five acres, fifteen of it cleared. And you had about ten acres of woodland back of you. I would never have let that land been broken up, just in honor of my father. But you know you can't do what you want. You'll always have some members of the family are going to pull off and do things, and they wanted to sell and get rid of it. I don't know what each one got, but I didn't get anything because I was off at school. If I had stayed here and watched things we'd have it now. For whatever it sold for a different one, is worth ten times as much now.

"When I was a kid we would go down there to Mill Landing and meet my father and my uncle when they came back from the Coast Guard, and bring them home. Old man E. R. (Zeke) Daniels' store was there. He was about the wealthiest man in property on the island. They claimed Clary Pugh had more cash money, but old man Zeke had more property. He owned several boats, I think he owned

the *Hattie Creef. Pompano* was another boat Uncle Zeke owned. I remember his son Preston well. He used to come by home flyin' on a motorcycle.

"Oh, yeah, they allowed us to go in that store. My aunt and another lady used to cook down there for him. And George Pledger, who used to live in front of us across the highway, he worked with him for just about all his life. Old man Zeke was very liberal, just like old man Acie Evans. I came home some years ago and I met his son Charlie so he said to me, he said, 'Nick, have you been over t'see my father?' I said, 'No, I haven't.' He said, 'Would you go over and see him? He's getting quite feeble. He thought so much of you, I know he'd be glad to see you.' So I went over to see him. He was just a fine old gentleman.

"See, some of the people were just like that. People like I'm tellin' you about, like the Evanses, the Creefs — one my very best friends was Albert Evans. His father was the blacksmith here. My father used to get him to make all his carts. He always had a nice horse cart so that during bad weather — we had to walk about a mile and a quarter from my home to the school. But when it was bad weather my brother used to drive us to school.

"My father died on October the thirtieth, nineteen seventeen. He and another man, Kitt Miller, were coming back from Pea Island in Miller's boat. And the engine quit. And the tide carried them out to sea into a storm.

They said they could see them from shore for a long time. They were trying to make it back but they couldn't against the current.

"My mother was the finest little black woman I have ever known. After she was widowed she never married. She talked to a lady when my father passed, Miss Ella Dunbar, who was a teacher here, about what to do about putting me and my sister in the right place. We were the two youngest. I was twelve when my father passed, and she was fourteen. I only had one sister and five brothers. All older — I was the youngest.

"So Miss Ella Dunbar told her the best thing to do was to put my sister and me in the Normal School in Elizabeth City. 'Cause she was getting a small pension from the government because of my father's death, and till my sister and I were eighteen we would draw enough money to go to school. But my mother could not stand to see us go. She found a lovely place for us to board. Mrs. Mary Hargood's. She had a big home then on Southern Avenue extension. I loved her, she treated me like her own son. My mother stayed there a few days with a friend of hers after she dropped me off. But when she got ready to leave it was all she could do to leave me. And she would come over there and get some work around the school, they had a farm there, vegetables and beans. Not that she — well, she did need the money, but she did it to be near me.

"In fact my first year at State

Normal, that was at Elizabeth City, it was interrupted by the flu. We had gone there my sister and I for about two or three months and the school closed down on account of the flu epidemic. They opened up after a few months, but I didn't go back till the following year. I stayed there until twenty-five, 1925, when I finished high school.

"I enlisted in the Coast Guard the 15th of August 1942. And I stayed there exactly thirty-seven months. Here's a copy of my discharge. I was seaman first, then I changed to fireman. I wasn't anxious to go to sea, and I had a better chance to go to shore duty as a fireman. See that there? If you stayed in over three years and didn't come back late or anything you got the Good Conduct medal. Sixtynine dollars a month. That was big money then.

"I was up in Long Island right after a German sub put those spies ashore there. I was stationed with the fellow, John Cullen, the boy who turned them in. Cullen when he intercepted those spies all he had was a nightstick. And they offered him five hundred dollars as a bribe to let 'em through. Their mission was to blow up the bridge between Newark and New York. They said they was rumrunners. They gave him $480 — shortchanged him — and he hightailed it to the station and reported it. Within minutes they had all of Long Island cut off. I don't think they treated Cullen right. They had so many ninety-day wonders. Why in the world didn't they make him a lieutenant? What if he had just put that money in his pocket?

"When I enlisted I was working as a redcap in Penn Station. Before that I had two or three jobs. I worked as a postal clerk. That was during the Depression and I almost starved. I was a temporary sub, I only worked during the summer, and they gave me all the work. What I did was I took the examination for subway conductor and when I got out of the service they offered me either one. I could go back to the railroad or I could go there. So I went back with the railroad.

"I wore these legs out in eighteen years at the railroad. I had a family to take care of and going to school too. I went to school days from nine to three and I had to be at work at the railroad at four thirty. But every dollar counted. Every time I took a passenger to a train, or picked up a passenger, that was an extra dollar. It didn't bother me then — I could run up and down, didn't even stop to wait for the escalator.

"I'd get sometimes three passengers off the same train, they were waiting on the platform for a redcap. Sometimes you'd make two dollars a night, sometimes twenty or thirty. Some would give you a dime, some would just pay for the tags, for the railroad. The highest I had was several ten-dollar tips. But I tell you the worst job I had was Gene Tunney. He came down the station late, so another fellow, Killer Wiggins and I, we ran

down to the train just as hard as we could. And just there in time to put his bags on. You know what he handed us? One dollar! Millionaire! That wasn't even enough to pay the tags. Why couldn't he have accidentally pulled out a twenty?

"I admired Jack Dempsey as much as I disadmired Tunney. When I was in service he was a lieutenant commander. He had charge of us in New York, he used to come around and inspect our work in the sail loft. Very soft-spoken, he never spoke above a low monotone. He may have been a terror in the ring, but personally he was a fine man.

"I stayed with the railroad while I went to Long Island University for three years under the GI Bill. Then I resigned and came home and did another year's work at North Carolina Central; and then I started teaching.

"I taught in Washington County for about fourteen years. The first years I taught at the local high school and the last year I was transferred to the Plymouth high school, and that's where I retired from. The Washington County school was predominantly black. After they integrated I was transferred to Plymouth. But of all the black and white students, of all the thousands I taught during those fifteen years, I didn't have more than three ornery ones. Ninety nine and nine tenths per cent were fine students I could reach. These contrary ones, they just didn't want to do their work. I remember one boy from Creswell I used to get on. He was about to fail, but I gave him a D minus to let him go. When he finished school he came and gave me his school picture. I said, 'James, I appreciate it. I guess you always felt I was being too hard on you.' He said, 'No, Mr. Meekins, I wish you'd been a little bit harder.' I was so surprised you could have knocked me down with a feather.

"I taught English and social studies. I really love literature. I took extra hours in college. For a major I needed forty some hours. I think I had seventy hours in English. I follow most of those New England writers. One of my favorites is Channing. And Longfellow and Emerson, and Theodore Parker. Hawthorne—I liked most of Hawthorne. But The Scarlet Letter, I liked it and hated it. Hester suffered too much.

"William Ellery Channing was one of my favorites. He was speaking about books. He said, if I can give you this: 'In the best books, great men talk to us, give us their most precious thoughts, and pour their souls into ours. God be thanked for books. They are the voices of the distant and the dead, and make us the heirs of the spiritual life of ages past. Books are the true levelers. They give to all, who will faithfully use them, the society, the spiritual presence, of the best and greatest of our race. No matter how poor I am, no matter that the prosperous of my own time would not enter my obscure dwelling. But if the sacred writers will enter and take up their

abode under my roof; if Milton will cross my threshold and sing to me of Paradise; Shakespeare, to open to me the world of imagination, and the workings of the human heart; Franklin, to inject me with his practical wisdom; I shall not pine for want of intellectual companionship. I may become a cultivated man, though excluded from what is termed the best society in the place where I live.' That's one of the best things I got from Channing.

"I tried to be emphatic, or dynamic, in my presentation of literature, and my students still ask me for 'Gunga Din' or 'The Raven' when I see them. I memorized quite a few things. Last year we went to Hatteras High School, it was Negro History Week. And they gave us such a warm welcome and asked us to come back. One of the teachers there sent me a thank you letter and forty students had signed it. I don't want to look for it now. But she said 'After you left, the students talked more about you than they did about the senior prom.' Evidently I made a pretty good impression.

"We recited some things from Negro writers. Like Kelly Miller. He was Dean of Men at Howard University. He wrote a World War One history. And one of the memorable things in it was an open letter he wrote in 1917 to President Woodrow Wilson. The other was Frederick Douglass, his speech that he made in Rochester on the Fourth of July of 1852. Did you ever read that? He said, "Fellow Citizens: Pardon me, and allow me to ask, why am I called upon to speak here today? What have I or those I represent to do with your national independence?. . . To drag a man in fetters into the grand illuminated temple of liberty, and call upon him to join you in joyous anthems were inhuman mockery and sacrilegious irony." He knew his Bible; he knew the lament of a woe-smitten people, when the ancient Israelites said, "By the rivers of Babylon, there sat we down; and we wept when we remembered Zion." He thought it was rather ironic during the Fourth of July, to celebrate liberty while he had four and a half million brothers in slavery. His mistress, the white lady, taught him to read. He ran away to Baltimore and worked on the docks. But he sent back and paid for his freedom! The language that he uses is marvelous. You wonder now, how did he master such language?

"And then Paul Lawrence Dunbar, our first renowned Negro poet; he wrote a lot in dialect. Let me give you one they liked:

*The Lord had a job for me, but
I had so much to do.*
*So I said, get somebody else, or
wait till I get through.*
*I don't know how the Lord came
out, but He seemed to get along.*
*But I felt kind of sneaky like,
'cause I knowed I'd done him wrong.*
*Then one day I needed the Lord,
I needed him right away.*
But way down in my accusin'

heart, I could hear him say,
*Son, I've got too much to do;
you get somebody else, or wait till   I
get through.*
*Now, when the Lord has a job
for me, I never try to shirk*
*I drop just what I have on hand,
and does the good Lord's work.*
*And my affairs can run along,
or wait till I get through.*
*Nobody else can do the job that
God's marked out for you.*

"I was glad to take those things to Hatteras. And you know, that was the first time. I'd been far as Pea Island, and all these years I'd heard so much talk of Hatteras, but I'd never been down there.

"You know, most of my reading I did before I was eighteen years old. I read night and day. But in after years my eyes bother me. When I got in service I had 20-20 vision. But now, when I have plenty of time, I can't read more than five or ten minutes. The reading that I did before I finished high school kept me through college. So many things I had read then I could draw on. It just came in mighty handy in later years.

"My father, he wasn't a highly educated man, but he was self-educated. He bought books. One of the finest books he bought was by William Ellis, *Billy Sunday: The Man and His Message*. World War History by Kelly Miller. He had all about the Galveston Flood, Spanish-American War, the white slave trade. He read all those during his leisure time in the Coast Guard. He had some wonderful books. I wonder how he selected them. But I guess the salesman would come down to the station. I can't find them now.

"I recall he had a power boat called the *Henrietta*, after my mother. It was the best boat around there. And so we were coming across the Inlet, and he revved up the motor. And I wondered why. And about the time he revved up the motor the boat moved to the side. She had hit the current in the channel. So he caught me by the waistband and told me to look over the washboard of the ship. I looked over there and as far down as you could see the water was clear; but you could see that current cuttin' the sand from the bottom. Now little did he dream that was going to be his doom.

"Little things like that I remember about him and I'm proud. As I said, the October 30th, 1917, was my saddest day. I was at school, and there was a boy, Haywood Wise, he was my buddy since we could remember. Eleven, twelve years old. He was superintendent of the Sunday School here for thirty-five years. He passed a few years ago. Now, when the word came that my father had been blown out to sea, we had been out playin'. It hit me so I got up and went over and sat down by myself. Haywood had stopped playing and sat by me too. He didn't know what to say, but he felt my hurt was his hurt. And after that I got my books and started on that mile home.

And he walked half the way with me. In Hutchinson's book *This Freedom* he says "In our successes, our hours of triumph, there are a hundred eyes that shine with ours in those. But it's defeats you want her to tell. The lights that are gone out; the springs that spring no more; the secret sordid things that hedge you in, that draw you down; those, to have somebody to tell those to." That's what a real friend means to you.

"I went on home. And my home, for the next week, which had been so quiet and peaceful, was bedlam. My mother for nights walked the floor. Maybe she was hoping against hope; hollering and crying for nights. Aunt Victoria Daniels, Nancy Midgett, the neighbors did all they could to console her. But she didn't want to be consoled.

"I don't know why people do things like that, but a month or so later somebody put a article in the paper that Theodore Meekins and Kitt Miller had been picked up by a German tramp steamer and were making their way home. That gave us some terrible false hopes. It was a hoax. They never did find Kitt Miller, but six months later my father — what remained of my father — washed up on the beach down there between Oregon Inlet and Pea Island. And they could only identify him by his underwear and his dental work.

"I came back here September before last. After I retired I stayed in Washington County. I had so many friends there. I hadn't been in a rush to come back. I had feelings for the old homestead, but I had some unpleasant memories too. But my wife wanted to come home. She has three brothers here.

"I might say what ought to be my happiest time was when I wanted a son, and when my son was born — in fact all my children. I had two boys and three girls. I was mighty joyful about that. And thank God they've never given me any problems or trouble, and they're self-sufficient and independent. And they all went to college.

"My oldest son is in the Coast Guard. When he got out of college he enlisted in the Navy, so I got him to switch. This is his picture when he was commissioned. He flies the helicopters. This is my baby girl; she lives in Durham. My other son is in Minnesota. I have one daughter in Los Angeles and my other daughter is a nurse in New Haven. See, all of them are just as far from me as the ends of the country, but I hear from them every week.

"I have so many nieces and nephews here. Must have a hundred of them. Too many! They come to me, speak t' me, 'Uncle Nick,' and I have to get them to tell me who their mother is.

"I feel somewhat depressed when I think of how I'm unable to reach so many young people. Those kids the other day — suicides — sometimes I'm just dumbfounded. As much as I took in psychology I never really learned how to reach somebody. The human mind is so intricate! It seems the more I studied the more nonplused I became.

"The best approach I know is to show them that, you're not alone. There's others have had greater problems than you. I had something prepared for when I went back to Hatteras. I think it would be about as good as any, come to think about it. Dwight Hillis, in *The Battle Of Principles*, has one part on Abe Lincoln. He gave it in such beautiful language. I'll try to give it to you. He said that when the country was threatened, the very existence of government, that God needed a man like Lincoln. He said, "Lincoln was the man who had walked for fifty years under cloudy skies. He was the most picturesque figure in history. He was the strongest, the gentlest, the saddest, the most pathetic figure in history. God chose him. He passed by the palaces and went to a cabin in the wilderness. And he took this little baby in his arms and called to his side his favorite angel, the Angel of Sorrow. And said to him, 'Take this little child of mine, and make him great.' Said, 'Take from him everything that he loves. As he climbs the hills of adversity, let his footprints be stained with his own blood. Till his face is more marred than any man of his time. Then bring him back to me, and I will have him free four million slaves.' So he said, 'God, and sorrow, made Lincoln great.' If kids could think about the problems that others have had, that they're not alone, their depression would be lifted.

"Well, my worst drug is my beer and my pipe, but I'm addicted to that TV more than anything else. Sometimes I have to crawl around on the floor to get over to it. I can't do a lot of walking, but I get stiff if I sit still too long. Hard to believe I was the captain of the football team, isn't it? I could really move then.

"I have some regrets about things I might have done differently. But you know, I don't have any real fear. Yes, I believe there's an afterlife. I tell you, there has to be. Whether it's beyond purgatory or not. If there is such a thing as Purgatory, then maybe it isn't necessary to have a Judgment, if you can be cleansed before a future life. Too much a belief in one might contradict the other. You might be punished in this world. There seems to be some judgement here. But there has to be some reckoning. "I try to do like, what did William Cullen Bryant say in 'Thanatopsis'

Thou go not, like the quarry-slave at night,
Scourged to his dungeon, but, sustained and soothed
By an unfaltering trust, approach thy grave,
Like one that wraps the drapery of his couch
About him, and lies down to pleasant dreams."

Photo: DCTB

Gigantic red drum proliferate in local waters.

Photo: DCTB

Fishing on one of the many Outer Banks piers nearly always ends up with fresh fish for dinner.

Inside
Bodie Island \

Bodie Island is not an island as it was long ago. Storms and shifting sands have closed inlets at a northern area known as Whalebone Junction. (The area in and around the intersection of Routes 158 & 64 is known as Whalebone Junction.)

Bodie Island (pronounced "body") begins where the Cape Hatteras National Seashore begins. In early times, livestock roamed freely on Bodie, and there were a number of gun clubs built here in the 1800s, when sportsmen took advantage of the vast marshes and migratory waterfowl. When commercial fishing boats began to come in through Oregon Inlet it became the location of a lighthouse. Today, Bodie Island is a preserved marshland, a place where birds and wildlife claim a portion of the barrier islands for themselves with a lighthouse of their own.

Bodie Island

ATTRACTIONS

BODIE ISLAND LIGHTHOUSE
AND KEEPERS' QUARTERS
Bodie Island   **441-5711**

Bodie Island Light, one of the four famous lighthouses of the Outer Banks, is at the end of a road, west of NC 12, about six miles south of Whalebone Junction and opposite Coquina Beach.

Built in 1872, the 150-foot brick structure is noticeable by its horizontal black and white stripes. It was the only light between Cape Henry, Virginia and Cape Hatteras when it was built. Over this 120-mile shoreline, Bodie Island Light provided important warnings for mariners coming too close to the Graveyard of the Atlantic.

It is the third lighthouse to stand at or near Oregon Inlet since it opened in a hurricane in 1846. The first developed cracks and had to be destroyed, the second was destroyed by the Confederates to confuse Federal shipping. It is located somewhat farther inland as nature has built up the southern end of the island.

The wide expanses of marshland behind the lighthouse are perfect for a short walk. There are cattails, yaupon, wax myrtle, bayberry and other vegetation. A short path and overlooks are provided.

The double-keepers quarters were operated as a visitor center until five years ago when the building's condition gave park service officials quite a scare. The building was closed to the public after workers discovered electrical shorts.

Although three years passed before funds became available from the U.S. Department of Interior to restore the building, throughout the restoration which began in 1990, great care has been given to protecting the building's unique history and the exterior. Restoration stopped for a brief period when funds ran out. However, a year ago, work got underway again and when completed in spring of '92, the keepers house will look very much as it did in an 1893 photograph.

Field mice, nesting behind the walls had gnawed away at the electrical wiring. In addition to the mice, termites and wood borers and other bugs had literally eaten the building to pieces. Walls and ceilings had been covered by layers of fiber board and acoustical tile. Some of the old plaster walls, built with sand collected off the beach, have been saved. Drywall has been used to cover and preserve them.

To save the building from the harsh coastal environment and the ravages of time, further work has been underway. Where possible, floorboards, window panes, window frames, doors and brick fireplaces have been retained.

The most difficult work has been to restore the floors. Workers lying on their backs on the sand maneuvered in an area no more than 18 inches deep under the house to shore-up floor joists.

The work has been time-consuming, but a significant pencil-drawing was recovered from inside the plaster walls. The artist was John B. Etheridge, a carpenter who helped in a former remodeling of the building back in 1955. That year the Park Service took over the building from the Coast Guard. Etheridge was a descendant of the family that sold 15 acres to the government in 1870 (for $150) as the site of the Bodie Island Lighthouse and quarters.

John Gaskill, 76, of Wanchese, is the son of Vernon Gaskill, who served as the last civilian keeper at Bodie Island Lighthouse. He recalls the days when the lighthouse was the only thing between the area just north of Jockey's Ridge and Oregon Inlet -- between 1919 and 1940. He cut the grass around the lighthouse with a push mower and helped his father strain the kerosene before it was poured into the lighthouse lanterns. This prevented particles from clogging the vaporizer that kept the light burning.

The Keepers Quarters are expected to be open to the public this summer. We were unable to confirm the exact date, but an interesting side-trip to the grounds of this historic lighthouse is a must for history buffs as they drive along the Cape Hatteras National Seashore highway.

COQUINA BEACH

Bodie Island   **441-7425**

This wonderful, wide, desolate beach is one of the best swimming

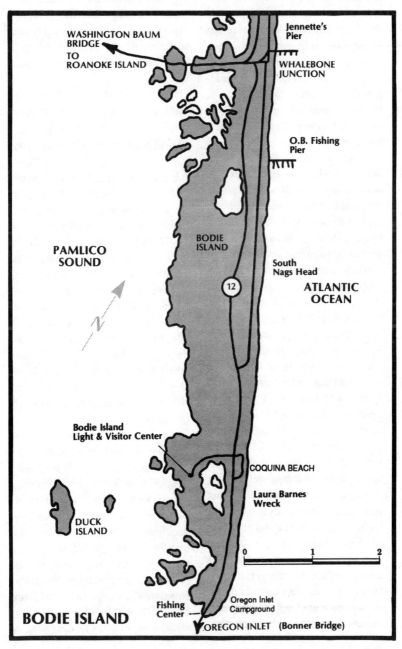

WASHINGTON BAUM
BRIDGE
TO
ROANOKE ISLAND

Jennette's
Pier

WHALEBONE
JUNCTION

O.B. Fishing
Pier

BODIE
ISLAND

PAMLICO
SOUND

12

South
Nags Head

ATLANTIC
OCEAN

Bodie Island
Light & Visitor Center

COQUINA BEACH

Laura Barnes
Wreck

DUCK
ISLAND

0   1   2

Oregon Inlet
Campground

BODIE ISLAND

Fishing
Center

OREGON INLET (Bonner Bridge)

beaches on the Outer Banks. The sand is fine and almost white; the beach is flat. The National Park Service has added public restrooms and showers, otherwise it's as natural as it was long ago. The beach is guarded from mid-June through Labor Day. By the way, the name comes from the little shells," Coquinas," found underfoot in the surf, like millions of tiny bronze coins.

Unfortunately, the Halloween Storm of 1991 hit Coquina Beach with powerfully high seas and the picnic area and half of the parking lot was completely destroyed. The entrance to Coquina Beach is closed on the northern end, but continue your drive to the southern entrance, a short distance away, if you'd like to swim or fish on this stretch of beach. The bathhouse sits on a dune and escaped with only minor damage during the storms. There was, however, plenty of sand to shovel. The dunes are some of the highest on the Outer Banks, or at least they were before the recent storms. I've enjoyed solitude here on many occasions and listened to children playing hide-and-seek around the base of the dunes where the wind has sculpted nooks and crannies. (Climbing on the dunes is discouraged by Park officials and all who are environmentally aware of this fragile area where sea oats and other beach grasses grow.) Bodie Island and Coquina Beach are a part of the National Seashore and will remain protected from development. The area lends a sense of change or a place of transition from the towns gone-com-mercial on the northern portions of the barrier islands to the villages struggling to retain their remoteness on the southern end -- Bodie Island Lighthouse keeping a watchful pose over it all.

OREGON INLET COAST GUARD STATION

Coquina Beach   987-2311 or 473-5085

Much of the history of the Outer Banks centers around the lighthouses and the lifesaving stations. The United States Lifesaving Service was the forerunner to the U.S. Coast Guard. It was in 1873 that Congress allocated funds to establish lifesaving stations for the east coast. Of the 29 stations planned all but four were to be located on the North Carolina coast. The station at Oregon Inlet was one of these. Actually, there were two lifesaving stations built in the area. One was Bodie Island Station on the north side of Oregon Inlet and the Oregon Inlet station was located on the south side of the inlet.

Violent, storm-tossed seas played havoc with the lifesaving stations as much as delays or poor construction practices. Other lifesaving stations were built and faced the same conditions. There is a government report, issued in late 1888, which states that four stations, including Caffey's Inlet Station and Oregon Inlet Station in North Carolina, were under reconstruction. (The other two were Dam Neck Mills and False Cape lifesaving stations in Virginia.) Less than a decade later, disaster struck again at the Oregon Inlet Station. Just before the turn of the century, the station had been reconstructed and Keeper M.W. Etheridge was assigned there.

Again in 1933-34, modernization took place and a new 4-story lookout tower was added. The tower had a catwalk displaying the coat-of-arms of the U.S. Coast Guard, which the lifesaving service had become by then.

In 1972, a new extension was added then, recently, the old station was abandoned when the southward migration of the Oregon Inlet threatened everything in its path. However, a stone groin built by the state of North Carolina to protect the Bonner Bridge from the drifting inlet also saved the lifesaving station. Such is the fickleness of the sea. A brand new station is now operating behind the Oregon Inlet Fishing Center.

OREGON INLET MULTI-MISSION COAST GUARD STATION

Oregon Inlet   987-2311 or 473-5085

The new Multi-Mission Oregon Inlet Station, completed in August of '91, is home base to Coast Guard operation in this area now. The 10,000-square-foot building feature traditional cedar shake siding and houses a communications room, maintenance shop, administrative center and berthing areas. The Coast Guard bases all their boats up to 40' cutters here, and there are two piers to handle the vessels.

LAURA A. BARNES
Coquina Beach

As you enter the southern end of Coquina Beach, you'll notice the remains of a shipwreck on the dunes. The *Laura A. Barnes* was one of the last coastal schooners built in America. Built at Camden, Maine in 1918, she was under sail from New York to South Carolina in 1921 when the 120-foot ship ran into a nor'easter that drove her onto the beach, just north of where she now lies. The entire crew survived. It was in 1973 that the National Park Service moved her remains to Coquina Beach for safekeeping. During the storms of 1991, she resisted the surge of the ocean, but appears to have taken on an additional load of sand. The *Laura A. Barnes* serves as a startling reminder of the closeness of the ocean.

OREGON INLET FISHING CENTER

Bodie Island   441-6301
FAX: (919)441-7385

Oregon Inlet is one of the centers of sport fishing activity on the Banks — especially of deep-sea Gulf Stream fishing. From this National Park Service-leased marina, dozens of charter boats operate, catching thousands of dolphin, wahoo, marlin, sailfish, tuna, and other sport fish every year.

Since they are concessionaires of the Park Service, the thirty- some charter boats that operate from here charge the same prices. You can reserve a full day offshore, including

We Make Your Fishing Dreams Come True

OREGON INLET FISHING CENTER

919-441-6301

OREGON INLET, N.C.

Blue Marlin, White Marlin, Sailfish, Tuna, Dolphin Fish (Mahi Mahi), Wahoo, King Mackerel, Spanish Mackerel, Big Blue Fish, Taylor Blues

- ◆ Offshore Gulf Stream & Canyon Trips
- ◆ Inshore, Inlet and Sound Headboat Fishing
- ◆ Fish Cleaning Service
- ◆ Complete Line of Tackle for the Surf and Sea
- ◆ Automotive & Marine Fuels

- ◆ Small Boat Launch Ramps
- ◆ Mastercard & VISA accepted for Charters & Merchandise
- ◆ Restaurant with Breakfast Buffet from 5:00am
- ◆ Box Lunches Available upon request

◆ Located in Cape Hatteras National Seashore on the beautiful Outer Banks of North Carolina

Oregon Inlet Fishing Center

North End of Oregon Inlet Bridge on NC 12 • P.O. Box 533, Manteo, NC 27954

(800) 272-5199 • (919)441-6301

bait and tackle; full-day trips in the Inlet and the sound; and half-days in the Inlet and sound (see The Outer Banks Fishing Guide section for what you can expect to catch). You can make reservations at the Booking Desk (the number above) or with the captains themselves...and we recommend you make them well in advance during the summer, for Oregon Inlet is one of the busiest places on the Banks come June.

Don't feel quite up to an 1100-lb. blue marlin? A less demanding sport is head boat fishing, aboard *Miss Oregon Inlet,* a 65-ft. diesel boat out of Oregon Inlet Fishing Center. She carries up to 46 fisherpersons on half-day inlet and sound bottom fishing cruises, catching spot, croakers, gray trout, bluefish, mullet, sea bass, etc. All bait and tackle is included in the price. Schedule: Early spring and late fall, one trip daily, departing at 8:00 a.m. and returning at 12:30. During the season (Memorial to Labor Days) there will be two trips daily, 7:00 a.m. to 11:30 a.m. and 12:00 to 4:30 p.m. at a cost of $20.00 per person. A non-fishing Twilight Cruise Tues, Thurs, Fri, and Sat, at 5:30 p.m., at a cost of $6.00. If you've not fished the salt sea before, a head boat is a rewarding and much less expensive way to start.

Aside from charter and head boats, the Center also supplies a fish-cleaning service, restrooms, and five boat ramps into the sound. The marina restaurant is open from 5 to 9 a.m. for breakfast, and also offers a box lunch

service. The tackle shop carries a complete line of surf and deep-sea fishing equipment, as well as basic snacks, drinks, and camping consumables.

Everything at Oregon Inlet is organized around the angler; the fish-cleaning service will take your fish right off the boat to a truck, and there are mounting services to do your lifetime trophy up proud. Don't miss the outdoor display of mounted deep sea game fish, including a World's Record 1,142-lb. Atlantic Blue Marlin caught off the Inlet in 1974.

Finally at the south end of the piers, a scenic overlook displays the bronze prop of SS *Dionysus*, a Liberty ship sunk offshore as part of the state's artificial reef program.

The Oregon Inlet Fishing Center is nine miles south of Whalebone Junction, west of Highway 12 on the turnoff to the right just before the bridge. This is also a relatively inexpensive place to gas up.

OREGON INLET
Between Hatteras and Bodie Island

Driving south from Nags Head, through Bodie Island, you'll soon find yourself lifted skyward on an immense concrete bridge. From a hundred feet in the air you can see for miles — to seaward, over Atlantic swells; to soundward, over the vast calm sheet of the Pamlico.

This is Oregon Inlet, the Bank's major avenue for trade and fishing for over a hundred years, and still the major outlet for today's heavy commercial and recreational traffic.

Oregon Inlet opened during a hurricane in 1846, and was named, as was the custom in those days, after the first ship to make it through. Its opening brought shoaling to Ocracoke Inlet, and economic ruin to the once-flourishing town of Portsmouth.

Today it too is shoaling, and its consequences may be just as dramatic.

The Herbert C. Bonner Bridge, built in 1964 to provide access to the southern Banks, may have hastened this process by impeding the free tidal flow through the inlet. (Note, as you pass over it, the mile or more of new land under the bridge supports to the north.) But it is more likely that simple beach migration, the eons-long march of the Banks to the south and west, is the real cause. Whatever the causative factors, the inlet has required nearly round-the-clock dredging for the last few years, and now the silting is overtaking the Corps of Engineers ability to dredge; in fact Oregon has been completely closed for days at a time in recent years. In 1989 erosion at the southern side of the inlet accelerated dramatically, destroying much of the former Coast Guard station and requiring emergency repairs to the bridge.

The controversy over clearing or stabilizing the inlet, or whether it can be stabilized at all, has been going on for some years now. A long rip rap jetty might keep the channel open, at great expense, but it too would have to be dredged, and there is no guarantee that it would work for more than a few years.

The Oregon Inlet jetty project was approved by Congress in 1972, but permits for the rubble structures have never been granted. Since then, over 200 acres of North Point have been lost to the sea. Jetty opponents have argued that jetties would accelerate erosion south of the inlet; they proposed letting nature take its course.

Meanwhile, the boatbuilders and trawling companies of Wanchese, have been hit with skyrocketing insurance rates. Many of them have moved south, to the Morehead City area. It is too soon to write Wanchese off as a fishing port, but there is no doubt that the situation there is serious.

The four-day March, 1989 nor'easter and the damage it caused to the bridge supports spurred renewed effort to get a project started, and a $20 million revetment and groin was completed in 1991.

The potential closing of the inlet also leads to the question: where will the next inlet be? Historically, the closing of an inlet has seemed to portend the opening of a new one somewhere else. All that water in the sounds has to go somewhere. We don't know, and no one can really predict, where an inlet will open. But it can happen pretty quickly, when those winter waves come crashing over the barrier dunes.

Another sobering reminder of the precarious nature of human "mastery" over nature occurred in October of 1990, when hurricane-force winds blew a dredging barge into the Bonner bridge, stranding 5,000 tourists and residents. It took four months to repair the 370 feet of damaged bridge. This incident led to new studies of alternatives to the bridge, including tunnels and a return to ferries, but as of this writing the Bonner seems to be the only feasible means of access, given the nature of the bottom in this area and the heavy traffic demands in the summer months.

U-85
Off Bodie Island

As you stand on Coquina Beach, the sun bright overhead, look straight out to sea. If you could take your car and drive outward for fifteen minutes, you would be over one of the strangest yet least known attractions of the Outer Banks. Only fifteen miles straight out, over a hundred feet beneath the glittering sea, the first Nazi submarine destroyed by Americans in World War II lies motionless in the murky waters of Hatteras.

Almost undamaged, except for rust and the encroaching coral, it lies on its side, bow planes jammed forever on hard dive. Its hatches gape open to the dark interior, where silt swirls slowly between dead gauges and twisted air lines. Its cannon points upward, toward the dim glow that is all that remains of the sun at eighteen fathoms. Its conning tower, flaked with corrosion, lies frozen in a roll to starboard that will last until its steel dissolves in the all-devouring sea.

Here, at 35 55' N, 75 18' W, it is still World War II. Here, and all along the coasts of the Outer Banks, dozens of wrecks lie half buried in the sea bed. It is from here, from the silent hull of a 750-ton Type VIIb U-boat, that we can begin a journey back to the months when the Outer Banks was a battle line, when the German Navy patrolled and ruled our shores.

To Spring, 1942.

Adolf Hitler declared war on the United States on December 11, 1941, four days after Pearl Harbor.

In Europe the war was two and half years old. Deep in the Soviet Union, Nazi and Red forces churned the mud in a precarious balance outside the city of Moscow. In the West the British, in from the first, had come close to strangling in the noose the U-boats had drawn around their island. German submarines had sunk over a thousand ships, over a million tons of material and food; but as 1941 ended, quickly built escorts, ASDIC, and a convoy system were loosening the knot. In his operations room at Kerneval, Occupied France, Admiral Karl Doenitz wondered: where, now, would he find easy sinkings for his thinly stretched submarines?

On the eleventh of December, he knew.

Operation *Paukenschlag* (Drumroll) began on the eighteenth of January, when the Esso tanker *Allen Jackson* exploded a few miles off Diamond Shoals Light.

Within weeks, the entire East Coast was under siege, and it was almost defenseless. Most of our ships had been sent to the Pacific, or to the North Atlantic run, where two of them, *Reuben James* and *Kearny,* were torpedoed even before war officially began. Aircraft? Almost none. To defend the east coast of the United States in spring 1942, there was a total of ten World War I wooden subchasers, three converted yachts, four blimps and six Army bombers.

When the U-boats arrived, it was slaughter. They struck on the surface, at night, often not even bothering to dive. The stretch of coast off the Banks was their favorite hunting ground. Armed with both deck guns and torpedoes, they would lie in wait at night, silhouette the passing coasters against the glow of lights ashore, and attack unseen by the men aboard. Ship after ship went down in January, February, and March: *Rochester; Ocean Venture; Norvana; Trepca*; *City of Atlanta; Oakmar; Tiger*; and scores of others. Oil and debris washed up on

the beaches, and residents watched the night sky flame as tankers burned just over the horizon.

The "Arsenal of Democracy" was under blockade; and from the protected pens at Lorient and St. Nazaire more raiders, fresh from refit and training, sailed to attack a coast where in three months of war not one German submarine had yet been the target of an effective attack.

One of them was the U-85.

U-85 was a Type VIIb, specially modified for the Atlantic war. A little over seven hundred tons displacement, two hundred and twenty feet long, she was a little larger than a harbor tugboat, or the *Calypso*. She had been built in northern Germany in early 1941, the second year of the war. Her commander was Kapitan-leutnant Eberhard Greger, Class of 1935.

Greger and U-85 spent her first summer working up in the deep fiords of occupied Norway. On August 28 she left Trondheim for her first wartime cruise. On September 10, the wolf tasted blood for the first time. Greger latched on to a Britain-bound convoy. U-85's first five torpedoes ran wild. Throughout that day and the next he ran eastward, staying with the convoy on the surface, just over the horizon. The diesels hammered as U-85 slashed through heavy seas. The convoy's escorts, American destroyers, tried repeatedly to drive her off with gunfire and depth charges. Each time, she submerged and evaded, then came back up and hammered ahead again, rolling viciously, but gradually drawing ahead to position for a new attack.

The next afternoon she reached it, and Greger sent U-85 dashing in on the surface. Boldness was rewarded: at 1642 he made a solid hit on a six-thousand-ton steamer, and, in the next half hour, struck at two more of the heavily laden merchantmen. Then the destroyers closed in for a close depth-charge counterattack. At a little past midnight, September 11, Greger brought her up slowly, and then crept toward home for repairs.

U-85's second war cruise was less dramatic. Battered by heavy weather off Newfoundland, shrouded by fog, she never made contact with her prey, and engine trouble eventually sent her back to St. Nazaire.

For her third war cruise, a new man came aboard. He sounds like a sailor Goebbels would have exulted over; young (26), tall (six feet), blond and well built; but this German must have been different from the Nazi stereotype. For one thing, he kept a diary; and it is thanks to Erich Degenkolb that we know as much as we do about his ship's last cruises.

According to Degenkolb — we can imagine him wedged into his cramped leather bunk, diary on his stomach, listening to the waves crash against the outside of the hull — U-85's third war cruise was her most rewarding, both to Doenitz and to her crew.

Operation Drumroll had begun, and U-85 was one of the first reliefs to be thrown into the battle. On the way across she sank a 10,000-ton steamer and took a near miss from a plane off Newfoundland. "Off New York," as Degenkolb wrote in his diary in February, she sank another steamer after a seven-hour surface chase. She chased convoys throughout the month, probably in the Western Atlantic approaches to New York, till her fuel tanks sloshed near-empty, and then set course for home, crossing the Bay of Biscay submerged and arriving in St. Nazaire again on the twenty-third of February.

A month's refit and leave, and it was time to sail again. At 1800 on March 21, 1942, with a brass band on the pier, with a blooded crew, a confident captain, and a well-tried ship, U-85 set out once more for "Amerika."

The drumbeat of the U-boats had grown louder through February and March. No censorship could conceal the fact that ships were being lost. The explosions on the horizon, the oil on the beaches, the boatloads of huddled men being debarked at every seaport told the story too plainly for anyone to deny.

The Navy and Coast Guard, along with civilian authorities, were struggling with this new meaning of the once-remote war. Vice- Admiral Adolphus Andrews, directing the East Coast antisubmarine effort, found that aside from the lack of ships and planes, he had inadequate operational plans and even less clout. He couldn't even get the use of the destroyers and planes already in Norfolk assigned to the Atlantic Fleet.

One of the results of this unfortunate combination of censorship and unpreparedness was, typically, rumor. U-boats were refuelling, people whispered, in isolated inlets along the coast, and they had been seen in Chesapeake Bay itself. Citizens reported odd lights along the shore at night...obvious signals to someone out at sea.

One of the most persistent rumors concerned landings along the Outer Banks. German sailors, it was said, had actually slipped ashore, were mingling with the locals and even seeing movies, as ticket stubs supposedly recovered from sunken U-boats proved. Alas, a good story, but probably untrue. The Germans did land specially trained spies later in the war in Quebec and at Narragansett, Long Island; but according to the Coast Guard, Navy, and FBI, that was it in World War II. No U-boat captain must have had much desire to hazard his craft close inshore, or risk losing a skilled *obermachinist* so that he could report on the latest Errol Flynn epic. All that *can* be proven is that where news does not exist, gossip and invention will swiftly take its place.

And in March and April 1942,

reality was bad enough. Eight ships had gone down off North Carolina alone in January; two in February, as the first team of submarines headed back across the Atlantic; and then fourteen in March, as they were relieved. Once the "pipeline" of the eighteen-day cruise out of France was full, there would be eight boats on station all the time.

The Outer Banks were suddenly the focus of world war.

Cape Hatteras was dreaded by every merchant seaman on the East Coast. The "Graveyard of the Atlantic" was earning its name anew in the age of steam, and a new cognomen besides — "Torpedo Junction." On March 18, for example, the U-boats met an unescorted "convoy" of five tankers, and torpedoed three, plus a Greek freighter that stopped to rescue crewmen from a black sea filled with blazing oil.

This was how it was: in March 1942, three ships were going down every day, one every eight hours. But even worse was the closely guarded secret that the "exchange rate" — the magic number in antisubmarine warfare — was zero. Not one U-boat had yet been sunk off America.

It could not continue this way. Either the U-boats would be driven under, or all coastwise shipping would have to stop. America, the Allies, could not afford losses on this scale much longer.

It might not be too much to say, as Churchill later did, that it was the war itself that hung in the balance.

USS *Roper*, DD-147, was a fairly old ship in 1942, as warships go. At a little under 1200 tons, she wasn't all that much larger than U-85.

She had been born in Philadelphia, at William Cramp & Sons, in 1918. *Roper* evacuated refugees from Constantinople in 1919 and then spent a few years in the Pacific before being laid up in San Diego in 1922. Recommissioned in 1930, she spent the slow years of the Depression on reserve maneuvers and patrol duty in Hawaii, Panama, and the Caribbean. In 1937 she was transferred to the Atlantic Fleet.

When war began in Europe, the pace picked up. The old four-piper rolled from Key West to Yucatan, and then north in 1940 to the coast of New England. In early 1942, she ran a convoy to Londonderry, passing the U-85, then on her third war patrol; they may have crossed each other's paths for the first time then, somewhere in the empty spaces of the North Atlantic.

In March, the rigorous glamor of convoy duty ended; she was ordered back to the coast for more patrol. Patrol — steaming endlessly through fog, storm, calm, night. Her crew carried out innumerable late-night actions: radar contact, a breakneck steam to intercept, the depthcharging that was always futile. Whales? Escaping U-boats? Her crew never knew. Perhaps some day, in a war that everyone knew now would last a long time, they would have their chance to fight. But for now, it was more of the same, everlasting patrol.

Kapitan-leutnant Eberhard Greger sailed U-85 on her fourth sortie on March 21, beginning the long transit submerged. In a few days, though, he was able to bring her up, and dieseled west through seas "as smooth as a table," as Degenkolb, relaxing belowdecks, jotted in his journal. They took some damage from a storm on March 30, but repaired it and continued the cruise.

At this stage of the war, Germany's submariners were confident men — especially off America.

By early April she was on station, ranging the coast from New York to Washington. On the tenth, Greger took his boat below to sink a steamer with a spread of two torpedoes. But targets were scarce.

He decided to head south, toward the easy pickings off the Outer Banks.

On the night of April 13, as U-85 hammered through calm seas at 16 knots, Degenkolb made his last entry: "American beacons and searchlights visible at night."

Lieutenant-commander Hamilton W. Howe, captain of the *Roper*, was tired. His crew was tired.

The ship itself, twenty-four years old, was tired. But they were alert. The old four-piper did not yet have the new gear Allied scientists were racing to produce. But she had enough. A primitive radar and sonar. Depth charges. And plenty of guns — nice to have, if only a U-boat would play the game for once and surface, instead of skulking away underwater while the horizon crackled with flame from dying ships.

At midnight on the 13th, *Roper* was running southward off Bodie Island. The lighthouse, still operating, was plainly visible to starboard. The night was clear and starry, and at 18 knots the knife bow of the old DD pared phosphorescence from the smooth water. Most of her crew was asleep below.

On the bridge as Officer of the Deck, Ensign Ken Tebo was awake and alert. At six minutes past midnight, the radar suddenly showed a small pip a mile and a half ahead. The ship had been plagued with these small contacts all night. Another small boat, Tebo thought; probably a Coast Guard craft, on the same mission as the destroyer — patrol. But he felt immediately that there was something strange, something different, about this one.

He ordered an eight degree change of course, to close slowly, and to present the smallest possible target — just in case. In seconds — the captain always slept in full uniform at sea — Howe was on the bridge.

Tebo explained the situation quickly. He still had that strange feeling. *Roper* was overhauling, but too slowly. At 2100 yards range the two men saw the wake of whatever it was up ahead. White, narrow, it glowed in the starlit seas. Howe ordered an increase in speed to 20 knots. It still might be a Coast Guard boat. But Howe made his decision. At the clang of General Quarters, seamen rolled from their bunks and ran to man their guns, the torpedo batteries, the depth charge racks astern, and the K-guns, weapons that threw the drums of explosive far out over the ship's side, widening the carpet of concussion that could crush the hull of any submerged enemy.

Aboard the speeding U-boat, most of the crew was asleep. Degenkolb had thrust his diary into his pocket and turned in. On the darkened conning tower, only a few feet above the sea, an officer and two lookouts stared ahead. They anticipated no trouble. A U-boat had a tiny silhouette, almost impossible to see from a ship's deck at night.

After a time, one of the lookouts turned 'round and tapped the officer on the shoulder. There seemed to be something astern. A target? The submarine's rudders swung, and she began to creep to the right.

Below, her men slept on.

Aboard the *Roper*, now only a few hundred yards astern, Lt. William Vanous, the executive officer, stood panting atop the flying bridge. Commander S.C. Norton was beside him. Below them the two men could hear the pounding of feet on metal as the bridge team manned up. The starlight showed more men on the forecastle, running toward the three-inch guns. Beside them, the searchlight operator was swinging his lamp around, and they heard the clang as BMC Jack Wright charged the No. 1. 50-caliber machine gun.

Vanous strained his eyes ahead. At the end of a white ribbon of wake a black object was slowly drawing into view. Could it really be a submarine? It was awfully small. He noted happily that the men on the bridge below were keeping the ship a trifle to the side of the wake; most U-boats carried torpedo tubes in their pointed sterns as well as in the bow.

Yes, thought the German officer ahead of him, there is something back there. And it was very close. He reached for the alarm toggle, and below him, under the waterline, Degenkolb suddenly awoke.

The two ships were turning. The submarine was slipping to starboard. In a few moments its stern tubes would point directly at its pursuer. Howe ordered the helm hard right, and called into the voice tube, "Illuminate!" Above him, with a sputtering hiss, the searchlight ignited. Vanous coached it out into the darkness, and caught his breath. The beam had swept across the conning tower of a submarine with five men running along the half-submerged deck toward her gun.

Someone shouted to Wright, and with an ear-battering roar the chief began firing. The machine gun tracers swept forward, hung over the black boat, then descended, dancing along the thin-skinned ballast tanks, then reaching up the deck toward the frantically working gun crew. Forward, a second machine gun opened up. The glare of the searchlight wavered, but held. In its weird light men began to fall.

At almost the same moment, crewmen along the destroyer's side pointed and shouted at a sparkling trail in the water: a torpedo!

Inside the hull of the U-85, other men heard the clang of machine gun bullets on metal. They ran for their stations, forty men in a hull no wider than a railway car. The ship shuddered as a torpedo went out astern. Erich Degenkolb swung a locker open and pulled out his yellow escape lung. Could Kapitan Greger submerge and escape? He hoped so, desperately. But from the sounds that came through the steel around him into what the U-boat men called the "iron coffin," it seemed that U-85's luck had finally run out.

On the *Roper's* bridge, Howe had no time for thoughts and no time for feelings. It was a U-boat, and it was *surfaced*. The ship was still shuddering around in her turn. "Open fire!" he shouted.

On the exposed forecastle, in the mounts on deck aft, the three-inchers began to fire. Their target was only 300 yards away now, almost pointblank range. But it seemed smaller. It was submerging. In a moment it would be gone.

The *Roper's* men thought they saw their last round hit just at the base of the conning tower, where it joined the U-boat's pressure hull.

With the sound of a solid hit in their ears, the *Unterseeboot*-men knew their battle was lost. The ballast tanks were already filling, and the machine gun and shell fire must have holed them too. U-85 was on her last dive. There was only one way for her men to live now, and that was to get out of her narrow hull before it slipped forever under the icy sea.

Erich Degenkolb joined the crowd struggling under the ladder. Seconds later he found himself topside. The deck was familiar, but fire was still drumming on the sinking boat. A blinding shaft of light picked out every splinter, every weldment of the hull. He stumbled from the blaze of fire and sound over the side. The water was freezing cold. Gasping, he came up, stuck the mouthpiece of the lung between his teeth, and tried to inflate it. His heavy clothes were dragging him down.

Suddenly the firing stopped. The light went out. He drifted, seemingly alone, for a few minutes, feeling the cold of the sea gnaw into his bare hands, into his face.

Then, all at once, a string of deeper detonations brought his attention up, into the night.

The last thing he saw was the American ship. Immense, black, blazing, it loomed over the sinking shell that had been his home, over the struggling men in the water who had been his friends. And from its sides, in brief bursts of reddish light, he saw the depth charges leap into the night and splash on either side, amid the waving, screaming men.

When the black ship slid under, Howe doused the light. He was suddenly conscious of how conspicuous he was. Lights, shooting...the killers, it was common talk among destroyermen, often operated in pairs.

A few minutes later, the sonar operator reported contact. The destroyer, darkened and silent now, wheeled and headed toward it.

"Prepare for depth charge attack," said Howe.

"Men in the water ahead, captain."

"All stop."

Her screws slowing, *Roper* coasted forward. From the bridge he could see them now. One of them was even shouting up at him... *"Heil Hitler."* But he was thinking. He held course. He knew they were there. But the contact was solid. It might be another sub.

"Fire depth charges," said Howe.

Astern, from the fantail, the launchers exploded. The charges arched out, hit, and sank, and seconds later 3300 pounds of TNT went off in the midst of forty swimming men. *Roper* made no more attacks that night, but lingered in the area of the sinking, echo-ranging and with every lookout alert. At about six the sun rose, lighting the scene of recent battle. Oil slicked the low waves; life jackets and motionless bodies drifted in slow eddies as the destroyer nosed back and forth, sniffing for the vanished enemy. At 0850, obtaining a ping on a bottomed object, she made a straight run and dropped four more depth charges. A great gush of air and a little oil came up when the foam subsided astern. At 0957, Howe dropped two more depth charges over the largest bubbles. At last he concluded that it was over. The U-boat was still down there, but she was dead. Coached from aircraft from shore, still watching for that constantly-feared other sub, the *Roper* lowered a boat, and began dragging bodies aboard.

One of them, his face and body swollen and discolored from the depth charging that had killed him, was Erich Degenkolb.

The first U-boat! The news was electrifying. At long last one of them had been destroyed, by an American ship, and in the very area where for four months now the wolves had hunted with impunity. The story was immediately released to the press. But this was not the end. *Roper* continued south on her patrol, but the remains of U-85 were far too valuable to be left undisturbed.

Over the next weeks, divers explored the shattered boat. A hundred feet down, clumsily-suited Navy men clambered over torn metal, pried open hatches, traced fuel and air lines and manifolds, and tried unsuccessfully to raise the hull with compressed air. They were unable to get inside and it was impossible to raise the wreck without a major salvage effort — not an easy option off Cape Hatteras in April.

In the end, they left her there, possibly with some of her crew still inside the now-silent hull, under the canted conning tower, with its painted device of a wild boar, rampant, with a rose in its mouth. The divers, the ships were needed elsewhere. There were valuable cargoes to be recovered. And from now on, there would be casualties from the other side as well — U-352, sunk off Morehead City in May; U-576; U-701; dozens of others. And, last of all, U-548, sent down a hundred miles east of the Chesapeake Bay entrances three years later, in April, 1945.

The U-boat threat was anything but over, but on the Atlantic horizon more light was dawning than that of burning tankers. In the months after April, 1942, American strength increased steadily in our home waters. The threat was overcome, this time; the enemy was steadily shoved back, first to the center of the ocean, then to his home waters. Finally, with the loss of France in 1944, he could deploy only the few war-worn boats that could slip out from Germany itself past close blockade into the North Sea.

Lieutenant-commander Hamilton Howe retired as a rear admiral in 1956. He lives in Winston-Salem, North Carolina. Captain Kenneth Tebo retired in 1961, and lives in Falls Church, Virginia. Captain William Tanous died the same year in a naval hospital in Annapolis. Erich Degenkolb, N 11662/41, lies in Hampton, Virginia, in plot #694 of the National Cemetery.

Kapitan-leutnant Eberhard Greger's body was not recovered.

U-85 lies rusting on a white, sandy bottom, fifteen miles east of where Bodie Island light still glitters out over the troubled seas of Hatteras.

Photo: Michael Helminski

A female Green-Winged Teal makes her landing.

Photo: DCTB

Pea Island National Wildlife Refuge is home to thousands of snow geese during the winter months.

Inside
Hatteras Island

*F*or many, the southern leg of the Outer Banks, Hatteras Island National Seashore and its small villages, is the grandest of all places. The natural beauty, desolation, migratory waterfowl, expansive beaches and dunes provide a startling contrast to other areas farther north on the barrier islands.

This portion of the Outer Banks begins just south of Bodie Island. The seashore highway lays a ribbon-like path into silence where water and sky meet and acres of marshland reveal a captive yet protective habitat for waterfowl and wildlife. Stalks of seasoned vegetation, wild flowers, beach grasses and wind-blown trees provide shelter from scorching summer sunlight and often-blustery winter winds for the variety of small creatures that live here.

When you can hear only the roll and hiss of the sea and the chatter of wildlife, you begin to appreciate what preservation means. Farther along the highway, you get a glimpse of how life for humans is more seasonal, or at best, rugged in most every way.

The Pea Island National Wildlife Refuge separates the towns of the north and central barrier islands from those small towns and villages farther south and Cape Hatteras, the "elbow" which turns west almost in retreat from the wild Atlantic.

Pea Island, administered by the US Fish and Wildlife Service, provides miles of unspoiled beauty and, if you're inclined, several overlooks and nature trails to get a closer look.

The National Park Service campground at Oregon Inlet is available for those who prefer life under the stars or out there on the beaches where fishing and swimming provide the only activity for campers during the day. The Oregon Inlet Fishing Center on the west side tempts you to a day at sea on charter boat trips from the marina.

An occasional village appears as the drive continues. Each year brings more businesses and services to these remote areas, where people come to get away from more heavily populated towns. Shops, restaurants, cafes, motels and cottages line the short lanes from the highway to the ocean and sound. There are fewer reminders of how rugged life was as more development occurs. Nevertheless, recent storms which created ocean overwash along portions of the highway slowed down future growth, thus preserving the best fishing, the best beaches and natural habitats for those who tread lightly or are willing to work at their recreation rather than have it built-in with luxurious complexes.

Descendants of early settlers remain fiercely protective of their culture, their lifestyles and manner of speech. The Hatteras people are different from those who settled in villages like Nags Head or Kitty Hawk. They have accepted the summer visitors and know their economy relies on those who come to fish in fall or spring, but they know all to well the ever-present threat of storms, of another side of life.

Rodanthe, Waves, Salvo

These three villages are scattered along the road toward Buxton and Hatteras. Each community has its own business area, comprised mainly of bait and tackle shops, grocery stores, small restaurants and gift shops. Visitors will find something different and should take time to explore these small town rather than passing them quickly by for the more storied Hatteras Village or Ocracoke. Many come here for fishing or windsurfing. There are fishing piers and scattered throughout these villages, and the wide, open sound for water sports. And, if you like looking back over time, you'll appreciate the Chicamacomico Lifesaving Station. You'll note the houses here are built high off the ground and small churches are tucked in between, in more secure

places. The beaches are beautiful in this area, and for many are reason enough to leave the more populated areas of the Outer Banks behind.

Avon

Avon is primarily a summer community, but it has experienced more growth than other village. A large shopping center is anchored by Food Lion and includes other small shops for convenience foods, clothes and water-sports gear. Real estate development has occurred largely because of the width of the land here. Larger and newer homes are being built and a few housing developments are selling lots with amenities like pools and clubhouses.

Buxton, Frisco and Hatteras Village

The southern "arm" of Hatteras Island — from the "elbow" at the Cape west and south, toward Ocracoke — is more populated and more habitable than the open land to the north. More of it is privately owned, in contrast to the overwhelming proportion of National Seashore land on the rest of the Island. Higher and more stable geologically, the southern arm is primarily a maritime forest habitat, often thick with live oak and red bay, dogwood and loblolly pine. It offers more shelter from wind and storm, and has borne a small and hardy population from the earliest Indian times. His-

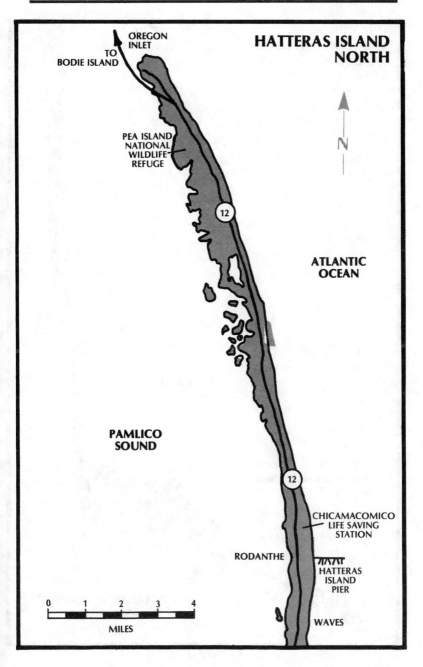

HATTERAS ISLAND
NORTH

N

TO BODIE ISLAND
OREGON INLET

PEA ISLAND NATIONAL WILDLIFE REFUGE

ATLANTIC OCEAN

PAMLICO SOUND

CHICAMACOMICO LIFE SAVING STATION

RODANTHE

HATTERAS ISLAND PIER

WAVES

0 1 2 3 4
MILES

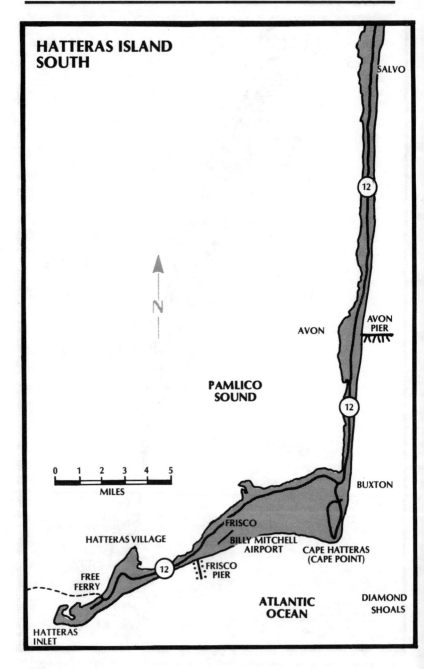

HATTERAS ISLAND SOUTH

SALVO

12

AVON PIER

AVON

PAMLICO SOUND

0 1 2 3 4 5
MILES

BUXTON

FRISCO

BILLY MITCHELL AIRPORT

HATTERAS VILLAGE

12

CAPE HATTERAS (CAPE POINT)

FREE FERRY

FRISCO PIER

ATLANTIC OCEAN

DIAMOND SHOALS

HATTERAS INLET

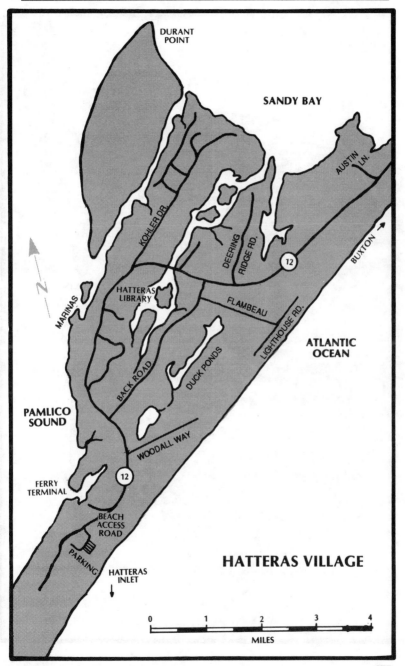

HATTERAS VILLAGE

DURANT POINT

SANDY BAY

AUSTIN LN.

KOHLER DR.

DEERING RIDGE RD.

12

BUXTON

MARINAS

HATTERAS LIBRARY

FLAMBEAU

LIGHTHOUSE RD.

ATLANTIC OCEAN

BACK ROAD

DUCK PONDS

PAMLICO SOUND

WOODALL WAY

FERRY TERMINAL

12

BEACH ACCESS ROAD

PARKING

HATTERAS INLET

N

0 1 2 3 4

MILES

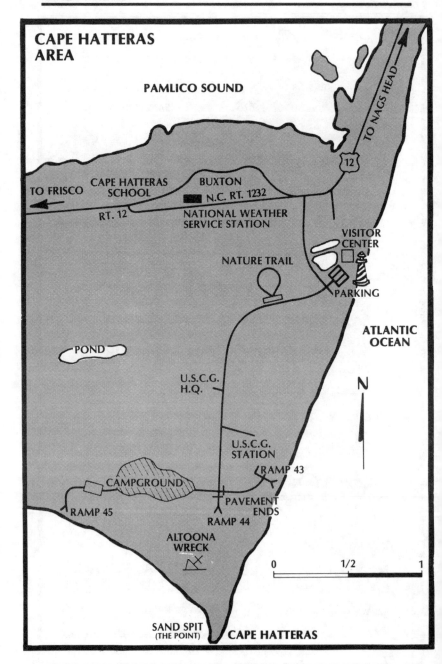

CAPE HATTERAS AREA

PAMLICO SOUND

TO NAGS HEAD

US 12

TO FRISCO

CAPE HATTERAS SCHOOL

BUXTON

N.C. RT. 1232

RT. 12

NATIONAL WEATHER SERVICE STATION

VISITOR CENTER

NATURE TRAIL

PARKING

ATLANTIC OCEAN

POND

N

U.S.C.G. H.Q.

U.S.C.G. STATION

RAMP 43

CAMPGROUND

RAMP 45

PAVEMENT ENDS

RAMP 44

ALTOONA WRECK

0   1/2   1

SAND SPIT (THE POINT)

CAPE HATTERAS

torically, they made their livings from the sea; supplanting this, many local people are still at least part-time commercial fishermen.

Buxton, just inland from Cape Hatteras itself, is a rapidly growing town at the moment. The fishing flavor is strong here during the spring and fall seasons. Buxton is a Mecca for sports fishermen and Atlantic Coast surfers. (See the "Outer Banks Fishing Guide" section and "Surfing Along the Outer Banks.") And the "Canadian Hole," located just outside of Buxton, draws windsurfers in droves from all over the country.

A winding, pleasant road runs west from Buxton towards Frisco. On the way you will pass several campgrounds and many roads leading back into new real estate developments, both on the ocean side and on the higher land overlooking the sound. Previously forested, this road is taking on the look familiar along the rest of the developed areas of the Banks.

Hatteras Village, at the western tip of the island, is second only to Wanchese as the Banks' center of commercial fishing activity. We have seen upwards of sixty drop-netters (gill netters) run out from there during the late fall and early spring. At the docks, during this time of year, you can see tons of trout coming in under the watchful eyes of wharf cats, gill nets being dried, all the activity of a busy fishing port. Trout, croakers, big blues and king mackerel are packed in shaved ice, trucked out in five thousand pound lots and end up in Fulton's Fish Market in New York City within twenty-four hours. Most of these boats come from other towns, and spend the season out of Hatteras, fishing in the neighborhood of the Light. Feel like a different kind of vacation? Sometimes, it you're young and hearty, you can talk yourself into a billet aboard one of these hard working craft.

Sport fishing, for marlin and other big sport fish, is another Hatteras specialty. The Hatteras Marlin Tournament is perhaps the biggest single week in Hatteras Village. Fifty or sixty private boats, carrying some of the East Coast's leading politicians and businesspeople, attend this invitation-only championship, one of the most prestigious in the country. The Tournament is hosted by the Hatteras Marlin Club, in the Village, and takes place the second week in June.

Hatteras Island

ATTRACTIONS

PEA ISLAND NATIONAL WILDLIFE REFUGE

N. end of Hatteras Island   987-2394

Once you cross Oregon Inlet, leaving the Herbert C. Bonner bridge behind, you're in Pea Island. On your left is the surf, on your right the marsh. And everywhere, everywhere — are birds.

Pea Island was founded on April 12, 1938, when Congress provided that Pea Island be preserved as a haven for wildlife, specifically as a wintering area for the Greater Snow Goose. Roosevelt's CCC was put to work stabilizing the dunes with bulldozers and sea oats, sand fences were built, dikes were constructed to form ponds, and freshwater marshes and fields planted to provide food for wildfowl. The refuge was seldom visited by tourists until the Oregon Inlet bridge was constructed in 1964. Now Pea Island is one of the most popular spots on the island with naturalists, bird-watchers, and just plain lovers of wildlife.

Both bird watchers and wreck lovers will want to stop at a Rest Area some 4 1/2 miles south of the Bonner Bridge. To the surf side, if you walk over the dunes to your left, you will be able to glimpse the remains of the Federal transport *Oriental*. The black mass is thought to be her steel boiler, all that remains of the ship that went ashore in May, 1862. To the sound side, a short walk leads to an overlook of North Pond and New Field, where special crops are sown each year for the use of the waterfowl that winter over in the milder climate of the Banks. (See "North Pond Trail.")

While there, you may see some of the Refuge's guests. The 5,915 acres of the Refuge are an important wintering ground for whistling swans, snow geese, Canada geese, and 25 species of ducks. Many other interesting species, such as the Savannah (Ipswich) sparrow, migrant warblers, shorebirds, gulls, terns, herons and egrets can be found here during the winter months and the spring and fall migrations. During the summer months several species of herons, egrets, and terns, along with American avocets, willets, black-necked stilts, and a few species of ducks nest at the Refuge. Oceanic species can be expected during most any season but are most common from late summer through fall into late winter. Following storms, many species unusual for this area have been observed. In all, over 265 species of bird have been identified repeatedly at the Refuge or over the ocean nearby, with another 50 species of accidental or rare occurrence. Mosquito/bug spray is recommended here March through October. Also see the section on ticks in the back of the book.

Regarding Loggerhead turtles: volunteers patrol Memorial Day to Labor Day looking for nests, relocating them if necessary and guarding hatchlings on their way to the sea. To volunteer, contact the Outdoor Recreation Planner at Alligator River 473-1131.

The Refuge is controlled from the Headquarters, some 7 1/2 miles south of Oregon Inlet.

NORTH POND TRAIL
Pea Island

This self-guided nature trail, a favorite with birdwatchers, starts five miles south of Oregon Inlet Bridge, and two and a half miles north of the Pea Island Refuge Headquarters. Parking area and a restroom building mark the beginning of the trail. The trail is roughly a mile long and will take you half an hour to walk briskly to the sound and back.

The trail itself is on top of a dike between two man-made ponds. (It's easily negotiable. Though interrupted by a stepped viewing platform about 200 yards from the road, we judge a wheelchair could negotiate around it, if you have a strong helper.) The ponds and dike were constructed in the 1930s and early '40s by the CCC. Wax myrtles and live oaks stabilize the dike and provide shelter for songbirds. Warblers, yellowthroats, cardinals, and seaside sparrows rest here during their spring and fall migrations.

On either side you'll look out over an intensively managed ecosystem of pond and field. The fields are planted with such bird goodies as rye grass and fescue. In winter you can see hundreds of snow geese and canada geese resting and eating, and cattle

egrets in summer. Pheasants, muskrats, and nutria live here year round.

The diketop view in ideal for birdwatchers. Bring a tripod-mounted scope of at least 15x, and probably 25x will be better; the ranges are long over the pond. However, this trail isn't just for birdwatchers. It's just a nice break from the near-continual pressure to buy and consume that is now part of the Outer Banks experience. A warning: bring insect spray; check for ticks after leaving.

PEA ISLAND REFUGE
HEADQUARTERS
Highway 12   987-2394

On the sound side, 7 1/4 miles south of Oregon Inlet, is the headquarters building. There's a small parking area and a Visitor Contact Station manned by Refuge volunteers (Monday through Friday, April to November, 8 to 4). Though visitor services there are limited, you may want to stop in. Information is available on bird watching and use of nature trails. Special public programs are offered during the summer months.

We talked with personnel there about what you can and cannot do on the Refuge. You're not allowed to hunt. No camping, no open fires. Dogs must be on a leash. Four wheel drive vehicles are not permitted on the beach. Firearms are not permitted within the confines of the Refuge. Headquarters personnel say that even on the road, driving straight through, shotguns and such must be stowed out of sight.

Photo: DCTB

The Chicamacomico Lifesaving Station in Rodanthe is being restored to its former slendor.

Those hunting farther south on Hatteras are advised not to flaunt their equipment on the Refuge. Beach fishing is permitted. Fishing, crabbing, boating, etc. are allowed on the ocean or soundside, but not in Refuge Ponds.

We might suggest one side trip from the headquarters building. It's only a few hundred feet, but it takes you back a century in time. East of the building, across the highway, and over the dunes, in the surf or on the beach, you'll find a few remnants of concrete foundation. Those bare chunks are the remnants of Pea Island Station, the only US Lifesaving Service station to be manned entirely by blacks. How it came to be so, and what they accomplished, is a little-known story that deserves to be told here.

Established with the rest of the stations in 1879, Pea Island was at first, like the others, manned by entirely white crews. Like the others, it had black personnel, but they were confined to such menial tasks as caring for the tough little ponies that dragged the surfboats through the sand.

But this first crew let the Service down. They were dismissed in 1880, one year later, for negligence in the Henderson disaster. The authorities then collected the black personnel from the other stations, placed them under the charge of Richard Etheridge, who was part black and part indian, and set them to their duty.

They fulfilled it magnificently. In dozens of disasters, the Pea Island Crew risked life and health in rescuing the crews and passengers of the vessels that came driving ashore in northeaster and hurricane. Etheridge became known as one of the best-prepared, most professional, and most daring men in a Service where professionalism and selflessness were a matter of course.

Probably the most famous of their rescues was the *E. S. Newman*. That story is recounted in the dry summary prose of The Annual Report of the Operations of the United States Life Saving Service for the Fiscal Year Ending June 30, 1897:

"Oct. 11 (1896), American Schooner *E. S. Newman*, Pea Island, North Carolina.

"Sails blown away and master obliged to beach her during hurricane two miles below station at 7 P.M. Signal of distress was immediately answered by patrolman's Coston light. Keeper and crew quickly started for the wreck with beach apparatus. The sea was sweeping over the beach and threatened to prevent reaching scene of disaster, but they finally gained a point near the wreck. It was found to be impossible to bury the sand anchor, as the tide was rushing over the entire beach, and they decided to tie a large-sized shot line around two surfmen and send them down through the surf as near the vessel as practicable. These men waded in and succeeded in throwing a line on board with the heaving stick. It was made fast to the master's three-year-old child, who was then hauled off by the surfmen and carried ashore. In like manner his wife and the seven men composing the crew were rescued under great difficulties and with imminent peril to the life-savers. They were all taken to station and furnished with food and clothing, and during next three days the surfmen aided in saving baggage and stores from wreck. On the 14th three of the crew left for Norfolk, and on the 21st the remainder departed for their homes, the vessel having proved a total loss."

BIRDING ON PEA ISLAND

Virginia Valpey, a Refuge volunteer, contributed this advice to the Guide on birding:

Pea Island is a particularly fine birding area, especially during the spring and fall. There is a variety and an abundance of bird life passing through the "Atlantic flyway" over Pea Island, one of several air routes that migrating birds use regularly during their semi-annual trips north and south.

The beginning birder should arm him or herself with a good field guidebook and a pair of decent seven to ten-power binoculars. Among several excellent field guides on the market, the most familiar is Roger Tory Peterson's *A Field Guide to the Birds* (Houghton Mifflin Co., Boston.) This guide and others are available at any good bookstore. (In this area, the National Park Service sells them at the Wright Brothers National Monument in Kill Devil Hills.) The easiest time to spot birds and identify them is spring. In most species, the males are more vividly colored during the mating season than at other times. Also, many "passerines" (perching birds) can be located — and often identified — by the particular song sung by the males to mark their territory during nesting season. Pick a warm (not hot), dry day, in the early morning, when birds are feeding. (Woodland birds tend to take a siesta during the hot midday). Dress in drab clothing that doesn't rustle, so that you can hear — and won't startle — the birds. Move slowly and quietly, listening and watching for movement in the trees or bushes. When you see movement, without taking your eyes off the spot, raise your binoculars to locate its source.

Some helpful hints for beginners trying to identify birds: first of all, determine the size of the bird. Compare your bird to one you are already familiar with — a robin or a bluejay, say, or even a pigeon. Note the dominant color, and then note the color of its beak, its throat, breast, wings, back and tail.

Pay close attention to the beak — shape as well as color. Seed-eating birds such as cardinals or sparrows, for instance, have relatively large, conical-shaped beaks suitable for cracking seeds, while flycatchers, which actually catch insects on the wing and thus have no need for this less aerodynamic appendage, have a slender bill.

Notice whether the bird has wing bars and, if so, how many. Does the tail have a band across it? A different color under the tail? What shape is it? Finally, pay attention to what the bird is doing. A flycatcher won't scratch around on the ground like a towhee, and you won't find a woodpecker sucking pollen like a hummingbird or probing in shallow water like a dunlin.

Don't be discouraged if you can't identify everything right away. Start a life list to increase your pleasure in birding enormously. You will probably find that even if you are a rank beginner, you can probably list a dozen birds that you already know. Note the date, the species, and the location where you first identified the bird. You'll enjoy looking back over this list many times, and you will find you are eager to add to it. Good birding!

WILDFLOWERS ON HATTERAS ISLAND

Driving south from Oregon Inlet, roadsides afford a mixed wildflower population during most of the year.

The nearness of the warm Gulf Stream tends to keep temperatures from reaching extremes, and late autumn blooming plants such as the Goldenrods (Solidago) sometimes bloom well into January during a mild winter. Early Cresses (Barbarea) and Chickweeds (Stellaria) begin their flowering in February so there are almost always a few wildflowers on hand.

If you have chosen a late spring visit, roadside plants may include Blue-eyed Grasses (Sisyrinchium). This small, lily-like plant is in the Iris family and is recognizable by its startling bright blue color. It grows in large colonies that create carpets of blue along the highway in wet ditches and other damp places. Avon is a good place to see both this and a tiny, white orchid called Spring Ladies' Tresses (Spiranthes vernalis). Its leaves resemble grass and the flowers are borne pole-style on a single twisted stem.

Groups of Yuccas are also fairly common; they are huge and tough with long, dangerously pointed, fibrous evergreen leaves encircling the thick, trunk-like stem. Fat, cream, bell-shaped flowers bloom in a large cluster that rises above the plant's leafy parts. The hairy, prickly Yellow Thistle (Cirsium horridulum) blooms at this time too. Its hefty size makes it easy to spot, and its large, fluffy looking flower head is palest yellow. A couple of high climbing vines are worth looking for. Yellow Jessamine (Gelsemium sempervirens) has a thick trumpet-shaped flower of brilliant yellow. It blooms in April. Coral Honeysuckle (Lonicera sempervirens) has smaller, narrower flowers of a similar design and is a firey orange-red. Both are evergreen.

Summer brings quantities of Gaillardias (Gaillardia pulchella) or Jo Bells, as they are known locally. Introduced here years ago, these low growing, hardy plants are so salt resistant that you may see them near your

Photo: DCTB

Cape Point on Hatteras Island draws anglers almost every day of the year.

oceanfront cottage. Looking a lot like daisies, they are abundant along sandy roadsides and come in mixtures of red and yellow or occasionally solid yellow. Both the Yellow and the White Sweet Clovers (Melilotus officinalis and Melilotus alba) are common — especially near the villages of Avon and Buxton. Seaside Croton (Croton punctatus), in the same family as the Poinsettias of Christmas fame, bloom near the ferry docks in Hatteras Village as well as quite near beaches. Mowers generally make their appearance by the end of June and from then on, staying ahead of them can be difficult. Everything looks like a short lawn after their passage.

From late summer through early winter, Goldenrods (Solidago), Asters and Bonesets (eupatorium) may all be seen along most roadsides. Bushes with berries become colorful at this time. Yaupon Holly (Ilex vomitoria), from which the old timers made tea, shows red berries beginning in November. Bayberry bushes (Myrica pensylvanica) on the north end of the island bear clusters of silver covered, waxy berries. The foliage smells spicy. Flowering Water Bushes, (Baccharis halimifolia) resemble clouds of white feathers and the Beauty Berry Bushes (Callicarpa americana) produce dense clusters of intensely fuschia berries along their branches. Patches of Hairawn Muhly (Muhlenbergia capillaris), a highly salt resistant grass, looks like purple or pink fog banks on the ocean side of the highway near Salvo.

Cape Hatteras, like much of the rest of the Outer Banks, is home to many other salt-resistant wildflowers and weeds. On the widest part of the island near the Cape itself is Buxton Woods, a genuine maritime forest of some three thousand acres. Its dense canopy provides good protection from most salt spray, and a variety of plants flourishes within its borders. The forest covers a series of ridges which are old or relic dunes and low, wet, freshwater valleys called swales. There are also a number of shallow ponds called sedges and a few somewhat deeper ponds.

The best viewing of forest plants is along the Buxton Woods Nature Trail, built and maintained by the National Park Service. The trail is near the Cape Hatteras Lighthouse, but make a right turn instead of the left you would make to enter the lighthouse grounds. There is a clearly visible sign on the right marking the trail's beginning and a parking area with plenty of spaces. Small, well placed plaques provide good information about plants and other items of interest to be found on the looped path. Since its length is only three quarters of a mile, it's a pleasant walk.

A late summer little mint named Blue Curls (Trichostema dichotomum) may be found at the trail's entrance as may Golden Aster or Silkgrass (Chrysopsis graminifolia) with its dusty looking, grass-like leaves. There is Common Bladderwort (Utricularia

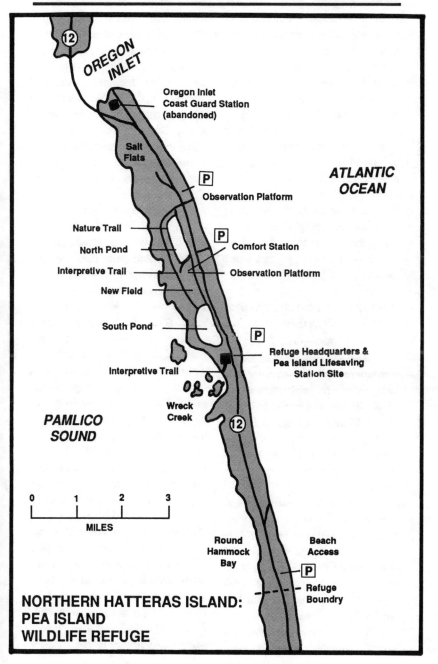

NORTHERN HATTERAS ISLAND: PEA ISLAND WILDLIFE REFUGE

vulgaris) in the waters of Jennette's Sedge which runs along the edge of the trail's right fork. The thready underwater leaves of this meat eating, freshwater plant have small bladders which entrap tiny water-dwelling animals which the plant then uses as food.

You will doubtless encounter many more plants than have been mentioned. If curiosity is running high, book stores offer some good basic wildflower guides.

Barbara Midgette's excellent *Cape Hatteras Wildflowers* contains color photographs and complete descriptions of flowering plants found locally.

CHICAMACOMICO LIFE SAVING STATION
Rodanthe

The buildings, once boarded up, with broken windows, and rusted padlocks, are now restored to their stately beauty, thanks to a group of dedicated citizens who refused to see the historic buildings fade into oblivion. For Chicamacomico was one of the most famous Life Saving Stations on the Outer Banks.

In 1874, Chicamacomico Station was part of a daring new concept in lifesaving. In that year the U.S. Life Saving Service was building a chain of seven stations along the Banks, at the points of greatest danger for oceangoing vessels. (See "The U.S. Life Saving Service" for their story.)

And Chicamacomico Station at Rodanthe, Number 179, was foremost.

Under three Keepers — Captain Little Bannister Midgett III (Ban), Captain John Allan Midgett, Jr., and Captain Levene Westcott Midgett — it guarded the sea along the northern coast of Hatteras for 70 years. Number 179 and the Midgetts are still legends in the Coast Guard. Since 1876 seven Midgetts have been awarded the Gold Life Saving Award and three the silver; six worked or lived at Chicamacomico.

The Station was active through World War II, until the Coast Guard closed it down in 1954. It languished unused for some years thereafter, and many readers will remember its sagging, rotting roof, its boarded-up windows.

Today, like so many previously unappreciated reminders of the Banks' seagoing heritage, it is being restored. The Chicamacomico Historical Association, Inc., a nonprofit organization established for its preservation, has cleaned up the interior, restored the exterior, and has opened displays in the main station building. They've received some federal and state grants, but only on a matching fund basis. So you can help doubly with a check to the Association at P.O. Box 140, Rodanthe, NC 27968. Be a Lifesaver!

During the summer, Chicamacomico is the site of commemorative life saving drills held by the National Park Service. Schedule: every Thursday at 2 p.m., from mid-June to the end of August. Bring your cameras. Admission is free.

THE WRECKS OF NORTHERN HATTERAS

One of our nicest memories is the sunny, still day of late winter when we scrambled over the dunes of northern Hatteras with two friends after a storm. On the bare beach we found a freshly-uncovered wreck. We were able to date it to the mid-nineteenth century by the method of fastening sheathing to ribs. We searched the sand in the still silence and found mementoes: a tiny bottle that might have held opium or perfume, a spar with emaciated iron fittings still attached, a broken teacup, a quaintly shaped whiskey bottle with the rotting remains of a cork. No treasure chest — not that time.

Yes, literally hundreds of ships have gone ashore on these beaches in four hundred years. And most of them are still here. Wood, buried in sand along the Banks, holds up surprisingly well. The continual wrestle of beach and sea yields them up from time to time. Michael McOwen, who flies a light plane out of Manteo, made out the ribs of an old sailing ship one day in about thirty feet of water off the beach; he snorkled out as soon as it got warm enough and had himself some fine tautog and porkfish. And there are more modern ships as well: in February, 1948, while being towed to Charleston, LST 471 parted her lines and drifted ashore at Rodanthe. Personnel from the then-still-active Chicamacomico Coast Guard Station rescued three of the crew with beach apparatus. Previous visitors will remember that the pilothouse was visible for some years, up till 1985, when a storm tore it apart and sent part of the hull crashing into the fishing pier. The remainder of it is (at least at time of writing) buried by sea and sand. But it will be back one day, like all the other ghost ships of the Outer Banks.

Find an established entry onto the beach then begin your search. Wrecks, like gold, are where you find them.

U.S. COAST GUARD FACILITY, BUXTON

Buxton   **995-5881**

Formerly the Naval facility at Buxton, the grounds and buildings were turned over to the Coast Guard in June of 1982. It's not normally open for visitors, but retired military, dependents, and military personnel may use the few remaining facilities. There's a limited commissary, a small exchange, small mess hall, recreational facilities (tennis, basketball, and beach swimming), and a small dispensary.

Insiders like:
Taking windsurfing or sailing lessons.

Insiders' Tip

The hours, at all military bases and stations, are subject to change, but don't plan on anything being open after 5 p.m.

THE ALTOONA WRECK
Cape Point

Driving to the end of the Cape Point road, you will see Ramp 44 straight ahead. Don't try to drive over, or even to, this ramp in a regular car. A four-wheel-drive vehicle will make it over the soft sand between the road and the ramp; a two-wheel-drive one will not. We speak from experience, as we tried to and lost...and towing fees in Buxton are, to say the least, uncompetitive. Instead leave your car on the solid ground near the road and walk over the ramp. Walk on over the ramp and continue on the foot trail that veers off at a forty-five degree angle at the base of the dune. At the edge of the seawater pond — about a 10 minute walk from where you parked your car — you'll find all that remains of the sea-savaged *Altoona*.

The *Altoona* was a cargo ship, a two-masted, 100'-long schooner out of Boston. She was built in Maine in 1869. In 1878 she left Haiti with a load of dyewood bound for New York. She was driven ashore on the Cape by a storm on October 22, 1878. Her crew of seven was rescued, the deck cargo lost, but the cargo in the hold was salvaged. A few years sufficed for the shifting sands to bury her. She re-emerged in 1962 in a storm, and was quickly broken apart by the sea. The bow and part of the hull, still with greenish copper teredo sheathing on it, lie pointing south. A few odd pieces of her ribs and beams lie scattered between her and the Atlantic.

DIAMOND SHOALS LIGHT
Off Cape Point

From the lighthouse, or even from the eastern shore of Cape Point, you may be able to see on a clear night a sudden white flash of light from far out at sea. Time it; if the flashes come every two and half seconds, you are looking at the Diamond Shoals Light, some twelve miles out at sea southeast of the lighthouse, marking the end of the Shoals that have claimed so many ships.

Through the years, there have been numerous attempts to build lighthouses out there, on the shifting sandbars; all have failed. Three lightships have been on station there since 1824. The first was sunk in a gale, in 1827; the second lasted from 1897 until 1918, when it was sunk by the German submarine U-140; and the third remained in service until 1967, when it was replaced with the present steel structure.

How long will it last?

THE MONITOR
Off Cape Hatteras

Every American knows the story of the *Monitor* from schoolbooks. How, during the Civil War, the Confederates built the first ironclad warship from the hulk of the Union

Photo: DCTB

Fishing on the Outer Banks can be as exciting or as peaceful as you like.

frigate *Merrimack*, renaming it the *Virginia*. How, in the early hours of March 8, 1862, the tent-shaped ship steamed out of Norfolk to challenge a Union blockading force of six wooden ships — and how, by the end of the day, she had sunk two of them and damaged another. Broken the blockade, and written a new chapter in naval history.

The *Monitor* was an even more daring innovation. Built by John Ericsson, a Swedish-American engineer, the "Cheesebox on a raft" was a low-slung ironclad whose main battery was carried in a futuristic revolving turret. Arriving in Norfolk in the nick of time — the next day — the *Monitor* battled her adversary throughout the ninth, and finally, the fight at a draw, the Virginia retreated back under the guns of Norfolk.

Neither of these first ironclads lived very long. The *Virginia* was destroyed by retreating Confederates; the *Monitor*, ordered south, foundered off Cape Hatteras during a New Years' Eve storm in 1862. And there she lay for a hundred and twenty years, unseen by human eye, even her location unknown.

She was rediscovered in 1975, resting quietly upside down, just as she sank, in two hundred feet of water 25 kilometers south-southeast of Cape Hatteras.

Since then, the *Monitor* has been designated the first National Underwater Marine Sanctuary, and has been the object of repeated dives and evaluations by government agencies and underwater archaeologists. A few small artifacts — bottles, silverware, that sort of thing — have been recovered, and in 1983 the ship's distinctive four-bladed anchor was located and raised by a NOAA/East Carolina University expedition.

So far, aside from a collection of artifacts at the Visitor Center, there's nothing to actually see of the *Monitor*. But someday there might be. NOAA is considering the feasibility of raising the turret, which is relatively complete, and possibly other parts of the ship's hull for preservation and eventual display.

CAPE POINT, CAPE HATTERAS NATIONAL SEASHORE
Buxton

As you continue that leisurely drive south along the length of Hatteras Island, you will come to the sharp elbow in the road that leads into Buxton. To your left, beyond a small cluster of motels, you can hear the surf booming; to the right are the trees of a

---

Insiders' Tip

Insiders like:
Walking the beach after a storm hunting for unique shells.

small forest — here, on the Banks! As highway 12 curves to the right, signs point to the left, toward the Lighthouse and the Coast Guard Facility. Resist your first impulse to turn, continue about 200 yards past the turn for the Facility, and turn left there to the Cape Point area of the Cape Hatteras National Seashore.

The approach is beautiful in and of itself. It is a winding drive between brush-covered dunes, with the white and black striped lighthouse looming on your left. There's a nice photograph on your left, about halfway there, where the lighthouse is reflected in the water of a pond.

The Cape Point area contains a number of attractions and recreational opportunities: the Visitor Center, the Lighthouse, a shipwreck, a nature trail, and a campground. Surfing and surffishing are permitted year round, and a protected (lifeguarded) beach is available for swimming near the campground (by Ramp 43) in the summer.

HATTERAS ISLAND VISITOR CENTER

Near Hatteras Lighthouse   995-4474

Built in 1854, this two-story frame house was for many years the home of the assistant keepers of the light (the smaller home just to the east was the quarters of the Keeper himself). Today it's a National Park Service Visitor Center, the central one for the island of Hatteras, and extensive historical renovation was completed in 1986 to restore the building to its original condition. The Principal Keepers Quarters has been restored too.

Along with a helpful ranger at the information desk, it now houses a well kept museum devoted to Man and the Sea at Hatteras. The exhibits and displays center around shipping, the Cape at War, Making the Cape Safe, the lighthouses themselves, and the heroism of the Life Saving Service, later to become the Coast Guard. There's information on the rescue of passengers from stranded ships in storms, and a small but well-stocked bookstore carries related books. Last but not least there are clean restrooms.

In addition to its own exhibits, the Center is where you can obtain a schedule for the activities the Park Service conducts on Hatteras Island during the summer, and at a reduced pace in spring and fall. They change each season, of course, but here are samples of what's offered:

SEASHORE ARTS — What you can create with things you pick up by the sea.

HATTERAS HISTORY — What it was like at Cape Point a hundred or more years ago.

FISH WITH A RANGER — Surf-fishing...how to do it. Bring your own bait.

CATCH A SAFE WAVE — How to boogie board.

BIRD WALK — Bird-watching with an expert around the Point.

Most of these programs, as well as others, are conducted weekly. Pick up a schedule at the Center, or call the number above, for exact times and dates.

The Center is open from 9 to 5 daily September through May, and 9 a.m. to 6 p.m. in June, July and August (hours subject to change).

Closed Christmas Day.

CAPE HATTERAS LIGHTHOUSE
Cape Point

For over a hundred and seventy-five years, mariners rounding stormy, dangerous Cape Hatteras have searched for the glimmer of Cape Hatteras Light to assure them of safety. Sometimes they found it in time; sometimes, as the bare-boned wrecks on the point testify, they didn't.

Hatteras has been a place of danger for ships since the Europeans first began crossing the Atlantic. Its typically turbulent weather is caused by the confluence of two currents: the warm, northward-flowing Gulf Stream, and the southbound, inshore Virginia Coastal Drift. An eight mile finger of shoal water, the Diamond Shoals, and the low, featureless nature of the Banks coastline conspired to lure hundreds of ships to rest in the 'Graveyard of the Atlantic'.

The first lighthouse at Hatteras Point was raised in 1802. When we first began to write about the Outer Banks, not that many years ago, its sandstone ruin was still visible about three hundred yards south of the present lighthouse. A blizzard in March, 1980 finally took it, so utterly that you can now search the beach for a single piece of crumbling sandstone. It was ninety feet high, with a feeble whale oil light, and proved inadequate. Also, as the century progressed, it became evident that erosion would soon overtake it. It was heightened and improved, but as the years went by, erosion weakened it, and by the late 1860s it had to be replaced. The War between the States had left its mark, too; the Confederates, retreating in 1861, took the light's lens with them.

The new lighthouse was built in 1869-70, of 1 1/4 million Philadelphia-baked bricks, at a cost of $150,000. It's built on a crisscross of heavy pine beams, with its foundation eight feet deep in the sand. A granite base sits atop that, and then the brick begins, carrying the lighthouse up to the light at 180 feet, and from there to the very tip of the lightning rod two hundred and eight feet above the foundation. The first light installed was whale oil, with a special Fresnel lens to flash its beam far out to sea. The eye-catching spiral paint job was added to make the lighthouse visible far out at sea during the day, so that ships could determine their position by taking bearings from a known point. When it was completed, the old lighthouse was dynamited. The new lighthouse was in service from 1870 to 1935, when it was abandoned, due to beach erosion. The erosion halted, and in 1950 the lighthouse was reactivated by the Coast Guard. Today its 800,000 candlepower electric light rotates every 7 1/2 seconds, reaching out more than 20 miles to sea.

From the Visitor Center you can walk across to the lighthouse. As you can see, the beach migration that destroyed the first beacon here is seriously threatening the second. The sea seems to hate lighthouses; it either strands them inland, as it did at Bodie Island, or it eats them, as it does lighthouses on the French side of the English Channel — and as it ate the great Pharos of Alexandria, the first lighthouse ever. Perhaps it is in revenge for the ships these lights have cheated them of...This threat became critical in December of 1980, when the high tide came within fifty feet of the structure's base! There were intense efforts to save it, including sandbagging and the dumping of rubble; but most geologists now agree that the beach built back naturally — at least for a time.

As a result, though, the National Park Service, the state of North Carolina, and the "Save Our Lighthouse" campaigners (whom we helped) have mounted an intensive effort to thwart the Atlantic Ocean. Various experts proposed options ranging from moving the lighthouse bodily inland to letting it "go gently into that good night." The current plan is to attempt to move it, and studies are now underway to determine the best way to do this. The National Academy of Sciences has recommended that the lighthouse be moved 600 feet inland, and the National Park Service has decided that a move would be the most

appropriate and long term solution for saving the structure. Nothing is permanent on the Banks. But one thing is certain: this striking structure is one of the quintessential symbols of Hatteras. Of the men who for centuries have battled its seas, and the women who battled to build their lives and families waiting at home. We hope it's been saved for generations to come.

BUXTON WOODS NATURE TRAIL
Cape Point

The Nature Trail is 3/4 mile long, leading from the road through the wooded dunes, vine jungles, and fresh-water marshes of Buxton Woods. It's one of the best nature trail on the Banks. It is a must...don't miss it.

Beginning on the right side of the road south from the lighthouse to the Point, the trail winds at first among low sand hills, then into the maritime microforest that has gradually established itself on this broadest part of the island. Its natural beauty is enhanced by small plaques, masterfully written, explaining the changing surroundings in terms of the closed, fragile ecosystems of the Banks; the water table, the role of beach grass and sea oats in stabilizing dunes, the beach microforest and its stages of development, and the harshness of the Banks environment of wind, sand, and salt.

There are cottonmouths on this trail, unmistakably fat-bodied rough-scaled snakes in various dull colors (brownish, yellowish, grayish, varying almost to black), though they are rare. Don't stick your hands or feet where you can't see. If you encounter a snake, allow it time to get away; generally it will retreat. The local people advise extra caution when encountering a cottonmouth during chill weather, in spring or fall. During this period, they say, the snakes are less confident of their ability to get away from you, since they're rather sluggish in cool weather, and they're more likely to attack. In mid-summer they will often scurry off quickly. If they stand their ground, though, we advise retreat!

It might also be a good idea to glance over the section on ticks and chiggers in the Directory before starting out.

We don't recommend this trail for handicapped or very small children, but for everyone else, it's a must.

Picnic tables and charcoal grills are located just south of it for lunch.

BILLY MITCHELL AIR FIELD
Frisco

This is a small no-frills landing strip located about a mile south of Highway 12 just west of Frisco. Named after the controversial Army aviator who conducted some of his bombing tests near here in 1921, the strip is 3,000 feet long, 75 feet wide, oriented NE/SW, and asphalt paved. An exhibit at the pilot's shed provides a history lesson.

FRISCO NATIVE AMERICAN MUSEUM
Frisco   995-4440

From the outside this looks like a gift shop, but inside we were taken aback to find rooms of Joyce and Carl Bornfriend's personal fifty-year collection of Native American artifacts. Hopi drums, pottery, kachinas, weapons, jewelry — it's real. Actually this type of hodgepodge of good pieces and curiosa is what all museums were like in the early 1800s (the *Kunstkamera* in Leningrad, for example). Lectures to school groups, etc. can be arranged through a non-profit educational foundation. Worth a stop on a rainy day. Open daily except Monday. Call for an appointment for groups.

THE "GRAVEYARD OF THE ATLANTIC" MUSEUM
Hatteras Village

We'll jump the gun a little here with advance notice of this planned museum for the Village. Now being developed for a site on National Park Service land near the ferry terminal, the museum's general concept and story line have been approved. We look for it to begin building circa 1993 with a combination of federal, state and contributed monies. You can help. Contributions to the Graveyard of the Atlantic Museum, P.O. Box 191, Hatteras Village, NC 27943.

THE U.S. LIFESAVING SERVICE

In 1874, the U. S. Lifesaving Service was a daring new concept. In that year the Federal Government began building a chain of seven stations along the Banks, at the points of greatest danger for oceangoing vessels. Each station was supervised by a Keeper, and had permanent winter crews of six skilled, strong, and brave surfmen. They quickly proved their worth in an area known to all seamen as the "Graveyard of the Atlantic." Ships had a habit of coming ashore on the Banks in storms; the strong northeast winds and seas that developed during winter storms drove them helpless into shoal waters, where pounding surf soon broke them up. Those who tried to swim ashore or row in life boats usually perished, battered to death in the icy water by waves and debris, or — even if they made it ashore safely — freezing slowly on a deserted coast.

The mission of the Lifesaving Service was to rescue those on grounded ships...and a demanding, often suicidal mission it was, too. The surfmen stood watch all along the coast, in the foulest winter weather. Once a wreck was spotted, they had to return to the station, get boats, rescue gear, and the rest of the crew, and then drag everything in heavy carts through the soft sand to where the stricken vessel lay. There they might go out to her by boat, driven not by engines but by strong arms on the oars; might attempt to swim out; might fire a line with a Lyle gun and pull the ship-

wrecked mariners and passengers to safety one by one by breeches buoy high above the deadly surf. In the wrecks of the *Metropolis* (1878), *A..B. Goodman* (1881), and dozens of others, these hardy men, for the most part native Bankers, distinguished themselves in courage and seamanship.

Some flavor of what they went through is preserved between the faded blue covers of the Annual Reports of the Operations of the U.S. Lifesaving Service. A century old now, their pages fragile as old iron found in the surf, their laborious prose still evokes the terror of gigantic, freezing surf, the incredible heroism of these common men. Here, shortened a bit and paragraphed more closely to modern tastes, but otherwise unchanged, is the story they tell of one day in the Life Saving Service: the disastrous 24th of October, 1889.

"Wreck of the schooner *Henry P. Simmons.*

"October, 1889, was in general a very tempestuous month, but there can be little doubt that the most destructive storm experienced on the Middle Atlantic coast of the United States during the month was that which reached the coasts of Virginia and North Carolina on the afternoon of the 23rd, and raged with great violence and with but slight intermission until the evening of the 27th. The easterly wind blew at times with the violence of a hurricane, and drove the sea into mountainous billows which endangered all craft so unfortunate as to be within its influence. The low beaches of Virginia and North Carolina were literally strewn with wrecks, and the hardy crews of the Sixth District were kept exceedingly busy saving life and property. The storm had come with such suddenness that many coasters were unable to reach a harbor, and this will account for the great number of casualties.... In three instances...there was lamentable loss of life, the particulars of which are here given.

"The vessels involved were the schooners *Henry P. Simmons, Francis E. Waters*, and *Lizzie S. Haynes*; all three being wrecked within a few miles of each other, the first two in the night of the 23rd and the Haynes on the following day. The case of the Simmons was a particularly harrowing one, as, owing to the long duration of the storm and the great distance from the shore at which she sunk, it was not until the morning of the 28th that anything could be done by the crews of the neighboring stations....

"The *Henry P. Simmons* was a fine, staunch three-masted schooner of about six hundred and fifty tons, hailing from Philadelphia, Pennsylvania. She carried a crew of eight men all told, and was commanded by Robert C. Grace, who owned an interest in her. She had sailed from Charleston, South Carolina, on or about October 17th, on her way to Baltimore, Maryland, deeply laden with a cargo of phosphate rock for use in the manufacture of fertilizers. The place where

she sunk is a mile and a half to the northward and eastward of the Wash Woods Station....

"The voyage was without special incident until the afternoon of the 23rd, when the gale set in from the northeast and with it a high and dangerous sea, which caused the vessel to plunge deeply and ship a great deal of water. The sole survivor, Robert Lee Garnett, a colored man, says that the deck was so constantly deluged by the seas that at 8 o'clock, when the fury of the storm made it necessary to take in the already closereefed mainsail, the men were unable to handle it for fear of being washed overboard; and all hands were driven to the rigging for safety. The helm was lashed amidships, and with no one to guide her the schooner was thus practically helpless, and drifted completely at the mercy of the wind and waves. Rain was also falling in torrents, so that it was impossible to see anything around them, and the poor fellows were quite ignorant of their distance from the shore, knowing only that they must be in the vicinity of False Cape, Virginia. The laboring of the vessel had also caused her to spring a leak, and this added to the peril of the situation, for she was liable to sink at any moment.

"In the midst of these dangers the men, by watching their opportunity, would descend to the deck and work the pumps until again driven to the rigging by the seas. At half past 10 o'clock that night the schooner struck with a crash on what is known as

Pebble Shoal...and there she bilged and quickly filled with water. The top of the cabin was almost immediately swept away, and the vessel settled into the sand until the hull was wholly submerged, leaving nothing but the masts above water. What passed during the remaining hours of that dreadful night is a blank, beyond the statement of Garnett that at 3 o'clock in the morning (24th) the steward, a colored man, unable to hold on any longer, fell into the storm-lashed sea and was lost. This greatly shocked the rest.

"When day dawned the scene from the rigging of the wreck was a wild and terrifying one. The wind still raged and the waves broke into surf as far offshore as the eye could see through the pelting rain and spoon drift, while to the leeward lay the low sand hills, which ever and anon came into sight and were then hidden by the towering billows that madly chased one another shoreward, and were there scattered with thunderous roar into a smother of foam and spray upon the desolate beach.

"The first intimation the Wash Woods crew had of there being a craft in the offing was after midnight, when the incoming patrolman from the north beat reported a faint white light, apparently some distance off. This he had answered with his Coston danger-signal. It should be stated here that the storm tide had risen so high that it swept completely across the low parts of the beach, the water in some localities being over the lower floors of the stations. Under these conditions patrol duty was attended with the greatest difficulty and danger, the men having in places to wade hip-deep and being frequently driven to the knolls for safety.

"The next patrol upon returning at daylight brought news that a vessel had sunk during the night well off shore; the masts at that time showing above water about two-thirds of their length, while the end of the jib boom was just visible between the seas. The vessel lay with her head shoreward. And it was scarcely light when the patrolman passed her, he saw nothing of the crew. Another surfman was at once dispatched up the beach to obtain more definite information, and returned with the report that he could see several men in the rigging. It was impossible to handle the beach apparatus just then, by reason of the condition of the beach, but as soon as the water fell off on the ebb tide the men set out with the long-range gear and after a hard tug reached the scene at about 10 o'clock in the forenoon.

"In the meantime...the second mate had been swept from the rigging and another man shared a like fate an hour or so later. Thus but five men were in the rigging when the station crew arrived, and shortly afterwards another fell into the sea.

"An attempt to reach the craft with a line thrown from the wreck-gun failed utterly, the shot dropping into the water about half way. It was thus demonstrated that, owing to the great distance, the beach apparatus was practically useless...the schooner was at least one thousand yards off. Indeed the purpose of the keeper in firing the gun was more to reassure and encourage the poor fellows than from any hope of reaching them with the line. At the same time the surf was so high and dangerous that no human power could have forced a boat through it. The hands of the beachmen were practically tied. They could do nothing but watch and wait for the storm to abate and the sea to run down, and the outlook for this was not promising. Here, on the one hand, was a sunken vessel with her crew in the rigging, looking imploringly to the shore for help, and, on the other, a band of sturdy men skilled in the handling of boats in the surf and equipped with the most approved appliances for the saving of human life from the perils of the sea, but withal powerless to save. Yet this was the exact situation.

"At noon the party on the beach was reinforced by the arrival of the False Cape crew from the north...but their coming did no good, since the storm continued with unabated violence all day, and absolutely nothing could be done. With the approach of darkness driftwood fires were lighted and kept blazing all night to encourage the hapless sailors on the wreck. On the following day, (25th) at 8 o'clock, the tide being low, an effort was made with a picked crew to launch the boat, but although the gale had slackened a little, the surf was still tremendously

high and the attempt failed. The agony of suspense the poor fellows suffered must have been terrible, as cold, wet, and hungry they clung with the desperation of despair to the dripping shrouds, watching for the relief which could not reach them, waiting for their awful doom. Towards noon one more unfortunate fell exhausted from the rigging and disappeared. This left but three remaining alive..."

The beach was vigilantly patrolled that night, an extra force of men being out watching for a lull... Three attempts were made (on the 26th) to reach the *Simmons*, but every time the boat was driven back full of water, the wind having changed to the southeast and set in more fiercely than before, with, if possible, a higher sea. Two of the remaining men were washed out of the rigging during the day in plain view of the people on the beach, and the day closed with but one man left on the wreck. The weather on the morning of the 27th was no more favorable, the wind falling in torrents, with a continuance of the southeasterly gale. Towards evening, however, the storm had nearly spent itself, and there was promise of a shift of wind to the westward. This was what the lifesavers had been hoping for and it gave them encouragement, though there must necessarily be one more night of horror for the sufferer in the rigging before the sea could run down sufficiently for him to be reached. If he could hold on a few hours longer he would be saved.

"By midnight the wind had canted to the southwest and subsided to a moderate breeze. The sea also fell rapidly, so that at 5 o'clock in the morning of the 28th, before daylight, the surfboat was again moved down to the edge of the water in readiness for a launch. Life belts were then strapped on by the picked crew of oarsmen from the Wash Woods and False Cape crews, including Keeper O'Neal of the last-named station, and with the veteran keeper, Malachi Corbel, at the steering oar, a bold and successful dash was made through the heavy line of breakers at the bar. Once through these the boat was not long in reaching the sunken wreck, which, in the darkness, had to be approached with some caution to avoid entanglement in the cordage hanging from the spars. To the great relief of every man in the boat a faint response came to the keeper's hail, and presently there crept out into view the form of the sole survivor of the dreadful tragedy. He had been ensconced within the sheltering folds of the mizzen gaff-topsail, and this protection, with the aid of a splendid physique, had enabled him to withstand the great hardships to which he had been exposed. He had been without food of any kind for over four days, his only sustenance having been rainwater caught in the sail, and his survival was simply marvelous. Once in the boat no time was lost in transferring him to the shore, where restoratives from the medicine chest were quickly administered, and he was then conducted to the station, comfortably clad in warm garments from the supply box of the Women's National Relief Association, and otherwise cared for.

"...Five of the bodies of the drowned seamen were subsequently recovered at various points along the shore, that of the captain being found on November 19th, nearly four weeks after death. All were given decent burial, the body of Captain Grace being afterward claimed and removed by relatives....

"**Wreck of the Schooner Francis E. Waters.**

"Next in order is the wreck of the schooner *Francis E. Waters*, of Baltimore, Maryland, which was capsized and driven on the coast of North Carolina about two and three-quarter miles north of the Nag's Head Station, (Sixth District,) the same night that the *Henry P. Simmons* stranded, October 23, 1889. The entire crew perished. As shown in the preceding account, a furious storm raged all that night. Nothing was known of the disaster on shore until the next morning, when the schooner was discovered bottom up in the breakers. The story is necessarily brief. It appears that the *Francis E. Waters* left Georgetown, South Carolina, with a cargo of lumber and shingles for Philadelphia, Pennsylvania, on or about October 20th, her crew consisting of six men. The much-dreaded Frying Pan and Hatteras Shoals had been safely passed and the prospects seemed good for a quick voyage up the coast when, in the afternoon of the 23rd, the freshening easterly wind and the gathering clouds gave portent of the coming storm. By sundown the wind backed to the northeast and increased to a gale of terrific violence, the night becoming, in nautical phrase 'as dark as a pocket.' This, together with a tempest of driving rain and the blinding spray flying shoreward from the crests of the breakers, produced atmospheric conditions upon the shore absolutely impenetrable to human vision. There was also an extraordinarily high tide, so that after midnight almost the entire expanse of low beach was submerged, compelling the patrolmen for their own safety to take to the higher and remote parts of the shore, thus increasing the distance between themselves and the outer line of the breakers on the bar, where vessels might be expected to fetch up. This distance was fully from one-half to three-quarters of a mile, and in some places probably greater. The patrols of the Nag's Head and Kill Devil Hills Stations, between which the unfortunate craft stranded, met regularly and exchanged checks up to the time stated, but after that the surf and rising tide swept over the beach in greater volume, and cut such deep gullies in the sand that the man who took the north beat from Nag's Head at 3 o'clock in the morning of the 24th was unable to get nearer than within half a mile of the point where he should have met the south patrol from Kill Devil Hills.

"Therefore, after peering as far as was possible through the storm towards the end of his beat, he turned back, reporting upon reaching the station that he had been unable to get through, and that he had seen objects which he took to be lumber or wreckage of some kind floating in the swash of the surf. This it should be remarked is not an unusual occurrence.... The patrol from the Kill Devil Hills Station, who should have met the patrol from Nag's Head, upon arriving at the halfway place and not finding anyone, pushed on south to ascertain the cause of the man's nonappearance. He had not gone more than a quarter of a mile beyond his own beat when, in the early gray of the morning, for it was now about 6 o'clock, he was startled by the discovery through the rain and mist of a vessel half submerged and bottom up in the breakers out on the bar. His first thought was for the crew, but there was not a soul to be seen on the ill-fated craft, so after satisfying himself on that point, and taking a long and searching look in every direction as far as the weather would permit, he retraced his steps to the station and reported his grim discovery to the keeper. The latter (Keeper Partridge,) at once telephoned the news to Keeper Van Buren Etheridge at Nag's Head; the wreck lying within the latter's patrol limits. Etheridge immediately turned out his men, and as the launching of a boat was out of the question, proceeded with such appliances as he thought might be needed to the locality of the wreck, the party arriving there at about half-past 8 o'clock. It was plainly to be seen that there could be no one on the half-buried hull against and over which the surf was dashing incessantly. A man could not have maintained himself there for a moment. The surfmen were therefore deployed along the beach in quest of bodies, and before long the search resulted in finding one corpse, that of a negro, entangled in a part of the rigging attached to a broken mast which had washed up some distance from the wreck, and been left by the now receding tide. This body was decently interred later in the day, there being no marks upon it which might lead to its identification.

"...A second body, that of a white man, was cast ashore nearly two weeks afterwards at a point at least thirty miles to the southward, and recovered by the crew of the Gull Shoal Station. It was identified as the body of R. W. Lecompte, of Cambridge, Maryland, one of the schooner's crew, and relatives came and removed it....

"It is therefore supposed that, losing her canvas or springing a leak and becoming water-logged and unmanageable, she let go her anchors to avoid drifting into the breakers, when, the ground tackle failing to hold her, she fell off into the trough of the sea, rolled over on her beam ends, and in that condition drifted ashore before the gale and sea. This view is supported by the fact that after the subsidence of the gale, and the sea had gone down sufficiently to permit the launching of the surfboat . . . the crew found a quantity of wreckage outside the bar about a quarter of a mile from the shore, and this was attached in some way to the anchors on the bottom. Or it is possible that she capsized under too great a press of sail in the effort to work away from the treacherous sands under her lee...."

"Wreck of the Schooner *Lizzie S. Haynes.*

"The third of the group of three disasters in the Sixth District attended with fatal results during the great October storm was that of the *Lizzie S. Haynes*, a three-masted schooner owned in Bath, Maine, which was wrecked between the Oregon Inlet and Pea Island Stations, on the coast of North Carolina, in the forenoon of October 24, 1889.

"The northeast storm was then raging in all its fury, and there was a frightful sea. Her crew numbered seven men, and of these all but two perished.

She was a vessel of four hundred and thirty-seven tons and was bound from Savannah, Georgia, to Baltimore, Maryland, with a cargo of yellow-pine lumber. From the accounts received it appears that she was first sighted by the crew of the Oregon Inlet Station at about half past 8 o'clock, a mile or two distant to the northward and eastward, and could just be dimly made out through the blinding rain, as she plunged and rolled in the turbulent waters under scant canvas and with her head pointed offshore. It was soon evident that she was making no headway, but, on the contrary, was drifting to the leeward toward the land very fast. As she came nearer it was noticed that her crew had taken refuge in the rigging, a sure sign of her helpless condition. Two men could be seen in the fore shrouds, three in the main, and two in the mizzen. Keeper Paine, anticipating difficulty in rescuing them while such a high surf was tumbling in upon the beach, telephoned the news at once to Keeper Etheridge of the next station south (Pea Island), and asked his aid.

"By 9 o'clock, when the schooner was nearly abreast of Oregon Inlet, Paine and his men had set out with the breeches-buoy apparatus to follow her down the shore, but she drifted so rapidly before the gale, and the beach was so deeply flooded in places that it was found impossible to keep up with her. She struck at twenty minutes to 10 o'clock, three hundred yards from the beach, at a point three and three-quar-

ter miles below Oregon Inlet and a little less than two miles north of the Pea Island Station. She was thus within Etheridge's beat. The latter, as requested by Paine, had promptly left his station with a spare shot-line, (a No. 7,) the medicine chest, and a bag of blankets, and being therefore lightly burdened and having the shorter distance to travel, he and his crew reached the scene first. Thinking that the sea would force the schooner along the bar still further south, and nearer to his station, Etheridge dispatched his men back with the horses for his own beach apparatus, while he proceeded on north to meet the Oregon Inlet crew to lend them a hand, and at the same time consult with his brother keeper. The latter arrived abreast of the vessel at 10 o'clock, before the Pea Island crew could return.

"In the meantime a distressing and terrible accident had befallen the hapless people on the schooner, which practically sealed the fate of all but two of their number. It happened about five minutes before the Oregon Inlet crew arrived. The two crews were at this moment hurrying to the scene from opposite directions with their life-saving appliances, when...the Oregon Inlet crew, then but a short distance away, were horrified by the sight of all three of the schooner's masts breaking off by the board, leaving nothing standing above the deck but a stump of about twenty feet of the mizzenmast. The masts fell toward the stern and carried all but one of the crew to the deck, that one falling overboard and being immediately swept out of sight.

"This appalling and exciting incident infused fresh energy into the little band of jaded life-savers as they pressed forward, and within five minutes of the time of their arrival the Oregon Inlet crew had thrown a line over the wreck. The line landed near the stump of the mizzenmast. This was not more than ten minutes after the spars fell. The lumber of the deck load was already coming ashore on every sea, and this, with the broken spars, the sails, and the rigging, formed quite an entanglement between the vessel and the beach.

"Only two men could be seen on board, the rest either having been severely injured or killed outright by their fall. These two were the captain and the steward. The latter caught the shot-line as it came near him, and both men began hauling it off in order to get the whip or larger line which would follow, but before they could gather much of it in the shot-line fouled the wreckage, and in the effort to free it it was broken or cut in twain. A second line was quickly fired from the shore as successfully as the first, but the current setting along the beach was so swift and strong, and there were so many other difficulties to contend with, the principal of which was the inability of the two men to haul off the line through the wreckage, that notwithstanding the most persistent effort it was nearly 4 o'clock in the afternoon before the poor fellows on the wreck, weakened and exhausted by exposure, could complete the rigging of the apparatus to the stump of the mast a few feet above the deck.

"When this was at last done the two men turned their attention to the mate, the only other member of the crew remaining alive, and made strenuous exertions to place him in the buoy first. But, injured as he was and suffering also from exposure, he had become delirious and resisted the efforts for his removal to the shore. The captain and steward were unable to manage him either by persuasion or force, and as night was nearly upon them, they reluctantly abandoned him to his fate and resolved to look out for themselves. The captain therefore got into the breeches buoy and was drawn safely to the beach, the steward following him just as darkness closed upon the scene....

"The two rescued men, thoroughly used up, were conducted to the Pea Island Station as quickly as possible and properly cared for. As the tremendous surf on the rising tide had gradually pushed the schooner farther onto the shore, the crews of the two stations... returned to the beach and waited for an opportunity to board the wreck, hoping from what the captain had told them to be able yet to save the mate.

"The opportunity...came with the ebb of the tide, which about midnight left her in such a position that the men were enabled to wade out to her.

Quickly climbing on board they found two bodies, one the mate's, the other that of a seaman, the rest having been washed away. Both bodied appeared to be dead, but as the mate's was still supple, though cold, it was landed without delay and carried to a house on the beach, where, with restoratives from the medicine chest, all possible means were resorted to for its resuscitation. These efforts were kept up for two hours, until the stiffening muscles gave indubitable proof that life was beyond recall. Thus five of the little band of seven men composing the schooner's crew, who but a few hours before were in the full flower and promise of manhood, became the victims of the storm.

"...The two bodies recovered from the wreck were provided with decent burial near the life-saving station. The rescued men remained at the station for a week, until able to travel to their homes, and during this period the crews of the two stations were engaged whenever opportunity offered — for as shown in the account of the loss of the *Henry P. Simmons* the bad weather lasted for several days — in recovering such articles as it was possible to save from the wreck.

"The following is the captain's letter:

"Oregon Inlet, North Carolina,
"November 1, 1889.

"Mr. S. I. Kimball,
General Superintendent U.S.Life-Saving Service, Washington, D.C.:

"I desire to express my thanks for the prompt service rendered by the keepers and crews of the Oregon Inlet and Pea Island Life- Saving Stations at the wreck of the schooner *Lizzie S. Haynes* on Pea Island, October 24, 1889, and would state that no default on the part of the life-savers or defect in the working of their gear was responsible for the loss of life that occurred on that day.

"W. A. Sawyer,
"Late Master of Schooner *Lizzie S. Haynes.*"

The U.S. Life Saving Service was merged with the older Revenue Cutter Service in 1915 to form the U. S. Coast Guard. Its aircraft, surface craft, and support personnel, from stations at Coquina Beach (Oregon Inlet), Buxton, and Ocracoke, still guard the Banks and their offshore waters today.

Hatteras Island

RECREATION

WATERFALL PARK
Rodanthe   **987-2213**

As you travel south on Hatteras Island, you'll find the only water slide and go-kart track south of Oregon Inlet. Other motorized cars and boats create a haven for family outings. There is a 36-hole miniature golf course for those who prefer something quieter. The races, in cars which perform just like regular automobiles, can thrill the most experienced driver and competition for the road is tricky. This full range amusement park is open from Memorial Day through Labor Day from 10:00 a.m. until 10:00 p.m. everyday.

HATTERAS ISLAND FISHING PIER
Rodanthe   **987-2323**

This National Park Service pier is located in the small village of Rodanthe, the northern most village of the Hatteras Seashore as you drive south. A motel and restaurant are included on the grounds and are open from April 1 to November 30.

Louise Twine is the pier manager and the pier shop provides bait, tackle, ice, rental equipment and everything you need to fish. There is handicapped access to this pier and the price to fish is $5/day. There's plenty of parking, and those who know fishing recommend this pier for large channel bass.

AVON FISHING PIER
Avon   **995-5480**

This pier has undergone extensive renovations and has a 471-foot extension over the water. Managed by Fran Folb, it's open from Easter until Thanksgiving, 24-hours a day. The pier fee is $5/day for adults and $3/day for those under 12 years of age. Many species of fish are hauled in from this pier according to local anglers. You can expect flounder, trout, sea mullet, king mackerel and red drum.

BUXTON STABLES
Buxton   **995-4659**

How many of us haven't dreamed of racing down an empty beach on the back of a sleek horse? Well, you can do just that at Buxton Stables. Reservations are recommended, but there are a dozen Appaloosa and quarter horses and one Shetland pony for the youngsters. Some lessons are available. The basic charge is $20/hour per person. The stables are open year round, from 8:00 a.m. until 5:00 p.m. in the summer, but closed on Sundays.

WINDSURFING HATTERAS
Avon   **995-4970**

This facility just keeps getting better and is a popular place for lessons, rentals and clinics. A complete line of many brands of surf wear and equipment is for sale here and their site for sailing in Pamilico Sound is one of the best. Catamarans, jet skis, boogie boards, roller blades and windsurfing gear can be rented. They're open from 8:30 a.m. until 8:00 p.m. everyday and close only in January. Many special events are held just over the soundside bridge out back of the shop. Call for the schedule.

FOX WATER SPORTS
Buxton   **995-4102**

Ted James came here from Florida to make boards, which he does here. He also sells a variety of surfwear, has equipment rentals and provides windsurfing lessons. He has been teaching for years, and word has it there's almost no one he can't get sailing. Two or three consecutive hours are recommended for lessons at $35/hour. This is one of the best surf shops on the lower Outer Banks. They close before Christmas and open again around April 1. Hours are 9 to 9 in summer; 9 to 6 otherwise.

CAPE HATTERAS PIER
Frisco   **986-2533**

Also known as Frisco Pier, this is another National Park Service pier on Hatteras Island. It's located about 2 miles west of the village, keeping in mind that as you drive south into Buxton the road then turns west. The pier points south into the ocean and is closest to the Gulf Stream. It's 600 feet long and many species of fish are caught here night and day. There's a snack bar in addition to the bait and tackle shop. Rates on the pier: $5/day, $25/week, $100/season for individuals, $150 for a family and $130/couple. Open from about April 1 to the end of November 6:00 a.m. until 11:00 p.m.

OCEAN EDGE GOLF COURSE
Frisco   **987-2258**

Located in the heart of fishing territory, the new (1991) nine-hole golf course covers 16 acres of dunes just off the main highway. The golf

**THE ONLY COUNTRY ON THE BEACH
CAROLINA 92 FM**

WNHW, the only station on the Outer Banks offering a mix of modern, traditional and cross-over country music, with CNN and local news, sports, weather, fishing information, beach conditions, community promotions, tourist information, and daily updates of what's happening on the Outer Banks and surrounding areas. Located at 92.5 on the FM dial, Carolina Ninety-Two serves Northeastern North Carolina with offices in Nags Head. Stay informed and entertained with the only country at the beach, WNHW, Carolina Ninety-Two!

course offers an alternative to fishing and many have found its three par-4 holes and six par-3 holes a good challenge. There is a clubhouse, pro shop and lounge which includes a snack bar. Locker facilities are available. It's open year round and the public is welcome.

TRENT WOODS GOLF CENTER
Frisco   995-6325

Situated in Trent Woods among tall pines, live oaks and fresh water ponds, the 18-hole championship miniature golf course is a perfect choice for family recreation after a day on the beach, or on an overcast day. You're in the heart of nature in this well-planned facility and it's a great place for a birthday party or other occasion.

CHARTER FISHING

Buxton, Frisco and Hatteras Village are home to several marinas which offer fishing charters, sight-

seeing and scuba diving.

TEACH'S LAIR MARINA
Hatteras Village   986-2460

This is one of the best known and largest marina in the village. It has 92 slips and accommodates boats from 10 feet long up to 53 feet, all with full hook-ups except sewage. There's a boat ramp and a tackle shop with a wide range of fishing gear, ice and bait. There is a dive boat and dry storage for boats and campers. Charter boats operate from here. Rates for all day charters run around $650. There are also camp sites next door, with full hook-ups. All this is conveniently located near the ferry terminal.

HATTERAS HARBOR MARINA AND GIFT STORE
Hatteras Village
986-2166 or 1-800-356-6039 (for charters)

Located on the soundside just over a mile from the ferry terminal, this marina boasts some of the most modern accommodations for the big fishing boats available on the Outer Banks. As many as two dozen boats operate from here and charter reservations are easily made by calling 1-800-356-6039. There are 46 slips with 110/220V power, accommodating boats up to 60 feet long. Exxon products are available.

This is the place for big boats, as the basin is dredged to seven feet at mean low water.

The marina store carries everything you need and the gift shop is filled with interesting items to take back home in case the big one was released...or got away!

ODEN'S DOCK
Hatteras Village   986-2733

Oden's is one of the oldest family-owned boat docks in Hatteras Village. There is a full line of supplies, a repair shop and Texaco marine products available here.

INDEPENDENT FISHING CHARTERS AND OTHER WATER EXCURSIONS

Capt. Spurgeon Stowe, 986-2365, operates *Miss Hatteras* and *Little Clam* out of Oden's Dock. For a real adventure, give yourself a half-day or full day on the high seas. Sightseeing excursions, evening cruises and seafood cruises are also available. If it's fishing you're doing, be ready to go early in the morning!

Capt. Steve Gwin, 995-5091, also offers departures for all day or half-day fishing trips. Excursions to Diamond Shoals and Portsmouth Island are also available, departing from Buxton.

BURRUS FLYING SERVICE
Frisco   986-2679

Bring your adventurous spirit and camera for a flight-seeing tour over Cape Hatteras and Ocracoke Island. Call in the evenings and sign up. You'll take off at Billy Mitchel Airfield in Frisco. There's a ticket office near the post office. Flights over Cape Hatteras Lighthouse, Diamond Shoals, Hatteras Inlet and on to Ocracoke Village and Portsmouth Island provide a thrill you won't forget. Rates are $24/person for a party of two and $19/person for a party of three.

HATTERAS LIBRARY
Hatteras Village   986-2385

The village has a rather large library of 10,000 or more books. It's located across from Burrus' Red & White, in the Civic Building. Hours are from 10 to 6 Monday through Thursday, 1 to 7 on Wednesday and closed Friday, Saturday and Sunday.

HATTERAS INLET FERRY TO
OCRACOKE
Hatteras Village

The ferry trip is free and links Hatteras with Ocracoke Island on an enjoyable 40-minute trip. The ferries accommodate cars, large camping vehicles and some trucks. The frequency of trips makes your wait bearable, but do expect a line during summer months. Reservations are not required.

For a full schedule, see the Ferry chapter of this book.

Hatteras Island

SHOPPING

Every year it seems like there are more shops on Hatteras Island. While the explosive growth of a few years ago has slowed down, there are still a few more new spots each time we give ourselves the pleasure of a trip "down south." Though more shops than ever are adopting the year round schedule of their neighbors to the north, the pace is slower and most shops still close for at least a month or two during the winter.

Though you don't have the vast variety of shops you'd find in Nags Head or Duck, the ones you do find in the Hatteras area are interesting and carry fine quality items. And besides, the calm pace of wandering in and out of shops dotted down the road -- rather than saturating the area -- keeps the dreaded "shopping frenzy" at bay.

RODANTHE
The Sea Chest, 987-2303, has a wide variety of antiques and gifts. Myrna Peters opened her shop about 10 years ago. She's a collector and you'll spend a lot of time inspecting, browsing and talking about everything from antique dolls to decoys. The **Island Convenience Store**, 987-2239,

is a one-stop shopping place. They have groceries, bait and tackle and a small deli. **Bill Sawyer's Place**, 987-2214, has an assortment "general store" items, too. You'll find the woodcrafts especially interesting. **The Waterfowl Shop**, 986-2626, is a sports photography gallery that features the work of Richard Darcey. There are other gifts as well, like decoys, tide clocks and windspeed indicators.

Pamlico Station features **Lee's Collectibles**, 987-2144. You'll find t-shirts, beach supplies, gifts, jewelry, mugs, cards and antique bottles. **Michael Halminski Studio and Gallery**, 987-2401, is another interesting place to shop or visit. Michael has been a well-known Outer Banks photographer, and his beautiful nature shots are featured in the North Carolina aquarium.

AVON

Picnics, 995-4966, is the place to go in this area for pastries and breads baked daily, whole bean coffees, a complete line of deli meats and cheeses and ice cream. If you need a party platter, they'll take care of it for you. **Hatteras Wind**, 995-6055, has a good collection of handcrafted wooden gifts.

The shopping center anchored by **Food Lion** now has other shops as well. **Bubba's Bar-B-Q**, 995-4385, is an all time favorite. It moved here last year from another location down the road. Don't expect to travel past without noticing the smoked ribs aroma, which will make you hungry even if you just finished eating. **Beach Bites**, 995-6683, is a new deli and bakery. This place is home to the Outer Banks Elephant Ear, a large, sugar-dusted light pastry. They have homemade everything, like 8-grain bread, sourdough bread, bagels muffins and soups. **Tory's**, 995-6720, has fine ladies apparel, jewelry, accessories and a good

selection of swimwear. **Baggies Surf Shop**, 995-6722, is next door with more swimwear, windsurfing gear, body boards and accessories.

Avon Shopping Center, 995-5362, is a local's favorite for freshly cut meats, but they also have most everything else you'd expect from a general store. Amoco gas is also sold on the premises.

Ocean Atlantic Rentals, 995-5868, has opened a new store here and has chairs, umbrellas, strollers, cribs - - you name it. Whatever you forgot, they will have. **T-Shirt Whirl**, 995-4111, has opened its new store with one of the largest selections of tee's on the Outer Banks.

Avon Waterside Shops has **Windsurfing Hatteras**, 995-4970, for everything you'd want to get in some serious windsurfing. Lessons and rental equipment are also available. **Home Port Gifts**, 995-4334, is one of the nicest stores on the entire Outer Banks. They've been open for about 5 years now and work with many local crafts people to offer an abundance of fine wares, antiques, jewelry, accessories for the home and all sorts of other gifts.

Carol's Seafood, 995-4232, is where you'll find the freshest fish, crabs, shrimp and scallops.

BUXTON

When you arrive in Buxton, you'll discover the shops are more spread out and range from the general store, bait and tackle shops to spe-cialty shops. **Daydreams**, 995-5548, is a big store, and it needs to be to handle the regular shoppers. They have earned a reputation for having exceptionally stylish clothes, with name brands not usually found at other stores in the area. Clothes for men, women and children are offered, along with accessories and jewelry. **Hatteras Outdoors**, 995-5815, adjoins Daydreams and has all the clothes for sports enthusiasts. There's equipment, accessories, rentals and lessons, too. **Cape Sandwich Co.**, 995-6140, has snacks, great sandwiches, soups and desserts.

Red Drum Tackle Shop, 995-5414, is a place you'll enjoy. Get the latest in fishing information and select gear from their complete line of custom rods, bait and tackle. A fish mounting service is also available. **Dillon's Corner**, 995-5083, opened 11 years ago. It started as a bait and tackle store, but has expanded into a complete fishing center now. It's owned by Ollie and Kathy Jarvis. She has expanded the store to include a gift shop, **The Fisherman's Daughter**, specializing in local crafts, works of art by California artist George Edenfield, pottery and jewelry.

Natural Art Surf Shop, 995-5682, is owned by Scott and Carol Busbey. It has been around for a long time and has the reputation for being "the surfer's surf shop," meaning they specialize in surfing rather than all water board sports. Scott, who has his own line of boards called In The Eye, makes custom boards and does repairs while Carol makes clothes such as skirts, shirts, shorts and dresses, mostly in soft, cotton prints. Children's items are included.

Ormond's, 995-5012, is probably the oldest department store in Buxton. It has fine sportswear for the family. **Fox Water Sports**, 995-4102, features custom boards made by owner Ted James. Boards, booms, sails, harnesses, surfing accessories and clothes are also featured here. Rentals are available. Lots of t-shirts and swimwear fill this interesting shop. **Times Past Antiques**, 995-4022, buys, sells and trades interesting treasures from other times.

Buxton Village Books, 995-4240, is packed with fiction, non-fiction, best-sellers, sea-faring tales -- in other words, lots of good books. There are some used paperbacks, too. Owner Gee Gee Rosell has a great selection of cards, some office supplies, illustrations suitable for framing and a FAX service. A couple of furry-friends, especially "Buddy" the bookstore cat, will more than likely give you a slight nod. If not, Gee Gee will make up for it with interest, humor and charm. She writes a column for the local newspaper and is definitely at home in her delightful bookshop.

Buxton's supermarket, **Conners Cape Hatteras** market, car-

Photo: Phillip Ruckle

Hatteras Island is acknowledged as having the biggest and most consistent surf on the East Coast.

ries everything you need in the line of groceries and basic supplies. For fresh baked goods, **Orange Blossom Pastry Shop**, 995-4109, is loaded with delicious homebaked pastries and breads. They have giant apple fritters, referred to as Apple Uglies, that we definitely do not pass up, regardless of any diet.

FRISCO

Browning Artworks, 995-5538, is the only exclusively North Carolina fine craft gallery. You'll be impressed by the creations of crafts people who make blown-glass, porcelains, pottery, baskets, stoneware, fiber art, decoys and jewelry. The works are attractively displayed and, of course, are for sale. Linda and Lou Browning are the proprietors and select only the finest works available for the serious collector who knows good artwork. A bridal registry is maintained for residents and visitors. They will ship your selections back home or to other destinations. Linda and Lou and their staff are all very knowledgeable about each item in their shop and its artist.

Pirates Chest, 995-5118, is an older store, but filled with a variety of things like scrimshaw, coral and shells from far away places. Local shells, books and a large selection of handmade Christmas ornaments are found here. The works of local artists are featured and they sell hermit crabs! **All Decked Out**, 995-4319, is a furniture factory owned by Dale Cashman. Dale and his crew build outdoor furniture and will ship anywhere in the US. **The Gingerbread House**, 995-5204, is a delightful shop for early morning baked goods. They also have fabulous pizza and sandwiches. **Scotch Bonnet Marina Gift Shop**, 995-4242, has great fudge, custom and silk-screen T-shirts, hermit crabs and other gifts.

HATTERAS VILLAGE

At **Summer Stuff**, 986-2111, you can buy everything from clothes and shoes to toys and gifts. There's plenty to choose from here. **Blue Ridge Trading Co.**, 986-2257, is an interesting store featuring jewelry, shells and loads of T-shirts. **Nedo Shopping Center**, 986-2545, is really just one store, but it carries lots of different things you'll need for fun and sun on the beach and beyond. There's tools, small appliances, kitchen and bath supplies, books, toys, sporting goods, fishing equipment, clothes and more. **Lee Robinson General Store**, 986-2381, opened long ago, but the old store was replaced by a replica several years ago. We're glad they kept their old, beloved look, with a wide front porch and wooden floors. Owners Belinda and Virgil Willis have always carried everything you would usually need for a vacation at the beach, and still do. But they also have something you wouldn't necessarily expect to find at a beach general store: a huge selection of fine wines. **Ocean Annie's**, 986-2665, opened a fifth store on the Outer Banks in the spring. You'll see the same fine quality pottery and woodcrafts from all over the country plus gourmet coffees as in their other shops. **Burrus' Red & White** and **Oceanside Bake Shop** are recommended when shopping for eats. Carol opens the bakery at 4 a.m. and closes around noon in the off season, but is open until around 4 p.m. in the summer. **Hatteras Harbor Marina Store Gift Shop**, 986-2166, has jewelry, sportswear and other items in addition to one of the largest charter fishing fleets on the island.

Photo: DCTB

A 55 1/4-pound channel bass caught 11-10-82 by Dominic Quattrone of Mercer, N.J. during Cape Hatteras Surf Fishing Tournament.

Captain Ernal Foster
A Life On Hatteras

Yep, I got to get cleaned up some in here one of these days."

Captain Ernal Foster looks slowly around the interior of what he calls his "equipment building." Against the walls are stacked bundles of hand-tied nets. In the roof beams are bamboo poles, rods, old outriggers striped red and white. Covering the plank floor are heaps of bronze propellers, fighting chairs, Pflueger Altapac reels, old cans of Athey and Pettit paint and varnish. "That's my father's sail bag over there, with his needles and palms. And his sea chest, there in the corner. One of these days. Come on, let's talk in the house." The gray house on the sea side of Hatteras Village looks small and commonplace from Highway 12. But inside, its pine panelled walls are covered with mounted marlin, sailfish, swordfish. The furniture is oak, from old ships; Hazel shows you a Singer that washed ashore in the 1890s. Even the bathroom doors came from a vanished schooner.

Foster is not a large man, but at 76 his shoulders still bulge under his loose shirt as he lowers himself into his armchair. The steady eyes are the color of a blue marlin's back. And then the only sound is the soft voice, and faintly from outside the endless crash of the surf.

"I was born and raised on this spot, spent most of my life here. My father, he was raised down here on this hill, but they claim his father was a Yankee. My mother was born and raised here. I grew up one of seven children. Three girls, four boys. I happened to be the oldest boy.

"When I grew up there wasn't much to do round here. We boys entertained ourselves. We had shove-skiffs we made — wasn't no harbor here then, we kept the boats out in the sound, on stakes, and you went back and forth on a shove-skiff. You didn't row, you had oars and you shoved back and forth. We boys, we sewed some sails out of these burlap bags. Them skiffs didn't have centerboards on them, they was flat-bottom — and on a northeast wind, we'd race down to the point beach, three or four miles, four or five of us. And then we'd shove back. If it was southwesterly we'd shove down there and race back home. And we had horses to chase and catch, and ride on the beach. And we played cat. How do you play cat? Take socks, and unravel the yarn and make a ball out of it. You throw the ball at the man, and if you hit him he'd be out. Didn't have no money for baseballs. We boys had teams. When anybody lost there'd be a fight. But we had games like that. I don't know how we could have had a better time.

"Then when we got to our teens boys and girls would get together at their homes, and get some cocoa, try and get some sugar, and we'd have a cook-candy. And some of the boys didn't get invited, when you'd set the candy out to cool they'd come around and steal it. When we did taffy you'd pull it out, a boy and a girl. If it didn't break she'd have candy in both hands and you could kiss her. Then on Fourth of July we'd take our boat and go to Ocracoke, to the dances. I had me a Ocracoke girl. Ever heard of Aycock Brown? He married my girl friend.

"My father started working me when I was a boy. He didn't let me lay around. When I was small, on Saturdays I'd go out with him fishing. In the winter the shad, they had a lot of good roe into them, I'd take and bust them and get a bucket of roe out of them and take it home.

"When I was thirteen I was mess-cooking at the factory for sixty- five men, two dollars a week. That was down in Southport. That's thirty miles below Wilmington, on the mouth of the Cape Fear River. My father was captain of a menhaden boat, and they moved the factory from Portsmouth down to Southport. That was a lot of money. You went to the movies — silent, they didn't have no talkies then — Friday nights, ten cent movies, get you a bag of peanuts for a nickel. Only sound in the movie house would be the poppin' of them peanuts. In World War One we moved to Beaufort, fishing that menhaden boat. When the war ended in 1918 I was in school there.

"When I come to be fourteen my father turned the boat over to me. I had a two-cylinder Lathrop in to her. Straight drive, you didn't have clutches then. You had to learn how to handle that switch. You had to know how to judge the wind and the distance comin' in. One time when we were going up the sound when I was sixteen she kicked back and smashed that finger there. So I still got a mark from that engine. I hauled cars across to Ocracoke with that boat. Down the shore side there I got two skiffs and I put 'em side by side and put planks on 'em. Then I'd put the cars on 'em and tow 'em across. Got ten dollars a car. See, boys were working away from home, Philadelphia and them, and they'd come home want to show their car off. Didn't have a road, but just flatten your tire down fourteen or fifteen pounds you could ride in the sand. Catch low water and you could ride the surf line. I've gone from here to Oregon Inlet in an hour. Course you didn't have traffic then.

"I used to have to hunt when I was a teenager. They had a private club there my father took care of. That's an unpleasant job, working for rich people. It was on the Sound, up on the Reef about four miles from here. In about six feet of water. We had blinds up on the reef and we had about 65 geese there in the yard. We were guides. They come down to go hunting, we had to go put the decoys out. We had metal pegs you tied their foot to it. Use about fifteen to eighteen to a battery. Live geese. See, they outlawed that.

"I think the hardest work I ever done was pushing a clam-rake. You only got fifteen cents a hundred for 'em in the thirties. That's hard work, worse'n any. You'd get three and four hundred clams a day. And you get you a can of sardines for a nickel, a coca-cola for a nickel, some crackers, well you had to catch a hundred clams to pay for your lunch. And pound netting for my father, that was hard work. And fishing in the ocean, and we pulled our nets by hand. They don't do that no more. Those nets out in the equipment house my mother and I knotted in the thirties. It all used to be cotton, linen. We used to buy the twine and tie them. We'd make our wooden gages the size we want the net. You don't tie too many yards in a night...we used to haul eleven hundred yards of net, get on the stern and pull them in by hand. About the second week of that you'd be gettin' in good shape. That's the way we used to work. But everything's push a button now.

"My father started going to sea when he was fourteen years old. His name was Charlie. He got eight dollars a month. He worked his way up to mate. He was on a three, four-mast schooner, I don't remember the name. He used to sail down to the West Indies, all that way.

"Ain't too much I know about my mother. She was born here in the woods and she never liked to go places. We lived in Beaufort for two years and then we come home. We were coming out of Beaufort Inlet and she told my father, this is my last trip to sea. Over the years she never had any use for the water. I had my first boat and she wouldn't never go to the dock to look at it. It didn't mean a thing to her. She was a Ballance. Her family was mostly fishermen, that was all there was here. They practically owned this beach down below the ferry dock. They just let it go; it wa'n't worth nothing. There was a local man here in the twenties taking it up for taxes and he sold it to some Yankees. And they had a fence across it all the way to the ocean, which was wrong. So I pried into that. A good friend of mine, the governor of North Carolina, said they'd back me in a test case. Some of them got mad at me over that. Then when the Park Service came along in the fifties they was the first to sell, because they know they'd lost their rights. Park Service, best thing that ever happened to this island.

"I started the sport fishing out of here in '38. And the first summer I went it was a hundred dollars for four day trips out to the Gulf Stream. Twenty-five dollars a day was money then.

"What made me get into fishing? I just wanted to. I left home to keep from fishing. I went to New York, went two years in the Coast Guard in rum-running days. Then I worked in a sheet metal shop out in Long Island. It was pretty work, I spent five years putting copper roofs on them big summer homes. Then in '33, after the election, money people just closed up. And you can't live up there without work. So I came home. That depression running me home was the best thing ever happened to me. I lost the boat we had in '35, out on Diamond Shoals, my brother did. So then I built the *Albatross* in '37.

"I got my lumber. It grows on the swamp, over on our mainland. Other people calls it white cedar, but we call it juniper. Cost me 4 1/2 cents a foot and the framing three cents a foot. I carried it down to Marshallburg and a man there built my boat. When I got her home she cost me eight hundred and five dollars. Without a engine. I want to the bank and borrowed seventy-five dollars, put a shaft in her. And I bought a Buick for fifteen dollars. Man said, drive it home, ain't nothing wrong with it. I said, don't want the car, just want the engine! Local man, Lloyd Styron here, he put her in for me. He said, Pay me when you make it. I borrowed a propeller. I borrowed a steering wheel. I borrowed a gas tank. That's how I started out in the *Albatross*. A lot of people don't believe a lot of this, but that's just the way it happened.

"It didn't take too long to pay that $75 back. Man at the bank said

Ernal, just let that ride. I said no, I want that note! Because it was on my boat.

"So we went along. Later on I got a Chrysler engine, Airflow, straight eight, '34 model. But I got it hot and busted it. Then Burris, who owned the Texaco station, said, Ernal, I'll get you a engine. Six hundred dollars, a Chris Craft. So I went to the bank and borrowed it. This was in thirty-eight. That was some engine. We went along. Money was scarce. We were getting half a cent a pound for croaker, three cent for trout. I got that note paid off in December of 1941. And the second week after I got her paid off I got my notice from the Army.

"Draft! That killed me. I had a row with the girl in the office. I said, I'm thirty-two years old. I'm living, taking care of my father and mother. How can I support them on $21 a month? She said, that's your problem. She give me two weeks to think it over. Lloyd and I was the two oldest, he was thirty-seven, but we was drafted first! There was some paid off, so they wouldn't go. Think so? I know so.

"So I went to Norfolk, got in the Coast Guard. The Hooligan Navy. I knew I would, I'd been fishing for a year with this commander. I went in as a first class petty officer. Eighty-four dollars a month. I married Hazel here in '42. She's one of those Midgetts, they say the first one washed ashore in a whiskey barrel. Her grandfather you might have heard of, he saved a lot of people.

"I never been across the Atlantic. My brothers did, they were in the Navy. I was one of the lucky ones, I was here for four years. Baltimore was the farthest I got away from home.

"I was on a boat — harbor duty, sabotage, patrolling. We used to patrol the pierheads and Newport News, and the bridgehead. One merchant ship there come in with blood comin' out of the scupper holes. Had a mutiny on it. And when they paid off ships I stood guard. They paid off in cash, men come in one door of the mess hall and out the other. Wouldn't let but one man in at a time. I didn't like being guard — a gun's something I never had any use for. I got me a shotgun back there I bought in 1929 and I never had any use for it.

"Then for eighteen months I was on a patrol boat out of Morehead when they was sinking of these ships out here. It was bad. I didn't sleep when we were out on patrol — I was afraid one of those subs would blow us out of the water. This was a old 75-foot chaser they built to chase the rum-runners. We had a one-pounder on the bow and a fifty-caliber machine gun. I could throw a shell about as far as that one-pounder would shoot. We carried four depth charges. You dropped one of those, it was full speed ahead or it would knock the caulking out of your hull and you had to head for the ship-yard.

"During the war you couldn't even rest here at night. It would jar you off your bed, almost knock the lights out and shake your windows. The con-cussion. You'd look out and see two or three ships burning at one time. I've fished over a lot of 'em. My son says oil's still flowing out of one of them.

"And then they took my boat! I get so mad about that I don't like to talk about her. They had here down there in Fort Macon and painted her gray. They used her for a play toy.

"I had a time getting her back. I had a big row in the captain's office. 'You've been paid for that boat,' he said. I said, 'Show me where it's paid for.' I knew it hadn't because when they sent me the papers I put them in the stove and they went up the chimney. So he said, 'Well then we got a boat for nothing.' We had it out but when I was leaving I said, 'Captain, there's bigger men than you are.' He figured I was just a sailor. But I wrote to my congressman. I knew him since I was a boy. And I wrote a lawyer in Washington, DC, which his father was some of my mother's people. And about two weeks I was called back in the office, and the captain invited me to sit down. And he wanted to help me get my boat back then.

"It was in bad shape. Painted gray inside and out, and they had burned the engine and clutch up. But I accepted it as it was. I wanted her back.

"I got back in forty-six. I'd had some lung trouble, spent six months in the hospital. Later on they found a growth in my lung. Took part of it out, some of my ribs. Doctor told me I couldn't work no more in the winter. So I figured then I'd just stick to my charter fishing. Didn't anybody else want to, they'd leave them on the dock to go shrimping. So I turned around, and instead of building a home I built the second boat, in '48. I had a little disability, but they cut that off in '52. So then instead of building a house we built the third boat. Then in '55 we finally had to tear down the old house, and I built this one. And we finally got it so we can live in it.

"Then my son Ernie was getting up in age, and we wanted him to go to school. So we saved. We cut a lot of corners. No automobile, nothing. We could have asked for a handout from the government, but we didn't. My father always told me the government owes you nothing. You got to make your own way. And I never got on that social security till I was sixty-eight, cause I was working. Ernie's a schoolteacher up in Manteo now, and he comes down here summers. After I had the heart trouble I turned the boats over to him.

"But I got into this charter business, and just liked it. It was something different every day. At first we fished wrecks. Then we fished billfish. Out in the blue water you don't know what you're going to catch. It does something to you. When you see the fish come out'n the water walking on their tails. The more you do it the more you get encouraged. And it made you feel good to catch a fish.

"I used to have some nice customers. I've fished governors, ambassadors, senators. Ray Trallenger, from the New York *World*. Senator Duff. I used to have a bunch of girls, too. One of them got sick on me out catching bluefish. She was redheaded. Blondes, lightheaded people get sick easier than darkheaded. All over I used to have coming in here. Those days it was a week or ten days at a time, man and his wife. If you didn't catch a fish, well, you'd catch one tomorrow. It's not like that anymore. It's groups, five and six, and if they don't catch a boatload of fish they're mad.

"The most beautiful thing I ever saw at sea was a school of marlin. I thought at first it was porpoises. It was in the small tuna season. And they were knocking them in the air, then they'd jump. And there might be ten or fifteen of them in the air at the same time. And the sun was shining, and the water run off their back. A person hasn't seen it can't imagine it. It's blue and changes. And when they went into the air the sun would shine on them, the water running off almost like a blue rainbow. It's the only time I ever seen that.

"We don't have them out there like they used to. Used to be you'd hook two or three at a time. Big marlin. They're being overfished.

"The man who wrote this book about the Albatross Fleet, John Cleveland, he was the first one to release a marlin. He started fishing with me in `58. And he made me release the biggest sailfish ever caught on this coast. I imagine he was ten feet long. They live after they're released, if they're not bleeding. Sometimes I just cut the wire, but if I can, I sit on the stern and shake the hooks out of 'em. I don't like to kill fish if you're not going to use them.

"These tournaments are just disgusting. A bunch of millionaires had this tournament, up at this club. And they lie, steal, cheat — it's sad. Instead of having a fun tournament, money got involved, and they'll do anything to win. Used to be they'd release them. Then one of those yachts was fishing close to my boat and he lost the fish, a hundred yards back when he jumped off. And he called in that he released a fish! Now they have to bring them in, they stopped trusting each other. But there's all a new group there at that club now. I walk up there at night and I don't know anybody. Some of them there now got a glass in each hand and one in their mouth. To drown their problems. They're not happy people.

"Fishing is going to go up and down. But now there's laws, and limits. That's federal. State don't mess with it. But I don't like that. And now I got to pay tax on my boats, same as commercial fishermen. Another thing I don't like is people selling their fish off my boat. If they don't want to take them home and eat it themselves, I say release it. But there's more people fishing now. Used to be I was out for five, six days and I was the only boat out there.

"I never used charts. Or compass. I never used Loran. I carried a boat to New York with no chart. Every place on the coast is in my mind just like you're on a highway. I know how much time I make and I just go where I want to go. I can't tell anybody the courses, but it just comes to me. My family is all natural born watermen. Now they got depth recorders. Colored depth recorders! They got temperature gauges! I used to use my finger.

"You know, I think if the people today had to live like we had to live they'd see it differently. Young people today, all they think is money. They get sixteen, they got to have them a car! You got to have money to live, but if you get to craving it you can forget living. I never worried to pile up a lot of it. I wouldn't be doing anything different if I was rich. I done what I set out to do and I'm happy.

"I look back over the years and how I had to struggle. And in a way I still ain't got nothing. But I got Hazel, home, children, we got a lot to be thankful for. Two years ago I had a heart problem, they told me I couldn't go to the dock no more. I guess I let little things get to me too much. When the boat broke down, things like that. Had to give up everything! But I haven't. I invited those doctors down in August and took them out fishing.

"I still mess with the boats every day, piddle around. But now I try not to let things bother me. I sit on the dock and whittle. Don't make nothing but a mess. And I wait for my boats and my boys to come back in."❧

Photo: Michael Halminski

Don't be surprised to find yourself all alone on an Ocracoke beach, even on a weekend.

Inside
Ocracoke Island

A thirty-minute ferry ride across the waters of Pamlico Sound brings you to Ocracoke Island. There is no charge for this ferry, which is a form of public transportation for islanders and visitors.

The gentle roll of the ferry accompanied by sea gulls in flight often provides the first-time traveler a feeling of awe -- out on the water, the sight of habitable land where sky and water wash together off in the distance. You're allowed to get out of the car and walk around. This means opportunities for friendly exchanges among passengers and for tossing bread to the sea gulls that hover overhead, cawing greedily. They'll even eat right out of your hand when the competition gets heavy. Often the captain encourages feeding the gulls from the stern, for obvious reasons, if you think about it; and we recommend wearing a cap and closing car windows and sun roofs to be on the safe side!

Disembarking from the ferry on Ocracoke Island releases you on a 12-mile ride along the dunes and soundside forests of cedar and pine before you arrive in Ocracoke Village. Roll the window down and smell the cedar mixed with salt-air. Waterfowl are plentiful in the wide expanses of marshgrass and narrow canals. Depending on the time of day and year you arrive here, you'll be enchanted by some of the most beautiful nature scenes on the Outer Banks. This area is a part of the National Seashore and will never be developed. There are parking lots provided at several points along NC 12 for easy beach access. The miles of desolate beaches will ease you into a new adventure -- slowing your pace -- alone with the sea.

Ocracoke Village occupies the western portion of the island. Life here is quite different from other Outer Banks towns and villages. It would appear that a lazy island life is afforded all who live here. The pace is slower and many islanders live off the bounty of the sea and small island stores and shops. Days are long. Bike rentals are popular in the Village -- often replacing cars as a means of getting around.

Most of the island is still just as uninhabited as you drive down it as it was on a spring day in 1585, when seven English ships appeared off Ocracoke Inlet.

Sir Richard Grenville was in command, a seasoned, experienced soldier. He had about three hundred troops aboard his fleet. His mission, entrusted to him by Sir Walter Raleigh and the Queen, was to establish a permanent English base in the New World. He was to fail at Roanoke Island; but that summer no one yet suspected the fate that awaited those first colonists. The Banks welcomed him in characteristic fashion, leaving his flagship, *Tiger*, hard aground on the bar. He and Ralph Lane took advantage of the delay to explore north and west in smaller vessels (see 'Ocracoke Pony Pens,' in this chapter — these hardy ponies may stem from stock lost from the *Tiger*). When the ship was floated and repaired, he headed to Roanoke, leaving the island sleeping and deserted once again.

It's thought that the name 'Woccocon,' which was applied to the island at first, was derived from the neighboring Indian tribe the 'Woccons.' But its precise derivation, like that of so many Outer Banks names, is unclear, as is its subsequent degeneration through 'Wococock,' 'Occocock,' 'Ocreecock,' and other variations to the present 'Ocracoke.' Spelling held a low priority in those days, a state to which the English tongue seems to be reverting.

Most of the island remained in its wild state, with sheep, cattle and horses released by the early owners to graze freely. But the gradual increase in colonial trade in the early 18th century saw more and more ships using the Inlet, in those days deeper than it is now (too, ships, were of shallower draft). In 1715 the colony of North

Carolina established Ocracoke as a port, setting aside land on the western tip of the island for the homes of pilots (for midwesterners and other non-seagoing types, a 'pilot' meets incoming ships at sea and guides them safely in. Pilots are generally older men, brine-encrusted, who know the configurations of sand bars and channels from painful experience).

A new problem also arose: pirates. They interfered with the pilots, terrorized the inhabitants of the islands, boarded and robbed ships at sea, murdered crews and passengers and made themselves generally unwelcome. John Cole, Robert Deal, Anne Bonny and dozens of others operated along the Caribbean and Southern Atlantic coasts in the early eighteenth century.

But it was the notorious Blackbeard, standing out as the worst of a bad lot, who left his name stamped on the Outer Banks, and on Ocracoke, one of his lairs. Much of his early career lies somewhere between conjecture and legend. It is thought that he started as an honest English tar named Edward Drummond, born, perhaps, in Bristol.

He may have started, like many pirates, as a privateer — a sort of seagoing guerrilla. But by 1716 he had turned pirate, calling himself Edward Teach. He had found his metier, and his rise was rapid. He seems to have been a man of organizational ability, for in short order he was in command of a sizeable fleet of ships, and some

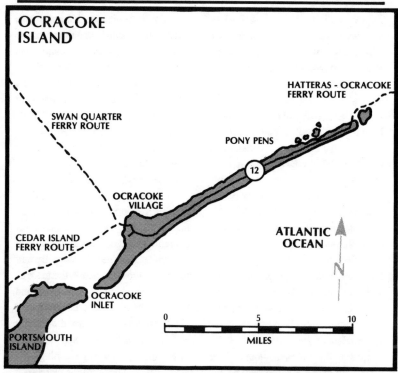

OCRACOKE ISLAND

SWAN QUARTER FERRY ROUTE

HATTERAS - OCRACOKE FERRY ROUTE

PONY PENS

12

OCRACOKE VILLAGE

CEDAR ISLAND FERRY ROUTE

ATLANTIC OCEAN

N

OCRACOKE INLET

0   5   10

MILES

PORTSMOUTH ISLAND

hundreds of men.

He also understood advertising. An evil reputation is a great thing to a terrorist, for it weakens the other side's morale and leads to quick capitulations. Blackbeard was a master in dressing for success and winning through intimidation. Tall, broad and with a bushy coal-black beard, he festooned himself with cutlasses, dirks and loaded pistols. In battle his beard was plaited, with little ribbons to add a festive air. Lighted cannon fuses dangled from under his hat, an affectation of dubious safety with primed flintlocks in his belt, but unquestionably effective in giving him the air of the very devil.

And a devil with political clout. He bought Governor Eden, of North Carolina, and was able to move ashore to Bath with his booty in 1718. Like many men, he became bored with retirement, and before the year was up he was out raiding again part-time. Eden stayed bought and did nothing, so a few citizens went north to ask a favor of Governor Spotswood, of Virginia.

Spotswood sent the Royal Navy. In November of 1718, Lt. Robert Maynard left the James River, heading south in two sloops manned with sailors from British men-o'-war. Maynard must have had confidence in himself; his two small sloops had no cannon, only small arms. The shallow-draft boats were able to penetrate where larger warships could not go, and Maynard was able to track Blackbeard's *Adventure* to Ocracoke Inlet.

Dawn, November 22. Ocracoke Inlet resounded to the boom of pirate guns and the crackle of British musketry fire. The *Adventure* grounded, but her well-laid cannon took heavy toll of the Royal Navy men. Maynard ordered them below, then stood ready on deck as his sloop drifted down on the larger ship.

They met. Teach's men launched a volley of grenades and swarmed aboard. The sailors came up from below to begin a merciless hand-to-hand struggle. The pirate chief and the lieutenant faced each other. An exchange of pistol balls wounded the pirate, but in the next moment he had broken the officer's sword with his cutlass. Another sailor sliced the massive buccaneer in the neck, but he fought on...then collapsed. The battle was over. The pirate's head was cut off and hung from the rigging for the trip back, that all might see he was dead. The body was thrown overboard, where, island legend has it, it swam seven times round the ship before sinking. Most of the rest of his crew were taken to Williamsburg and given a fair trial before they were hanged. His treasure? Probably there was none — he spent what little money the coasting trade yielded. But legends persist....

With the pirates cleaned out, trade flourished. Most of the seaborne commerce of North Carolina, and much of that of Virginia, came through the inlet, and gradually families settled there to service the ships. There were sporadic Spanish incursions and raids in the 1740s and 50s, and at one time they even had a camp on the island. Eventually peace came between England and Spain and they went home.

It was in 1753 that the village became a recognized town, and then there were only about a hundred inhabitants. Most of the island remained in a wild state. The inlet was fortified in 1757. Across the water, the town of Portsmouth was also growing up, and the little port of Beacon Island Roads, as the two towns were commonly called, was doing well when the Revolution arrived. Much of Washington's army was supplied through Ocracoke, and coastal North Carolina trade remained intact although the British patrolled outside, landed troops and engaged in various futile retaliations.

After the war, the lighthouses were built by the new government, the first in 1798 on Shell Castle Rock, the second (the present one) in 1823. But even as they went up, the golden age of Ocracoke was drawing to an end. Hatteras and Oregon inlets opened during a storm in September of 1846, and as these were deepened by outflow, Ocracoke Inlet began to shoal. The fort was abandoned by the Confederates in 1861 and the Government sank several ships loaded with rock in the channel to seal it. Such seagoing traffic as remained to the Banks — for by now oceangoing ships had grown much larger and deeper — shifted to Hatteras Inlet. After the war the village declined to a hundred or so inhabitants, who subsisted as fishermen, boatmen or lifesavers. Many went to sea, and not all of them returned.

It took a war to bring new life. Silver Lake Harbor (formerly Cockle Creek) had been dredged out in 1931, and in 1942 a naval base was established there. As cargo ships burned offshore, as oil and debris and dead bodies drifted ashore, telephones and paved roads were brought to the villagers. The base was closed in 1945, but in the mid-50s the National Seashore and the highway brought a new source of revenue: the tourist.

Today tourism has taken over from fishing as the island's main livelihood (though the same road service that has brought visitors also made crabbing commercially feasible). And they do come, more every year, in a two-season economy of tourists in the summer and anglers in the fall. Regret it or welcome it, the nineteenth century is giving way to the twentieth fast in Ocracoke Village. Electricity came in 1938 and the first paved road in 1951. In the late seventies an ABC store, a doctor and a night spot arrived; in 1985, television, in the form of a 3.5 meter dish and cable; in 1987 the first multistory hotel and the first lakefront condo opened. Gift shops are proliferating and sadly so are signs.

But a walk or a bike ride will show you that Ocracoke hasn't been spoiled yet. There's still no barber shop, no movies, no crime, not one fast-food joint. Many of the streets are only sandy paths, still unpaved and not likely ever to be. Walking them on a soft summer's night is as close to inner peace as many Americans will ever get. Even some of the paved roads are so narrow and winding that two Caddies will scarce pass abreast.

And still, to the north and east...Ocracoke Island stretches out unpopulated and untamed. The sea roars against the rows of dunes; the road, silent and empty, shimmers amid the beachgrass and yaupon. Toward the Sound the ponies graze warily, and Ocracoke is quiet by the jealous sea.

Ocracoke

ATTRACTIONS

OCRACOKE PONY PENS
Soundside

'Ponies'? The word conjures up a picture of something small, shaggy and friendly. None of these adjectives, however, exactly fits the semiwild Ocracoke ponies. They're not really that small, perhaps thirteen or fourteen hands high. They are shaggy, in the winter. But they are definitely not friendly.

History, economics and even anatomy have been used to try to explain the derivation of these hardy russet-colored animals that, in former days, roamed wild on the length of the island, as well as on Hatteras Island. A popular version goes as follows. In 1585, the vessels carrying the first colonists to Roanoke made their first landing at Ocracoke Inlet, where the flagship, *Tiger*, grounded. Sir Richard Grenville ordered the ship unloaded, and its cargo, which included a brace of horses purchased in the West Indies (then under Spanish rule), was put ashore while the *Tiger* was taken off the shoal. The usual method of getting horses ashore in those days was to let them swim; and it is thought that some escaped, and began their wild existence on the Banks. Other theories say they came from Spanish shipwrecks,

or, more prosaically, were introduced by the early Bankers as a ready source of horseflesh. The rugged, wild ponies have been proven of Spanish mustang descent by the number of lumbar vertebrae and number of ribs. A current research effort involving genetic tracking may answer the question once and for all.

At one time there were more than a thousand of them, roaming free, subsisting on marsh grass. As civilization came to the Banks they were penned and sold off. When the Cape Hatteras National Seashore was established they were taken over by the Park Service. There are now about twenty-five ponies in the herd.

The Pony Pen is located some six miles southwest of the Hatteras-Ocracoke ferry landing, on the sound side. Park Service signs will direct you to a wooden observation platform overlooking the mile-long fenced pasture. Don't count on seeing the ponies, especially in rough weather; they have shelters down near the southwest end that they retreat to. *Don't* cross the fence into the pasture. These are wild ponies, and they can bite and kick.

HAMMOCK HILLS NATURE TRAIL
Opposite Ocracoke Campground

Ocracoke's not all sandy beaches and small town. This 3/4-mile nature trail shows us a cross-section of the island, from dune through maritime forest to salt marsh. Learn how various plants adapted to conditions of salt and stress. A pleasant walk, the trail takes about half an hour to complete. Bring the camera. There are some biting insects in summer and you should review the notes for snakes for "Buxton Woods Nature Trail" for snake warnings.

OCRACOKE ISLAND VISITOR CENTER
Near Cedar Island and Swan Quarter Ferry Slips
928-4531

The Ocracoke Island Visitor Center is run by the National Park Service as part of the Cape Hatteras National Seashore. It's in Ocracoke Village, at the very southwest end of Highway 12, on Silver Lake. To reach it from 12, just stay on the highway past the Island Inn until you reach the Lake and a T. Turn right and continue around the shore of the lake in a counterclockwise direction till you see the low brown building to your right. Parking is available there.

The Center has an information desk, helpful people, a small book shop and exhibits. It's also the place to make arrangements for use of the Park Service docks.

It's open seasonally; Memorial Day through Labor Day. That means that things are pretty quiet during the winter, as they are in the rest of the village, but during the warm months the Rangers offer a couple of dozen "Discovery Adventures," all free, presented several times each week (check at the desk for what, where and when). In the past these have included beach and sound walks, interpretations of the life and times of a pirate, day or night walking tours of the village, bird-watching, history lectures and quite a few more. Once you've looked around the village for a couple of days you may appreciate the Park Service's thoughtfulness in arranging things for you and the kids to do.

OCRACOKE COAST GUARD STATION
Silver Lake   (Business) 928-4731
Emergency   (SAR line) 928-3711

The southernmost of the chain of five Coast Guard stations along the Banks is Ocracoke. Its complement of twenty-one men maintains a 44-foot motor lifeboat and several other, smaller vessels for search and rescue, law enforcement, servicing aids to navigation and environmental protection. In an average year, they respond to 250 calls for assistance from fishermen and boaters. The station building was built in 1938 to replace an older one on the same site. The formerly open station is now more tightly secured, but a weekly tour gives a thorough look at the station, its piers, its boats. Check at the NPS Visitor Center for time and dates of tours. Bona fide group tours can be arranged a week in advance by calling the business number.

OCRACOKE ISLAND MUSEUM AND VISITOR CENTER
Silver Lake

To the east of the NPS parking lot in Ocracoke, you'll see a two-story white frame building, recently restored. The house was built by David Williams, the first chief of the Ocracoke Coast Guard Station. In 1989 it was moved to its present location on NPS land. The Ocracoke Preservation Society, a group of interested local people, and the Park Service restored the building for use as a museum and visitor center. Like the restoration at Chicamacomico, this benefits both local residents and tourists.

OCRACOKE CIVIC CLUB
24 hour answering machine
928-6711

You can call during business hours if you have specific questions about Ocracoke, or write: Civic Club Box 456, Ocracoke, NC 27960.

OCRACOKE VILLAGE - A WALKING TOUR
West end of Highway 12

The little village of Ocracoke is a world of its own. Reclusive, hidden, romantic...these are words used by those who know her. A haunt of writers, artists and lovers, this small lost hamlet at the world's end (or at least at the end of the highway, a phrase that has a touch of the mysterious itself) is unlike any of the other towns on the Banks.

Things have changed since WWII and the coming of paved roads, but not all that much. The roads are still narrow, the people friendly but a touch reticent, with manners and a speech of their own distinct from mainland North Carolina. We love Ocracoke, and you will too.

For a short walking tour of the village, park in the lot opposite the Visitor's Center. Turn left out of the lot and walk down Route 12, along the shores of the Lake.

The village waterfront, formerly quite sleepy, is beginning to resemble St. David's, Bermuda. You'll pass many small shops (see Ocracoke Shopping for profiles) and some large new hotels: the Anchorage, Silver Lake's new addition, Harborside, Princess Motel. For the tour, keep walking till, on your right, you see a small brick post office.

Opposite the post office, a sandy, narrow street angles to the left. This is Old Howard Street, one of the oldest and least changed parts of the village. Note the smallness of the old homes, the cisterns attached to them for collection of rain water and the detached kitchens. If you've been to Colonial Williamsburg you will recall seeing these detached kitchens under somewhat more monumental circumstances. Continue past Village Craftsman, unless of course you want to check out the local crafts.

After some four hundred yards Howard Street debouches on School Street: turn left for the Methodist Church and public school. The church is usually open for visitors, but use discretion; there may be services in progress. (Also, please wipe your feet as you go in; the sand doesn't look good on the carpet.)

If you enter, note the cross displayed behind the altar. Thereby hangs a tale, and not so ancient a one. The cross was carved from a wooden spar from an American freighter, the *Caribsea*, sunk offshore by U-boats in the dark early months of 1942. By the strange workings of circumstance, the *Caribsea's* engineer was James

Baugham Gaskill, who had been born in Ocracoke. He was killed in the sinking; and local residents will tell you a further strange fact; that several days later a display case, holding, among other things, Gaskill's mate's license, washed ashore not far from his family home.

There's been a Methodist church on Ocracoke since 1828. This building was built in 1943, with lumber and pews salvaged from older buildings. A "historical sketch" pamphlet is generally available in the vestibule for visitors.

If you'd like to walk to the lighthouse on the tour — it adds about another half mile — turn right (west) and follow the road past the Island Inn about five hundred yards. You will see the lighthouse towering on your right. After inspecting it (see Ocracoke Inlet Lighthouse) return to the church and school.

The next leg of the tour takes you around the north corner of the school and past the playground on a narrow boardwalk. This leads you out onto the paved road beyond it to the east. Turn left. This was the first paved road on the island, and was constructed by Seabees during WWII. Turn right after a third of a mile (first stop sign). A few minutes' walk along this narrow, tree-shaded road will bring you to the British Cemetery. You have to watch for it; it's on your right, set back a bit from the road, and shaded by live oak and yaupon. The big British flag makes it a bit easier to spot. It's not an impressive site; very small, very understated; entirely appropriate. The *Bedfordshire* was a trawler, one of a small fleet of twenty-four antisubmarine vessels that Churchill loaned to the United States in April 1942 to help us against the U-boats. She was a small ship, only 170 feet long, displacing 900 tons and armed with a single 4-inch deck gun, but full of fight. She had no chance; she was torpedoed off Cape Lookout during the night of 11 May by U-558. Six bodies washed ashore. Four were interred here by the Navy and Coast Guard, and the little cemetery is maintained by the USCG.

Each year a ceremony here commemorates their sacrifice. The fiftieth anniversary, in 1992, is planned to be especially impressive, with multinational participation.

To return to the Visitor Center, walk west till you reach the lakeshore, then turn right.

OCRACOKE LIGHTHOUSE
SW corner of Ocracoke Village

This, the southernmost of the four famous lighthouses of the Banks, is also the oldest and the shortest. It's the second oldest operational lighthouse in the United States as well. Yes, it's still "flashing" away, — one long flash from a half hour before sunset to a half hour after sunrise — still warning mariners away from the ever-changing shoals offshore.

When it was built, in 1823, this was a busy port. The present lighthouse replaced a still older one, the Shell Castle Rock lighthouse, which had been built in 1798 but which was rather left behind when the inlet moved south.

The Ocracoke Inlet Lighthouse houses a 360-degree non-rotating light with a range of 14 miles. Focal plane height is 65', overall height of the structure is about 75'. The brick walls are five feet thick at the base. That pretty, textured white surface is mortar, hand-spread over the bricks. The two-story white house you will find nearby was originally meant for the lighthouse keeper. It underwent extensive reconstruction in the late 1980s, to Historic Preservation standards, and now serves as quarters for Ocracoke's Ranger and the maintenance supervisor. The light itself is operated by the Coast Guard and cannot be entered.

To reach the light, turn left off Route 12 at the Island Inn, and go about 800 yards. A white picketed turnoff on the right allows you to park your auto or bike and walk the last few yards to the base of the structure.

SILVER LAKE MARINA

At Visitor's Center   928-4531

Silver Lake is the Park Service-run marina in Ocracoke, and is the only large one there. It is run differently from a commercial marina in that there are no dockage fees and no reservations. The marina has no slips, only four hundred feet of frontage on Silver Lake with tie-up facilities. Water is available, and so are power hookups

($1/night). The basin has been dredged to eighteen feet.

Basically, the way to get a slip is to arrive at the right time. If there's one open just pull in and tie up. There's a fourteen-day limit in the summertime. Actually, the rangers tell us that it's possible to get a slip there even in the summer, although it gets crowded on weekends.

If the marina should be full when you arrive, don't panic. Just anchor out in the lake, staying out of the channel and out of the way of ferry operations.

O'NEAL'S DOCKSIDE

Behind the Community Store

928-1111

O'Neal's is your friendly hunting and fishing center, owned by Charlie O'Neal. This is where you book your offshore fishing charters on the *Miss Kathleen, Seawalker, Bluefin* and *Outlaw*, and where you can charter trips to Portsmouth Island. They also sell a full line of supplies, boat gear, and fuel.

OCRACOKE TROLLEY

Trolley Stop, Highway 12   928-4041

It's one thing to see Ocracoke Island through your own eyes, and another thing altogether to see it through the eyes of a local, someone who knows every nook and cranny of the island. The Trolley runs three times a day during the week and twice on the weekends and takes you past some of Ocracoke's history you'd never know was there on your own.

The narrated tour includes the Coast Guard Station, the WW II Naval Base, several Sam Jones homes, the British Cemetery and Howard Grave Yard, a WW II Mine Control Tower, the Civil War headquarters for the Union Forces and lots more.

Reservations are required for buses or groups numbering over 25, but for others, just show up at the Trolley Stop (you can grab a quick bite there too while you're waiting). Tours leave at 10:30 a.m., 2:30 p.m., and 5:00 p.m. Mondays through Saturdays. (No tours on Sundays.)

OCRACOKE FISHING CENTER

Silver Lake   **928-6661**

Part of the Anchorage Inn operation, these five 200-foot piers and new building act as a center for charter boat operations to the sound, Gulf Stream and close inshore. There's a minimum six-foot depth alongside. Docking ($.60/foot/day) includes showers, pool, telephones and other extras. Gas and diesel are available and the boat ramp is two dollars. There are marine supplies and a small tackle shop. Open March 1 to November 30.

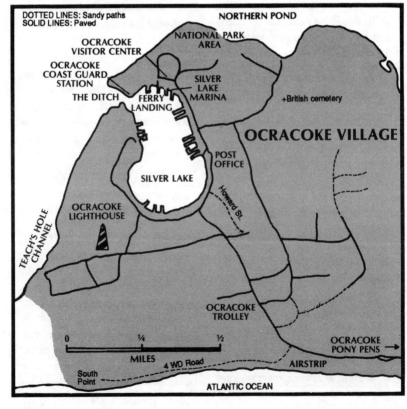

Ocracoke

RECREATION

Fishing from the surf or on a charter trip, windsurfing, biking, walking, swimming and horseback riding are the choices for recreation on Ocracoke Island. There are several Park Service access roads to the beach for 4-wheel drive vehicles and once you're on the beach, it's possible to fish, swim, play volleyball, windsurf and sail when the conditions are right. Mainly though, Ocracoke is for activity or recreation of a non-vigorous nature -- wind surfing being the exception!

A hiking trail (see Hammock Hills Nature Trail under Attractions in this chapter) is located about 6 miles from the village, on the right as you approach from the ferry terminal. Take plenty of film for your camera. Insect repellant for most times of the year is recommended.

Bike rental places are scattered throughout the village. One convenient spot is right on the road next to the Island Ragpicker.

Horseback riding is available on Ocracoke Island through Seaside Stables, 928-3778. There's a two-hour minimum; all day and evening riding is available. Reservations are required.

Charter boat trips can be arranged at most inns and motels as well as the marinas in Ocracoke. Trips are available to the Gulf Stream, to Portsmouth Island and the sound.

Photo: DCTB

Ocracoke

SHOPPING

Shopping in Ocracoke is casual, interesting and easily managed on foot. Small shops are scattered throughout the village and set unobtrusively along the main street, on sandy lanes or in private homes. You'll also discover that some dockside stores take on the ambience of general stores and carry everything you need. Ocracoke Village shops offer a variety of local crafts, artwork, quality accessories for the home, antiques, beach wear, books and magazines as well as T-shirts and even a few souvenir mugs. The best part is the subtle charm of just happening upon a studio-type shop or gallery, rather than a series of stores set apart from other aspects of life in the village. ·

Let's start with the **Ocracoke Variety Store**, 928-4911, on Highway 12, before you enter the village.

"Hutch" and Julia Hutcherson, the owners, are most always there ready to talk about the village, their own lives and other years while you shop for groceries, beach wear, magazines, camping supplies, wine or beer. Their selection of t-shirts is the best we've seen. "Hutch" worked for A & P for many years and the store reflects that expertise. It has good light and with wide aisles the food and product arrangements are easy to find. Julia and "Hutch" are very helpful people and they keep on hand all the menus of the cafes and restaurants of the Island. So, even if you're not shopping for anything specific, stop by and take advantage of this information. They're open all year.

A short distance down the road, is **Whittler's Bench**, 928-7201. Tom and Shirley Mason opened their shop about 6 years ago. Tom was a freelance journalist and wrote for the Miami *Herald* in other times. He carves de-

coys known as Mason's Mason Decoys. His works are sold as copies and
you can hardly tell them apart from the
more famous Mason originals! Their
store displays quilts, pottery and baskets, and the upstairs gallery exhibits
a variety of artwork by local artists.

Island Ragpicker, 928-7571,
will catch your eye with an attractive
mixture of bells, baskets and rugs spill-
ing over the porch railings and hanging from the ceiling. Started a few
years ago as a place to sell their beautiful handmade rugs, the owners
Mickey Baker and Carmie Prete offer
other fine quality crafts, including
many by local crafters, handmade
brooms, cards, jewelry and some clothing. They have a nice selection of
books and gifts. And, the soft music
you hear as you browse is available on
tape. The store also serves as Ocracoke headquarters for LegaSea, an
environmental group united to oppose
offshore drilling on the Outer Banks.

Recent legislation indicates that the
efforts of this group, augmented by
determined Outer Banks citizens, has
stalled, if not permanently stopped,
the threat of oil drilling off this beautiful coast. We applaud this group for
their leadership and belief in the power
of the people. Ask for more information about this issue if you are interested; Carmie and Mickey have been
at the head of the very active Ocracoke
coalition of LegaSea so can more than
fill you in.

As you go along the main street
in the village, you'll see the **Merchant Mariner**, 928-6141, which displays attractive gifts, greeting cards
and a nice selection of clothing for
infants and children. The shop also
offers a selection of swim wear. An
usual combination of items throughout the shop makes an interesting visit.

Out back is **The Old Post Office Shop and B. W.'s Surf Shop**,
928-6141. The older part of the build-

ing was actually the Ocracoke Post Office from 1954 until 1967. Brian Waters has kept the old combination mail boxes and they are used to display shoes and other merchandise. A boutique clothing store, it carries casual and beach clothing and accessories for men and women.

The **Community Store**, 928-3321, is on the waterfront and a place where you can shop all year for essential items as well as rent videos and VCRs. Got a question? Then ask it — either inside or of someone sitting on the porch — and more than likely you'll discover another piece of history. When you approach this store, you'll smile and appreciate the reminders of another era. Feet shuffle and clonk on the wood floors inside. And, as you grab an ice cream from the cooler, you won't miss the quiet groaning of the overhead fans. The owners, David and Sherril Senseney also own **The Gathering Place**, 928-3321, across the parking lot on the Harbor. This century-old building boasts a front porch for a place to rest and look at the boats, dockside. But go on in and enjoy the local crafts, artwork, pottery and, would you believe, antique collectibles, such as old records, shoes and kitchenware. One room upstairs is an art gallery.

Island T-Shirts, 928-6781, is located in the heart of the village and has a great collection. The wide range of sizes and numerous designs make this shop hard to beat anywhere.

Kathy's Gifts & Clothing, 928-6461, located on the waterfront, occupies the first floor space of the Princess Waterfront Suites motel. Owner Kathy Cottrell has a lovely selection of accessories for the home and a fine collection of women's wear, t-shirts and jewelry.

Harborside Gifts is one of the pleasant surprises for visitors to Ocracoke. The owners know about quality and carry a wide selection of sportswear for the family, as well as some gourmet foods, books and magazines. Check out their interesting t-shirts. And, above your head you'll discover the model train that runs throughout most of the store.

North Carolina crafts are in abundance at a shop owned by Philip Howard. **Village Craftsmen**, 928-5541, has become a local landmark in the past 20 years — not a landmark easily discovered unless you're willing to explore a narrow sandy lane known as Howard Street. It's a nice walk from the main street, but please use some insect repellant in warm weather! Once there, you'll discover a wide assortment of crafts, pottery, rugs, books, soaps, candles and jams. Philip himself is an artist and his work is sold in the shop. An Outer Banks dulcimer, handmade on Hatteras by Adolph Caruso, will charm you. The necks of these instruments are a hand-carved duck's head or other coastal animal. Other musical instruments, such as precisely tuned wind chimes, door harps, catpaws and strumsticks, will invite you to a different setting and mood in this secluded, wooded hideout on Ocracoke Island.

Sunflower Studio, 928-6211, is located along one of the back streets in the village. A gallery owned by Carol O'Brien, it features fine art, one-of-a-kind jewelry and crafts. We also love their sign out front.

Albert Styron's General Store is located on the street as you approach the Ocracoke Lighthouse. Dating back to 1920, the store has recently been renovated but retains the appearance of an old general store. Some of the older fixtures remain. A wide selection of natural foods, homemade pies, cakes and cookies are available here. It was nice to notice the recycling containers outside.

If you're interested in "piratical piratephernalia" -- read, a great collection of things in the pirate mode -- then you shouldn't miss this place. Managers George and Mickey Roberson have created a gift shop and exhibit that tell the story of Edward Teach, alias "Blackbeard the Pirate," in this shop on the Back Road. See our introduction to the Ocracoke section for more information of this dastardly fellow, or, better yet, visit **Teach's Hole**, 928-1718 and ask the experts.

Black Anchor Antiques & Collectibles, 928-6301, is an interesting place to browse and select a favorite item from yesteryear. In a far corner, you'll come upon an array of old clocks just ticking away! No two are alike and the volume of clicking-ticking reminded us to slow down and enjoy some nostalgic moments and visit with Sally and Darrell Dudley for awhile. Darrell has an incredible collection of weathervanes out on the porch, perhaps the only brass moose in North Carolina. Sally's vintage jewelry, hand-shaped vases or hats give a nudge down memory lane.

The gleaming white lighthouse in Ocracoke serves as a landmark on land as well as sea.

Photo: DCTB

Elizabeth Ann O'Neal Howard
A Life On Ocracoke

*T*he bridge of time can be crossed in one direction only. But we can, by listening to those who have crossed it before us, find out much about the journey. And about how things were, back then.

The house is small and white behind its picket fence and its two live oaks. The lane is so small it has no name. "But we call it Curiosity Lane," says Elizabeth Howard, laughing like a mischievous thirteen-year-old. "Because everybody who lives here is so curious. Come on in! Let's sit in the living room. I talk better from my chair."

"I was born in nineteen ten, in what we call the Trent Woods. It was beautiful up there. I wish I could take you up and show you. There wasn't a many of houses; we all lived in that one little neighborhood; there were three houses, and then one farther down, and then that was all. It's up on the Bay. I better not say what the name of that bay used to be...when I was born there were six of us, me and my two brothers and my father and mother, and then there were my cousins.

"My daddy when he was young, he went to sea. He was born up in Trent too. There was forty-seven acres and there was my grandmother, my uncle and aunt, and my father and mother. And my uncle and my father each had three children, so there were six of us. My mother had four children, but my oldest brother died. He saw a duck, and he shot the duck, and he went in to get it. And it was freezing cold, and he caught pneumonia and died four years before I was born. Doctor MacIntyre gave him medicine but it didn't pull him through.

"I can go back in my family to seventeen hundred and fifty-nine. William Howard came and bought the island in 1759. And with him came John Williams, who was a pilot. And he witnessed the deeds. Then two months later John Williams came back and bought half of the island from William Howard. I married a Howard; but I'm an O'Neal. And my mother was a Williams. So I am about...fifth generation from John Williams.

"The O'Neal that I came from, I can't go back farther than 1774 on the O'Neal side. That's when Elizabeth Jackson married John O'Neal. And they had ten children. And I came from Christopher O'Neal, who was the youngest boy.

"My grandfather Horatio Williams was an old sea captain. My mother and her sister sailed to New York City on his vessel, the *Paragon*. And he gave them money and told them to go ashore and buy whatever they wanted. My mother's sister bought a bedroom suit, and my mother bought cashmere and embroidery and ribbons and things. For her trousseau. There were three men on the vessel, and he sent them ashore to look after them. But they all three got drunk and she and her sister had to get back to the boat the best way they could.

"When I was two and a half years old, my father bought the house that's around the corner. And they moved down here to the creek side of the island. Then later my father bought the store on the Lake. My daddy was then in the Lifesaving Service, so my double-cousin and my brother operated the store. So I've lived in this neighborhood seventy-three and a half years.

"When I was a little girl we played bob-jacks, little things made out of metal and you throw the jack up and catch them. We didn't use a ball. And we played what we called hop scotch, and croquet, and dolls. I had a lot of books with paper dolls in them; and we also cut the pictures out of the catalog and played with them.

"We had what you call a Hot Blast — a big stove that would hold wood and coal. In our living room we had a two-burner stove that looked like a piece of furniture. Kerosene. And then the kind you carry around in your hand, we had those in the bedrooms. And a fireplace in the living room, but I never used that when I was young, and now I'm old I still don't. In the kitchen we had a big iron stove with a reservoir to keep the water hot. That burned wood.

"In the summer my mother would cook on the oil stove to keep the kitchen from getting hot. In the winter she would use the wood stove. For breakfast we would have ham and eggs, or hot rolls homemade; or you could have oatmeal; or grits; or fish if you liked. I never liked fish for breakfast, I didn't like the smell. We had our main meal, what we called dinner and is now called lunch, in the middle of the day. Because when you don't have 'lectric, dark especially in the wintertime comes early. That's an old kerosene lamp there that belonged to my mother. For dinner we had chicken, it could be baked or stewed; we had lamb, my daddy had sheep on the Banks. We had oysters, fish, crab, clams, wild duck, hog meat. The hogs lived in pens in people's yards. My father had cattle down below and every week he would kill a heifer and sell it in the store. He had a refrigerator in the store that would hold sixteen cakes of ice, and twice a week he would get ice and have a man cut the meat up and he would sell it. The sheep lived on the banks, from where the pony pen is now to the town. They just roamed free. My daddy's branding iron was a diamond shape. My daddy would buy the stock and the feed and my uncle would do the work.

"Our water came from cisterns. And some people had rain barrels. A cistern catches rain water from the roof. And a lot of people had wells and lift pumps. Well, honey, you had to bathe in a wash tub or a wash basin. I played in the dirt and I took a bath every day. You were never put to bed dirty, I can tell you that. The cleanest people on earth are right here on this island. And that still goes in our family.

"I saw my first airplane in 1916, 1917. I was six or seven. It was at a funeral, it was a family connection. People were standing around out in the yard and heard the roaring of the plane. And everybody fell on the ground. They were frightened, they didn't know what the plane was there for. It was World War One. Wouldn't you have been frightened?

"I don't know how old I was when I first went off the island. I took the mail boat. It was a bugeye. It took nine hours. It went out every day, except in the hurricane of '44. I got seasick. When I was a little girl I never wanted to travel around. Later on I wanted to but I never did. And now it's just too hard. I don't really want to any more.

"I could go anywhere I wanted on the island when I was a little girl. But I couldn't wear pants, my daddy wouldn't let me. I wear them now, but he never saw me in pants. I had pretty dresses. My mother had three boys, so she knew how to make boy clothes, but she wasn't too good at making girl clothes; so my aunts, my blood kin and my aunt by marriage, made all my dresses. I had three or four silk dresses, Sunday dresses, and maybe seven or eight cotton I wore the rest of the week. The Sunday dresses I would wear all day. And I remember the minister's son lived right across from us, and this little boy and I were playing, and we got in to some briars and I tore my silk dress. And my mother didn't spank me. She never spanked me for tearing my dresses. She only spanked me when I talked back to her.

"I wasn't allowed to go barefoot either. My daddy wouldn't let me go barefooted because we had horses in the yard. He was afraid of lockjaw. I wore Mary Janes, with straps, patent leather. But when my father wasn't home I used to go across the street with the parson's children and take my shoes off and play in the sand.

"At Christmas we would have a tree and Santa Claus would come. And everybody would go to the church, to the exercise on Christmas Eve. The Methodist church, that's all we had then. There would be a tree there too, and it's traditional that everybody who goes gets a bag of candy and peanuts, raisins, apple, orange in that bag. All of my life that happened, and I don't know how many years before. And on Christmas Eve night all the children had recitations, and we would put on a pageant. I can't remember anything I recited, but I remember one little boy, I can always remember the things I don't need to — he had a recitation that went, "Who's old Santy, I don't know/Great long whiskers hangin' down so." That little boy's name was Thomas Gilbert Jackson. He is still living here.

"You gave presents, you gave every member of your family presents. I remember when I believed in Santa Claus, that is I didn't know but what there wasn't a Santa Claus, I remember my cousin taking me to the other side of the Lake, to John McWilliam's store. She got a little toy cooking stove, and little frying pan, little pot, and then she bought a little clothesline and pins, and a big ball. Maybe I was a little stupid, but I didn't think anything about it. Oh, and a little tea set, and a little piano. And we left and I never thought about it and my mother hid everything for Christmas. But I searched, and I found it and I was in trouble. To this day I can never put anything back in a drawer the way I found it. But the next year the other children told me there wa'n't any Santa Claus. I don't know how I thought he got here — probably on the mail boat.

"What did we do in the winter? Some people quilted; I don't but I have some beautiful ones that were given to me. Do you know what a Chautauqua is? The Chautauqua came twice a year. And there were dances for the adults maybe every weekend, and in the summer every night. At the dance hall. One was down near the docks and the other was at the Pamlico Inn. And then there was one at the Odd Fellows' Lodge. When I grew up I danced at all of them. And people had parties in their homes. Dinner parties, and parties for the children. And candy-pulling, where you make candy and pull it and put it on a plate and let it get hard. And people would put on shows, they still do. Of course we had radios. But no one on the island knew how to fix them. So we just bought new ones when they wouldn't work any more.

"I grew up fast. All through my childhood I was taller than most children my age...when I was ten years old my father left the store in the neighborhood and moved down to the waterfront. My first cousin went with us and my mama sent me down there too. I had chores to do; I had to empty the Pepsi container, where they'd throw their empty bottles, and I had to take the trash out, sweep the front porch, and I had to take the oranges that were going bad out of the orange box, and the apples, and the grape box, had to throw away all the things you couldn't sell. The name of the store was Big Ike's. His name was Ike. It was on the waterfront. When I was a little girl the big boats couldn't get into the creek. The sailing vessels had to anchor out in the sound and you'd have to send a man out in his skiff and get my daddy's goods off the boat and bring it to my daddy's pier. You could pole out with a big oar.

"I was about twelve years old when a man from Hatteras came over here selling Model T Fords and my daddy bought one. And you know what he paid for it? Five hundred dollars. And Dallas Williams and David Williams bought one from the same man. Then later Captain Bill Gaskill bought a great big truck. He had the Pamlico Inn, that was where they took boarders — tourists. Tourists came here before I was ever born. This picture was taken in 1915 when I was five years old...this hotel had a hundred rooms. And I remember we were looking at that truck and somebody said, 'Captain Bill, is that a Ford?' And he said, 'It's all I can a-ford.'

"The cars could take you to the beach, but frankly you pushed more than you rode. If we left the island, going to Hatteras, we rode the high-water mark. We'd have to leave the car down at the inlet and took the Coast Guard boat across. On the other side we'd visit among our relatives and come back the same way we went.

"During the depression there wasn't any money here. People who were in the Coast Guard, or the light-house, it didn't hurt them. But it hurt our family. It knocked the props from under my father. Because if you have a business and nobody has any money you can't sell anything, and if you do it just goes on the books...but even at that, nobody here went hungry. You couldn't here, you had fish, crabs, oysters were plentiful. That's what they'd give you at the store. Everybody had gardens.

"I finished the eighth grade here, then I went to school in North Carolina. Most children did that. I was fifteen when I went away to school. It was a private school which I thought was the army — you got up by the bugle and you went to bed with the bugle. It isn't there any more.

"After high school I wanted the bright lights and glitter, and the five and ten cent store. I had a job offered to me in Raleigh, to work with a doctor. I wrote to my mother telling her that and she wrote telling me to come home, my father needed me. So I came home. And I worked in my daddy's store. And after that I worked for Robert S. Wahab at what used to be the Wahab Hotel. They had the hotel, a skating rink, a movie theatre, and the dance hall, the Spanish Casino.

"That's another thing, why people came to Ocracoke and lived during the summer. Malaria, on the mainland. And you wouldn't get it on Ocracoke; these salt water mosquitoes don't carry malaria. All the little houses along the sound side were the people who came here during the summer to get away from the malaria.

"I married a Howard, Robert Wahab Howard. Did we grow up together...yes and no; I was three years older than he was and he grew up to me. That's a picture of him over there in his Navy uniform. He was a good-looking man, and he was smart. He was only in for the duration of the war but he made permanent chief. He could have stayed in. I wanted him to, but one day he took me aside and said, 'I got something to say and I want you to listen. If I stay in we won't have much time together. I want a home and a family, and I want to be home with my family. So don't tell me any more you want me to stay in the Navy.' I always thought he could have gotten the pension...but he died when he was only sixty. I thought then, he must have known. We were married in 1942. August the seventeenth.

"My daughter was born in the house around the corner from me. She wasn't supposed to be. I was supposed to be in Washington N.C., Little Washington the Tarheels call it. But she came early when I was getting dressed to get on the mail boat. I was making coffee when I felt the first pains. They brought a bed downstairs and that's where they put me. They had a registered nurse here and a practical nurse, Lola Williams, and they delivered my daughter. Lola stayed with me for ten days. And I remember my father said to my mother, 'Helen, that child will talk sooner than any child ever talked.' And my mother said, 'Why do you say

that?' And my father said, 'Because she's been in that room with Lola and Elizabeth for ten days and they haven't shut up once.'

"In World War Two things changed. You could go down to the naval base, if you had family in the Navy, and you could buy anything you wanted — a gold watch or anything. They had entertainment, USO shows. I never saw a ship actually get torpedoed; but we could hear it, boom boom booom. And you could step up on my daddy's porch and see the blaze. In that respect it was scary here. Everything was blacked out. The lighthouse had a blind on it. I asked my daddy one night, 'Papa, if the Germans take Ocracoke what will we do?' He said, 'Well honey I don't know what you'll do, but I think I'll kill m'self.' And my sister-in-law's a full-fledged German.

"Now things are changing here like everywhere. I don't think people here are as friendly as they used to be when I was growing up. People used to share their food. And we still do in this neighborhood, and I'm sure in the other neighborhoods too. But not everybody's like that. They can't afford to be. One thing, we don't have too many original families here any more. That's the Williamses, the O'Neals, the Garrishes, the Howards, and the Gaskills. And the Scarboroughs and the Spencers. They're all originally Ocracokers. Well, I won't say all the children are originals because their fathers or mothers may have come from some other place. I'm actually all Ocracoke. O'Neal and Williams and Tolson and Jackson. English and they say the Williamses are Welsh. Isn't it different where you live, where your grandmother lived, than it is now? I don't want to say things that will offend anybody, but when I grew up Ocracoke had the best class of people.

"The nicest thing about it still is that people here have more freedom. You don't live in fear here as much as in the cities. When my little girl was little she could run anywhere on the island, and in fact we'd let her take people around. Nothing has ever hurt me so I've never been afraid of things.

"My granddaughters now, for instance, they're nineteen and twenty-one. And they come and stay with me every summer. They wear pants. So that's changed. But I remember something my daddy said to my mother once, when I was fifteen and my cousin and I wanted to go to Hatteras for a dance, the Woodmen of the World opening, and stay overnight with our relatives. My mother said I shouldn't go, that her mother would never have allowed her to. But my father said, 'Let them go. Time changes. And people have to change with it.' I always remembered that because like it or not I think he was right.

Outer Banks
Restaurants

*S*eafood and lots of it is the mainstay of Outer Banks restaurants. From the in-shore and off-shore waters, many species of fish are available on menus as catch-of-the-day or traditional entrees.

Select from broiled or fried fish or culinary delights with special butters and sauces. Some restaurants have seafood trios, small portions of several fish filets. Others serve seafood, stuffed with crabmeat or shellfish stuffed with crabmeat.

Speaking of crabmeat, Outer Banks She-Crab soup, chowders and crabcakes are standard fare at most area restaurants. Soft shell crabs are the rage in spring. Crabmeat cocktails are plentiful in the appetizer section of most menus.

If you're into picking your own crabs, more than likely you'll do it at your own cottage, on an outdoor picnic table. Buy them already steamed or freshly caught to steam them in your own kettle. Restaurants on the Outer Banks have phased out the all-you-can-eat-steamed crabs affairs, where butcher paper, mallets and knives were the only table-dressing. The local seafood stores carry steamers with racks, seasonings and know-how for these great American feasts of summer.

Oysters and clams provide additional temptation when you're visiting the Outer Banks. Raw bars are noted at many restaurants. The same for scallops. They are plentiful and served in a number of ways: fried, sauteed and broiled.

Shrimp are plentiful and prices are very good at local stores for buying them by the pound for a quick steam. Shrimp served in restaurants range from large ones stuffed with crabmeat to creole dishes or simply sauteed or broiled.

Check out the restaurants in several villages, buy from local stores or catch your own. Seafood is plentiful on the Outer Banks, and a well-prepared seafood dinner is about the best cap to a day on the beach that we can think of.

OUTER BANKS STYLE CLAM CHOWDER

Every seafaring area takes its clam chowder seriously. Chowders come in three basic varieties. Manhattan Clam Chowder has a tomato base and may be on the spicy side with hints of Tabasco, thyme, basil and oregano. New England Clam Chowder is generally considered to have a milk base and has salt pork, onion and always potatoes added. The Outer Banks variety (call it Hatteras style, Wanchese style or whatever) uses neither tomato or milk, but prefers to feature the clams in their own broth or liquor. Other ingredients may include diced potatoes, chopped onions, celery, parsley and the chef's choice of spices which enhance the clam flavor. Chowder will sour very easily if it is not handled properly, especially if made in big batches. Chowder chefs agree that the cover on a pot of chowder should never be left on while it is cooling because the condensation will spoil it. A chowder should never go into the refrigerator until it has completely cooled to room temperature. Any skin that forms on the top of a cooled chowder should be carefully skimmed off. A chowder always tastes better on the second, or even third day, if it doesn't ferment first! Chowder is not easy to make and even harder to keep. It is little wonder that chowder chefs are so sensitive and proud of their vulnerable creations.

It is very possible that no two Outer Banks clam chowders are the same. Perhaps they are not even the same at the same restaurant from one day to the next. It is the challenge and delight of the would-be chowder gourmet to sample the field and declare his or her own preferences.

HUSHPUPPIES

Many seafood restaurants on the Outer Banks serve up a basket of hushpuppies with their entrees. Hushpuppies are a traditional Southern deep fried corn meal bread. The corn meal, flour, baking powder, salt, sugar, egg and milk batter is dropped by the spoonful into deep hot fat and allowed to fry until it is golden brown.

Some Southern areas add finely chopped onion to their mix and like to fry the hushpuppy in the same oil used to fry the fish. But the quintessential Outer Banks hushpuppy cook eschews the onion and the fishy hint to his or her creations in favor of a sweet, almost cake-like quality that is achieved by increasing the flour and sugar ratio and frying in oils reserved just for hushpuppies.

Hushpuppies can vary in diameter. Some cooks believe that the size of the round crispy breads is the secret to their texture and taste. Others guard their batter recipes in the conviction that they have discovered the perfect hushpuppy formula. Many restaurants on the Banks have loyal followers who are convinced that their hushpuppies are the best.

To tell the truth, few restaurants make hushpuppies from scratch anymore. There are excellent commercial mixes which get "doctored" so that the cook can claim it as his or her own. The quantitative and qualitative difference may actually be very small.

By legend, and this is perhaps a true one, hushpuppies got their name as southern cooks prepared the evening meal. Hungry hunting dogs would hang around the kitchen and bark for their share of the meal being prepared. The harried cooks, trying to get a meal completed for a waiting family, attempted to appease and quiet the dogs with bits of corn bread batter dropped into the hot frying fat. The little fried dough balls were thrown out the kitchen door with the admonishment, "hush puppy!"

PLANNING & PRICING

For many years almost all seafoods served on the Banks were deep fried. Today, the broiler and grill are just as popular, and there is a trend toward even further preparation diversity as chefs trained in other traditions come to cook on the Outer Banks.

The establishment of liquor by the drink on the main resort strip (Kitty Hawk, Kill Devil Hills, Nags Head) in 1981 heralded a remarkable surge in new restaurant construction, renovation of established places and rethinking all along the beach. The bar and lounge business has contributed to upgrading restaurant menus, decor and service wherever it has been allowed. Beer, wine and brown bagging are available on Roanoke, Hatteras and Ocracoke Islands and in Corolla. (See Service Directory-Liquor Laws for more information.)

The restaurant competition on the Outer Banks is keen. The prime vacation months account for a large percentage of a restaurant's income, so the good business person cannot afford to be outmaneuvered by menu pricing. Competitive enterprise seems to be working here to the consumer's benefit.

We see a basic uniformity of entree pricing for the most popular items. For example, a flounder filet stuffed with crabmeat, presented in restaurants of equal ambiance and kitchen quality, will cost about the same price. For our readers' convenience we have established four categories as a guide to menu prices. The costs are based on dinner for two persons which includes appetizers, entrees, two vegetables or side dishes, desserts and coffee. Specials and other factors can lower the basic check total just as cocktails, wine and flaming tableside desserts can increase it. For restaurants that don't serve dinner, the guideline is based on relative expense.

Restauranteurs with pocket calculators can easily challenge our best intentions in offering these guidelines. Personal choices and menu changes will prove us wrong in some cases. But we hope you'll bear in mind that these are only meant to be guides and adopt our dining-out attitude: Enjoy your favorite offerings on the menu and be prepared to pay the bill. Here are the guidelines that are reflected in the restaurant profiles to follow:

A basic meal for two under $25 **$**

A check for two of $26 to $40. **$$**

A check for two of $41 to $55. **$$$**

Over $55 for two. **$$$$**

These guides do not reflect the 6% NC sales tax or the gratuity which should be at least 15% for good service. Some restaurants offer discounts and specials for early evening dining in order to encourage their patrons to avoid the peak dining hours. It is no secret that in-season, and on shoulder season weekends, the waiting lines at popular restaurants are long. Few restaurants will accept reservations except for large parties. We list a season of operation for each restaurant. But please note: while we make every effort to get accurate information, in a competitive, active market like the Outer Banks, even the best-laid plans can get scrapped mid-season. If you're visiting off-season, it's best to call ahead before you make dinner plans.

The restaurants profiled in this guide are arranged by mile marker, north to south, Corolla to Ocracoke.⊷

Photo: Michael Halminski

Besides tourism, fishing is still the lifeblood of the Outer Banks, so you can rest assured that the seafood found here is as always fresh.

Northern Beaches

RESTAURANTS

Just a few years ago, Sanderling Inn provided the only restaurant on the northern beaches. There are more to choose from these days and while they don't have the large spacious dining rooms for seafood feasts that you find in Nags Head or other Outer Banks villages, the atmosphere is casual, the food is good and there are some wonderful surprises.

ELIZABETH'S CAFE & WINERY
Scarborough Faire, Duck   261-6145
$$-$$$ MC, VISA, AMEX

This was the year of international recognition for Elizabeth's. Voted by *The Wine Spectator* magazine as one of the best in the world meant that this cafe and winery met high standards for its wines. Gaining in popularity by those who enjoy fine wines in combination with fine foods, Elizabeth's will delight newcomers. The ambience is warm and casual. A fireplace is lit for early spring, fall and winter dining. Service is excellent and the waiters are knowledgeable about wines, which is a plus for those who are just learning. The menus change continually for lunch and dinner. Fresh ingredients and classic dishes with fresh seafood offer some of the best dining on the Outer Banks.

It's a small place, so make reservations or come early. In summer, there is some outdoor dining on the deck which is nice during lunch. In the evenings, outdoor dining is sometimes accompanied by live music especially on week ends. Elizabeth's is open all year.

BLUE POINT BAR AND GRILL
The Waterfront Shops, Duck   261-8090
$$-$$$ MC, VISA

The Blue Point has become one of the most popular places on the Outer

Banks. Those Two Guys, John Power and Sam McGann, have hit on a good thing with their classic, 1940-style diner on the soundfront. The small bar is a welcome place to have a cocktail or eat lunch. The menu is creatively nouvelle and always changing. The homemade soups, unusual seafood dishes, or steak and potatoes, and great salads tempt your palate. And, while the regular food is anything but regular, the desserts have gone out-of-sight, with Ms. Phyllis' creations. The pecan pie topped with whipped cream and an ample sprinkling of cinnamon is almost sinful. We won't mention the chocolate concoction with almond crust, dribbled with Chambourd (raspberry) sauce.

Dining at Blue Point, or the Point as it's called by locals, can't be matched. Never mind the noise or that the tables are close together on the inside. The outdoor eating, a real enclosure of the deck, is sometimes noisy, too. If it's not the ducks and geese, it's all those people enjoying good food, good conversation — letting the good times roll. A stop here is a must. Open for lunch and dinner all year.

BARRIER ISLAND INN

Duck Road, Duck Village   261-3901
$$$ MC, VISA, AMEX

Barrier Island Inn was one of the first good restaurants on the northern beaches. As you come around the curve just past the shops of the Village, you'll see the flags flying at the sailing center which is located outside on the soundfront of Barrier Island Inn. Right

away you know you'll have some activity to watch while you dine during most of the year. The views from inside are spectacular, the food and friendliness just as good. The bar offers locals and visitors a chance to mix with a shuffleboard table, large screen TV and its own menu of small meals. In summer, outdoor dining is available. The Inn is open all year for breakfast, lunch and dinner.

SANDERLING INN RESTAURANT

Sanderling, north of Duck   261-3021
$$$$ MC, VISA, AMEX

The restored lifesaving station, Caffey's Inlet Station No. 5, has become a wonderful place for year round dining. The cuisine is a nice blend of very good American food with some special Carolina recipes that will appeal to you. The wine list is very good and the desserts are all homemade.

The popularity of Sanderling is noted on the special dining nights, food-tastings and wine-tastings plus all the holiday feasts you can imagine. New Year's Eve at Sanderling is a traditional event carried out in grand style with dinner, champagne and music. The Sunday Brunch buffet draws the crowds for sumptuous foods.

Sanderling is open all year and dining here provides you with expansive ocean and sound views from the oceanfront dining room. If you prefer a quiet, private ambience perhaps the smaller Boat Room will catch your mood.

Reservations are accepted and

children's portions are available at dinner.

MONTERAY CAFE
Monteray Plaza
Whalehead Beach, Corolla 453-8833

As we go to press, Monteray Cafe has not quite opened; however, it's due to open in mid-June. Bob and Jan Kannry operated a restaurant in Nags Head a few years ago that was so popular, locals are still lamenting its loss (it burned). But, now we will sob no more, since Bob and Jan are again on the scene in Corolla.

A cafe-bistro approach is used in the 100-seat cafe with a wine bar. There will be an extensive wine list, and Bob and Jan are experts on the subject. The menu offers what is known as free-style or international cuisine. This French method allows the chef to go to the market daily and obtain the freshest seafood, vegetables and other ingredients for the day's meals.

There will be tables and booths available in Monteray Cafe which will be decorated in shades of green, maroon and ecru. It sounds like a winner for the north beach area, and you can rest assured that many loyal "diners from the past" will make the hour drive from Manteo to be regulars here.

NICOLETTA'S ITALIAN CAFE
Corolla Light Village Shops 453-4666
$$ MC, VISA

This small Italian cafe opened last October and already has a fine reputation for a wide variety of foods, well-prepared by award-winning chef and owner Ron Nicoletta. There are several choices of Italian seafood, chicken and veal entrees and pastas -- very good food and offered with a small but very select wine list. All sauces are homemade. After years of experience with east coast hotels, Ron brings his love of fine cuisine and his expertise in preparation to the Outer Banks in impressive style.

This charming cafe features a black and white floor, white table cloths and fresh flowers on the tables and black chairs for a clean yet sophisticated and happy ambience. A separate room is available for private parties. There's a wine bar as well. Nicoletta's is open for lunch and dinner all year except some weekends during the winter months.

Nicoletta's Pizzeria
Corolla Light Village Shops 453-4004
$ MC, VISA

A charming addition to the Corolla scene, Nicoletta's Pizzeria opened in April of '92 for lunch and dinner. The decor is mauve, burgundy and black, with lots of plants situated among the eight tables and mother-of-pearl looking chairs. A juke box brings a youthful ambience to this second restaurant in Corolla owned by Ron Nicoletta.

Pizza, calzones and other Italian dishes are all homemade and delicious! In addition, an assortment of cold subs is on the menu. It's open all year, too.

Kitty Hawk

RESTAURANTS

We were here.

FAST EDDIE'S

The Marketplace, Southern Shores

MP 1   **261-8585**

No credit cards

Fast Eddie's is a new concept in dining. Owned by the Miller family its decor is bright, informal and a cross between a family restaurant and a dance hall with bar. The hamburgers are the greatest, featuring beef freshly ground by the butcher and cooked the way you want them. There's always a line in the summer, but while you're waiting you can run over the menu board high up on the wall until you're sure about your selection. The butcher shop, the bakery and ice cream shop and the bar offer many selections of good food to eat in or carry out. There's a juke box and on the upper level of Fast Eddie's you'll find the Outer Banks Shag Club congregating on Monday nights for line dancing and celebrating good beach music. The shiny hardwood floor is perfect for a real work out. Stop by, order something to eat, dance the night away, or just watch.

SPORTSMAN'S RESTAURANT

Route 158, MP 4   (919) 261-4600

No credit cards

A very popular restaurant run by the Lacy McNeill family, the Sportman's is big on friendliness, all-you-can-eat specials and good prices. A breakfast here could include a wait-

ing time, as it's probably the most frequented breakfast eatery on the beach. Informality and large portions keep people coming back year after year. The Sportsman's serves breakfast lunch and dinner almost all year. It's a popular place with visitors and locals for good food at very reasonable prices.

STATION SIX

Beach Road, MP 4-1/2   261-7337

MC/VISA

Station Six is a wonderful place to dine. The building is a former life-saving station and invites small intimate groups for excellent dining overlooking the ocean. There is live music here most evenings during the summer, and a wait on the deck for pre-dinner cocktails is refreshing. Linen table cloths and fresh flowers add a special touch. There's a new chef this year and owner Mimi Adams insists on the best, so give it a try. Station Six is open from Easter till Thanksgiving.

KEEPER'S GALLEY

Route 158, MP 4-1/2   261-4000

MC, VISA

R.V. Owens has a reputation on the beach for good food, and Keeper's Galley supports his reputation. The Owens family has several other restaurants as well that are all known for exceptional quality. You'll be more than satisfied with the choices here. It's open for breakfast, lunch and dinner all year except in the late winter months when the staff gets to take a

Drawing by Jerry Miller.

Bodie Island lighthouse.

break from all that good service and food. The nautical decor, polished wood and sea-faring nets attractively arranged, make this a great place for families as well as intimate dining. It's located next to the Days Inn Motel on the east side of the highway.

either side of the building. There are some interesting stories-in-pictures facing the glass enclosure to keep you occupied while you wait for your order. Call ahead for carry-outs. The decor is as good as any seafood shack in the world.

JOHN'S DRIVE-IN

Beach Road, MP 4-1/2   261-2916

John's has been an institution on the Beach Road for years. The fresh fish sandwiches or creamy ice cream shakes and sundaes are worth driving miles to reach. Locals can't get enough of the good food here, for take out or to eat at one of the picnic tables set on

CAPT'N FRANKS

Route 158, MP 4-1/2   261-9923

If it's been awhile since you tried a real southern hot dog, Capt'n Franks is a must stop. The Hess family has been serving hot dogs to the Outer Banks for nearly 20 years. Just walk up to the place and there's an assault on your senses you won't forget. The

Photo: Phillip Ruckle

assortment of toppings for hot dogs stretches the imagination and the french fries with cheese is a different twist. Capt'n Franks has picnic tables outside and carry out service. Call ahead for carry-outs whenever possible at this busy place. Open all year except Sundays in the winter.

KITTY HAWK PIZZA
Route 158, MP 4-1/2   261-3933

One of the best places to eat on the beach is Kitty Hawk Pizza. You'll keep coming back. Locals and vacationers love the pizza and other treats on the menu. The low prices are attractive as well. The emphasis on Greek food, seldom found on the Outer Banks, is a nice surprise. The booths and recently added Mediterranean Room afford large crowds or a table for two. It's more than a pizza parlor and for this author, it's a favorite place to stop in, eat some good food and write for an hour or longer during the off-season when taking up space isn't a problem.

It's comfortable, has some of the friendliest people on the beach and incredible plants...if you find the beginning or the end of the philodendron, it'll be worth the trip.

TRADEWINDS
Route 158, MP 4-1/2   261-3502

If you're in the mood for Chinese food, Tradewinds is a good choice and one of the very few restaurants that doesn't specialize in fresh seafood. Tradewinds is located in a strip shopping center on the east side of the highway yet stands alone when it comes to Mandarin-style dishes. They're willing to cook dishes to your specification -- if you prefer lightly steamed vegetables without a sauce -- or a variation on the good food they always serve. Carry out is popular here, but the generous portions of perfectly cooked Chines dishes -- they do have a large variety on the menu -- are served best in this dimly lit restaurant. They're open for lunch and dinner all year.

Kill Devil Hills

RESTAURANTS

STACK 'EM HIGH
Route 158, MP 4-1/2 & MP 9
261-8221 & 441-7064

$-$$ **No credit cards**

These two popular breakfast eateries -- one in Kitty Hawk and the other in Kill Devil Hills -- will get you started on any vacation morning. Their specialties are good pancakes, good service and convenience to both ends of the beach. The owners Kiki and Perry Kiousis opened their Kill Devil Hills restaurant over ten years ago and they know how to fix breakfast. Several varieties of pancakes are available as well as English muffins, Danish pastries, and cereal; ordinary eggs, bacon and sausage for die-hards, too! There's a limited lunch menu, but just get there soon after the noon hour or they'll be closed. Both locations are open from early spring through Thanksgiving.

SLIPPERY SANDS AT AVALON PIER
Beach Road, MP 6   **441-0527**

$-$ **MC, VISA**

Good food, friendly, attentive service and wide open views of the Atlantic Ocean are found here! The restaurant is under new management and is a great place for breakfast, lunch and dinner almost any day in season. Fresh fish, of course, is the best choice and the usual side orders of french fries, cole slaw. It's worth getting up and going for an early breakfast at 6:00 a.m. It doesn't get much better than having breakfast while the sun rises over the ocean! Lunch and dinner are served almost all year until around 9:00 p.m. Try an early weekend breakfast at 2:00 a.m. -- night fishing brings on a big appetite. Stop by and see Sam Bryan, now in charge of this small, delightful pier restaurant.

AWFUL ARTHUR'S
Beach Road, MP 6   **441-5955**

$$ **MC, VISA, AMEX**

This is very popular spot on the Beach Road across from Avalon Pier. It expanded a year ago and even with a second floor lounge is still crowded. But it's casual and folks at the beach love this place, especially for their steamed seafood -- our publisher will travel all the way up from Manteo (a 40-mile round trip, mind you) just to pig out on the Alaskan crab legs...oh, okay, for the Bass Ale on tap, too) . The seafood is great, the ambience is real "salty" and the local people pack in here all year. Famous Awful Arthur's t-shirts are seen all over the east coast.

FINELY RON'S
Route 158, Bypass MP 5-1/2 441-1664

$$$ **MC, VISA, AMEX**

Located in Seagate North Shopping Center, Ron and Jean Davidson lavish their expertise on their diners.

They have over 20 years combined experience and offer a variety of interesting choices. Lobster specials are popular. Soups are homemade. Finely Ron's is open all year and they offer a children's menu. You'll find a nice, cozy ambience, table cloths and fresh flowers.

NEWBY'S

Route 158, Bypass MP 6   441-7277
$ No credit cards

Newby's has become an Outer Banks institution with excellent sandwiches, subs, yogurt and ice cream. It's a favorite choice for lunch for residents and vacationers will approve of the informality -- stop in before or after a day at the beach! They're open late and open before noon, all year except as noted on their outdoor board.

JOLLY ROGER RESTAURANT

Beach Road, MP 7   441-6530
$$ MC, VISA

Jolly Roger's is a local favorite and is open 365 days a year for breakfast, starting at 6 a.m. Mon. through Sat., 7 a.m. on Sunday, lunch and dinner until 10 p.m. In the lounge, food is served until 1 a.m. The food is good, portions ample and you'll have

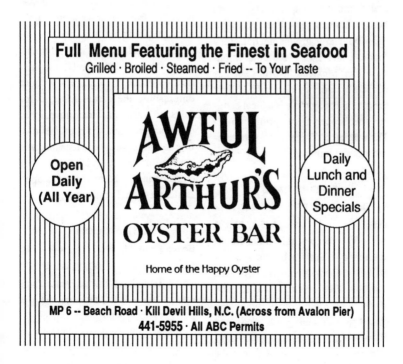

a "jolly time" here. There's live music nightly and the menu proudly presents home-style Italian dishes, local seafood and steaks.

PAPAGAYO'S

Beach Road, MP 7-1/2   441-7232
$$ MC, VISA

The old Croatan Inn is a landmark on the beach but now it's dressed in a sort of rustic, Mexican decor with interesting, tasteful cuisine. If you look closely, though, you'll see remnants of the old Inn, especially upstairs in the lounge or on the oceanfront deck. The view from one area of the dining room along the ocean is great, the food and friendliness superb. The dining here is fun and sometimes gets a bit noisy with large groups and hot, spicy foods. Outer Banks seafood, cajun-style fish, Mexican favorites such as enchiladas and chimichangas highlight the menu. Papagayo's is a local hangout and is open from spring through Thanksgiving. There's live entertainment in the lounge.

PORT O' CALL

Beach Road, MP 8   441-7484
$$$ MC, VISA, AMEX

The menu at this Outer Banks landmark restaurant boasts a continental cuisine with entrees like broiled shrimp stuffed with crabmeat, a whole array of seafood entrees, plus veal, chicken, beef and good soups and chowders. Fresh fruit and salads compliment your dinner choice and the desserts are excellent. A children's menu is offered.

Frank Gajar opened this restaurant in the mid-70s and his collection of Victorian furnishings in the Gaslight Saloon or the upper balcony offers a romantic touch for quiet dinner. Not at all typical of the Outer Banks, it's a great place and its popularity brings people back time and time again.

A Sunday Buffet is a must while you're at the beach. The Thanksgiving buffet is a highlight of a quieter time at the beach. A variety of live entertainment is on and off the small stage in the Gaslight Saloon. Last but not least, the gift shop/art gallery are attractions on their own. Furnishings and gifts from around the world are displayed in an unusual shop.

Overall the service and ambience of Port O'Call reflect the sophistication of the Victorian era without diminishing the casual lifestyle for folks on vacation. Hanging painted glass lamps, window treatments of a fine hotel-restaurant and brass accents are used throughout, adding a touch of extravagance. The restaurant is open Easter through Thanksgiving.

THAI ROOM

Beach Road, MP 8-1/2   441-1180
$$ MC, VISA, AMEX

This beach road restaurant opened about five years ago and is a popular year round place for locals. The wide choices of excellent cuisine are not the ordinary for oriental tastes. If you're ready to try something dif-

Photo: Michael Halminski

ferent, you'll be glad you chose the Thai Room. The menu notes the level of spiciness, so when you decide on your main entree whether it's Thai Beef Curry or spicy Chicken with noodles, or one of the many variations of shrimp, lobster and fish, let the waiter know how you like your spicy -- hot, medium or with a light touch. The soups and egg rolls are delightful.

The decor takes you away from the beach nautical, found all around the beach, and the owners can offer suggestions if you're reluctant to dive into a new adventure in dining. Carry out is available. They're open for lunch and dinner most of the year.

ETHERIDGE SEAFOOD RESTAURANT
Route 156, Bypass, MP 9-1/2
441-2645

$$ **MC, VISA**

The Etheridge family has become an Outer Banks tradition when it comes to dining on fresh seafood. This restaurant opened in 1986 to offer the fresh seafood the Etheridge fishing fleet hauls in from over in Wanchese. The decor is nautical, of course, but a round dining room provides a different ambience, especially in the semi-private corners labeled "Stamtisch," which is German for meeting place.

Etheridges is a popular place for locals and visitors alike. The seafood is some of the best on the beach, the service is very good and you'll be please with a decision to dine here.

They offer a children's menu and some non-seafood dishes. Open for lunch and dinner seven days a week from March through December.

PIGMAN'S BARBEQUE
Route 158, Bypass, MP 9-1/2
441-6803

$-$$ **MC, VISA**

Pigman's rib-man Bill Shaver opened Ye Old Ham Shoppe in 1985 and about a year ago, moved to a new location to open this fabulous rib restaurant. You might wonder if you're at a pet shop when you meet "Joker," Bill's blue and gold macaw and his pet pigs "Auggie" and "Piggy Lou" -- who manage to keep their good dispositions despite the bill of fare that draws rib-lovers from all over. If it's barbeque you're hungry for try beef, pork or tuna served with super cole slaw and fries. The red and white exterior is attractive, the aromas irresistible for year round eating. Opens at 10 a.m. and closes around 8 p.m. most of the year, but during the vacation season, they're open until 9:00. It's the place to go for barbeque, eat in or carry out.

CHARDO'S
Route 158, Bypass, MP 9   441-0276

$$$ **MC, VISA, AMEX**

Chardo's is an elegant Italian restaurant specializing in seafood and meats with northern Italian flavors. Their pastas are wonderful and fresh sauteed or steamed vegetables accompany entrees. Salads, prepared with originality and flair, are an interesting combination of vegetable chunks, salami and flavorful dressings. Service is formal and attentive by a well-trained staff. The bar is away from the main dining area, which is nice, and several smaller rooms offer an intimate atmosphere for a special occasion. A favorite of locals diners, it will appeal to vacationers who've been on the beach all day and want to go out for a nice dinner. You can linger without feeling rushed, but it's a good idea to call for reservations. Children can be served half-portions at half price. The wine list features the top California wines. They're open all year.

MILLER'S SEAFOOD & STEAK HOUSE

Beach Road, MP 9-1/2   441-7674

$$ MC, VISA, AMEX

The Miller family has restaurants all over the Outer Banks. For diners on a budget, but accustomed to good food and friendly service, this restaurant will appeal to many. A family restaurant where all-you-can-eat dinners are a favorite, Miller's fits the bill for informal dining near the beach. Seafood is served fried, broiled and sauteed. The menu offers prime rib and filet mignon along with beef ka-

bob and surf and turf combination.

The restaurant also offers breakfast, has a moderately priced children's menu and is open March through November.

OSPREY ISLAND GRILLE

Route 158, MP 10   441-6894

$$ MC, VISA

This attractive restaurant is a favorite with local diners and owner Chuck Voigt has mastered the art of well-prepared, inexpensive lunch and dinners. The menu is limited, but the flavors run the gamut from Italian to Mexican. Seafood and cajun seasoning are used in some dishes. The portions are ample and the quality of food good. Daily specials are offered and the restaurant features a salad bar. The dessert are all homemade with a very good key-lime pie one of my favorites. Open all year with full bar service.

SHIP'S WHEEL

Beach Road, MP 10   441-2906

MC, VISA

The Van Curen family has a reputation for great food at reasonable prices here on the Outer Banks. Sons Keith and Michael run the restaurant now located on the beach road. Break-

---

Insiders like:
Soft shell crab sandwiches (during the molting season), a specialty on the Outer Banks.

Insiders' Tip

fast at the beach is a tradition and you won't be disappointed here. The big plates (almost as big as cafeteria trays) are loaded with a variety of good pancakes, waffles, eggs and omelets. Lunch and dinner are backed up with a great salad bar and feature seafood, fried or broiled. They're open seven days a week March through November.

GOOMBAYS GRILLE & RAW BAR
Beach Road, MP 8   441-6001
$$ MC, VISA

Goombays is new on the Beach Road this year in the location of the old Whaling Station, but owner John Kirchmier is a 10-year veteran of Outer Banks restaurants and bars -- owning or managing several popular places like Quagmire's and Horsefeathers. Goombays features great appetizers, pastas, burgers and sandwiches for lunch and dinner. The bar is fun and colorful. The separate raw bar can't be beat. Caribbean casual reflects John's acquaintance with that area where white provides a nice contrast to tropical colors. A new restaurant features a new t-shirts and there's no exception here. Goombays shirts are cleverly designed originals and before the summer is over, we'll probably see them everywhere.

John promises good food with soft shell crabs, fresh fish and seafood leading the way. These entrees plus the long list of appetizers are moderately priced. Open all year from 11:30 a.m. for lunch til 10:30 p.m. for din-

ner. The bar is open until 2:00 a.m.

COLINGTON CAFE
999 Colington Rd., I mi. west of Bypass
480-1123
$$ MC, VISA

An intimate Victorian cafe situated in the trees on Colington Road, this is one of the most popular spots for moderately priced dining. The renovated older home contains three small dining rooms in which well-prepared French cuisine is offered for dinner only. They're open from 5 p.m. until 9:30 p.m. every day except in January. Homemade crab bisque is featured and their daily specials offer excellent pasta dishes and a mixed grill with hollandaise. The mixed-grill changes daily to include the freshest seafood in season.

CASPER'S RAW BAR & RESTAURANT
Colington Rd., 1-1/2 mi. west of Bypass
480-1897
$$ MC, VISA

Casper's is a small cafe across the road from the water and nestled in the trees. They're open for lunch and dinner every day from Easter to Thanksgiving or just after. During the remainder of the year, it's a nice place to have dinner. You'll find table cloths and linen napkins for dinner and a slightly less formal table setting for lunch. Owner Tom Brown told me they raised their own Black Angus beef and cut their own pork. Veal is offered and of course, great seafood and pasta dishes. They have lobster, shrimp, crab, fish and clams. They also cater to family dining with a children's menu.

frame house as you drive down Colington Road. They're open daily from Easter through Thanksgiving for dinner and at other times, Thursday, Friday and Saturday. There is a children's menu and families will enjoy the variety of steaks, chicken and seafood dishes in a nautical decor.⁂

BRIDGES SEAFOOD RESTAURANT
Colington Rd., 2 mi. west of Bypass
441-6398

$ MC, VISA

Bridges is located in a small

Nags Head

RESTAURANTS

SWEETWATERS

Route 158, MP 10-1/2   441-3427
$$ MC, VISA, AMEX

This restaurant is open for lunch and dinner all year except January and February. Lots of greenery and light natural wood reflect a casual ambience. The menu offers many choices of food from great burgers, pasta dishes and salads to grilled seafood and steak. There is a full-service bar and the lounge is a popular place for meeting friends and generating a lively evening. Sweetwaters is a good choice for brunch in season and the price is moderate.

KELLY'S RESTAURANT & TAVERN

Route 158, MP 10-1/2   441-4116
$$$ MC, VISA, AMEX

Kelly's has become an Outer Banks tradition. Mike Kelly, proprietor, gives personal attention to the service and friendliness of this special place. Kelly's is a large restaurant and a busy place. From the moment you get in the door, you'll be attracted to the decor which reflects the maritime-rich environmental history and wildlife focus of the area with mounted fish, birds and other memorabilia from the Outer Banks. Dinner is served in several rooms upstairs and downstairs. Dinner in the widow's watch, three levels up, offers a quiet romantic evening for special occasions. There's always a crowd at Kelly's but diners can enjoy cocktails in the lounge while waiting. It's also a great place to go for after-dinner entertainment. Kelly's is open for dinner only and it is one of the most popular places for locals.

The menu at Kelly's offers many seafood dishes, as well as chicken, beef and pastas. There's a raw bar for those who like to feast on oysters in season and steamed shellfish. Home-made breads accompany dinner. Deserts are always good after a leisurely meal. A children's menu is available. Open all year.

TORTUGA'S LIE

Beach Road, MP 11   441-RAWW
$-$$ MC, VISA

This is one of the most fun restaurants on the beach. The laid-back island atmosphere is coupled with friendly owners (who are almost always there...we can't figure out when they sleep!) and delightfully prepared food. You can choose from a menu that features everything from Gator Bites (yep, the real thing) to sandwiches to fresh seafood cooked in imaginative and delicious ways. And, while you typically wouldn't point out french fries as a high point of a restaurant, their's are the best we've ever had.

While you're waiting for your food, you can be amused reading all the license tags nailed to the ceiling or talking with other diners -- it's a small place that promote congeniality. Locals also frequent this spot for their Black and Tans -- a combination of Bass Ale and Guiness Stout that goes down like smooth cream. If you're a beer lover and haven't discovered them yet, make a point to while you're here.

PIER HOUSE RESTAURANT

Beach Road, MP 12   441-5141

$ MC, VISA

Here's a great place to eat an early breakfast or fresh seafood for lunch and dinner. This pier restaurant affords great views of the ocean. The ambience is casual and on days when the fish are running it could get crowded. It's nothing fancy, but offers characteristics not found in other places except at the beach. Fresh seafood, cole slaw, hush puppies and daily specials top the menu. Seafood is fried, grilled, broiled and steamed -- any way you like it!

THE WHARF

Beach Road, MP 12-1/2

$ 441-7457

You won't miss this popular beach establishment on the road across from the oceanfront due to the que of people out front. The line forms early and moves along while you visit with friends or meet new ones. There is a menu, but the ever-popular "all you can eat" buffet is the main target for folks who get hungry around 6:30 in the evening. The service is efficient in an atmosphere of beach informality. You'll not be disappointed unless you're looking for a setting for a ro-

mantic dinner for two! They're open from Easter through October and have become a summertime tradition for vacationers and locals alike.

MIDGETTS SEAFOOD RESTAURANT

Route 158 Bypass, MP 13 $$

Midgett is a legendary name on the Outer Banks. The menu here features family recipes from way back in the 1920s. The 100-seat restaurant opened two years ago and was built by a father and son team. The ambience is quiet and nautical without being pretentious.

Jeffrey Wade Midgett put away his tools after helping his dad, Jeffrey Gray Midgett, build the place, and is making a good impression with his duties as chef. The menu features a bounty of seafood entrees, as well as ribs, chicken and beef. The desserts are all homemade -- you'll love the key lime pie.

Midgett's has early bird specials from 4 to 6 p.m. and a senior citizens' menu.

There's a big porch in case you have to wait for seating. Overall, Midgett's has a fine atmosphere and excellent food. They're located just south of Jockey's Ridge.

WINDMILL POINT

Route 158, Bypass, MP 16-1/2

441-1535

$$$$ MC, VISA, AMEX

Magnificent views of the sound

at sunset, dotted with colorful sails of windsurfers delight diners who come here. Famous for the memorabilia from the S.S. *United States*, this restaurant provides excellent cuisine to match the views. There are two dining areas, tastefully furnished down to the table cloths, napkins and chairs that hug rather than hold you. Service is fast and unobtrusive. The upstairs lounge, which features the kidney-shaped bar from the ship, is a pleasant place to wait your call to dinner. Again the views from "up on deck" are great.

Favorites on the menu are the seafood trio lightly poached or grilled with a nice sauce or a seafood pasta entree of scallops and light seasonings. Chef Vanischak's creations get better every year. Open for dinner only all year.

THE DUNES

Route 158, MP 16-1/2   441-9953
$ MC, VISA

When there's a large crowd or your own family is a bit on the big size, this restaurant will accommodate with its three huge dining rooms and plenty of parking. Breakfast at The Dunes is a favorite and they have everything in every combination you'd imagine early in the morning in addition to a very popular Breakfast Bar. Large portions hold true for lunches which offer great burgers, fries and cole slaw or crunchy clam strips and other seafood. The rib-eye steak sandwich is a good choice if you've gone without breakfast or your beach appetite has grown.

Dinners feature local, well-prepared seafood at moderate prices to go along with the huge salad bar. They offer a children's menu and provide fast, friendly service. Open daily March through November.

PENGUIN ISLE SOUNDSIDE GRILLE

Route 158, Bypass, MP 16   441-2637
$$$$ MC, VISA

As night falls on the sound, the sunset creates a sense of calm and a variety of wildlife can be spotted in the low-lying marshlands of Roanoke Sound right outside the windows of this popular restaurant. But, no penguins in these parts! The menu carries the story of its name.

Residents and visitors to the beach come to this restaurant for an outstanding dinner. The dining room or the Gazebo lounge offer views of the water from almost every table. There's a deck for outside enjoyment and live music most nights in season. Owners Mike Kelly and Doug Tutwiler combine their talents to create a distinctive restaurant. Kelly is the same of Kelly's in Nags Head. It means you never get too much of a good thing. Penguin Isle serves a more nouvelle cuisine with a New Orleans touch, featuring, of course, fresh seafood. Residents come time and time again. Visitors will love it, too. Penguin Isle is open most of the year for dinner only.

DAIRY MART

Beach Road, MP 13

441-6730 $

Soft ice cream came on like gang-busters in the 60s and here is a holdover from those times, though thoroughly modern, clean and still serving great food. It's a drive-in where you order and eat at picnic tables adorned with umbrellas for a spot of shade during summer. In addition to the best ice cream and variations on the same, owners Ron and Carol Rodrigues serve the best quick sandwiches, fries and onion rings around. The "Big Daddy Burger" or "LittleMamma" are favorites (make sure you have a big appetite before tackling a "Big Daddy"). For some, the ice cream is the meal for hot summer days. They're open from May to October, but closed on Wednesdays.

OWENS' RESTAURANT

Beach Road, MP 17   441-7309
$$$ MC, VISA

Owens' is an Outer Banks legend serving wonderful fresh seafood meals from it's renovated building that looks like an old Nags Head Lifesaving Station. They've added on to it because the popularity couldn't be contained in the small, older building. People have returned time and time again during the more than 45 years they've been in business. The legend of many generations of the Owens family is not a well-kept secret. So, when you drive down the beach road to have dinner, be prepared for some wait time. They have several large dining rooms, but the Station Keeper's Lounge upstairs is a nice place to start your evening with the Owens family. In season, they have light entertainment.

But let's talk about dinner here.

Seafood, and lots of it, comes fresh and prepared in favorites like Crabmeat Remick, Coconut Shrimp and Crabmeat Norfolk, and of course the Seafood Platter is out of this world. There's a mixed grill for those who appreciate prime beef with their seafood. We opted for marinated chicken with our seafood and they were most obliging. Appetizers are very good, especially their homemade soups. Service matches the quality of food -- excellent. Desserts are wonderful, if you have room after managing the more than ample portions of your chosen dinner. Just go ahead and finish it off -- don't leave wondering if you've missed something. Owens' is open from April until after Thanksgiving for dinner only.

SAM & OMIE'S
Beach Road at Whalebone Junction
441-7366

$$ **MC, VISA**

Sam & Omie's probably should be listed as an Attraction in our guide due to its long-time popularity, but we'll take space here to brag about this place which has been around for over a half-century. This weather-beaten building situated at the "official end" of the beach road, is the scene of people enjoying good, moderately-priced food, story-telling, fresh oys-

ters in season, drinks or a game of pool on the billiard table located in the back room. The walls are adorned with sports mania and photographs include some long ago Redskin football greats. There are nautical treasures as well to keep you busy looking around while waiting for dinner.

You'll find breakfast here a time to get caught up in local lore and good food. Some folks hang around for lunch which features salads and sandwiches. Try their soft crab sandwich and iced tea for lunch. All meals are priced lower than most places. And, it's only fair to let you know this big open place can get smoky by evening. Open almost all year.

R.V.'s
Nags Head-Manteo Causeway
441-4963
$-$$ **MC, VISA**

R. V. Owens of the Owens' Restaurant family is holding forth here. It's one of the most popular places on the beach. In addition, he covers a lot of ground north to south with his newest restaurant in Kitty Hawk, Keepers' Galley (see the restaurant section for that town).

If you want to eat at the bar, OK. Another option is to be seated on the enclosed porch for lunch or dinner of food which, of course, features traditional Outer Banks seafood with legendary Owens' quality and quantity. Local folks pack in here during the week and on weekends; the gazebo raw bar, located on an attached deck

overlooking the water takes on a life of its own and stays open late. Some menu favorites are discovered right up front in the appetizers, which are big enough for a good feed. Prices are reasonable, the ambience is light and lots of fun. They're open from early spring through mid-November for lunch and dinner.

TALE OF THE WHALE
Nags Head-Manteo Causeway
441-7332
$$ **MC, VISA, AMEX**

This fine family restaurant is a step above some of the seafood restaurants around the beach. The ambience is friendly and yet lends a softness to an evening of seafood dining. The decor is nautical and dark, perhaps cooling after those long days in the sun.

The specials feature everything from mixed grill to broiled shellfish. Combination platters can be served fried or broiled. Desserts are wonderfully cool and tasty if you have room! During the summer, live entertainment is featured regularly in this soundside restaurant which offers a beautiful view across the marshlands and waters. Tale of the Whale is open from mid-April till the end of October for dinner only.

THE OASIS

Nags Head-Manteo Causeway   441-7721

$$ **MC, VISA**

The Oasis was built in the 1940s, which qualifies it as one of the oldest restaurants on the beach. Bought from the original owner by Violet Kellam in 1950, it became the home of the "bar girls," comely waitresses whose portraits now fill the lobby, and known for its lace cornbread. The family sold the restaurant in 1980 and its name was changed to The Dock. Then, several years ago, Violet's grandchildren -- Mike, Mark and Kellam France -- bought the place back, really spruced it up, and renamed it The Oasis.

They've brought back their specialty, lace cornbread, a family secret for years -- it's more like a crunchy hushpuppy than cornbread -- but the barefoot girls are just a memory. They've also started opening for breakfast and lunch as well. They open at 7 a.m. for breakfast, lunch starts at 11:30 until around 2 p.m., then dinner starts at 5 p.m. and continues until at least 9:30 (later if there's the demand). This is a pleasant place with a great view, where a full dinner and drinks won't cost you an arm and a leg. They're open May through November.

Roanoke Island

RESTAURANTS

MANTEO

CLARA'S SEAFOOD GRILL

On the Waterfront   473-1727

$$-$$$ **MC, VISA, AMEX**

Clara's combines a family tradition for excellence with waterfront views across Shallowbag Bay to bring you a wonderful dining experience. While your food is being prepared in the traditional style of the Owens' family, who also own Owens' Restaurant and RV's in Nags Head along with Keeper's Galley in Kitty Hawk, you can watch the boats sailing in and out of the marina and waterfowl diving for fish. Just across the way, the *Elizabeth II* is visible. The ambience is comfortable and casual, but there's a touch of sophistication about dining here.

The menus is extensive -- what you'd expect from years of family tradition. Regardless of the many excellent seafood dishes on the menu, one of the non-seafood favorites is Clara's Pasta Faschoul, tasty black beans on pasta, garnished with tomatoes, green onions and ricotta cheese. The Greek Lemon Chicken, Manteo Fish En Bag or Broiled Shadboat (fish and shellfish sampler) are other creations. All of Clara's special grill items and traditional seafood entrees satisfy your appetite. The Pastry Chef makes special treats daily for tempting des-

Clara's ...
for Fine Dining in Manteo.

Take a break from the bustle of the beach and relax over a memorable meal at Clara's, on the beautiful Manteo waterfront.

Enjoy the serenity of Roanoke Sound from your table, while you enjoy fine cuisine prepared by the Owens family - a name synonymous on the Outer Banks with good food and good fellowship.

Casual, yet elegant, Clara's will quickly become your favorite in Manteo. Brown bagging allowed for alcoholic beverages; beer and wine available.

CLARA'S ON THE WATERFRONT IN MANTEO • 473-1727

Open Daily for Lunch and Dinner

serts to top off an excellent meal.

For the '92 season, Clara's has added a steam bar, offering oysters, shrimp and crab legs. We've already found this nice for when we want a tasty treat or a smaller meal.

Clara's offers a good selection of wines and imported beers. Brown bagging allowed. The service is excellent and you'll enjoy waterside dining at Clara's from March through Christmas.

DARWIN'S CAFE, THE NATURAL SELECTION
On the Waterfront
473-6113   **$**

What began as a health food store has become a very popular small cafe specializing in vegetarian foods. There's an assortment of soups and salads as well as deli sandwiches. They also have homemade desserts and fresh-baked muffins. The daily specials they offer are truly delicious, as well as inventive. They have a huge selection of beers and wine. Don't let the "health food" idea throw you off if you're typically a meat and potatoes person; you can get that if you want it, but the featured specials and regular menu items will make you feel like converting - at least for *one* meal.

DUCHESS OF DARE
Budleigh Street   **473-2215**
$$ **MC, VISA**

This is a favorite gathering place for locals and it's situated in the heart

of the business, municipal and civic area. Locals get here early for breakfast and enjoy the Walker family's cooking at lunch and dinner, too. When was the last time you ate at a counter? Try it here and listen in on the latest talk around town. Sunday brunch draws a good crowd and at other times the good seafood, vegetables and salads satisfy your hunger pangs. All desserts are homemade. The price is right for family dining. Open all year from breakfast through dinner hour.

POOR RICHARD'S
Downtown Manteo, on the waterfront
473-3333
$ **No credit cards**

Richard Brown owns and operates this cheery and convenient sandwich shop overlooking the sound and the *Elizabeth II*. It has become a Manteo "thing" at lunch when, it seems, every local within easy walking distance descends on the place between noon and 2 p.m. They come for good reason. Richard serves up a great selection of made-to-order sandwiches. His tuna salad and all the grilled sandwiches are especially good. Soups, chili, salad plates and ice cream are also available.

Poor Richard's is open for most of the year. During the busier months it opens early for breakfast with scrambled egg and bacon sandwiches, bagels with cream cheese and other light breakfast options.

BUTCH'S HOTDOGS
Downtown Manteo, on
the waterfront
473-3663

$ **No credit cards**

If you're a dog lover -- and we don't mean the kind that slobbers all over you and wags it tail -- you'll want to mosey into Butch's. You can get regular or foot longs, smothered with all the fixin's, just the way you like them. Or, try their cooked-fresh-daily turkey salad or turkey breast sandwiches. You get a freshly baked cookie with your order. And, shoot, go ahead and take Fido something...he's probably hungry, too.

THE WEEPING RADISH BREWERY
& BAVARIAN RESTAURANT
Main Hwy.

473-1157 **$$-$$$**

Most major credit cards

You'll see the Bavarian-style restaurant through the trees on Main Hwy., adjacent to the Christmas Shop. The shade of pine trees and gardens make this a delightful place to relax before a meal at this unusual restaurant. The name, Weeping Radish, comes from the radish served in Bavaria as an accompaniment to beer. The radish is cut in a spiral, sprinkled with salt and packed back together. The salt draws out the moisture and gives the appearance of a "weeping radish."

An authentic German atmosphere prevails and guests are tempted by a variety of German dishes such as veal, sauerbraten and sausages. Homemade noodles, or spaetzle, and cooked red cabbage are two of the side dishes served here. Traditional American food is served, too.

A brewery opened in 1986 and offers a pure, fresh malt brew of German tradition, without chemical additives. This "nectar of the gods" is a big

reason why this is a favorite spot with locals and tourist alike. Enjoy lunch in the outdoor beer garden. The Weeping Radish is open all year.

GARDEN PIZZERIA
Main Hwy.

473-6888 **$$**

This is a delightful small eatery shaded by those wonderful Manteo pines and offering some of the best pizza we've tasted anywhere. You can order for take-out or eat inside or out on the small deck. The White Pizza is topped with ricotta, mozzarella, provolone and romano cheeses, broccoli, pepperoni and minced garlic. Have you ever? Don't miss out on the good food here, or the wide assortment of deli sandwiches, homemade salads and, of course, antipasto salads. Garden Pizzeria will make up party platters, vegetable or cold cut varieties for take out.

DARRELL'S

Main Hwy. **473-5366**
$-$$ **MC, VISA**

Darrell's is another favorite in a long line of restaurants owned and operated by the Daniels family. It started as an ice cream stand over 30 years ago and since the late 1970s has been a good restaurant which appeals to locals and visitors. The daily lunch specials are a real bargain and the portions are somewhat smaller than at evening meals. Popcorn shrimp and fried oysters accompanied by salads and vegetables are featured on the menu. They're open 11:00 a.m. till 9:30 p.m. all year except on Sundays.

THE CRAB DOCK

Main Hwy. **473-6845**
$-$$ **MC, VISA**

This is a new addition to the Manteo restaurant scene, having opened in early June. The Crab Dock has picked up on the current "steam bar" craze and serves crabs, shrimp, mussels, snow crab legs and clams along with soups and sandwiches. There's a kid's menu in case yours haven't yet developed their culinary tastes buds to accommodate the seafood -- that's fine, more for you. One of the nicest things about this spot is the huge deck out back overlooking the sound. You're literally on top of the water, which means there's usually some sort of breeze to keep things cool, and the nautical, laid back mood is all the more enhanced. Crockett's Seafood Market is right next door, so it would be hard to get any fresher fish. They serve lunch and dinner and have beer and wine.

VITI'S

Chesley Mall, Main Hwy. **473-6006**
$ **MC, VISA**

The Italian food offered here is not only well-prepared but also affordable -- two factors that have contributed to this small restaurant's success. They have nightly specials and offer beer and wine. The service is friendly and quick, so if you're hurrying to eat before going to the Lost

Colony, this would be a good choice. They're open all year, serving lunch and dinner.

DOUG SAUL'S BAR-B-Q
Main Hwy.

473-6464　　　　　　　　**$**

Some say the barbeque here is the best on the Outer Banks. Look for this tiny cafe along Main Hwy. at one end of a shopping center. The buffet also features fried chicken, cole slaw and other vegetables.

The ambience is friendly and centered around the conversations of the local crowd who like the ribs and barbeque sandwiches, the buffet as well as the casual atmosphere. The dining room, furnished with formica-top tables and vinyl chairs, is off to one side away from the buffet. Eat in or call for take-out.

ELIZABETHAN DINNER THEATER
At the Elizabethan Inn
Main Hwy.

473-2101　　　　　　　　**$$$**

"Pastime with goode companie, I love, and shall until I die. Grutch who list, but none deny; So God be pleased, so live will I!" - Henry VIII.

Enjoy the good company in modern times at the Elizabethan Dinner Theater. A renaissance feast and

---

"Pastime with Goode Companie"

Elizabethan Dinner Theater

Imagine yourself at a country inn in the 16th Century... greeted by an innkeeper who speaks in an Old English dialect... served up Elizabethan delicacies on reproduction pottery, entertained with the latest gossip, tunes and dances of the time. You may even find yourself singing along or joining in a jig. It's like a trip to Renaissance England!

Five Course Renaissance Feast
& Fun-Filled Performance

7:30-10:00
Summer: Tues. through Fri.
Fall: Fri. & Sat.

By reservation only
473-2101 or 1-800-346-2466

evening of delightful entertainment await you here in an upstairs medieval-setting at the Elizabethan Inn in Manteo. You and your family will enjoy a step back in time with troubadours and wenches who delight in serving good food and gathering you up in the most gentlest of ways to olden times of the 16th century.

Nicholas Hodsdon and Doug Barger, who play minstrel and innkeeper respectively, have just opened their fifth season. Nicholas is a talented musician, performing on a variety of handmade instruments for the banquet. Doug puts you at ease with a theatrical-welcome to the evening.

It's easy to see that patrons and hosts have an equal amount of enjoyment and, even though the experience is important here, the first concern, says Doug, is that people like the food.

The intent in olden times, and now, is to have the food as pleasing to the eye as it is to the taste. Herbs and edible flowers are grown on the premises and the wait staff (wenches) explain the "curatives" of several during the process of serving the meal.

The banquet consists of roast game hen, roast beef, fruits, cheeses, baked breads, vegetable pie, pickled roots, sallet (a salad of leaves, herbs and flowers) and other foods of the period. Desserts, also as pleasing to the eye and palate as the other food, are a traditional English Trifle and Gingerbread with lemon sauce. No alcoholic beverages are served.

As you would imagine, table service is missing a modern instrument we've all come to rely on -- the fork! However, the knife serves as a splendid substitute, and there are spoons.

Children get caught up in the drama as easily as do the adults. Doug, Nick and the "cast" have created an authentic evening, right down to the costumes which were designed and sewn by Doug. Many come here, enjoy the experience, and return as a part of their vacation pleasure.

Call for reservations. Performances and dinner begin at 7:30 p.m. Tuesdays through Fridays during the summer and Fridays and Saturdays during the fall.

PIRATE'S COVE RESTAURANT & RAW BAR

On the Manteo-Nags Head Causeway
473-2266

$$$ **MC, VISA**

Dine here on the water, where the masts, booms and bridges of fishing boats are at ease, dockside. The views from this second floor restaurant, above the Ship's Store, are beautiful. Pirate's Cove is under new management and the food is quite good.

You can enjoy an early breakfast (they open at 4 a.m.) before heading out to sea, or lunch and dinner as the fleet returns. Bring your camera.

Fresh, well-prepared seafood tops the menu here. Sandwiches and salads are available, too. For a special meal recently, the Baked Glazed Ham and the Flounder stuffed with Crabmeat were our choice of entrees and were very good. Beer and wines are served and brown bagging is allowed.

WANCHESE

QUEEN ANNE'S REVENGE
Old Wharf Road

Wanchese	473-5466
$$$-$$$$	MC, VISA

Named after one of Blackbeard's famous pirate ships that terrorized sea travelers off the Carolina Coast during the early 1700s, this restaurant continues to be a favorite on the Outer Banks. Well-hidden off the beaten path in Wanchese, Wayne Gray and Donald Beach have operated this restaurant since 1978. Some were skeptical about its success, located in Wanchese on a dead-end road. But the intent to serve only the finest seafood and beef in this pleasant setting has cast aside all doubt. Many return to dine here, and it's known as a place where recipes are exchanged, new ones are tested and a lot of time is spent in food preparation, with quality ingredients. The grounds are delightful and once inside you'll enjoy dinner in one of three dining rooms.

Food. Lots of it and it's good. There's a fine selection of appetizers, including Bouillabaisse, Black Bean Soup and North Carolina Crayfish Cocktail, cajun style.

The seafood here is excellent, featuring Blackbeard's Raving and Wanchese Seafood Platter. There's

Chateaubriand for Two carved at your table. The kind of seafood varies according to weather and fishing conditions, but it is only the best, the freshest and well-prepared .

The desserts are homemade and served in generous portions. There is beer and wine service, but you're in Wanchese where no liquor may be served, so the restaurant will serve set-ups if you'd like to brown-bag it.

Be prepared to wait in season. They're open seven days a week, June through September for dinner only and closed on Tuesdays during the winter.

FISHERMAN'S WHARF
Near the end of Highway 345

Wanchese	473-5205
$$	MC, VISA

Located at Mill Landing overlooking the fishing port of Wanchese, the dining room of this family-owned restaurant is rather ordinary and situated over the dock where fresh fish is unloaded from the fleet. But, this view assures diners, almost better than at any other Banks restaurant, that the fish they'll be served is as fresh and local as it gets.

The Daniel's family of Wanchese fishing-history operates this restaurant for lunch and dinner from April through October. Seafood plates, complete with homemade hushpuppies and good cole slaw, are the best selections from a variety of things on the menu. Save room for the homemade desserts. A children's menu is available. Open noon till 9 p.m. daily.

Hatteras Island

RESTAURANTS

EMILY'S SOUNDSIDE RESTAURANT

Waves   **987-2383**

$$ **Most major credit cards**

There's upstairs and downstairs dining in this attractive restaurant located in Waves. From nearly every spot in the dining rooms, you can see the water and spectacular sunsets in the evening. Jim and Emily Landrum have been serving fine meals since 1972. Their breakfast omelets are wonderful. Pancakes, eggs, potatoes, grits, fruit juice and, of course, coffee will start your day right.

Traditional seafood dishes, steamed or raw shellfish, beef and chicken are offered on the menu here at Emily's. The ribs are great. Soups and desserts are homemade. A breakfast buffet is featured on weekends during the summer and at other times when its called for. Open mid-March through most of December for breakfast, lunch and dinner.

WAVES EDGE RESTAURANT

Waves   **987-2100 or 441-0494**

$-$$ **MC, VISA**

Waves Edge opened several

years ago and has earned a good reputation for quality food and good prices. Located on the soundside of NC 12, the views are great. An upstairs lounge features light entertainment during the season.

Lunch specials include dishes like shrimp creole or meat loaf and mashed potatoes. There's a nice variety of salads, soups and sandwiches, too. All breads and desserts are homemade.

Dinner choices range from mesquite-grilled seafood to baby back ribs with lightly cooked fresh vegetables and herbs from their own soundside garden.

Waves Edge serves lunch (11:30 a.m. until 2 p.m.) and dinner (5 p.m. until...) seven days a week during the season, then after September, goes to five days a week. They offer a good wine list as well as beer, and carry out is available.

DOWN UNDER RESTAURANT & LOUNGE

Rodanthe Pier

987-2277   **$-$$**

The only oceanview dining on Hatteras Island is found at this restaurant featuring good food and good prices with a daily happy hour featuring steamed and spiced shrimp. Get an early morning start with a sun-rise breakfast here at this pier restaurant. They're open most of the year from 7 a.m. till midnight.

THE FROGGY DOG

Avon   **995-4106**

$-$$ **MC, VISA**

This is a real comfortable place to eat. They've enlarged their seating areas, but the natural wood finishes with a touch of nautical decor and plants provide the right ambience for all meals. Froggy Dog is open seven days a week, all year. Children's and senior citizen's portions are available.

But let's get to the food.

Breakfast is a combination of good food and local lore. Portions are big enough and everything is home-made. Lunches are great with salads and sandwiches. Dinner offers several entrees from broiled, fried or sauteed seafood to steaks and chicken. You won't be disappointed in the meals served by the folks at Froggy Dog. It has been a favorite place for a number of years.

SEA ROBIN RESTAURANT

Waterside at Avon   995-5931

$-$$ MC, VISA

Sea Robin has enlarged its seating capacity attesting to its popularity as a good place with good food. The restaurant is situated on the soundside of Avon and the views are wonderful. It's off the road and quiet.

They're open for breakfast with Eggs Benedict or Steak and Eggs for top choices. For lunch the choices range from steamed shellfish and salads to a list of sandwiches as long as your arm. They're truly ready to provide variety to all types of hungries! At dinner, the menu again features a full list of entrees from the Sea Robin Seafood Platter and Surf 'n Turf to Cajun Fish and Crabmeat Saute.

THE MAD CRABBER RESTAURANT & SHELLFISH BAR
Avon

995-5959 $-$$

Don't you just love this name!? The Mad Crabber is a real lively place, offering lunch and dinner daily, in season. They're not fancy, but they have good seafood. Steamed crabs and shrimp lead the way, accompanied by corn on the cob. If you're set on something else, try their good hot dogs. There's a game room for your enjoyment.

DIAMOND SHOALS RESTAURANT

Buxton   995-5217

$$ MC, VISA

A popular place with the locals, visitors also enjoy the big servings of good food and come back often. It's within walking distance of several motels in Buxton which means you can walk it off if you've eaten too much! They're open for breakfast and dinner all year and the service is friendly and efficient. Breakfasts are big and the all-you-can-eat dinners with plenty of seafood choices top the list in the evening.

THE PILOT HOUSE

Buxton   995-5664

$$$ MC, VISA

This soundside restaurant is designed to capture the spectacular views across the sky and water. There is a lounge upstairs which also has a view of the ocean -- well worth the climb.

Although the building is rather new, the Pilot House has been a long time favorite -- before the original restaurant burned down and since rebuilding. The decor is soft and on the nautical side, but not overpowering.

Fresh seafood is well-prepared and served in several combinations, or as the fresh catch of the day. Soups are homemade and you'll want to try the seafood bisque.

The Pilot House is open from mid-April to late fall, seven days a week for dinner only.

BILLY'S FISH HOUSE RESTAURANT

Buxton   **995-5151**
$$ **MC, VISA**

There's nothing real fancy here, but the ambience is busy and you're on-location, so to speak, where the one-time fish house has kept the evidence. Concrete floors with a slant for an easy wash and run off and picnic tables with a view of the water set the casual mood. And, in good weather, you can eat right on the dock.

Billy and Chalaron May turned their fish house into a restaurant and it captured an easy-going crowd which, surprisingly enough, enjoys some of the best seafood served anywhere, even when eaten on plastic table service. (There's a limit on how many dishes you can wash without the appropriate septic system, which is the problem here, near the water.)

Billy's is open for lunch and dinner from Easter till early December.

TIDES RESTAURANT

Off Hwy. 12, Buxton   **995-5988**
$-$$ **MC, VISA**

If you're not watching you'll miss the turn off to Tides, which is just past the business part of Buxton, across from the entrance to the lighthouse. Tides is hidden off the beaten path near to the right. It's a favorite place for early breakfasts and dinners, which features fresh local seafood.

We enjoyed our meal there, even though we were seated near the entry of the L-shaped dining room. The portions are large and the service is good here. Be prepared to wait in season..it's a popular spot.

THE GREAT SALT MARSH RESTAURANT

Buxton   **995-6200**

A quaint restaurant situated at the edge of the main road and overlooking the marshlands nearby, The Great Salt Marsh Restaurant is owned by Heidi Blackwood and Chyrel Austin. They've been open for a couple of seasons and this year a new lounge has been added to accommodate patrons during their wait for lunch or dinner. This indicates a good following by people who dine here on well-prepared New American or California-style seafood dishes, fresh salads and sandwiches, homemade soups and desserts. The service and ambience reflect special touches and attention to the pleasure of dining here. They're open for lunch everyday except Sunday and dinner everyday. Reservations are welcome for dinner.

FRISCO SANDWICH SHOP

NC 12, Frisco   **995-5535**

$ **MC, VISA**

You won't miss their sign out front, so stop in for lunch or dinner. It's open seven days a week during the summer and closed on Sundays the rest of the year. Owner Stan Lawrence and his staff know how deli-style sandwiches are made and it has kept them going for over 12 years. They've grown

from the original drive-in sandwich shop and now there's a place to sit down and enjoy the company of locals and visitors along with the good food.

BUBBA'S BAR-B-Q

NC 12, Frisco   **995-5421**

$ **MC, VISA**

When you get serious about barbeque, Bubba's is the right place. The pork, chicken, beef, ribs and turkey plus all the trimmings can't be beat. If it's take out or eat in, you will chew on the world's best, as far as we're concerned. Owner Larry Schauer (Bubba) and his wife (Mrs. Bubba) left their farm in West Virginia and came to the beach to do their cooking. Lucky for us! All their meats are cooked right before your eyes on an open pit with hickory wood. The cole slaw, cornbread and french fries are good, too! Homemade pies such as Sweet Potato, Peanutbutter and Coconut Custard are the favorites. Bubba's is open all year.

GARY'S RESTAURANT
NC 12, Hatteras   986-2349
$ No credit cards

Gary's has grown up from a fast-food style restaurant to a small cafe, where relaxing over a cup of coffee and great breakfast or enjoying a nice lunch (including homemade soups) or a cozy dinner will satisfy your appetite.

They're open most of the year at least for some meals, but during the early spring until late fall, you can get breakfast early -- say around 5:30 -- and the other meals, too.

The decor is soft blues and white, with tables nicely arranged throughout the dining room. The dinner menu features a list of Surf Side and Land Side entrees such as the Commodore's Choice Platter of oysters, scallops, shrimp and fish, and a NY Strip or Delmonico steak.

THE CHANNEL BASS
NC 12, Hatteras Village   986-2250
$$ MC, VISA

Situated on an inlet, this family-owned restaurant has been serving food forever -- well, almost. The Harrisons are a famous fishing family and you'll notice all the trophies in the foyer that belong to Shelby, (Mrs. Harrison)! They're coming up on thirty years of serving fresh seafood, some of which was caught aboard *Miss Channel Bass*.

The menu is loaded with seafood platters, either broiled or fried -- they even have broiled crabcakes that

are just as good as the fried ones but a lot better on your diet -- along with a steamed seafood platter, veal and char-broiled steaks. You'll enjoy all the food served here and the local chatter about the big fish caught from the big boats at nearby Hatteras Harbor.

BREAKWATER ISLAND RESTAURANT

Hatteras Village	**986-2733**
$$	**MC, VISA**

This family-owned restaurant is the latest undertaking by the hard-working Oden's of Hatteras Village. Things started out fairly simple years ago when Donald Oden just took care of his fishing business at Oden's Dock. Now they run the Hatteras Harbor Motel and a very nice restaurant located on the dock, which means on the water. The views are wonderful and so is the food. They serve lunch and dinner featuring fresh local seafood, prime rib and several pasta dishes. This is a place you'll enjoy and return to again and again.

Channel Bass Restaurant
P.O. Box 147 Hatteras, NC 27943 • 919/986-2250

Seafood Direct From the Ocean to You
Open 5:30 pm to 9:00 pm
Sunday 5:00 pm to 9:00 pm

Jackie and Shelby Harrison - Owners
Debbie-Brenda Harrison - Managers

"The Restaurant with a Reputation"

PONY ISLAND RESTAURANT

928-5701

"WHERE THE ISLANDERS DINE"

Featuring -
Steamed Shrimp
Daily Specials
Homemade Desserts

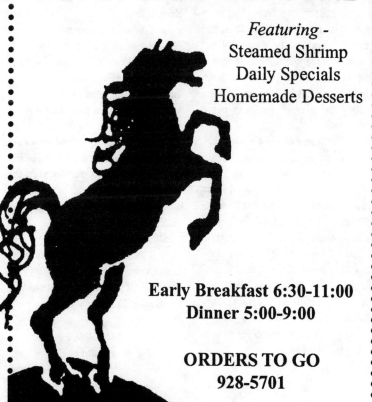

Early Breakfast 6:30-11:00
Dinner 5:00-9:00

ORDERS TO GO
928-5701

Ocracoke

RESTAURANTS

THE PELICAN RESTAURANT
928-7431

$$ **MC, VISA**

Located in the heart of Ocracoke Village, The Pelican Restaurant gives you the choice of dining inside in one of two rooms or being seated on the porch for a delightful breakfast, lunch or dinner. The old cottage, refurbished for the restaurant, is situated near the activity of Ocracoke Village, but trees and shrubs offer privacy from intrusions. The linen table cloths and fresh flowers add to its casual but pleasing atmosphere. A treat here is also the outdoor bar that serves beer, wine and special fruit drinks, making waiting for a table anything but a bother.

The menu offers a wide range of seafood fried in a light batter, sauteed or broiled. The Blackened Fish prepared with Pelican's special sauce is a favorite of diners as is the wonderfully-prepared quiche. A children's menu is available, as well as a great variety of breakfast items (you can't miss with their omelets), lunch sandwiches, soups, salads and dinner entrees. This restaurant is open seasonally, and the hours are 11:00 a.m. to 4:00 p.m. for lunch and 5:30 p.m. til 9:30 p.m. for dinner.

PONY ISLAND RESTAURANT
928-5701

$-$$ **MC, VISA**

A good casual restaurant, Pony Island serves more than adequate portions of a variety of well-prepared foods, and some delightful surprises await you. Nightly specials might present an unusual treat, such as a Chinese dinner or something with a flavor from the southwest. Or, you will get to choose from fresh seafood prepared in a variety of ways. If you've had a good day fishing and bring it in, they'll cook it for you, but be sure to clean it first.

Homemade desserts are a great finishing touch to their fine meals.

The Pony Island Restaurant is adjacent to the Pony Island Motel, and located less than a block off the highway. They're open from Easter until late fall and are one of a few places that serve breakfast. If you're up early, around 7:00 a.m. for a day at the beach or going out to sea for a day on the water, take advantage of their big breakfast biscuits, hotcakes, eggs and omelets. We go just to get their "Pony Potatoes," which are hash browns covered with cheese, sour cream and salsa...yum...a meal in themselves, especially if you get a second order as we usually do.

PAMLICO'S
928-6891

$$ **MC, VISA**

Pamlico's offers very good Italian food — a nice change of pace from seafood — but the seafood is well-prepared, as well. Homemade pasta dishes, pizza, soups and salads are popular menu selections.

Located some distance away from the hustle and bustle of the village on the main road, it's perhaps not a recommended casual stroll, but then again, however you get there, the food is good and the hospitality welcoming. Maria's is open from Easter until late fall for lunch and dinner.

THE BACK PORCH
928-6401

$$$ **MC, VISA**

Whether your dinner is served on the screened porch, in the small nooks or the open dining room of this well-known Ocracoke restaurant, you'll find it a most pleasant experience. The service is friendly and portions of food pleasing. John and Debbie Wells renovated this older building and refurbished it to blend with the many trees on the property. Its location off the main road adds to its appeal as a place for quiet dining.

The menu is loaded with as many fresh items as possible. All sauces, dressings, breads and desserts are made right in their kitchen and they hand-cut their meats. Nearly everyone asks to have one of their secret recipe — they are that good. Outer Banks seafood is plentiful in original

Photo: DCTB

The Ocracoke Lighthouse.

and unusual dishes, like Gratine' of Scallops Florentine, or their appetizers of smoked bluefish or crab beignets. Non-seafood dishes are a tasty option as well, our favorite being the Cuban black bean and monterey jack cheese casserole. Be prepared for some pleasant surprises, one of which is the freshly ground coffee. There are reduced prices and smaller portions for children and senior adults. The wine selections and imported beers are well-matched with the menu. Be on the lookout for *The Back Porch Cookbook*, authored by Debbie, and published in the Spring of '92...maybe some of those secret recipes won't be so secret much longer!

CAP'T. BEN'S
928-4741

$$-$$$ **MC, VISA**

Since the late 70s, Cap't. Ben's has been a favorite restaurant for locals and visitors on Ocracoke Island. Located on the main road before you enter the village, this casual restaurant beckons families to come on in and enjoy a good meal.

Ben Mugford is the owner and the chef. For over 16 years he has perfected some house specials. His crab balls and stuffed mushrooms are favorites. He offers some of the best freshly cooked seafood on the island and the portions are for the hungry.

Lunch is served from 11:00 a.m. and the Cap't. Ben Burger is the choice here. Lunch sandwiches are served with chips or fries and dinners with soup and salad. The wine list is quite adequate for the menu.

The decor is nautical and friendly. Cap't. Ben's is open from April through November, every day for lunch and dinner.

ISLAND INN RESTAURANT
928-7821

$$ **MC, VISA**

The meals served at this island restaurant are prepared by a native Ocracoker, Chester Lynn. For nearly 16 years he worked at the restaurant and has returned after a brief absence to carry through the traditions of southern cooking. Not southern cooking with grease and heavy breading, but southern cooking with the freshest ingredients, a light coating on seafood and all traditional recipes he has learned through the years. While the variety of foods served on three menus — breakfast, lunch and dinner — can keep him quite busy, Chester is always on the watch for unusual things for the dining room. The tables and chairs of this country restaurant, set in a large room on red tile floors, are all of a different style. Some of his antiques are from England. The table service consists of old china and flatware -- collectors' items with a history all their own. All this complements the food and creates conversation and a lasting interest in his discoveries. Some renovations are

planned this year to create an even more comfortable ambience.

Fresh seafood carefully prepared, omelets, homemade soups, biscuits, crabcakes and desserts are favorite selections.

Breakfast service begins at 7:00 a.m. Light fare of ample portions is offered for lunch. Dinner features a variety of seafood, lightly coated or broiled and served by a knowledgeable staff. The three meals create a one-of-a-kind restaurant in Ocracoke.

The Island Inn Restaurant is open from March through November. Smaller portions for children and senior adults are available at dinner.

HOWARD'S PUB & RAW BAR
$ **928-4441**

Howard's has been on the scene for awhile in Ocracoke, and is a fun, friendly place to go for a meal, beer and conversation. In fact, it's the only place open year round for late night snacks (until 2 a.m.), as well as breakfast, lunch and dinner. The knotty pine walls are adorned with important notices -- whatever people want to tack up -- and an interesting array of college pennants, photos of parties held here and other items lends a note of familiarity for those who visit.

Buffy and Ann Warner are from West Virginia where he was a senator and she worked in a state office. Their lifestyles have changed a bit and you can tell they love it.

In addition to a raw bar, subs and other foods are featured, and the daily special might be chicken wings, polish sausage or steamed shrimp.

There's a wide-screen TV and free popcorn, and live music at night in season and on weekends in the off-season. When we visited, a new deck was being added on the front and the kitchen was being enlarged to accommodate a new menu. They'll be adding burgers and fish sandwiches, among other casual food, by summer. It's the only raw bar on the island, and the t-shirts attest to the popularity of their "oyster shooter," which you'll just love if you're a raw oyster and Tabasco fan....This is a place you can't, and shouldn't, miss as you drive into the village.

CAFE ATLANTIC
928-4861

$$ MC, VISA

Located off to the side of the main highway, this traditional beach-style building was opened a few years ago by Bob and Ruth Toth. The views from the dining room look out across the marsh grass and dunes. The gallery-like effect of the rooms is created by hand-colored photographs by local photographer Ann Ehringhaus. There's a non-smoking dining room upstairs and a smoking section upstairs, a consideration we appreciate.

The Toths make all their soups, dressings, sauces and desserts from scratch. Lunches feature a variety of soups, sandwiches and salads. Dinner features mostly sauteed or grilled seafood, however, if it's fried seafood you desire, you can order that as well. Many of the pasta dishes, sandwiches and seafood choices are available for carry out.

Cafe Atlantic is open from spring until late fall and has a nice selection of wines and beers.

Photo: Michael Halminski

Outer Banks
Night Spots

*I*f the beach, water-sports, fishing, shopping and sight-seeing on the Outer Banks wear you out, you'll find a few night spots where live music and dancing will finish you off!

The Outer Banks lifestyle is a bit different than what you might expect from other resort beaches. It was established a long time ago, at least among *some* of the people on the Outer Banks, that if you get to bed early, then you won't be late getting up the next day for a fishing expedition to the Gulf Stream or to a hard-earned job. We won't, however, include the mass of college-age "kids" in this, who stay up partying until who knows when yet *still* manage to be at their 6 a.m. shift...ah, youth!

But there are places on the beach where you'll discover a way to unwind, if that's mostly what you want to do, and we've included some here. Drinks are available until around 2 a.m. at most places, some even serve food after midnight. Live music is becoming a drawing card for many restaurants and lounges, so here's the run down.

Duck

BARRIER ISLAND INN
Duck Village   **261-8700**

This is a soundside favorite in Duck village where folks enjoy fabulous sunsets and indoor recreation in the form of table-top shuffleboard. Live music starts around 9 p.m. Locals gather here and newcomers are likely to get caught up in the fun. There's food and beverage service till whenever. Open all year.

BLUE POINT BAR & GRILL
Duck Village   **261-8090**

Blue Point is a very popular place for locals and visitors. Its reputation is built on the great food and ambience, but there is a small bar that offers a place to lean on your elbows and talk it up. The deck and some areas of the porch can be just as entertaining. Live music is featured on weekends. Open all year.

Kitty Hawk

FRISCO'S

Route 158, MP 4   261-7377

A popular hangout for locals, this refurbished restaurant is a crowd pleaser. Always open for food, it's also a great place for some live entertainment on Thursday night and it's large enough to accommodate patrons around the "U-shaped" bar or at small tables in the lounge. Open all year.

STATION SIX

Beach Rd. MP 4   261-7337

A small cafe-type restaurant featuring live music on the deck across from the ocean and inside during cooler months, Station Six is open April through Thanksgiving. If the Jazz Trio featuring Laura Martier is playing, go see them...we're convinced this woman is destined for stardom.

Kill Devil Hills

AWFUL ARTHURS

Beach Road, MP 6   441-5955

It's loud, packed with people and as popular as it gets. There's occasional live entertainment here, but the real draw just seems to be the atmosphere -- table after table of youngish patrons having a good time at the beach.

THE DUNES LOUNGE AT THE SEA RANCH

Beach Road, MP 7   441-7126

There's live entertainment most nights at the Dunes Lounge and it's open all year. A small dance floor, large screen TV and the overall atmosphere attract a somewhat older crowd than other places listed.

PAPAGAYO'S CANTINA

Beach Road, MP 7-1/2   441-7232

Let the ocean breezes lift your spirits from this second floor, ocean-front lounge and deck. There's live music during the season most nights and on weekends during the off season. It's a popular place for locals and visitors who like Mexican food and margaritas.

PORT O'CALL GASLIGHT SALOON

Beach Road, MP 8-1/2   441-7484

The Gaslight Saloon is a favorite place of Victorian style, featuring dark wood panelling and a long mahogany bar. Antique furnishings and a small dance floor for enjoyment are available. Live entertainment is offered in season several nights a week and on weekends in off season.

Insiders know:
Taxis can almost always be found waiting outside popular Outer Banks nightspots. Take advantage of them if necessary.

Insiders' Tip

MADELINE'S at the HOLIDAY INN
Beach Road, MP 9-1/2   441-6333

A popular place for the local population, Madeline's features live entertainment or a DJ for top-40 music. It's open all year for dancing or meeting friends. There's an on/off cover charge.

Nags Head

THE COMEDY CLUB
at the CAROLINIAN
Beach Road, MP 10-1/2   441-7171

Listen to good, live comedy six nights a week and enjoy meeting friends at the Anchor Lounge. Consider making reservations for a night of laughter...this form of entertainment is popular!

KELLY'S
Route 158, MP 10-1/2   441-4116

A great restaurant and tavern, Kelly's has become synonymous with good times on the Outer Banks. Live music is featured all year. There's a packed house almost every night.

WOODY'S
Route 158, Bypass, MP 11
at Pirate's Quay
441-4881

This raw bar and grill is becoming one of the most popular places on the beach. There's lots of good food here ranging from prime rib to good seafood. Entertainment at Woody's features reggae and calypso music with

shows starting at 10 p.m. It's free cover before 10 p.m.

PENGUIN ISLE
Route 158, MP 16   441-2637

This is a popular restaurant with a large deck and gazebo-lounge for a variety of night life. Entertainment is featured by local and out-of-town musicians. A lively crowd, generally late 20s and older, congregates at this favorite night spot.

STATION KEEPERS LOUNGE
at OWENS' RESTAURANT
Beach Road, MP 16-1/2   441-7309

The crowd that gathers here in this small, intimate setting will enjoy live piano music or small groups. The natural wood and brass accented by Tiffany-style lights create a cozy ambience.

Hatteras Island

KINNAKETT TAVERN
NC 12, Avon   995-5959

A mostly-local hangout, it's just right for late afternoon and night-time gatherings. The food is good and they have a pool table, big screen TV, darts and video games to keep you entertained.

DOWN UNDER
Rodanthe Pier, Rodanthe   987-2277

Down Under stays open till around midnight and is a great place to go for night life on Hatteras Island.

They've added a sunset deck and have the only cold, frosty (almost ice-caked) mugs on the island that we've found. Food is served until 10 p.m.

BUDROE'S

Hatteras Village, NC 12   986-2630

Comedy and musical entertainment keep this a lively place for locals and visitors. A small dance floor and pool table invite participation in the night life of this quaint establishment.

Ocracoke

3/4-TIME DANCE HALL & SALOON

NC 12, Main Road   928-1221

When you get here, you'll have to shift gears to get into the flow of this more traditional dance hall. There's plenty of fun on the dance floor and great music from the stage. It's a surprising place on an otherwise remote, quiet island.

HOWARD'S PUB & RAW BAR

NC 12, Main Road   928-4441

Howard's Pub & Raw Bar is the place to go for late night entertainment and they're open all year. They serve food until 1 a.m. and feature live music every night in season and on weekends during the off season. In addition, they have a big screen TV for all the big sporting events.

Optional Nighttime Activities

Miniature golf, amusement rides, water slides and movies are listed in the Recreation sections by town or village and will appeal for family outings.

DOWDY'S AMUSEMENT PARK

Route 158, MP 11, Nags Head

This park features fast-moving rides like the scrambler or tilt-a-whirl and will evoke memories of the midway or carnival atmosphere. There's just enough to whet your appetite for this type of fun satisfied and the kids will probably take the upper hand on what's fun and what isn't! Open evenings from spring until Labor Day.

WATERFALL PARK

NC 12, Rodanthe   987-2213

This park spreads out on both sides of the highway going south to Hatteras. (We've covered it in Hatteras/Recreation in some detail.) If rides, go-carts, lots of noise and excitement are the thing for your family, there's plenty of it here. Open 10 a.m. until 10 p.m. in season.

FAMILY LIFE CENTER

Route 158, MP 11-1/2   441-4941

Located at the Ark on the west side of the highway in Nags Head, there's a low-key Christian atmosphere available for young people here. Indoor games such as ping-pong, basketball, video games and roller skating are available on Friday and Saturday nights. Thursday night is adult basketball night.

ELIZABETHAN DINNER THEATRE
At the Elizabethan Inn
Main Rd. (Hwy. 64), Manteo 473-2101

There's unusual but delightful entertainment a short distance away from the beach. For those who have enjoyed the combination of dining and drama, this 16th-century tavern promises an interesting and educational evening by a troupe of Elizabethan characters. The language of the roles played out here will delight adults and children. The food is adequate and no alcoholic beverages are served, even though the setting is a tavern.

Photo: Michael Halminski

Outer Banks
Rentals

*T*he choice for lodging on the Outer Banks is counted in an unusual assortment of motels and hotels from Corolla to Ocracoke. In addition to motel rooms, a wide variety of rental apartments, condos, homes and cottages is available, depending on your preference. Since vacation planning is a primary use of this guide, we've made this an extensive chapter, covering hotels/motels and cottages with information on rental companies, regulations and hints for successfully planning your Outer Banks visit. We start with cottages.

VACATION COTTAGES

The competition is stiff for rentals of cottages and condos in this area. Rental brochures outline specific procedures to reserve time and it's best to "shop and book" early in the year. Oceanfront rentals go quickly and are in sharp demand every year. Those who rent them one year will often get preferential treatment the following year.

Some areas of the Outer Banks will demand higher prices than others and, of course, the closer to the ocean, the higher the fee. Early spring and fall offer some great bargains for the beach. More people are giving consideration to these "shoulder seasons" and have discovered very enjoyable vacations. Winter rentals are also available, particularly on the northern beaches, if you prefer a cottage over a motel/hotel room. Some of these northern Outer Banks cottages are quite luxurious.

By reading information about each area in this book, you will be able to choose which area of the beach you'd prefer to visit...each has its own personality. Call the companies located in that area for rental information. There's a lot to choose from and it is a good idea to select several choices according to priority before making a call.

When you rent a home or cottage, your options for the family are greater. Eating arrangements, periods of rest and relaxation, and more elbow room for family members are important considerations.

THE RATE SEASONS

Rate changes are sometimes confusing and tend to change with the season. Additional discounts are sometimes offered during the first week of a new season. Check with each company for specific rate/date changes. Here's a general idea of what to expect.

In-season is from mid-June through Labor Day and is the most expensive.

Mid-season is from just after Labor Day through Thanksgiving and from Easter until mid-June.

Off-season is from around December 1 through pre-Easter week.

Costs are as much as 20-30% less in mid-season than in-season and as much as 50% less in off-season than in-season.

PETS

Some rental cottages are available for bringing along the family pet. Don't be surprised at the additional charges for spraying. Each company has a complete policy for your protection, your pet's protection and for the protection of the homeowner who allows you to bring that important member of the family!

OCCUPANCY

Each rental cottage is governed by rules and regulations which are spelled out in the rental brochure from which you select your place at the beach. Most cottage owners and rental companies on the Outer Banks discourage large groups of young adults or college students who, instead, can select their accommodations at some motels and hotels on the beach.

Groups who try to get around the rules governing occupancy stand to lose their money and risk eviction. So, it's hard to imagine why some take the chance. Anyway, most people who visit the Outer Banks are family-oriented and prefer a quieter lifestyle than those large, youthful, rowdy beach party types!

ADVANCE RENTS

Money paid in advance is no longer considered a deposit. It's now called advance payment or advance rent. The transaction is governed by the laws of the North Carolina Real Estate Commission involving renting or leasing property from another.

Details, explanations and rules are spelled out in rental brochures and again in your lease. Read the fine print and save yourself a potential headache.

Personal checks are usually accepted for these advance rents and some rental companies allow credit card transactions. Final payments made upon check-in are usually required in the form of certified checks, travelers' checks or cash.

CANCELLATIONS

Again, cancellations are spelled out in rental brochures and lease agreements, and you can expect few exceptions. Forfeiting money is a difficult experience. Make sure you read the small print and know what the policy is on cancellations.

SECURITY DEPOSIT

This is another fee often included in the total amount you will pay for use of someone else's cottage on the beach. It's exactly what it implies. If there is damage, expect a smaller refund or no refund at all if the situation warrants it. The rental company has the final word on this, as a part of the business transaction for the homeowner.

MINIMUM STAYS

During the off-season some options exist for partial weeks and weekend rentals. During the in-season it's practically impossible to rent for less than a full week, which in this market runs either Saturday to Saturday or Sunday to Sunday. Hotels and motels are more flexible. Measure the difference in cost.

COTTAGE LOCATIONS

Rental brochures are a sophisti-cated business tool and locations are described in great detail in them. If it's not on the oceanfront, descriptions often indicate how far it is to walk to the beach. Read the cottage and location descriptions carefully so that you'll know exactly what you're renting. Here's a thumbnail sketch of what the various location descriptions mean.

Oceanside means you can walk to the beach without having to cross a major street or road. There will be other rows of houses along narrow lanes or roads between your cottage and the ocean.

Cottages from Kitty Hawk to Nags Head are often located between the highways. What this means is that the house is located between the Beach Road (in some places marked as NC Hwy. 12) and the Route 158 Bypass. The Beach Road is two lanes (one in each direction) and not difficult to cross most of the time. Pavement gets hot, though, so plan to wear good shoes when you walk from a cottage between the highways to the ocean.

Soundfront, soundside or westside locations generally mean facing the waters of the sound, near the sound without crossing a major road, or not very close to the water of the sound, but on the west side of the Bypass.

WHAT'S FURNISHED

A rental cottage is a fully-furnished home, in most instances. The rental brochures will list the furnishings, like small appliances, TVs, VCRs, stereos, toasters, microwaves, etc. and note other items provided such as beach chairs, beach umbrellas, hammocks and outdoor grills.

Most of the time, all you bring are your sheets and towels; however most rental companies rent them, as well.

If it's important to keep track of the time, bring a clock or radio, otherwise, watch the sun and relax!

MAIL & PHONE SERVICE

Rental companies are a service business and the people who speak with you on the phone to assist you with the details of your personal vacation will go the extra mile and take phone calls and mail if it's required while you're here. But you can make it easier on everyone by taking care of things like this before you arrive. Obtain the phone number of the cottage you will be renting and leave this number with close friends or relatives in case of emergencies.

Some older cottages don't have telephones, so be sure you check this out. In any event, long distance charges are the responsibility of the renter. Rules on this are spelled out in detail in most all rental brochures and in your cottage upon check-in.

EQUIPMENT RENTALS

If you prefer not bringing everything from home several rental companies can make life a lot easier. Strollers with large wheels for easy movement in the sand, beach chairs, videos, cribs, high-chairs, cots, you name it! The following rental companies are listed for your convenience.

Ocean Atlantic Rentals: 1-800-635-9559. Locations in Corolla, Duck, Nags Head/Kill Devil Hills, Waves and Avon.

Metro Rentals: (919) 480-3535. Located in Kill Devil Hills. (They carry party supplies, folding chairs, etc. in addition to the usual items needed at the beach).

Lifesaver Rentals: 1-800-635-2764. Located in Kill Devil Hills.

Beach Rentals (at Ocracoke Island Realty, P.O. Box 366, Ocracoke, NC 27960. 1-800-242-5394.

RENTAL COMPANIES

We've listed some rental companies and their location on the Outer Banks for your convenience.

Atlantic Realty, 261-2154 or 1-800-334-8401 for out-of-state callers. Located on Route 158, Bypass at MP 2-1/2. Mailing address: 4729 N. Croatan Hwy., Kitty Hawk, NC 27949.

Managing rental properties from Whalehead Beach to S. Nags Head.

Britt Real Estate, 261-3566 or 1-800-334-6315 for out-of-state callers. Located north of Duck Village. Mailing address: 1316 Duck Rd., Duck, NC 27949. Managing rental properties from Duck to Corolla.

Cove Realty, 441-6391 or 1-800-635-7007 for out-of-state callers. Located between the Beach Road and Route 158 bypass at MP 13-1/2. Mailing address: 105 E. Dunn St., Nags Head, NC 27959. Managing rental properties in Old Nags Head Cove, Nags Head, South Nags Head and the Village at Nags Head.

Dolphin Realty, 986-2241, 800-338-4775. Located in Hatteras. Mailing address: P.O. Box 387, Hatteras, NC 27943. Representing rentals on Hatteras Island.

Kitty Hawk Rentals, 441-7166 or 1-800-635-1559 for out-of-state callers. Located on Route 158 at MP 6. Mailing address: P.O. Box 69, Kill Devil Hills, NC 27948. Also located in Duck 261-6600 or 1-800-849-3825 for out-of-state callers. Mailing address: 1450 Duck Road, Duck, NC 27949. Managing rental properties from Corolla to South Nags Head.

Joe Lamb, Jr. & Asso., 261-4444 or 1-800-552-6257 for out-of-state callers. Located on Route 158, MP 2. Mailing address: P.O. Box 986, Kitty Hawk, NC 27949. Also located on Beach Road, MP 11. 441-5541. Managing rental properties from Whalehead to South Nags Head.

Midgett Realty, 986-2841 or 1-800-527-2903 for in and out-of-state long distance callers. Mailing address: NC Hwy. 12, Hatteras, NC 27943. Managing rental properties from Nags Head to Hatteras Village.

Sharon Miller Realty, 928-5711, Ocracoke, NC 27960. Managing Ocracoke Island properties.

Ocracoke Island Realty, 928-6261 or 928-7411, Ocracoke, NC 27960. Managing Ocracoke Island properties.

Outer Banks, Ltd., 441-5000 or 1-800-624-7651 for out-of-state callers. Located on Route 158, MP 10. Mailing address: P.O. Box 129, Nags Head, NC 27959. Managing rental properties from Duck to South Nags Head.

Outer Beaches Realty, 995-4477. Located on Hwy. 12 in Avon. Mailing address: P.O. Box 280, Avon, NC 27915. Managing rental properties from Rodanthe to Hatteras Village.

Pirate's Cove Realty, 473-6800 or 1-800-537-7245. Mailing address P.O. Box 1879, Manteo, NC 27954. Managing rental properties in the development of Pirate's Cove.

R & R Resort Rentals, 261-4498 or 1-800-433-8805 for out-of-state callers. Located in Duck Village. Mailing address: 1184 Duck Rd., Duck, NC 27949. Also located in Corolla Light Village Shops. 453-3033 or 1-800-962-0201 for out-of-state callers. Managing rental properties from Southern Shores to Carova Beach.

Resort Central, 261-8861 or 1-800-334-4749 for in and out-of-state callers. Located on Route 158, MP 2-1/2. Mailing address: P.O. Box 767, Kitty Hawk, NC 27949. Managing rental properties from Corolla to Nags Head.

Resort Realty, 261-8282 or 1-800-458-3830 for out-of-state callers. Located in Kitty Hawk. Mailing address: 3608 N. Croatan Hwy. Kitty Hawk, NC 27949. Also located in Duck: 1-800-545-3908; Corolla: 1-800-633-1630; and Rodanthe: 1-800-345-3522. Managing rental properties from Corolla to Rodanthe.

Salvo Real Estate, 987-2343. Located on NC Hwy. 12. Salvo, NC 27972. Managing rental properties in Rodanthe, Salvo and Waves.

Seaside Realty, 261-5500. 800-395-2525 for out-of-state callers. Located in on Route 158, MP 3-1/2 in Kitty Hawk. Mailing address: 4425 N. Croatan Hwy., Kitty Hawk, NC 27949.

Representing rental properties from Corolla to South Nags Head.

Southern Shores Realty, 261-2000 or 1-800-334-1000 for out-of-state callers, 1-800-682-2002 for in-state long distance callers. Located on NC Hwy. 12, Ocean Blvd., Southern Shores. Mailing address: P.O. Box 150, Southern Shores, NC 27949. Managing rental properties in Southern Shores and Duck.

Sun Realty, 441-7033 or 1-800-346-9593 for out-of-state callers. Located on Route 158, MP 9. Mailing address: P.O. Box 1630, Kill Devil Hills, NC 27948. Other locations: Duck: 261-7911 or 1-800-843-2033. Kitty Hawk: 261-1152, 1-800-346-9593. Avon: 995-5865 or 1-800-843-2034. Salvo: 987-2766 or 1-800-345-0910. Managing rental properties from Corolla to Avon.

Surf or Sound Realty, 995-5801 or 1-800-237-1138 for in and out-of-state long distance callers. Lo-

cated on NC Hwy. 12. Mailing address: P.O. Box 100, Avon, NC 27915. Managing rental properties on Hatteras Island.

Twiddy & Co. Realty, 261-2897. Located in Duck. Mailing Address: 1181 Duck Rd., Duck, NC 27949. Managing rental properties from Southern Shores to Corolla.

Village Realty, 441-8533 or 1-800-548-9688 for out-of-state callers. Located on Route 158, MP 15. Mailing address: 1807, Nags Head, NC 27959. Managing rental properties in the Village of Nags Head.

The Young People, 441-5544 or 1-800-334-6436 for out-of-state callers. Located on Beach Road, MP 6. Mailing address: P.O. Box 285, Kill Devil Hills, NC 27948. Managing rental properties from Corolla to South Nags Head.

THE MOTEL MARKET

The familiar concept of a resort hotel or motel of more cosmopolitan beaches is a rare find on the Outer Banks. Most commercial properties here don't offer room service, assistance with luggage and such "big city" service. But, the comfortable ambience obviously more than makes up for these things, since hotels and motels are almost always filled to capacity.

Outer Banks accommodations range from family-owned and operated motels, bed & breakfast houses and inns to larger hotels. Rooms vary in decor and furnishings and amenities such as phones and TVs.

Many older beach-front motels are most suitable for anglers or families who vacation on a low-budget. They're comfortable, favorite meeting places for family-reunions or group fishing trips that might have started years ago, and often are not fancy enough to worry about getting sand everywhere. In other words, perfect for the beach. Rates will vary from one area to another on the Outer Banks.

Hopefully, in reading this book, you'll discover the necessary facts to allow you to choose suitable accommodations. We have noted the availability of non-smoking rooms and other information such as access to dining possibilities and swimming pools.

RATE GUIDELINES

Motel accommodations come in several basic categories. We've indicated range/cost for one night's stay for two people this way:

$25 to $52	**$**
$53 to $75	**$$**
$76 to $95	**$$$**
$100 and up	**$$$$**

The rates do not include local and state taxes.

Rates are based on proximity to the ocean, view and amenities.

The locations are indicated by mile-posts or beach town and sometimes both.

RATE SEASONS

Commercial motels and hotels

adjust their rates in much the same way as rental properties. Make sure you get confirmations on dates and accommodations as well as rates. In-season begins in mid-June and continues through Labor Day.

Mid-season or off-season rates, of course, are lower. Vacations taken the last weeks before each season begins could present some cost-savings. Again, it's important to take notes and ask for confirmations on all reservations.

N.C. law prohibits pets in motel or hotel sleeping rooms. In some instances, however, cottage courts and bungalows allow the four-legged members of your family.

EXTRA PERSONS

Children under 12 or staying in the same room as two adults are often allowed without an additional charge. Ask about the specific policy when you call for reservations.

Extra adults are not often allowed in rooms when they will exceed the bed capacity of that room. Again, ask and get confirmation of charges, even though it's sometimes small.

DEPOSITS

All motels and hotels require deposits to confirm your reservations. Policies vary from one property to another but the average is 25% to 33% of the total reservation costs, or one night's rate. The policy regarding payment of deposits or refunds of deposits is often according to each property.

Get clear on this part when reserving your place at the beach.

CHECK-IN, CHECK-OUT TIMES

Check-in times vary from around 2 p.m. until late arrival, when so specified or requested. Check-out times are generally at 11 a.m. for beach motels, hotels and inns. Times will be posted and, of course, you will be informed when making your reservations. If you plan to drive to the beach and take occupancy for a vacation, it's wise to know an exact check-in time. If you arrive early, there are public beach access points along the beach road which allow you to park and walk out onto the beach.

PAYING THE BILL

Many hotels and motels expect the balance of the reservation paid upon arrival. Personal checks are seldom honored for this final payment. Be prepared with travelers' checks or credit card. Expect to include in your final payment the state and local taxes, which should be quoted to you when you reserve space. Although many banks here have automatic teller machines, don't rely on last minute transactions to cover cash requirements. Plan ahead.

MINIMUM STAYS

Protecting prime time has become a way of business for motels and hotels. For that reason it's sometimes difficult to get a one-night stay. Established minimums are the rule. Week-long reservations are accepted, of course, and in some instances partial weeks are as well. Refunds on reservations not fulfilled are not to be expected. In other words, if you reserve a week, but for some reason can't stay the week, you're apt to pay anyway, except in dire circumstances. Make definite plans and know the details for your pleasure and convenience.

COTS & CRIBS

Infants usually stay free of charge if you bring a small crib. The motel or hotel might provide one for a fee. Cots also carry a cost and are added to the room fee. Since these items may be in short supply, reserve them early if you know you'll need them.

PARKING

Motels and hotels provide free parking for at least one car per reservation. Keep valuables with you and not in the car, which is sometimes exposed to excessive heat and sunlight. The responsibility for your car and whatever you leave in it is yours.

OFF-SEASON PACKAGES

Many motels and hotels remain open all year. The weather here makes it possible for this. Though not always hot and sunny, the Outer Banks attracts sport-fishing enthusiasts in the fall and early winter. Others are drawn to quiet, deserted beaches and mild winters, thereby allowing some accommodations to offer short-stay pack-ages, sometimes including discounts for meals at a variety of restaurants.

WEEKLY RATES

There's no way to note here an average weekly rate. Costs depend on proximity to the beach, yet some do allow a discount for a week's rental. Some offer one night free of charge. Our best advise is to ask when you're making your reservations.

MOTEL LOCATIONS

Any property that uses the term oceanfront must have rooms which face the ocean. These rooms may have balconies and views. Some, located on ground level or behind the dunes, may not have view although they are on the oceanfront. Ask what's available and clarify which location you prefer, as it would be disappointing being told you have an oceanfront room and upon arrival discover the oceanfront room is behind the dune. (The voice of experience, speaking!)

PERSONAL CHECK CASHING

Since you'll need a credit card, travellers checks or cash to settle the remainder of your accommodations bill, we thought a word about these matters would be smart. Unless you have established prior credit or have an automatic teller card, there are only a few local banks that will cash your check. Cash advances on credit cards are handled without question. *Banks on the Outer Banks are not open on Saturdays or Sundays*. Banking hours are 9 to 5 Monday through Thursday and 9 to 6 on Friday.

GOLF & TENNIS PRIVILEGES

Most any commercial motel/hotel property can offer these two amenities because several local golf courses and an indoor tennis center are open to the public. It's important to ask where the facilities are located in proximity to where your reservations are being made, if convenience is a factor. Ask about free passes and discount green fees.

GUARDED BEACHES

Nags Head Ocean Rescue and Lifeguard Service provide lifeguard service on our beaches from Nags Head to Kitty Hawk. Some areas are not guarded, so be aware if that's a concern to you. Many areas are red-flagged when stormy seas prohibit safe swimming. Pay attention to these flags! Lifeguard stands are located in front of many motel properties and at public beach accesses with adequate parking to ensure a crowd. The areas between the lifeguard stands are patrolled by a four wheel drive vehicle equipped for rescue. Ask when you make your reservations if your particular hotel/motel has a guarded beach if this is important to you.

Members of the Lifeguard Service and Ocean Rescue are especially trained in ocean rescue and are equipped with surfboards and life rings. Listen to their advice: if they say stay out of the water, they have good reason to say so. Believe us, they've seen too many vacations ruined because swimmers thought they could outsmart -- and outswim -- this Outer Banks surf.

RECYCLING

Citizens of Dare County take recycling seriously. In fact, you'll often find that volunteers at the recycling center also work in shops and rental offices of businesses on the Outer Banks. The North Carolina legislature set guidelines for compliance for all its counties and the permanent residents know what it means to keep the beaches clean and lighten the load of trash to area landfills.

Guests are encouraged to recycle, too. Rental companies have appropriate information about recycling centers located from Corolla to Ocracoke and there's information on the locations and operating hours of recycling centers for each town in our Service Directory. Thanks for doing your part to protect this beautiful environment.

Photo: Walter V. Gresham III

THOUSANDS DIE EACH YEAR . . .

YOU CAN MAKE THE DIFFERENCE!

Many animals are abandoned annually in Dare County . . . left to wander in search of a home . . . food . . . water.

The sad fact is that most of them don't find homes. They die as a result of starvation, injury, abuse or neglect.

We're working to change this. And you can make a difference.

PLEASE HELP US HELP THEM!

Send your tax-deductible contributions to:

Outer Banks S.P.C.A.
P.O. Box 3006
Kill Devil Hills, NC 27948
441-2766

Outer Banks
Accommodations

Northern Beaches

Accommodations

When you're vacationing on the northern beaches you're in an area without hotels, motels as known on others parts of the Outer Banks. The choice in this area is an incredible variety of private homes which are leased through real estate property management businesses. However, there's the old adage about "an exception to everything"...Sanderling Inn Resort fits here.

SANDERLING INN RESORT
NC 12, 1461 Duck Road
(919) 261-4111

$$$$ **MC, VISA, AMEX**

The Sanderling Inn Resort is situated on 12 acres of oceanside wilderness. The heavy stands of beach grass, sea oats, pines, fragrant olives and live oaks provide a natural setting for a luxurious vacation. The area is one of the most beautiful on the Outer Banks and has no commercial sector. It's 5 miles north of Duck Village. The Inn is built in the style of the old Nags Head beach homes of wood siding, cedar shake accents, dormers and porches on each side. If it's been a while since you've spent time in a rocking chair, on a porch overlooking the ocean or sound, be forewarned — it's been known to cause instant relaxation!

All the rooms at Sanderling welcome you to comfort and an understated elegance. Lounging robes, Caswell Massey soaps and toiletries, complimentary fruit, wine and cheese are provided for guests. A full breakfast and afternoon social hour with wine and hors d'oeuvres are complimentary to Sanderling guests.

The main lobby and gallery of Sanderling Inn provides a warm welcome to travelers. The mellow tone of polished wood floors, wainscotting and a English country decor begins here and is carried throughout all the rooms. The main Inn has 24 rooms and another 32 are provided in Sanderling Inn North.

A separate building also houses conference facilities and a Presidential Suite, complete with Jacuzzi bath and two decks — one overlooks the ocean and the other the sound. All rooms at Sanderling have remote color cable TV, telephones, and some have complete kitchens, others have refrigerators.

This is a complete resort with lovely beaches as well as a health club with two exercise rooms, indoor pool, separate whirlpool room, locker rooms, saunas, tennis courts, bike rentals and a natural walking or jogging trail. The nearby Audubon Wildlife Sanctuary and Pine Island Indoor Tennis and Racquet Club provide a wide range of choices for fitness and recreation.

The Sanderling Inn Restaurant (covered in detail in our section about North Beach Restaurants) is housed on the property in a turn of the century lifesaving station. The meals served here are what you've come to expect at an exclusive resort property.

Kitty Hawk

ACCOMMODATIONS

DAYS INN MOTEL

Route 158, MP 4-1/2   261-4888

1-800-325-2525 $$

Most Major Credit Cards

This Days Inn is located between the highway and the beach road. It's a short walk to the guarded Kitty Hawk beach and has its own swimming pool. The rates are very reasonable and children under 17 stay free. One of the newer properties on the beach, it is close to shopping and several restaurants. Keeper's Galley is a favorite local restaurant and is on the premises. Large rooms, most with

queen-size beds and attractively furnished for your comfort, are available in this year round resort motel. All rooms have color, cable TV and telephones.

BEACH HAVEN MOTEL

Beach Road, MP 4   261-4785

$-$$ MC, VISA

A small motel right across from a beach access on the beach road, the Beach Haven has rooms with a practical, homey touch rather than a standard motel. Items like coffee makers, hair dryers and porch chairs are provided. Owners Joe and Janet Verscharen live on the property to help make your stay here most pleasant.

BUCCANEER MOTEL

Beach Road, MP 5-1/4   261-2030

$$ MC, VISA

This is an older motel, now owned by Keith and Joy Byers. They've given the place a face-lift and it's a neat, friendly beach motel. The rooms are nicely furnished and decorated and they even have facilities for the handicapped. A separate four-bedroom efficiency can accommodate up to 10 people. The Buccaneer is right across the beach road from the oceanfront and has a dune deck and private access in order to get on the beach in record time. While there are no room telephones (a pay phone is on the premises), color cable TV and refrigerators are in each room. This friendly place also is a great place for kids. The property offers a small playground, and for the adults who like to catch and cook their own fish, a fish-cleaning station and charcoal grills are provided.

Kill Devil Hills

ACCOMMODATIONS

Severe storms of late fall and winter have taken a toll on the oceanfront properties in Kill Devil Hills and elsewhere on the Outer Banks. Some have done an excellent job of restoring the beach while others have not fared as well. Ask about the condition of the beach when you call for reservations.

THE FIGUREHEAD BED & BREAKFAST
417 Helga Street, MP 5-1/2, West of the Bypass
441-6929 or 1-800-221-6929 $

The Figurehead Bed & Breakfast opened in 1988 and overlooks the sound. Situated on a hill, the 3-story house has accommodations on all levels. The Keeping Room has a fireplace, perfect for chilly evenings in the off-season. The wide porch is a great place to sit comfortably in a rocking chair and watch the sun go down.

A view of the sound awaits guests from the Osprey Watch upstairs, which has a private sun deck and Jacuzzi. Safe Harbor, with a private entrance, bath and outside sitting area, is located downstairs. Sea One, with a private bath, offers privacy for a couple or the business person.

Owner Ann Ianni gives personal attention to all the details of a

convenient place by the sound. A continental breakfast is served. A picnic area for outdoor cooking and dining, complimentary newspapers and soundside access are all part of the charm at the cozy home. Ann has used soft colors, natural woods and a blend of old and new furniture to capture the spirit of seaside living. We consider The Figurehead an excellent option for accommodations.

THE MARINER

Beach Road, MP 7	**441-2021**
Non-smoking rooms	**$$**

MC, VISA, AMEX

This oceanfront property has experienced damage for two or three years, yet remains open with standard rooms which are well-maintained. All rooms have color cable TV, phones and refrigerators. Some two-bedroom apartments in the oceanfront building have been refurbished and about five years ago two- and three-bedroom efficiency apartments were built across the road. There's easy ocean access, the units are big and offer flexible living arrangements for families or groups. The recreation area has facilities for volleyball, shuffleboard and badminton. The swimming pool and beachside showers are right on the ocean. Indoor tennis is across the street. The Mariner is open from mid-February through the end of November.

SEA RANCH HOTEL

Beach Road, MP 7	**441-7126**
1-800-334-4737	
Non-smoking rooms	**$$$**

All major credit cards

The Sea Ranch was one of the first resort properties on the Outer Banks to include all recreational amenities, a restaurant, bar and retail shops. This nice oceanfront destination is a Quality Inn property and has had its battle with storms and beach erosion. The beach has been rebuilt to some degree. Luxury condominiums and a five-story oceanfront tower in addition a two-story oceanside building comprise this property. Room service is available, all rooms have color cable TV with HBO, refrigerators, microwaves, and some suites and apartments have glass-enclosed oceanfront balconies.

Amenities include Alice's Restaurant overlooking the ocean, a lounge with dance floor and nightly entertainment. The Nautilus Fitness Center is on the premises as well as the indoor pool. Alice's Looking Glass women's boutique and Shear Genius Hair Salon round out the retail shops. Its open all year and the rates are reasonable.

HAMPTON INN

Beach Road, MP 7-1/2   441-0411

1-800-338-7761

Non-smoking rooms $$

All major credit cards

There's a new name and a new look for this 97-room hotel directly across from the beach. Rooms feature mostly double beds, but some kings and a few singles are available. Rooms also have microwaves and refrigerators, but no utensils. An extensive breakfast buffet of fresh fruit, juices, sweet breads, coffee and tea will appeal to many. The reception and lobby/lounge are being refurbished, not only to accommodate the big breakfast buffet, but to allow a more casual place to meet, read the paper and enjoy afternoon cocktails and appetizers. Food and beverage service are available by the pool as well.

Walter Pope, manager, noted the upgrades such as new carpet, painting and better all around services for guests of Hampton Inn. There are four

handicapped units, parking and appropriate ramps at this property. The swimming pool has been resurfaced and the walk to the beach is less than 200 yards. They are open all year.

THE CHART HOUSE MOTEL

Beach Road, MP 7   **441-7418**

MC, VISA   **$**

David and Kristin Clark live in the large brick Colonial oceanfront house and offer a personal touch to their roles as host for the 18-unit motel. The Chart House, built in 1966, has become a legend on the Outer Banks and boasts large rooms, whether they're efficiencies or regular rooms. There is good beach here, rooms are more than adequate for the price and they're clean. Color TV and refrigerators are in every room. The efficiencies have fully-equipped kitchens.

For the children there is a playground. A small pool and patio away from the road and a dune-deck make staying here enjoyable. The Chart House is open March through November.

CAVALIER MOTEL

Beach Road, MP 8   **441-5584**

MC, VISA   **$-$$**

A variety of rooms is available at this courtyard motel on the oceanfront. Three one-story wings enclose the two swimming pools, volleyball court, children's play area and shuffleboard courts.

Parking is outside each room and the covered porch with outdoor furniture is just right for relaxation. An observation deck sits atop the oceanfront section.

Some units have shower facilities only, others have tub and shower, some have kitchenettes, all have refrigerators, microwave ovens, color cable TV and phones. It's a well-maintained property on the ocean and reasonably priced. Port O'Call, one of the nicest restaurants on the beach, is opposite and the Wright Brothers Memorial is nearby.

TANGLEWOOD MOTEL

Beach Road, MP 8-1/4   **441-7208**

MC, VISA   **$$$**

Tanglewood is a small oceanfront motel where the units are referred to as vacation apartments. Each one has a complete kitchen, with microwave, in addition to a full bath, of course. There is a swimming pool and picnic tables, plus a fish-cleaning table on the premises.

COMFORT INN

Beach Road, MP 8   **480-2600**

1-800-228-5150

Non-smoking rooms   **$$$-$$$$**

All major credit cards

One of the newer oceanfront motels on the beach, the rooms are standard motel rooms in the Quality Inn style. All rooms have a coffee pot; some have refrigerators and microwaves; all have color cable TV and phones. Most rooms have an ocean view. The property has an oceanfront pool and a hospitality room for meetings. Open all year.

DAYS INN - WILBUR & ORVILLE WRIGHT MOTEL

Beach Road, MP 8-1/2   441-7211
1-800-325-2525

Non-smoking rooms $$
Most major credit cards

An oceanfront motel situated on a wide area of the beach, this motel offers a lot of history from it's beginning in 1948. Originally built to resemble an old mountain lodge, it boasts an inviting lobby where guests read the paper and have coffee. It boasts balconies with old-time furniture and nice views. A shipwreck is located just north of the building, attracting off-the-beach divers or snorkelers.

Oriental rugs cover a large portion of the polished hardwood floors of the main lobby. The fireplace is large enough to take away the chill of cold mornings at the beach. Rooms in the older part are small, but the refurbished rooms are nicely decorated. Other sections of the building have larger rooms and very little storage space except in the kitchen. This Days Inn has a large pool and sundeck. There's also a barbeque pit for cookouts. Open all year except for December and January.

OCEAN REEF -
BEST WESTERN HOTEL
Beach Road, MP 8-1/2   441-1611
1-800-528-1234
Non-smoking rooms $$$$
Most major credit cards

The one-bedroom suites of this newer oceanfront hotel are decorated and arranged like a luxury apartment. The views are great and you'll find everything you need for a luxurious vacation at the beach. Each room has color cable TV and phones and a fully-equipped galley-style kitchen.

Upper floor rooms have private balconies overlooking the ocean. Some first floor units open onto the oceanfront pool and courtyard, others offer a private patio. One of the few properties on the beach to have one, the penthouse suite boasts a private jacuzzi and roof-top deck. There is a heated pool and a whirlpool located in the courtyard. The exercise room has the latest equipment and a sauna. During the summer season, bar and food service is available in the deli. Ocean Reef is open all year and is truly a luxury resort property.

COLONY IV MOTEL
Beach Road, MP 9   441-5581
Most major credit cards $$$

This modern family-owned and operated beach motel is very well-maintained with the most amenities of any place on the beach. Managed by Cindy and Tom Kingsbury, of the Neal family's second generation, they provide a lot of hospitality for moderate costs on the oceanfront here in Kill Devil Hills. A run-down the list will show: outdoor pool and patio, a 9-hole miniature golf course, 2 picnic areas with grills, a children's playground, a dune-top gazebo, a game room, horseshoes and other outdoor game areas. There is also a laundry. Continental breakfast is served every morning.

Rooms are nice size with two double beds (one has a king-size bed), phones, refrigerators and microwaves. Some rooms have direct access to the beach while others have a small balcony. The efficiencies have an eating area and combined with adjoining rooms create a good arrangement for family vacations. The motel is open February through December.

ECONO LODGE MOTEL
Route 158, Bypass MP 9   441-2503
1-800-446-6900
Non-smoking rooms $$
All major credit cards

Located on the highway rather than the Beach Road, this motel was built about 7 years ago and is very affordable. The 2 blocks to the ocean is manageable and the 40 rooms are all well-furnished and maintained. All have either king-size beds or extra length double beds, color cable TV with HBO, phones, tubs/showers and the property boasts an indoor heated pool for year round use. The motel offers an "Econo Traveler's Club": stay six nights and the seventh is without charge.

RAMADA INN HOTEL

Beach Road, MP 9-1/2   **441-2151**
1-800-2RAMADA

Non-smoking rooms   **$$$$**
All major credit cards

This five-story 172-room hotel was built in 1985 and is located on the oceanfront. A resort hotel/convention center, it is very popular for tour groups and small meetings. Rooms are standard with air conditioning and are nicely furnished. All have a balcony or patio, color cable TV with pay-per-view movies, a small refrigerator and microwave. A rare thing on the Outer Banks, room service and help with the luggage are available.

The meeting facilities are centrally located on the third floor overlooking the ocean. There are several meeting rooms or suites to fit a variety of needs.

For guests the enclosed swimming pool is located just off the second floor, atop the dunes and surrounded by a large sundeck. A flight of steps takes you onto the beach, where volleyball is the rage. There's a heated whirlpool and an oceanfront gazebo. Food and beverage service is available at the Gazebo Deck bar, adjacent to the pool.

"Peppercorns" is the name of the hotel's fine restaurant which serves breakfast and dinner year round and offers lunch on the deck during the summer. If you enjoy hotel accommodations rather than motel or rental cottage, you'll enjoy the Ramada Inn, complete with magnificent oceanfront views.

HOLIDAY INN

Beach Road, MP 9-1/2   **441-6333**
1-800-843-1249

Non-smoking rooms   **$$-$$$**
All major credit cards

Located on the oceanfront the 105 rooms of the resort property have been newly remodeled and you'll enjoy a visit here. The ocean views are breathtaking. The banquet and conference facilities have been expanded. There's a pool, Jacuzzi, and oceanfront bar. The rooms offer remote color TV with in-room movies. There's live entertainment at Madeline's, a full service restaurant and lounge. You'll find this a good place to stay and they're open all year.

TANYA'S OCEAN HOUSE MOTEL

Beach Road, MP 10   **441-2900**
MC, VISA   **$$**

Tanya's is an Outer Banks legend with its unique, individually designed rooms. The story goes that Tanya Young and a designer friend decided to do a theme room at the motel and it got out of hand to include a different design for each room. There's Carolina Party Room, Jonathan Seagull's Nest, and so on. No two rooms are alike. There are a few rooms which remain "normal" for motel rooms, if you prefer. Another nice thing about this motel is it's outdoor pool which is large and facing the sun all day. Each room has a refrigerator, color cable TV with HBO and some have waterbeds. Rooms are rather small, but they are very clean. Tanya's is open mid-March through October.

NETTLEWOOD MOTEL

Beach Road, MP 7	441-5039
Major credit cards	$-$

Locally owned and operated, the Nettlewood is a favorite of the older set who like to come to the beach in small groups, prefer a small, clean motel and don't need any extras. There are 21 apartments and 16 efficiencies located on both sides of the Beach Road. Rooms have remote control color cable TV. There is a large swimming pool on the premises.

QUALITY INN - JOHN YANCEY MOTOR HOTEL

Beach Road, MP 10	441-7141
1-800367-5941	
Non-smoking rooms	$$$-$$$$
Most major credit cards	

This is a nice family hotel conveniently located on a wide beach which is guarded by the Beach Lifeguard service during summer months. There is also a pool, playground and shuffleboard courts. Affiliated with Quality Inns, it is an older motor hotel but was heavily refurbished a couple of years ago. The main building was practically stripped, rebuilt, and redecorated.

The standard rooms have color cable TV, pay-per-view in-room movies and small refrigerators.

Surf fishing enthusiasts enjoy

staying here because of the wide beach. Children under 12 stay free. Rollaway beds and cribs are available for rent to accommodate extra children. The property is open all year.

Nags Head

ACCOMMODATIONS

For a more visual location of places to stay in Nags Head, we've divided the Beach Road motels into north and south. From MP 10, the "official boundary" of Nags Head to MP 13 is considered Nags Head north. From MP 14 to Whalebone Junction at MP 16-1/2, it's called Nags Head south. The entire area is accentuated with rental properties ranging from older, Nags Head-style cottages to timeshare condos, efficiencies and some delightful new and quite large beach homes. We've listed the rental companies who handle these homes in the section just before this one called Outer Banks Rentals.

NAGS HEAD NORTH

BEACON MOTOR LODGE

Beach Road, MP 11	441-5501
Non-smoking rooms	$$
Most major credit cards	

There are quite a few options at this oceanfront property for visitors who have a variety of needs while on vacation, whether it's a weekend in spring or fall or a week in the summer. They're oriented towards accommodating families, with one-, two- and three-room combinations ranging from efficiencies to motel-type rooms. All rooms are equipped with a small refrigerator and phones.

The oceanfront terrace accommodates all guests, and the oceanfront rooms open onto a large walled terrace affording wonderful views of the ocean from early morning until moon-rise.

Amenities include two children's pools, a large elevated pool, playground, patios with grills, electronic game room and laundromat. They're open from Easter through October.

OCEAN VERANDA

Beach Road, MP 11   441-5858

MC, VISA, AMEX $-$$

A well-maintained property, Ocean Veranda is under new management and anxious to please. They've done some refurbishing this year, including all new vanity tops in the baths and full-size refrigerators in every room. Rooms are large and have AC, 2 double beds, and color cable TV. Efficiencies have complete kitchens and can adjoin other rooms to accommodate large families. Rollaways and cribs are available for a small charge. Children under 6 are free. There is a small charge for extra person in rooms. There are 16 rooms and 15 efficiencies.

A nice breakfast selection is offered, compliments of the management, with fruits, juices, pastries, cereals and, of course, coffee. This is a

two-story property so the upper floors have a wider view, but you can't get much closer to the ocean. There are comfortable outdoor gatherings places as two gazebos are located at poolside.

Ocean Veranda is in the midst of everything on the beach and is open from March through November.

NAGS HEAD SOUTH

NAGS HEAD INN

Beach Road, MP 14   441-0454

Non-smoking rooms

1-800-327-8881

MC, VISA, AMEX $$$$

The identity as an inn is a little misleading here , as this sparkling white stucco building with blue accents is a relatively new addition to the Nags Head motels. It's quite a contrast to the old Nags Head style cottages nearby. There's covered parking and tastefully decorated rooms to accommodate you on the oceanfront.

Five-stories high, all rooms afford ocean views. Each has a small refrigerator and color cable TV with HBO. A heated all-weather swimming pool is located on the second floor deck. Open all year.

SILVER SANDS MOTEL

Beach Road, MP 14   441-7354

MC, VISA $-$$

This is one of the few motels not located on the ocean side of the beach road, but it's directly across from beach access. It's a small motel and has been renovated recently. Rooms have color cable TV with HBO, refrigerators and air conditioning. The walls are rustic pine and clean. There is a newer 2-story building which has balconies with oceanview on the upper floor. Another section offers 16 units near the swimming pool. For the location, you can't beat the price. Open from Easter until early December.

SURF SIDE MOTEL
Beach Road, MP 16
441-2105, 1-800-552-SURF

Non-smoking rooms   **$$$**
MC, VISA, AMEX, DISCOVER

This attractive 5-story motel is situated right on the oceanfront and all rooms face north, south and east for ocean views and some have views of the sound, as well. It's very moderately priced for what is offered. All ocean front rooms have refrigerators and are attractively decorated in soft muted beach tones and all have private balconies. There is air conditioning, phones, color cable TV and the honeymoon suites feature king-size beds and private Jacuzzis. Of course, there's an elevator for easy access.

The folks are very friendly and can accommodate you in an adjacent 3-story building which has rooms and efficiencies with either ocean or sound views. If you're in your room for any length of time, you'll be very comfortable. Otherwise, you can choose from an indoor pool which is open all year or an outdoor pool for swimming in warm weather.

Coffee and sweets are provided for early morning convenience and a friendly afternoon wine and cheese social hour is held for guests who stay here.

The *Surf Side* is available for charter fishing expeditions at Oregon Inlet Fishing Center and conveniently booked at the lobby-reception.

FIRST COLONY INN
Route 158, Bypass, MP 16
441-2343, 1-800-368-9390

Non-smoking rooms   **$$$$**

This refurbished landmark hotel of another era, has become a favorite for those who like the ambience of a quiet inn. It's history dates to 1932, when it was known as Leroy's Seaside Inn. The old Nags Head-style architecture of this inn, resplendent under an over-hanging roof and wide porches, has been preserved and now is listed on the National Register of Historic Places.

It was during the spring of 1988 that efforts began to save the dilapidated building from demolition. The Lawrence family, with deep roots in the area felt that the Inn was too valuable for the community to lose. The building was sawed into three sections for the move from its oceanfront location to the present site, three miles south, between the highways. It took two years of rehabilitation to return the inn to its original appearance. The interior was completely renovated and

now contains 27 rooms, all with traditional furnishings and modern comforts.

There's a spacious room for a deluxe continental breakfast. Upstairs there's an elegant but cozy library with books, games and an old pump organ -- a favorite place to read the paper or meet with other guests.

Each room is individually appointed in English antique furniture. Special touches like tiled baths, heated towel bars, imported toiletries, telephones, remote controlled TV, individual climate control and refrigerators are standard. Some rooms offer other special features such as wet bars, kitchenettes, Jacuzzis, VCRs and private balconies.

Some rooms have an additional trundle bed or day bed for an extra person. For the consideration of nonsmoking guests and the historic status of the inn, smoking is permitted only in the public areas and a few rooms. There is handicapped-access and one room which is designed for use by the handicapped.

Room service is available at no extra charge beyond menu prices from Penguin Isle Restaurant across the highway. Discounts and group rates apply under certain conditions and there is a policy of one night free for stays of seven days or longer.

This magnificent inn is open all year, has easy access to the ocean and is centrally located to many shops and restaurants in Nags Head.

ISLANDER MOTEL

Beach Road, MP 16　　　**441-6229**
MC, VISA, AMEX　　　　**$$$**

The Islander is one of the most popular small oceanfront properties on the beach. The buildings, attractive landscaping and well-maintained rooms are a strong influence here. Most rooms have a view and some have private patios or balconies. There is a pool and a private dune walk to the ocean.

The rooms are large and frequently refurbished. All have adequate sitting areas and refrigerators. Some with kitchenettes on the first floor offer complete accommodations for a pleasurable stay at the beach.

The Islander is conveniently located to all the restaurants, shops and Nags Head attractions. Because of the height of the dunes along the ocean here, some first-floor oceanfront rooms do not have ocean views. Check this out when making reservations. You'll find the comforts of this attractive motel more than adequate. Open from April through October.

BLUE HERON MOTEL

Beach Road, MP 16　　　**441-7447**
MC, VISA　　　　　　　**$$**

This family-owned motel provides reasonably priced, oceanfront rooms, a year round indoor swimming pool and a spa. It's considered one of the best kept secrets of the small motels in the area.

The Gladden family lives on

the premises and gives careful attention to the management of the property. It's located conveniently in the midst of fine Nags Head restaurants and offers a good beach to those who come here and want to relax.

There are rooms and efficiencies, air conditioned and heated. All have refrigerators, coffee pots, color cable TV and shower/tub combinations. It's open all year.

SEA FOAM MOTEL

Beach Road, MP 16   **441-7320**

MC, VISA, AMEX   **$$**

There are 29 rooms, 18 efficiencies and two cottages at this attractive motel on the oceanfront. The one- and two-story buildings provide some oceanfront and poolside views. The repeat clientele at this property will attest to its cleanliness and affordability. Children are welcome and there's even a playground for their use. A large pool, sundeck and shuffle-board are other recreational options. There's a gazebo on the beach for guests.

The tastefully furnished rooms have color cable TV with HBO, refrigerators, microwaves and phones. All are air conditioned. Some rooms, recently refurbished, have king-size beds. All units have balconies or porches with comfortable furniture.

Sea Foam Motel is within walking distance of good restaurants and Jennette's Fishing Pier. Open March through November.

OWENS' MOTEL

Beach Road, MP 16   **441-6361**

MC, VISA, AMEX   **$$**

The Owens' family has owned and operated this attractive motel for over 40 years. It was one of the first motels on the beach. Adjacent to their famous restaurant, it is well-maintained with care given to reflect its family atmosphere.

A newer three-story oceanfront addition was built about 10 years ago and it is a very reliable, no-frills motel. All oceanfront accommodations are efficiencies with large, private balconies. Each room has two double beds, tile bath and shower and a kitchen. The motel swimming pool on the west side, offers the choice of beach or pool. Color cable TV and air conditioning are available in all rooms. There's easy access to Jennette's Fishing Pier and a comfortable oceanfront pavilion with rocking chairs for the enjoyment of guests who stay here. Open April through October.

SEA OATEL
Beach Road, MP 16-1/2
441-7191, 1-800-221-2222
Non-smoking rooms $$$
Most major credit cards

This year round Quality Inn has an excellent oceanfront location to all restaurants, recreation, shops and Nags Head attractions. There are 111 rooms, all of which have been completely renovated. The exterior reflects major renovation and an invitation to enjoy 400 feet of oceanfront. The new blue roof is an easy identifying characteristic.

It's one of the nicest places on the south end of Nags Head. The front desk is open 24 hours a day, complimentary continental breakfast is offered and all rooms conform to the standards of Quality Inn. There's color cable TV with HBO, phones, a coin-operated laundry and snacks and ice is plentiful.

There is a sheltered cabana on the beach and everything you need for a visit to the beach. Open all year.

ARMADA RESORT HOTEL
Beach Road, MP 16-1/2   441-6315
1-800-334-3302
Non-smoking rooms $$$
All major credit cards

The Armada is a seven-story hotel which is being completely refurbished as we go to press. The exterior work is almost done and the concrete finish has a touch of pastel pink to give it a nice beachy appearance. The interiors, completed in early June, include new carpet, wall coverings and window treatments in all of the 105 rooms. The rates vary from month-to-month and according to room. Deluxe ocean rooms, ocean rooms, street-side rooms and suites are available.

The views of the beach from rooms facing the ocean are magnificent. The hotel is away from any busy areas of the beach and affords guests more than typical privacy while staying here. There's an oceanfront lounge for evening dancing and cocktails. The oceanfront pool and deck is a favorite gathering place, as well. Deckside beverage service are featured during the summer months. A full-scale continental breakfast area is located in the lobby area.

Corporate meeting rooms are being expanded and a new playground is being built for children. In other words, this oceanfront property will hold strong appeal for families and for business groups. Open all year.

FIN 'N FEATHER MOTEL
Route 64, Nags Head-Manteo
Causeway
441-5353

MC, VISA   **$**

A favorite small motel along the edge of the water, Fin 'N Feather has 10 rooms and is popular with those who come to the Outer Banks to fish and hunt. If you're planning to come in the fall or spring, make your reservations well ahead of time. Its location, near the Pirate's Cove Fishing Center, will please those who are

headed out for a day on the open seas. There's a boat ramp here, too, for those who bring their own.

The rooms are clean and comfortable with blue and white decor. Large windows open onto the water from either side, with stunning views.

Roanoke Island

ACCOMMODATIONS

THE ELIZABETHAN INN
Main Hwy., Manteo
473-2101, 1-800-346-2466

MC, VISA   **$-$$$**

The Elizabethan Inn is a full-

resort facility in the quiet town of Manteo. Contained within three distinct buildings of this comfortable hotel, there are 112 rooms, efficiencies and apartments and conference facilities.

Situated in town, the shaded picnic area and fitness center make this inn a delightful place to stay away from the beach, during season and off-season. There's a restaurant on the premises with banquet facilities for small and large groups. (The Elizabethan Dinner Theatre is located here and reviewed in the section on Restaurants.)

The small lobby is filled with interesting antiques and a friendly staff welcomes you to the historic ambience of Manteo and the Inn.

There's a small gift shop off the reception area.

All rooms have color cable TV with HBO, refrigerators and phones. Though the rooms in the original build-

ing are smaller than those in the Center Court or the Elizabethan Manor sections, all are clean, comfortable and perfectly suited for a quiet, Roanoke Island-style vacation. You will enjoy the friendly hospitality and convenience of this property to Manteo, the historic attractions and the comforts of a small town near the beach.

The Nautics Hall Fitness Center located here is available for guests of the Inn, of course, and is a big draw. There are two pools -- one outside and the other, Olympic size and heated, located indoors -- and the full range of equipment for intense workouts (reviewed in more detail in the section on Recreation). The Elizabethan Inn is open all year and offers special packages.

ROANOKE ISLAND INN

305 Fernando Street   **473-5511**

Most major credit cards   **$$$**

This white clap-board offers the atmosphere of a gracious, restored home with the comforts of a small, well-designed inn. The furnishings are homey and reflect genuine care by the Innkeeper. The ambience is laid-back and friendly. There's an eight-room addition which was designed for the privacy of the guests. Each room has its own private entrance, private bath, TV, phones and bikes for touring. There's an interesting collection of books and artwork related to the Outer Banks in the lobby, and a light breakfast is offered in the butler's pantry.

The grounds, situated on the waterfront in downtown Manteo, are private and comfortable too, with gardenia and fig bushes and other native plants. The coy pond out back provides "nature's music" to soothe and relax guest. You'll enjoy a stay here.

Generally, the Inn is open from mid-April to sometime in the fall.

SCARBOROUGH INN

Main Hwy.   **473-3979**

Most major credit cards   **$**

Located across from the Christmas Shop, this small inn is a delightful, friendly place to stay. A native of Manteo, owner Sally Scarborough long dreamed that she would have an inn someday and when her husband, Phil, a native of Wanchese and former Coast Guard officer, retired, her vision became a reality. Sally, with the help of designer-architect John Wilson, IV, has created a two-story reproduction of a turn-of-the-century inn. Each of the guest rooms is filled with antiques and other furnishings; most were refinished by Sally.

There's a story behind every room and its furnishings. Sally creates a casual, comfortable ambience with these stories and the attention to detail

Tranquil House Inn

Bed & Breakfast
•
Located on the
Manteo Waterfront
•
Roanoke Island
•
(919) 473-1404 or
1-800-458-7069

of each room. Antique sewing machines, expertly refinished, serve as TV stands. Some doors have been salvaged from an old church.

All the rooms at the Inn are located away from the street and have color cable TV, phones, private baths, small refrigerators and coffee pots. Some rooms have a wet bar. If you'd like your refrigerator stocked, Sally will gladly accommodate your wish. Complimentary morning coffee and donuts are served in the parlor.

Room rates vary and there are some suites. Travelers will appreciate the care and attention given by the owners and your stay here will be most pleasant.

DUKE OF DARE

Main Hwy.   **473-2175**

MC, VISA   **$**

Located on the main street but only a few blocks to the Manteo waterfront, this small motel provides the essentials of basic accommodations. The L-shaped motor inn has clean rooms and standard features, including color cable TV and phones. Some rooms have queen-size beds. There's a pool on the property.

The Creef family has owned and managed the motel for almost a quarter-century. Shopping is close by. This is an inexpensive, family-oriented motel and it is open all year.

TRANQUIL HOUSE INN

On The Waterfront

473-1404, 1-800-458-7069

Most major credit cards $$$

This 28-room bed and breakfast is located on Shallowbag Bay and a visit here will accommodate your desire for privacy and comfort. It's named after an old home which stood in about the same location from the time of the Civil War to the mid-1950s.

The rooms are all individually

decorated but all have a sitting area, private bath, color cable TV with HBO and a telephone. You'll feel welcomed by the hospitality and fine surroundings. Fresh flowers and a bottle of wine await your arrival.

Room service is available from nearby restaurants; a complimentary continental breakfast is also provided. The innkeepers also offer a baby-sitting service.

The long porches facing the bay open to sights of waterfowl and the *Elizabeth II* sailing ship docked across the way. Shops along the waterfront are a few steps away.

A marina is located just out the back for those who would prefer to arrive by boat. Bicycles are available for rent and car rental can be arranged. Tranquil House Inn is open all year.

DARE HAVEN MOTEL

Main Hwy.   473-2322

MC, VISA, AMEX $

This small motel is a favorite place for fishing enthusiasts who plan a charter from the waterfront, Wanchese or Pirate's Cove, or who bring their own boat and trailer. The parking is adequate for this.

Located towards the north end of Roanoke Island, the historic sites of Fort Raleigh and the Lost Colony are convenient. Some refurbishing has been done recently to give the rooms a fresh appeal. It is open all year.

WANCHESE

C.W. PUGH'S BED & BREAKFAST
Old Wharf Rd., Wanchese
473-5466

MC, VISA $

This charming house is over 100 years old and is situated next door to Queen Anne's Revenge (reviewed

in the section on Restaurants). It's in the process of being completely restored. There are four rooms, three of which are ready for use. There are baths on the first and second floors, a parlor and seating area for a full breakfast. Antique furniture and some reproductions are used throughout. One of the rooms will accommodate three people, two adults and a child.

The spacious lawn is appealing for those who like some elbow room. The winding lanes of Wanchese are perfect for bicycle rides.

It's situated near the end of the road, where at one time Mr. Pugh was a watchman, or lighthouse keeper, at Marshes Light, a house built on pilings out on the water. His duty was to help keep the channel waters open for passing ships in an area where shifting sands and numerous vessels came into the harbor. There is an electric light out on the sound these days.

Nancy Gray, whose husband Wayne Gray is one of the operators of Queen Anne's Revenge restaurant next door, has managed the bed and breakfast accommodations here for four years. Jim and Don Beach, the other restaurant owners, continue their work in restoration.

In a country setting, not far from historic Manteo or the beach, this is a good choice for those whose number one requirement is quiet and relaxation.

Hatteras Island

ACCOMMODATIONS

Accommodations on Hatteras Island offer vacationers clean, well-kept rooms and efficiencies. Most have swimming pools, but here on the southern portion of the Outer Banks, the need for luxurious accommodations with all sorts of recreational amenities has never caught on. For one thing, people who visit this part of the beach seem to want just the beach. Many are avid fishing enthusiasts or enjoy windsurfing and sailing. Some properties have been family-owned for a number of years and cater to guests who return year after year.

In other sections of this Guide we have indicated non-smoking rooms where available. For this section on Hatteras Island, most rooms have private entrances or are not connected by a hallway. While most proprietors have indicated they do not have non-smoking rooms, it's pretty obvious that with a private entrance to a clean, spacious room the notation of non-smoking rooms carries little importance, therefore we have omitted the designation. Enjoy your stay on Hatteras Island at one of these beach motels.

HATTERAS ISLAND RESORT
Rodanthe   987-2345, 1-800-331-6541
MC, VISA, AMEX $$

This is a large oceanfront resort that includes 32 motel-type rooms and efficiencies in a large 2-story building. The 25-acre oceanside property also has 35 two-, three-, and four-bedroom cottages arranged in clusters. All units have color cable TV and are comfortably furnished.

There are swimming pools for adults and children, a large patio area, volleyball and basketball and a well-stocked fishing pond. The Hatteras Island Fishing Pier is right out front on the Atlantic and it draws a lot of people to the resort. Open from late March till mid-December.

THE CASTAWAYS

Avon   995-4444, 1-800-845-6070
MC, VISA, AMEX $$$

Bea and Chappy Chaplin took over ownership here a couple of years ago and are making good progress is renovating and refurbishing this ocean-front inn. There are 68 rooms on five floors. Upper floor rooms have been refurbished and have wet bars with refrigerators and private balconies. Rooms on other floors are being refurbished and most have great ocean views, except on the lower floors which are behind the dunes.

Amenities here include a heated indoor competition size swimming

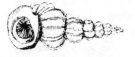

pool and Jacuzzi. The wide, unspoiled beaches at the Castaways are incredibly beautiful and quiet for swimming and sun-bathing or recreation. There is a boarded walkway to lead you over the dunes and onto the beach, where you can enjoy your retreat to the sea.

The restaurant and lounge is attractively decorated in a tropical island motif, rather than rustic-nautical found so often on the Outer Banks. The ambience works and getting into a real vacation here is no problem! The pace is leisurely and the food very good.

The property has its own pond and picnic area with tables and grills. The inn sits way back off the main road and affords the guest a quiet stay.

CAPE HATTERAS MOTEL

Buxton   **995-5611**
MC, VISA, AMEX   **$$$-$$$**

When you arrive in Buxton, you'll see the Cape Hatteras Motel situated on both sides of the road. Owners Carol and Dave Dawson have maintained this motel, some parts of which have been here for over thirty years, with an eye towards keeping what's comfortable and keeps families coming back. After last year's storms, they've cleaned up and helped rebuild the dunes. This motel has great appeal for those who love to fish and enjoy the beach. These units are standard rooms with no frills.

Some newer and more modern buildings, townhouses and efficiencies are located on the ocean and on the westside. These units attract many who come to windsurf at nearby Canadian Hole. There are lighted tennis courts, swimming pool with spa and some units are fully equipped for cooking your own meals. Some have king-size beds and most have been refurbished recently.

Cape Hatteras Motel knows what guests need to make their stay enjoyable. Restaurants are close by, making this a very popular place in season. Book reservations early.

OUTER BANKS MOTEL

Buxton   **995-5601**
MC, VISA, AMEX   **$-$$**

Located next door to the Cape Hatteras Motel, this motel offers efficiency units, two- and three-bedroom cottages and some beachfront houses. It is a very nice older property. Carol Dillon maintains it and says that close to ninety percent of her guests come back time and time again to stay here at the beach.

The rooms are pine paneled with tile baths. All units are air conditioned and have color cable TV with HBO. Screened porches are perfect for evenings outside listening to the ocean.

There's a coin-operated laundry, fish cleaning station and a guest freezer for storage of the big catch. If you enjoy soundside crabbing, there are several row boats for your use without changed.

With the particularly wide beaches here at Buxton, this motel is always filled with satisfied guests.

Open year round and a good choice. Book early.

LIGHTHOUSE VIEW MOTEL
Buxton   995-5680, 1-800-225-7651
MC, VISA $$

Lighthouse View is located on the curve in Buxton. There are 72 units here and all are different. The Hooper family has been serving vacationing families for over 35 years. Some accommodations here are standard motel rooms, others are 2-bedroom cottages located on the beachfront. There are some newer oceanfront villas. With all this in mind, it's safe to say that the variety offered here will turn up something to meet your needs. There's an outdoor pool and hot tub, color cable TV and air conditioning in this well-maintained complex. It's open all year and very convenient for surfers and fishing enthusiasts.

FALCON MOTEL
Buxton   995-5968, 1-800-635-6911
MC, VISA $

We've looked at many motels and, in our opinion, The Falcon has offered the best, inexpensive accommodations in the Outer Banks for several years. This motel appeals to quiet, family-oriented guests who appreciate moderate prices, good accommodations, and the environment. The style

is reminiscent of some older beach motels along the coast and that means sturdy, light-colored brick construction, larger than average rooms with adjoining baths and a wide, covered porch. Some rooms have refrigerators. Parking is right outside your door.

Falcon Motel is owned by Doug and Anne Meekins. They've refurbished the rooms since taking ownership a few years ago. All 35 rooms have a light-airy feel and reflect attention to detail.

There's a shaded picnic area amidst mature oak trees away from the road. They've added martin-houses, blue-bird houses and planted shrubs and flowers which attract the bird population of the area. An osprey platform is located on the soundside area beyond the trees. Anne exudes friendliness to everyone, especially those in search of family lodging who have an interest in birding and the overall environment of Hatteras.

The Falcon Motel is located within easy walking distance to several restaurants and shops. The beach is a block and a half away. There is a swimming pool and boat ramp. You'll enjoy your stay here. Open March through mid-December.

TOWER CIRCLE

Old Lighthouse Road

Buxton   **995-5353**

No credit cards   **$**

This small motel is located on Old Lighthouse Road off Highway 12. It's the closest motel to the Cape Hatteras Lighthouse. There are 30 rooms, some motel-type rooms and some efficiencies. You'll enjoy your visit here, as the Grays have owned the motel for twenty years and treat their guests like old friends, which many of them are. Many people return here so there's a homey atmosphere where folks sit on the porch and swap stories.

It's an older brick veneer property with juniper panelling in the rooms and modest furnishings. There is color cable TV and heat and air conditioning. Tower Circle is open April through November and it's just a short walk over the dune to the beach. An ideal place to stay if you're into surf fishing.

COMFORT INN

NC 12, Buxton

995-6100 or 1-800-228-5150

Non-smoking rooms   **$$-$$$**

All major credit cards

The Comfort Inn is the newest hotel on Hatteras Island. It is located in the heart of Buxton, close to the beach and shops. There are 60 rooms, including mini-efficiencies, offering a variety of accommodations. Non-smoking and handicapped-accessible rooms make this property attractive to visitors.

Barbara and John Murphy welcome their guests to this comfortable inn and give attention to all the details of your visit. A continental breakfast is served in the greeting room or lobby. The quiet ambience of this Outer Banks-style inn is found in the soft-colors used throughout its spacious rooms and grounds. There is a heated swimming pool and gazebo for outdoor relaxation, in addition to a wide lawn. A tower room and deck affords views of the ocean, the sound and nearby Cape Hatteras Lighthouse.

All rooms have color cable TV with HBO and refrigerators. Mini-efficiencies have microwaves and refrigerators (no utensils, however).

Comfort Inn of Hatteras Island offers special vacation packages and has ample parking for boats and campers.

CAPE PINES MOTEL

Buxton   **995-5666**
MC, VISA   **$**

This motel will have a strong appeal to those who favor the traditional 1-story motels with private entry to each room, convenient parking and a nice swimming pool out front. The grounds are well-maintained as well.

Steve and Hazen Totton have owned the property since 1988, and along with their daughter and son-in-law, they rolled up their sleeves and put a fresh face on what was becoming a mediocre place a few years ago. Not so now.

There's plenty of room to stretch out and relax around the pool and the lawn, which has picnic tables and charcoal grills. There's also a fish cleaning table and a pay phone on the premises.

This motel offers rooms, some have refrigerators, and fully-equipped efficiencies. Most have been completely refurbished since the Tottons took over. All units are air conditioned and have color cable TV.

DURANT STATION MOTEL

Hatteras   **986-2244**
MC, VISA   **$$**

Durant Lifesaving Station sits just behind the dunes from the ocean and serves as a focal point for this condo motel. The other buildings house apartments which are individually owned and furnished. All are similar with comfortable furnishings for your vacation at the beach.

The Lifesaving Station has been refurbished but some trappings of those early times have been retained. There's a lookout room several flights up and you can get a glimpse of what it must have been like to live here and work among the others who were a part of the lifesaving service. This large building has three inter-connecting apartments with ample privacy for individual guests or can be used for a large family reunion.

People who come here return often, as the motel caters to families during the summer season and to fishing parties in the off season. It's open from early spring through November.

SEA GULL MOTEL

Hatteras   **986-2550**
MC, VISA   **$$**

Everything is neat, clean and tidy at this well-maintained motel and it's situated just a few yards away from the ocean. The 45 rooms are large and comfortable. There's color cable TV, if the beach or the pool is not enough. Most nights you can just raise the window and catch the ocean breezes! There are some apartments with full kitchens.

There are a few shops and restaurants close enough to walk, but one of the nice things about this motel is its spacious grounds and boarded walkway to the beach. The people are friendly and have a good repeat business. Open almost all year.

GENERAL MITCHELL MOTEL

Hatteras Village   **986-2444**
MC, VISA   **$**

Named for Billy Mitchell, of the U.S. Air Service who directed the sinking of two retired battle ships off Hatteras to prove the potential of air power, this 30-year old motel is typical of some small motels built to accommodate those who like to fish and don't need a lot of extras. The rooms are clean and comfortable.

There are two buildings and the rooms have color cable TV and air conditioning. It's open all year and caters to the fishing and hunting crowd. There's a freezer for storage.

ATLANTIC VIEW MOTEL

Hatteras Village   **986-2323**
MC, VISA   **$**

The office of Atlantic View is close to the main road, but the motel itself is located down a sandy lane off the main road. The beach is a few minutes walk along a path to the dunes. This is a particularly nice place for families with children and there's a play area and swimming pool with a slide and a smaller kiddie pool.

Ray and Hal Gray built the Atlantic View over twelve years ago and the rooms are clean and comfortable. They cater to small families but some rooms connect to accommodate larger groups. For a family on a tight budget, this motel is a good choice.

Despite what the name infers, there are no rooms with a view of the Atlantic. Originally there was a motel on the site (built over sixty years ago) which had a view of the ocean. Since then, the dunes were built and this motel replaced the older one.

HATTERAS MARLIN MOTEL

Hatteras Village   **986-2141**
MC, VISA   **$-$$**

Hatteras Marlin Motel is owned and operated by the Midgett family

and located within sight of the harbor fishing fleet, restaurants and shops. There are 40 units in three buildings which contain the standard motel rooms and one- and two-bedroom efficiencies. Two new two-bedroom apartments have been built near the back of the property and away from the road. (The older buildings near the road share parking with Midgett's gas station and convenience store.)

The newest building is situated along a canal. You'll often see ducks waddling around in the grassy areas of the yard. All rooms are well-maintained and have color cable TV and air conditioning. There's a swimming pool and sundeck. Open all year.

Ocracoke

ACCOMMODATIONS

BERKLEY CENTER

Ocracoke 928-5911
No credit cards $$

Two buildings, situated on three acres, make up this 9-room bed and breakfast on the Ocracoke Harbor. The Manor House, originally built in 1860, was remodeled in 1950. The Ranch House dates from the mid-fifties but the architecture and cedar exterior create an impression of age and quality. Both buildings are furnished in reproduction antiques. All interior walls, floors and ceilings of the Manor House are made of hand-carved wood panels of redwood, pine

and cedar.

Berkley Center is adjacent to the Park Service and Ferry Dock, but away from the congestion that one might anticipate from seasonal visitors. The grounds are comfortably surrounded by trees. A Continental breakfast, consisting of fresh breads, preserves and coffee is available in the breakfast room of the Manor House. A guest lounge is also located in the Manor House and offers an opportunity to relax and enjoy the company of owners Ruth and Wesley Egan, Sr. He is better known as "Colonel," having retired from the USAF.

All rooms are spacious and have been furnished in classic fashion, most all have private baths with double sinks. Each room has a large closet. Two sets of 2 rooms share a large bath, ideal for a family. Berkley Center is open mid-March through mid-November.

PRINCESS WATERFRONT MOTEL

Ocracoke 928-6461
MC, VISA $$$

Situated on the edge of Silver Lake, the Princess Waterfront Motel is an older building, but very typical in appearance of Ocracoke Village. The first floor of the building features retail shops and the second offers spacious efficiency apartments for adults.

Opened in 1988 and owned by Scott and Kathy Cottrell, the units are equipped with a full kitchen, phone, remote-control color cable TV with

Showtime and modern furnishings. Since the building sits perpendicular to the waterfront, not all rooms have a full view of the harbor. The private dock is at the end of the parking lot. Guests have pool privileges at The Anchorage Inn, across the street.

ANCHORAGE INN

Ocracoke   928-1101

MC,VISA $$$

The Anchorage Inn overlooks Silver Lake and the village. An attractive red brick building with white trim, it was expanded from its original three floors to five in recent years. A penthouse on the top floor provides ac-commodations for owners Scott and Kathy Cottrell as well as non-smoking rooms for guests, all with king-size beds. An elevator provides access to each floor.

If you arrive in Ocracoke via the Cedar Island Ferry, The Anchorage Inn is visible amidst the booms, masts and lines of the ships in the harbor. Entering the village from the main road, it's situated on Silver Lake one block before you reach the ferry terminals.

Accommodations here offer views of the harbor and Ocracoke Village and are especially nice from all upper floor rooms. All rooms have some view of Silver Lake Harbor. A

pool, boat dock and ramp are available for guests.

The Anchorage Inn offers complimentary continental breakfast. Most guests are able to walk to restaurants, shops and the historical sights on Ocracoke Island. Bike rentals are available. Wind surfing equipment can be rented and fishing charters, which depart from the dock across the street, can be booked from the Inn reception or from each room, as all have direct dial phones. Each room has color cable TV with the Movie Channel.

PONY ISLAND MOTEL

Ocracoke   928-4411

MC, VISA $-$$

Located at the edge of Ocracoke Village and away from the Silver Lake harbor, the Pony Island Motel offers 31 rooms, 9 efficiency units and five cottages in a quiet setting. The grounds are spacious and owners David and Jen Esham have been hosts to families and couples who want solitude for nearly 20 years. The Pony Island Motel is over 30 years old but offers comfortable, air conditioned and heated accommodations.

The grounds are within walking distance of the Ocracoke Lighthouse and other Island attractions. Bike rentals are available. The large pool and deck, picnic tables and lawn offer plenty of elbow room for family activities.

The motel is open from March through November. Each room has color cable TV with Showtime. The Pony Island Restaurant, a locals' favorite, is right next door.

EDWARDS MOTEL

Ocracoke   928-4801

MC, VISA $

This older motel, located away from the center of Ocracoke and off the main route, is more of a summer house resort, and a cluster of cottages situated on a large yard. The Edwards Motel has been in the same family for twenty-five years. Ruth and David Sams bought it from Ruth's sister Mary and her husband Bernie Edwards. They offer inexpensive accommodations in a familial setting of green lawn, flower beds and pine trees.

With 13 units scattered over the large property, all have screened porches and some are small houses with living rooms, bedrooms and kitchen. There are some efficiencies which open onto a veranda in a larger building.

Edwards Motel is open from Easter weekend through the end of November.

Insiders like:

Feeding seagulls during ferry rides. Bring some bread or crackers and toss them into the air from the stern of the ferry.

Insiders' Tip

BLUFF SHOAL MOTEL

Ocracoke   **928-4301**

MC, VISA   **$$**

This small 7-room motel is located on the main street of the village. All rooms are comfortable and all have private baths and small refrigerators. These rooms have been refurbished with new carpet and paneling; every room opens onto a long porch. All rooms have color cable TV with Showtime.

Bluff Shoal Motel is close to everything and across the street from The Pelican Restaurant. The post office, community store and many shops in the village are within walking distance. Owners Mike and Kay Riddick keep their property open all year.

PIRATE'S QUAY

Ocracoke   **928-1921**

MC, VISA   **$$$$**

One of the newer properties on Ocracoke Island, Pirate's Quay is situated on the edge of Silver Lake. It is an all-suite hotel, each having a living room, dining room, full Jenn-air kitchen, one or two bedrooms and a bath and a half.

Jo Everhart owns and manages this unique facility. The views across Silver Lake from the decks of each suite are beautiful. Its proximity to the village makes walking or biking man-

ageable.

The upper floor suites have cathedral ceilings. There are two decks off each suite, which accommodates up to four adults and one or two children. A Jacuzzi bath and color cable TV with Showtime are included and each is beautifully furnished and equipped with all the dishes and cookware you need. An additional feature is the laundry, right on the property and available for guests.

Pirate's Quay has a waterfront gazebo and deep water docking facilities, and quiet beaches at the Silver Lake Inlet of Pamlico Sound.

THE ISLAND INN

Ocracoke   **928-4351**
MC, VISA   **$$**

The Island Inn, owned by Cee and Bob Touhey since just before the 1990 season, provides a variety of accommodations for adults and families with children in two separate buildings.

Originally built as an Odd Fellows Lodge in 1901, the main building has served as a school, a private residence and Naval Officers' quarters. It was restored by former owners and has been recognized in *Country Inns of the Old South*, and *County Inns, Lodges and Historic Hotels of the*

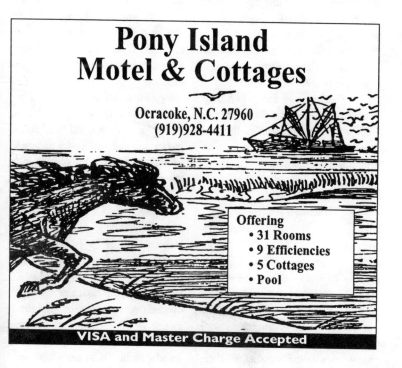

**Pony Island
Motel & Cottages**

Ocracoke, N.C. 27960
(919)928-4411

Offering
• 31 Rooms
• 9 Efficiencies
• 5 Cottages
• Pool

VISA and Master Charge Accepted

South.

The owners had their first date on Ocracoke Island and vacationed here for many years. They have returned to live and work, and the refurbishing of many of the rooms reflects their preferences in the style of this romantic, country inn.

There are rooms and suites located in the main building. All are furnished as a separate guest room in a private home with antiques and quilts, providing a restful ambience for guests. The rooms and suites for adults only accommodate a wide range of needs.

Across the street, a 19-unit, double-decked structure includes two honeymoon rooms with king-size beds and bay windows affording views of beautiful sunsets over Silver Lake. Families with children will find the casualness of the accommodations a welcome retreat.

The Inn also has a two-bedroom cottage for rent and a swimming pool which stays open as long as weather permits. Color cable TV with free Showtime is available in every room. The Inn is open all year.

OSCAR'S HOUSE

Ocracoke	928-1311
MC, VISA	$-$$

Oscar's House was built in 1940 by the Ocracoke lighthouse keeper and was first occupied by the World War II Naval Commander for the Ocracoke Naval Base. Stories abound about Oscar who lived and worked for many years on the island as a fisher-

man and hunting guide.

This four-room bed and breakfast guest house is located on the main road and is managed by Ann Ehringhaus, a local fine art photographer and author of Ocracoke Portrait, published in 1988.

No smoking is allowed in the bedrooms which retain the original beaded board walls. An upstairs bedroom and loft create a very comfortable setting for guests. All rooms are air conditioned and delightfully furnished. There are no private baths, but sharing is easily managed. The large kitchen with a big table is available to guests, however the stove is off-limits.

In addition, Oscar's house offers an outdoor shower and dressing room and a deck area which opens into a small private yard. Meals can eaten outdoors. Oscar's House is within walking distance to all shops and restaurants in the village.

Ann serves a full breakfast to guests and she will gladly adhere to special preferences for vegetarian or macrobiotic meals. This bed and breakfast is open from April to October.

BOYETTE HOUSE

Ocracoke	928-4261
MC, VISA	$-$$

Lanie Boyette-Wynn presides over this very pleasant motel which opened over ten years ago. The atmosphere is one of a quaint bed and breakfast, although the 12-unit, 2-story wood structure is a comfortable motel. Rocking chairs line the wide upper and lower decks fronting all rooms to provide a nice place to read and relax. The lobby accommodates a comfortable reading area as well, and offers the visitor a house selection of books to borrow.

Each room has a private bath, two double beds and color cable TV with Showtime. A sundeck at the back of Boyette House is perfect for sunbathing. The motel is open all year and within walking distance of Silver Lake and the restaurants in Ocracoke. If you'd like to be picked up at the boat docks or the airport, this can be arranged, free of charge.

SILVER LAKE MOTEL

Ocracoke   **928-5721**

MC, VISA, AMEX   **$$**

Silver Lake Motel is situated in a grove of trees along the main street of Ocracoke Village. The Wrobleski family built the two-story, 20-room motel in 1983 and have added another building since then. The wooden structure, with long porches and rooms paneled in California redwoods, has become well-known for its rustic appeal and comfort. Most of the furniture in the older rooms was built by the owners and the rooms have wooden shutters, braided rugs on pine floors and wallpapered baths that create an informal, restful mood.

In the newer building, there are 12 suites which can be rented in a variety of combinations. They, too, have wood floors and wall-papered baths, but the furnishings are more contemporary. There are wet bars and full kitchens. End units have their own 8-seat Jacuzzi, designed for relaxation while looking out over Silver Lake.

Each room has color cable TV with Showtime and all are air conditioned. A lounge, located on the second floor of the older building, serves beer, wine and soft drinks in the evening. A dart board hangs ready for use by those who enjoy the game.

The Silver Lake Motel offers families comfortable and attractive rooms and for those who will arrive by boat, a deep water dock is provided.

HARBORSIDE MOTEL

Ocracoke   **928-3111**

MC, VISA, AMEX   **$$**

This charming motel is located across from Silver Lake Harbor on the main street of the village. Its 18 rooms, panelled in knotty cypress, are well-kept and comfortable. There are four efficiencies available. All rooms have color cable TV and guests can use the waterfront sun deck, docks and boat ramp across the street.

Harborside has its own gift shop with a wide selection of clothing, books, gourmet foods and small gifts. Other shops and restaurants of Ocracoke Village are within walking distance. The Swan Quarter and Cedar Island ferry docks are close by, as

well.

This property has been owned by the same family for over 20 years and their hospitality and service have been well-established. All rooms are refurbished on a regular basis, which is the true mark of caring for the comfort of guests.

Harborside is open from Easter through mid-November.

SHIPS TIMBERS

Ocracoke   **928-4061**

MC, VISA   **$**

This small but historical bed and breakfast is located in the center of Ocracoke Village, on a gravel lane just off the main road. The house is over 75 years old and was built of timber from the *Ida Lawrence*, a ship that washed ashore on Ocracoke Beach in 1902. It is included on the National Register of Historic Places.

Owner Erik Mattsson, who is well-known in these parts for his special interest in water sports, caters to guests who enjoy kayaking, sailing and windsurfing. The three air conditioned rooms and a shared bath and a half are a popular place for families, too. The hospitality on and around its large porch and yard make this bed and breakfast more lively than some. Weekly rentals are available.

A light breakfast is served — fresh fruit and fluffy croissants — but Erik will whip up a hearty breakfast of French toast or pancakes if a guest stays more that a couple of nights. The Ships Timbers is open from March through December.

Photo: Michael Halminski

Tundra swans photographed at the Pea Island National Wildlife Preserve.

Photo: Michael Halminski

The ever changing Outer Banks landscape.

Outer Banks
Campgrounds

*T*he Outer Banks is an ideal place to camp out under the stars and listen to the ocean all night long. Long ago, there were campgrounds up and down the islands and this simple and unencumbered way of "life at the beach" was very popular; however, some sites have closed and the land has been developed. Camping is available in Kitty Hawk, Colington Island, Manteo, along the Cape Hatteras National Seashore, villages of the southern beaches and on Ocracoke Island. Some campgrounds have permanent residents in Kitty Hawk, Colington and Manteo but offer a few convenient spaces for transient campers. At the end of this section, we've listed those which have limited sites for vacationers. We've described others in more detail.

North of Oregon Inlet

COLINGTON PARK CAMP-GROUND

Colington Island   441-6128

Colington Island is close to the beach, but more closely related to the quiet, calm waters of the sound. This campground is heavily wooded and summer camping is very pleasant. There are 55 sites, all with water and power and picnic tables. Hot showers, toilets, a laundry, grocery and recreation room are on site as well. It's open all year and the rates start at $14.56/night for one camper or one tent with two people. There's a $2 additional charge for air conditioning. Lots of fishing and crabbing opportunities are nearby.

JOE & KAY'S CAMPGROUNDS

Colington Island   441-5468

Most of the sites here are rented yearly, but there are about 20 for transient use. The rates average $10-$15 for tents and there's a $2 charge for electricity and water, and $2 for extra people. Joe & Kay's is reasonable, cool shady area and a nice place for family camping. Crabbing is nearby. Open April to December 1.

OREGON INLET CAMPGROUND (NPS)

Bodie Island

There are several National Park Service camping areas along the Outer Banks and Oregon Inlet offers 120 sites. The sites are along the flat, sandy, windswept shores of the island. Turn east, or left, before you cross the Bonner Bridge. This is close to primitive camping as compared to other sites, as there are no utility connections, but water, cold showers, modern toilets, picnic tables and charcoal grills are available.

All NPS campground on the Outer Banks operate under a common policy and charge the same fees, except for Ocracoke, which is on the Ticketron reservation system. (See Ocracoke for details.)

Oregon Inlet is open from mid-spring till mid-fall on a first come, first serve basis.

It is recommended that campers bring awnings or other materials for shade, mosquito netting and long tent stakes for this sandy area. Fees start at around $10/night except in Ocracoke.

During the summer season, call 441-6644 for information on any of the NPS campgrounds on the Outer Banks.

Manteo

CYPRESS COVE CAMPGROUND
Main Hwy., Manteo   473-5231

An intown campground, Cypress Cove has conveniently shaded sites bordering the town of Manteo. Rates begin at $16 for one or two occupants of RV/Campers and $13 for one or two in tents. Pets are allowed provided they are quiet and on a leash. Call for reservations and other details

of Cypress Cove.

Hatteras

Camping on Hatteras Island is getting into some serious camping. There are more campgrounds and the spacious areas offer some of the best "out under the stars" living along the east coast. If you are a tent or trailer camper you'll love Hatteras Island.

Some Hatteras Island campgrounds are located on the oceanside where there is abundant open space, flat sand, plenty of sun and wind and no shade. Sunscreen and long stakes are essential. Other campgrounds are located on the soundside of the island amidst stands of pine and live oaks. These sites offer firmer ground, more shade and less wind. Mosquito control is being well-managed, but you'll find some in warm weather along the soundside wooded areas. Know your pesky critters such as chiggers, ticks and mosquitoes and decide. If you're a veteran camper, you'll know how to deal with them!

CAMP HATTERAS
Between Rodanthe and Waves on
NC 12
987-2318

Formerly known as Pea Island Resort, this 50-acre world-class campground is a complete camping facility. It has nightly and yearly campsites with full hookups, concrete pads and paved roads. There is a natural area for tents and everything else you'll need while camping. With 1000' of ocean frontage and 1000' of sound frontage, three swimming pools, club house, pavilion, marina, fishing, two tennis courts, a 9-hole miniature golf course, volleyball, basketball and shuffleboard courts, there is no need to go any further for family recreation. The grounds are extraordinarily well-kept, and it's clean and more organized than most campgrounds, with sports and camping areas separated. If you're looking for a top notch camping experience under the wide open skies, and close to other Outer Banks attractions, this one comes highly recommended.

CAPE HATTERAS KOA

Rodanthe   **987-2307**

In talking with Joan Berry who manages this large campground, they've added more sites and now have 269 with water and power and 66 with sewer connections. This campground is located 14 miles south of the Bonner Bridge across Oregon Inlet.

There are lots of amenities here: a dump station, laundry, two pools, Jacuzzi, playground, game room, restaurant, sailboard rentals, Kamping Kabins, a well-stocked general store and a full time recreation director in the summer. The ocean is just over the

dunes for fishing and swimming. A soundside swimming area is nice for smaller folks. Open March 15 to December 1.

NORTH BEACH CAMPGROUND

Rodanthe   **987-2378**

North Beach is in the village and right on the ocean. The 110 sites, all with water and power, offer ideal camping facilities. There are hot showers, toilets, a laundry, grocery store and the sea is right over the dunes.

Open March till December, this campground is south of Chicamacomico Lifesaving Station and during the summer, the Park Service conducts a Beach Apparatus Drill -- techniques and equipment used in lifesaving situations -- that is definitely worth attending.

OCEAN WAVES CAMPGROUND

Waves   **987-2556**

Camping in Waves at Clyde and Carolyn Bullock's place is very nice. They opened in 1985 on the oceanside and offer 68 spaces, 64 with full hookups, laundromat, game room and a pool. There's plenty of ocean fishing and swimming nearby. Open March 15 till November 30. Located off NC 12 in Waves.

SALVO CAMPGROUND (NPS)
Salvo

Salvo Campground is a very large, flat soundside camping area with 130 sites. The area is open for camping from late April till September on a non-reservation basis. The fee is $10. There are restrooms, potable water, unheated showers, grills and picnic tables. Plan on dealing with mosquitoes. This expansive campground is close to the sound and along NC 12.

KINNAKEET CAMPGROUND
Avon   **995-5211**

Avon is another small village of Hatteras Island which has seen enormous growth in the past few years -- they've added a traffic light and a supermarket! But, the soundside campground is off NC 12 and is geared towards trailers and mobile homes. No tents are accommodated at this time. Each site has a picnic table, access to hot showers, toilets and electricity. A dump site and running hot and cold water are available. Reservations are recommended.

CAPE WOODS CAMPER PARK
Buxton, Back Road   **995-5850**

There are 125 tent sites located here on the southern side of Buxton. This is a good example of the forested camping areas on the soundside of the island. Most all sites have shade as there are tall stands of poplar, pine and live oak trees. Cape Woods has two small lakes which contain bass and bream for fishing right there on the campgrounds. Ocean fishing is nearby. Most sites have water and power. Picnic tables, hot showers and flush toilets are available. Open March 1 through December 15 at $14/night and up, depending on services.

STOWE-A-WAY
Buxton, Back Road   **995-5970**

This is one of the smaller campgrounds on Hatteras Island. There are 20 campsites, all with water and electricity and some with full hookups. There is a bathhouse with hot showers, flush toilets and a picnic table at every site. The site is just around the corner from the Centura Bank in Buxton. Open year round.

CAPE POINT CAMPGROUND
(NPS)
Cape Hatteras

Cape Point is the largest of the Park Service's campgrounds on the Outer Banks. It's also one of the wildest! There are no utility connections, but there are flush toilets, cold showers, drinking water, charcoal grills and picnic tables. There are 203 sites, located behind the dunes on the southwest face of "The Point." Watch for Ramp 44. You'll need a 4-wheel drive vehicle to get traction for this soft sandy area. It's a short walk to the ocean and for surfers, this campground is located about two miles from the best surfing spot on the Atlantic. Bring netting to fend off mosquitoes, awnings for shade and long tent stakes for the sand. The fee is $10 per night and like most other NPS campgrounds, it is open from mid-spring to mid-fall on a non-reservation basis. A handicapped facilities area is also available.

FRISCO WOODS CAMPGROUND, INC.

Frisco   995-5208

This 18-acre campground is one of the best and it's located in Frisco Woods. Developed by Ward and Betty Barnett, the soundside location has abundant forest and marshland beauty. There are 200 sites, many with full hookups, electricity and water. There are tables and hot showers. Rates start at $13/night for one person.

Frisco Woods favors the tent camper rather than the trailer crowd because of its natural setting and siting. There's good crabbing and soundside fishing for recreation and virgin forest for long walks. If you like semi-wild, basic camping, this is the place. It's also very popular with the windsurfing crowd. Open March 1 till December 1.

FRISCO CAMPGROUND (NPS)
Frisco

Another National Park Service campground, it's located on the southern side of the island about 4 miles past Buxton on Highway 12. It's on the beach and is open from Memorial Day to Labor Day. There are 127 no-frills sites. It's one of the more isolated campgrounds and definitely for those who like their camping away

from civilization! There's a 14-day limit and fees are $10 per night, payable at the entrance. No reservations are accepted as it's first come, first serve. There are flush toilets, cold water outdoor showers, drinking water, charcoal grills and picnic tables.

HATTERAS SANDS CAMPING RESORT

Hatteras Village   986-2422

This well-maintained campground is located close to the ferry dock in Hatteras Village. There are 105 sites with water and electricity and some sewage connections are available. There are several very clean bathhouses throughout the resort. Some pull-through sites are also available.

There is an Olympic-size pool, game room and even a gift shop. A canal runs through the resort provides crabbing and fishing for the family. It's within easy walking distance of the village shops and restaurants. Open March till December with rates starting at $18.50. They offer some special rates which fluctuate during the season. You'll hear about them when you call for reservations.

Ocracoke

TEETER'S CAMPGROUND

Ocracoke   928-3511

MC, VISA

Teeter's is located near the heart of Ocracoke Village, next to the British Cemetery. Rates begin at $12/2-person tent to $20 depending on the services requested, which include cable TV hookups. Campers will appreciate the trees and grass on this campground.

Self-contained units are welcome year round, but as soon as it gets cold enough for water to freeze, the grounds are closed to others. There are hot showers, water and electric hookups and a few of the 25 sites here at Teeter's have sewage hookups.

BEACHCOMBER

Ocracoke   **928-4031**

MC, VISA

The newest campground in Ocracoke, it's located less than a mile from Silver Lake and from the nearest beach access. There's a long walk across the dune as well. The Beachcomber has 31 sites and rates start at $12 for tents and vary according to services, which include electricity and cable TV. Hot showers and fully-equipped bathrooms are available. They're open from early April through late October, depending on weather. Reservations for May through August are recommended.

OCRACOKE CAMPGROUND (NPS)

NC 12, east of town

There are 136 campsites on the oceanside of Ocracoke Island. There are no utility hookups, but there are cold showers, a dumping station, drink-

ing water, charcoal grills and flush toilets. There's a 14-day limit on stays at this campground.

We suggest bringing awnings, netting and long tent stakes for use in the sand to provide strong-grounding against the high winds which sometimes blow across this area. In fact, out here on the island, there is almost always a breeze, but there are insects, too, especially in summer months. The campground is sparsely vegetated and only three miles from the village.

Ocracoke is the sole NPS campground on the Ticketron reservation system. From Memorial Day weekend to Labor Day, you must either:

write Ticketron, PO Box 617516, Chicago, IL 60661-7516, or

go by the Ticketron office nearest you to make reservations. The charge is $12/night. Or, if you have VISA or MasterCard, you can make reservations by calling 1-800-452-1111. International callers, including Canada: (312) 902-1919. There is a charge for phone reservations.

Camping out on an island is often included in our dreams of getting away from it all. Camping out *here* gets right to the heart of the matter. This campground offers the most penetrating isolation of the Outer Banks!

A perfect summer day at the beach.

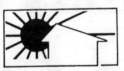

Inside
Outer Banks
Real Estate

*R*eal estate remains a good investment on the Outer Banks despite the 1991-92 economy. For most of the past year and up to the present time, there's a buyers' market for those who have a dream of owning a place at the beach. Lower interest rates (at press time) give additional incentive to prospective purchasers. While there's not much land on the Outer Banks, compared with other resort areas, there are many opportunities to own your place by the sea. The 1990s real estate drama is yet to unfold, but it's not likely to be a repeat of the 1980s. Most of the resort development of the 80s was planned with appreciation in mind. For the time being the values of lots and homes have stabilized and more than likely will remain so.

Following the slow down nationally as well as locally of the real estate market, the industry as a whole here seems to be getting a closer evaluation than was possible during the last ten or so boom years. This, in our opinion, benefits the buyer especially. The overall quality of construction, the planning and development are getting a closer look, creating stability.

When economic times are good, building is steady. In slower times, most builders have too much at risk not to do quality work. Land use and planning are constantly reviewed. Town planners and building code authorities generally have support for strong enforcement of codes and regulations. Continuing concern for coastal development dictates the way building is to continue. Water resources and water quality have come under careful scrutiny more recently. Development and environmental concerns don't have to be divisive. One supports the other over the long haul. The developers who care for the environment are obvious by the way building is carried out.

Perhaps, the only thing that could interrupt this focus on careful planning and development, other than a continuing slow economy, is a powerful storm. It has been a long time since the weather patterns have dealt the Outer Banks more than a one or two day nor'easter or one of those storms named after people! After the winter storms of 1991, however, the oceanfront is the exception. In a few areas, the oceanfront is not currently buildable.

If you're looking to buy a time-share, a fractional ownership segment, a townhouse or single-family home or lot, select a real estate firm, ask intelligent questions, listen for specific answers and make wise decisions. Here are some of the things you will probably want to consider: What type of property do you want? How much is affordable? Will it be rented? Where will the usual services come from, i.e. water, sewer, electricity? What area will offer the highest appreciation, lowest taxes, insurance, the best services? Where are the flood plains? What about fire and rescue services? Is the proximity of schools and churches a consideration? Medical facilities? Business opportunity? What about a nice, quiet get-away-from-it-all fishing retreat vs. a luxury mansion? What about a bulkheaded boat dock?

We've provided you with a rundown here of partial ownership properties, a look at some of the "brightest and best" developments in the area, a run down on real estate firms, architects, builders and designers. If you are in pursuit of the second American dream -- a home at the beach -- then this chapter will certainly get you started.

Timesharing

It's our understanding that timesharing is a deeded transaction under the jurisdiction of the North Carolina Real Estate Commission. A deeded share is 1/52 of the unit property being purchased. This deed grants the right to use the property in perpetuity. Always ask if the property you're inspecting is deeded timeshare because there is such a thing as undeeded timeshare which is the right-to-use a property which reverts to the developer in the end. What you are buying is the right to use a specific piece of real estate for a week per share. The weeks are either fixed at the time of sale or they rotate yearly.

Some disadvantages of being locked into a time and place have been partly removed by RCI (Resort Condominiums, Inc.), a timeshare bank. There are other similar operations. Members trade their weeks to get different time slots at a variety of locations around the world.

Qualifying for the purchase of a timeshare unit can be no more difficult than qualifying for a credit card, but be aware of financing charges which are higher than regular mortgages.

Most timeshare resorts on the Outer Banks are multi-family construction with recreational amenities that vary from minimal to luxurious, and sometimes includes the services of a recreational director. Timeshare units usually come furnished and carry a monthly maintenance fee. Tax advantages for ownership and financing are not available to the purchaser of a timeshare, so investigate from this angle.

Many offer "free weekends" which means you agree to a sales pitch and tour of the facilities in exchange for accommodations. Listen, ask questions and stay in control of your money and your particular situation. If you get swept away, you'll only have 5 days to change your mind if you so desire, according to North Carolina Time Share Act, which governs the sale of timeshares. But, if you can afford it, a relatively small amount of money to cover your vacation lodgings for years to come, along with the option of trading for another location, make timesharing a rather hassle-free and attractive option for a lot of people.

Timeshare sales people are licensed, which is to everyone's advantage, and they earn commissions. Some very good arrangements are out there;

some not so good. Check thoroughly before you buy.

BARRIER ISLAND STATION
Duck Village
Duck, NC 27949   261-3525

Barrier Island, one of the largest timeshare resorts on the Outer Banks, is situated on a high dune area of ocean to sound property. These are multi-family units of wood construction. There is an attractive, full-service restaurant and bar with soundside sailing center in addition to the beach. A full time recreation director is on board here for a variety of planned activities and events. Indoor swimming, tennis courts and other recreational facilities provide a full amenities package. This is a popular resort in a popular seaside village.

SEA SCAPE BEACH AND GOLF VILLAS
Route 158, Bypass, MP 2
Kitty Hawk, NC 27949   261-3881

There's plenty of recreation here. Tennis courts, two swimming pools, indoor recreation facility, weight room, game room and a lovely golf course await you at Sea Scape. The multi-family units are of wood construction. There's a shuttle to the beach from this west side resort. Some of the two-bedroom, two-bath villas have golf privileges, ocean views and access to a host of other amenities.

OUTER BANKS BEACH CLUB
Beach Rd., MP 9
Kill Devil Hills, NC 27949   441-7036

The round, wooden buildings of the Outer Banks Beach Club were the first timesharing opportunities to be built and sold here. There is an indoor pool and two outdoor pools in a great oceanfront location. One- and three-bedroom units also have access to whirlpools, tennis courts and a playground. There is a full time recreation director for a variety of activities and games.

DUNES SOUTH BEACH AND RACQUET CLUB
Beach Road, MP 18
Nags Head, NC 27954   441-4090

Townhome timesharing at this resort features two- and three-bedroom units with fireplaces, washers and dryers, Jacuzzis and hot tubs. A pool, tennis court, putting green and playground make up the recreational amenities.

Fractional Ownership

Fractional ownership, formerly called co-ownership, is very close to the same concept as timesharing. Here you share ownership of a building/house with other owners. Most fractional ownership properties are divided into 5-week segments for 10 owners with two weeks reserved for maintenance each year. The weeks of ownership are spread throughout the year with some weeks in prime time, others in the off season. At some resorts the weeks rotate through the years which means everyone is assigned the most favorable season at some point.

Fractional ownership can offer some of the tax benefits of vacation home ownership, depending on whether you occupy the property for the five weeks or rent it out. Appreciation is generally not as great on fractional ownership interests as on single family homes, but some of the more popular fractional ownership resorts on the northern Outer Banks have been quite profitable in resales.

This type of ownership is a comparatively inexpensive way to own a piece of the beach. The homes are luxurious and often include recreational amenities in addition to prime oceanfront or oceanside locations.

The resorts described in this section start on the north beaches and go south.

BUCK ISLAND
Ocean Trail (NC 12)
Corolla, NC 27927   **453-4343**

This is the newest, most exclusive and most expensive of fractional ownership resorts on the Outer Banks. The developer, Buck Thornton, met with great success in Duck with his first development in the area, Ships Watch. The homes are extravagant, well-designed and more than just well-

furnished. There are fireplaces, ga-
rages, marble and granite finishes and
more. Some homes have elevators. On
the outside, Buck Island is its own
self-contained community, and the
wide, white sandy beaches are some of
the best around.

PORT TRINITIE
Duck Road (NC 12)
North of Duck Village   261-3922

Port Trinitie is situated on a
deep oceanfront/oceanside property
that stretches across Duck Road to
offer some gorgeous views on the
soundfront. There are two swimming
pools and tennis court in addition to
the boat dock. Some of these homes
are single family and others are
townhomes. Port Trinitie is a favorite
location, just north of Duck Village.

NORTHPOINT
Duck Road (NC 12)
North of Duck Village

Fractional ownership is popular here at Northpoint though some
lots remain for individual ownership
and development. There is an enclosed
swimming pool, tennis and basketball
courts and a long soundfront pier for
fishing, crabbing and small boat dockage. One of the first fractional ownership developments on the northern
Outer Banks, it has enjoyed good values on resales.

SHIPS WATCH
Duck Road
Duck Village   261-2231
1-800-334-1295

Ships Watch is one of the most
successful fractional ownership resorts
anywhere. Each home is situated so as
to afford its owners maximum privacy
and views in a high dune area of Duck
Village. The oceanfront is exciting
and the recreational amenities include
tennis courts, outdoor pool, jogging
trails and a soundside pier. Parlayed as
a high-end property with all the trimmings, Buck Thornton and his associates have experienced great success
with this resort, conveniently located
in Duck Village.

Residential Resort Communities

We've listed a few of the newer
or more established oceanside and
soundside residential communities to
give you an idea of what's here on the
Outer Banks, starting as far north as
you can go and still be on the Outer
Banks. Most of these communities
offer recreational amenities and easy
access to the ocean and sound, although the off-road area of Carova
Beach is an exception. Living in this
remote 4-wheel drive area is unusual
but according to my friend, Marlene
Slate, who has lived in Carova Beach
for 7 years, it's "heaven"!

CAROVA BEACH
Off the paved road
Corolla, NC 27927

This subdivision has lots fronting on canals, sandy trails and open water between Currituck Sound and the Atlantic Ocean. Access to this area is by 4-wheel drive vehicle. Enter the beach at the ramp in Ocean Hill, be sure to read the rules of the road and enjoy a ride 14 miles out to Carova beach. You'll be riding on some of the widest beaches anywhere but it's recommended you drive at low tide. Most of the time it's just you and nature. (Driving into Virginia is no longer permitted and there's a posted area and gate to prevent crossing the border.)

THE VILLAGES AT OCEAN HILL
Ocean Trail (NC 12)
Corolla, NC 27927

The plans for this 156-acre single family development are really shaping up. After a slow start the community is experiencing a lot of new construction. The oceanfront clubhouse is underway and other amenities such as a soundfront pool, a lake, tennis courts and boat dock are ready.

COROLLA LIGHT RESORT
VILLAGE
Ocean Trail (NC 12)
Corolla, NC 27927

More than 200 acres comprise this northern Outer Banks resort. Construction began in 1985 and some very large, luxury homes are located here. When it all began, Corolla village was a sleepy, well-hidden oceanside community with a lighthouse, post office and a Winks store. The developer, Richard A. Brindley, and the marketing and sales team at Brindley & Brindley Realty, have created a beautiful ocean-to-sound resort that boasts an oceanfront pool complex, tennis courts scattered throughout the resort, a soundside pool and water sports center, and most recently an indoor sports center which houses a competition-size indoor pool, tennis courts, racquetball courts and exercise rooms. Two miniature golf courses complete the recreational amenities. The resort has its own water treatment facility and a wide range of luxury beach homes, townhomes and condos.

MONTERAY SHORES
Ocean Trail (NC 12)
Corolla, NC 27927

Monteray Shores, located on the soundside of this northern Outer Banks area, features magnificent homes with a unique Caribbean style. The red tile roofs, arched verandas, spacious decks and abundance of windows make these homes a popular option to the wooden structures found in most Outer Banks residential communities. While there are no oceanfront lots, the soundside clubhouse and recreational amenities provide a dash of sophistication and luxury to this area of the northern Outer Banks.

SANDERLING
Duck Road
Duck, NC 27949

This ocean-to-sound community of nearly 300 homes and lots is one of the most desirable residential communities on the Outer Banks. The heavy vegetation, winding lanes and abundant wildlife offer the most seclusion of any resort community on the beach. The developers have taken care to leave as much natural growth as possible and there are strict building requirements to ensure privacy and value. The Sanderling Inn Resort is located just north of the residential area. The homeowners have their own recreational amenities and access to the resort's facilities as well.

SCHOONER RIDGE
Duck Road
Duck, NC 27949

Schooner Ridge is located in the heart of Duck Village but its oceanfront/oceanside homes are well hidden from the hustle and bustle of the village proper. The high sandy hills fronting the Atlantic Ocean are perfect for the large single family homes with lots of windows and decks. Britt Real Estate handles lot sales and resales for Schooner Ridge. The community has indoor and outdoor recreational amenities. Bike paths wind through the area and all the shops of the village are within walking distance.

SOUTHERN SHORES
Ocean Blvd.-Duck Road
Southern Shores, NC 27949

Southern Shores is a unique 2600-acre incorporated town with its own government and police force. Although there is a shopping center on its western boundary, commercial zoning/development is not allowed elsewhere. This town has heavy maritime forests along the soundside fringe, wide open sand hills in the middle and beachfront property. Recently, the post office has officially recognized Southern Shores as a town so folks who reside here no longer use Kitty Hawk for mailing purposes. The heavy year round population attests to the popularity of Southern Shores. Development has been carefully paced through the years and there are still many lots which remain undeveloped. It is considered one of the most desirable places to live on the Outer Banks.

MARTIN'S POINT
Route 158
Kitty Hawk, NC 27949

Martin's Point is an exclusive waterfront community of magnificent custom homes. There are stringent building requirements, guarded entry and some of the most beautiful maritime forest found anywhere.

When you arrive on the Outer Banks via the Wright Memorial Bridge, the entrance to Martin's Point is on your immediate left at MP 0! The community is closed to drive-thru inspections, but if you're considering a permanent move to the Outer Banks, it's an area you'll want to look over.

KITTY HAWK LANDING
West Kitty Hawk Rd.
Kitty Hawk, NC 27949

This is a relatively new residential community of mostly year round residents. It's located on the far western edges of Kitty Hawk and to get there you turn at MP 4 on West Kitty Hawk Road and just keep driving until you see the signs. The community borders Currituck Sound, has deep water canals, tall pines and gorgeous sunsets.

COLINGTON HARBOUR
Colington Road
Kill Devil Hills, NC 27948

Development began over 20 years ago on this big island. There are a large number of luxury homes, complete with boat docks, but for the most part the average home is a beach-box. What makes Colington Harbour popular is its remoteness, private entry and many canals which offer "waterfront" living to most of its residents.

BAY CLIFF
Williams Drive, Colington Island
Kill Devil Hills, NC 27948

Bay Cliff is about three years old and not heavily populated yet. It is carved out of an incredible maritime forest, and there are restrictions on clearing land. The initial development was done with preservation in mind. The community has its own central sewage system. This means there's no need for septic systems here, as is the case in most beach development. Ben Cubler of BC Development is on site to show you around. There are 72 lots, some of which are already built out. Homes here are a bit larger than average, but the focal point of the community -- in addition to the nature trails and woods -- is its large soundfront clubhouse (the Claw Club) with pool, bar, game room and lounge. There is a boat slip at the clubhouse as no bulkheading is allowed for individual lot owners. The marshgrass and wetlands are protected, and rightly so. Once you've seen the sunsets and heard the sounds of nature in the forest and along the water's edge, you'll appreciate the careful planning and development.

THE VILLAGE AT NAGS HEAD
Route 158-S. Croatan Hwy.
Nags Head, NC 27959

It all began about 6 years ago and has become one of the best sellers on the Outer Banks. The golf course with beautiful clubhouse and popular restaurant, and the oceanfront recreational complex with tennis, swimming and a restaurant make this attractive residential community most desirable. Single-family homes, townhomes and condos provide something for everyone. The Ammons Corporation has developed this large community, which spans the highway, around MP 15. The oceanfront homes are some of the largest and most luxurious anywhere. There's lot to do when you live or vacation here. It's an excellent choice for beach-living or investment.

PIRATE'S COVE
Manteo-Nags Head Causeway
Manteo, NC 27954

Pirate's Cove is luxury waterfront property with townhomes and single family homes. Deep water canals provide each owner with a dock at their door, even though the centrally located marina is home to many large yachts and fishing boats. There's always activity here. Fishing tourna-

ments seem as important as sleeping to many of the residents (and locals and visitors can get in on the fun). Other recreational amenities include tennis courts, a swimming pool and hot tub. One of the prettiest settings on the Outer Banks enhances the Victorian-nautical design of these homes.

KINNAKEET SHORES
NC 12
Avon, NC 27915

The name comes from the first settlers of the area back in the late 1500s. Once a desolate stretch of narrow land between the Atlantic Ocean and Pamlico Sound, Kinnakeet Shores is a residential community which is being carefully developed. It consists of five hundred acres under wide open skies, beautiful marshlands and in one of the best windsurfing areas in the world. Recreational amenities include a clubhouse, swimming pools, tennis courts and a fitness center. This is the largest development on Hatteras Island and the homes tend to be quite big, reminding us of the northern beaches.

HATTERAS BY THE SEA
Hatteras, NC 27943

This rather small community of 36 lots on twenty-five acres is one of the last oceanfront areas available for residential living. There's not much land on the southern end of the Outer Banks and a good portion is preserved by the National Seashore designation. A large pool and some carefully de-

signed nature paths will be included here. Sunrise and sunset are unobstructed for homeowners.

Here are some Outer Banks real estate companies we think do good jobs:

Atlantic Realty, 261-2154, 800-334-8401 (out-of-state). Located at MP 2-1/2, Route 158, in Kitty Hawk. Representing the area from Corolla to Nags Head.

Beach Realty & Construction, 261-3815. Located at MP 2-1/4, Route 158, Kitty Hawk and North Duck Rd. near Sanderling, 261-6600. Representing the area from Ocean Hill to Nags Head.

Brindley & Brindley Realty & Development, Inc., 261-2222. Located at 1184 Duck Road, Duck Village, with an office in Corolla Light Resort, 473-5555 or 453-3000. Representing the area from Carova Beach to Kitty Hawk.

Britt Real Estate, 261-3566, 800-334-6315 (out-of-state). Located on Duck Rd. north of the village. Representing the area from Corolla to Southern Shores.

Cove Realty, 441-6391, 800-635-7007 (out-of-state). Located at 105 E. Dunn St., Nags Head. Representing the Nags Head and South Nags Head areas and specializing in Old Nags Head Cove.

Dolphin Realty, 986-2241, 800-338-4775. Located in Hatteras. Representing properties on Hatteras Island.

Gardner Realty, 441-8985. Located on the Beach Road at MP 11 in Nags Head. Representing the areas of Kitty Hawk, Kill Devil Hills and Nags Head, specializing in the area of S. Nags Head.

Hatteras Realty, 995-4600. Located on NC 12 in Avon. Representing the area of Hatteras Island.

Joe Lamb, Jr. & Assoc., 261-4444. Located on Route 158, MP 2 and on the Beach Rd. at MP 10, 441-5541. Representing the areas of Kitty Hawk, Kill Devil Hills, Nags Head and other northern Outer Banks properties.

Midgett Realty, 986-2141, 800-527-2903 (out-of-state). Located in Rodanthe and Hatteras. Representing

the southern end of the Banks.

Sharon Miller Realty, 928-5711, 928-5731. Located on Ocracoke Island. Representing island properties.

Ocracoke Island Realty, 928-6261, 800-242-5394 (out-of-state). Located on Ocracoke Island. Representing island properties.

Outer Banks, Ltd., 441-7156. Located on Rt. 158, Nags Head. Representing the areas from Corolla to Nags Head and Roanoke Island.

Outer Beaches Realty, 995-4477. Located in Avon with other locations on Hatteras Island. Representing the Hatteras Island area.

Pirate's Cove, 473-1451, 800-

762-0245 (out-of-state). Located on Hwy. 64/264 Nags Head Causeway. Representing properties in Pirate's Cove.

Resort Central, Inc., 261-8861, 800-334-4749 (in and out-of-state). Located on Route 158, MP 2-1/2, Kitty Hawk. Representing the areas of Kitty Hawk, Nags Head, Roanoke Island and Corolla.

Resort Realty, 261-8282. Several locations from Corolla to Rodanthe. Representing the entire Outer Banks.

Salvo Realty, 987-2343. Located on Monitor Lane in Salvo. Representing areas of Hatteras Island.

Seaside Realty, 261-5500, 800-395-2525 (out-of-state). Located on Route 158, MP 3-1/2, Kitty Hawk. Representing properties from Corolla to South Nags Head.

Southern Shores Realty, 261-2000, 800-334-1000 (out-of-state) or 800-682-2002 (in-state). Located in Southern Shores. Representing the areas north to Corolla and south to Nags Head.

Sun Realty, 441-7033, 800-346-9593 (out-of-state). Several locations from Duck to Avon. Representing the entire Outer Banks.

Surf or Sound, 995-5801. Located on Hwy. 12 in Avon. Representing properties on Hatteras Island.

Mercedes Tabano, 987-2711. Located on NC 12, Rodanthe. Representing areas of Hatteras Island.

Twiddy Realty, 261-2897. Several locations on the northern Outer Banks from Duck to north of Ocean Hill.

Village Realty, 441-8533, 800-548-9688 (out-of-state). Located at the Village of Nags Head. Representing the area in and around the resort.

Stan White Realty & Construction, 441-1515. Located on Route 158, MP 11. Representing areas from Kitty Hawk to Nags Head.

The Young People, 441-5544. Located on the Beach Road in Kill Devil Hills. Representing homes throughout the Outer Banks but especially main beach area from Kitty Hawk south.

Building Homes on the Outer Banks

Buying a lot and building a house at the beach is pretty close to nirvana for a lot of people. North Carolina law requires that building contractors have a license, helping to assure that that pleasant state of mind keeps with you. Some still get around the laws, so check qualifications and reputation before signing on the dotted line. Get in touch with owners of local homes to query them about their experience with their builder. Ask lenders. If you're itching to buy a lot or home, going to the real estate company first is fine, but you can reverse the situation and go to a lender first instead. They'll also know the reputable sales and construction companies all over the Outer Banks.

It's a good idea to get in touch with a designer or architect, too. When you're building on sand, these folks will know what's involved in the engineering and design.

Building a home in a coastal environment exposes you to more than a trifling of codes and restrictions. Send for informative pamphlets. Regulations set by the North Carolina Coastal Management Authority are for protecting the environment. Use them to protect yourself as well. CAMA will become a familiar acronym to you here as you go through the building process.

Local building codes and re-

strictions vary with each area of the beach. Get in touch with local planning boards. Although the builder obtains permits, it's good to know how he (we know of no women builders on the Outer Banks at this time) goes about that and what's required.

Before you buy, before you build, do lots of homework. The best real estate agents have lots of general information; some have specific information, which is what you need. Get educated with specific, printed information. The best builders know the ropes, too. Again, get enough information to know the process of building your home. Questions that come up "after the fact" can drive you up a

wall if you live out of town and the builder is out on the construction site driving nails and not in his office answering the phone.

A road tour of the Banks will reveal a wide variety of homes. It can get tough to choose what you want. And what about furnishings? Does that wall space allow for a proper-size bed or couch? What can be used on the windows?

We've listed a few designers, architects, builders and interior decorators for your use. We're not saying this list is inclusive, just that these are folks whose good reputation has been tested over time.

GENERAL CONTRACTORS

B.C. Development, Duck, 261-5050

Beach Realty and Construction, 261-3815

Cole Construction, Corolla, 453-2393

Dean P. Edwards, Inc., Kitty Hawk Village, 261-7858

Dog Point Builders, Frisco, 995-6340

Farrow Builders, Frisco, 995-5452

Olin Finch & Co., 261-8710, Kitty Hawk

Fulcher Homes, 261-3316, Kitty Hawk

Mancuso Development, Corolla, 453-8921

Newcomb Builders, Kitty Hawk, 441-1803

Newman Homes, Point Harbor, 491-8588

Beau Reid, Corolla, 453-8618

Sea Watch Builders, Southern Shores, 261-1793

Shotton Co., Duck, 261-5555

Snearer Construction, Kitty Hawk, 261-2228

Stan White Realty and Construction, 441-1515

Stormont & Co., Kitty Hawk, 261-8724

Bo Taylor Fine Homes, Nags Head, 261-2735

Waldt Construction, Duck, 261-3721

DESIGNERS & ARCHITECTS

Design Assoc. II, Southern Shores, 261-8498

Dixon Design Assoc., Corolla, 453-4279

Alex Engart, AIA, Duck, 261-1217

Jude LeBlanc, Southern Shores, 261-6869

Magnacorp., Duck, 261-4447

Real Escapes Ltd., Sanderling, 261-2181

Sandcastle Designs, Southern Shores, 261-2766

Steele & Assoc., Kill Devil Hills, 480-1400

John F. Wilson, IV, Manteo, 473-3282

INTERIOR DESIGN/DECORATING

Ambrose Furniture, 261-4836

Decor by the Shore, Kitty Hawk, 261-6222

Island Interiors, Southern Shores, 261-3614

Interior Techniques, Kitty Hawk, 261-4925

Interiors, Kitty Hawk, 261-4105

Mary Isaacs Interiors, Manteo, 473-1043

Photo: DCTB

Photo: DCTB

Birds, Fishing, and a Touch of Solitude
Gold & Silver Seasons

"Nature goes her own way, and all that to us seems an exception, is really according to order." -- Goethe

*A*lthough I grew up in this state, it wasn't until long after I had moved away, got involved in raising a family, and launched a career in a corporate environment that I discovered the Outer Banks.

I secretly wished all my life to live at the beach. Whenever our family planned vacations, there was never a question of whether or not to go to the beach -- just which one.

In my youth, I burned to a crisp on flat southern beaches, listened to beach music and learned to dance the Shag. Later on, I explored mid-Atlantic beaches and held private meetings with myself in solitude, shielded from the wind, behind boulders on the northeast coast. I watched in awe of nature's whims off the northwestern coast of Ireland. I looked for a small piece of beach along the Rhine River in Germany where vineyards and castles dotted the hillsides. I swam in warm, blue-green waters and squinted behind sunglasses on the blinding white beaches along the Gulf of Mexico.

Eventually, I arrived on the Outer Banks still searching for a beach...and finding one. During those summer days of 1987 when I was taking a course in "wave-ology" with a friend on the Nags Head oceanfront, my life changed forever.

I discovered a whole string of beaches, north to south, with many different characteristics. Some areas revealed fine, almost-white sand and a variety of shells. Other areas of beach trapped small pebbles on light-brownish sand. I found wide-open skies and heavy forests. The absence of bright lights and high-rise buildings was astonishing and appreciated. The rugged beauty of wind-blown trees and marshgrass, the stretches of uninhabited beach, the colorful sails of a windsurfer catching a breeze in high sun, the star-filled skies of quiet nights, the many shades of green and brown and the abundance of wildflowers and wildlife were pure luxury to my senses.

I ponder the silver sea in photographs I snapped in early morning light and realize that it could be any beach to someone else. It's not. I smile, remembering the rain clouds that moved in to change a vivid, blue sky to purple and thrn into a down-pour before I could haul myself and my stuff off the beach. I laugh at the photos of golden sunsets, recalling how a piercing sunset turned up the heat on the suntan I cooked one day. I stop looking at pictures and recall the sounds of silence, of aloneness on desolate stretches of beaches along the National Seashore on the south or Audubon Sanctuary on the north.

Pick a season. The whole year is good here.

A top priority is the water and a tan in summer months. Activities range from swimming, fishing and windsurfing to dining out, shopping or exploring art galleries. And of course, there are miles of beach to cover. Not to be overlooked is the sensational experience of coming off the beach and taking a shower outside; feeling a wet, plank floor underfoot while standing there long enough to cool-down a suntan and wash the salt and sand from your swimsuit, hair and body is outrageous. Sometimes you can look up at the open sky to spot an osprey or a small airplane -- it makes the day!

The water of the sounds between this narrow piece of land and the mainland provides a natural habitat for waterfowl and birds during the heat of summer. Huge flocks of brown pelicans fill the skies, fish jump out of the ocean. Fishing goes on all the time. You'll hear or create your own incredible fish stories, and watch the local newspaper turn into a "documentary" about people and fish during the summer.

After the summer's heat wears you down to a nub, the fall will set you free. A revival occurs at this time of year when the sun's angle is different and every bit of nature is gasping for breath after a summer bake. My body and spirit come alive in the fall when nights are cooler.

Fishing tournaments and the chance to go after the big one carry enthusiastiasm for many who relish the warm fall days out on the open sea. Thousands of birds begin to fly, high in the sky and way out over the ocean. Dolphins surface and dive to the delight of everyone on the beach. After the osprey leave, cormorants, Canadian geese, snow geese and mallards fly in. We're here on the Atlantic flyway. Take it in and feel the soft, salty moisture building up on your face.

During the month of September, I hear crickets and the ocean on quieter nights. I check the calendar for a late September or early October Harvest Moon. Seeing that reddish-blue-pinkish-orange ball rise out of the Atlantic Ocean gives me a chill and brings me down to Earth, and I often linger on the beach until it reaches a high point in the sky and begins to turn creamy. There's all-night fishing off the piers, great sunsets and a quieter beach. Large flocks of sanderlings flying across my field of vision capture the miracle of nature. How do they fly wing-tip-to-wing-tip, turn around and go again?

Finding a restful place down here on the Outer Banks in the winter is good. Pretend you're on safari and you don't know where anything is. (Use this book!) Where to eat, sleep and explore? Some beach shops close around Thanksgiving, others continue a flexible schedule. Life begins to achieve more balance -- the natural change of seasons and a slower pace.

The shorter days of winter allow for quiet walks and cozy evenings by a fire at home in a cottage or resort. There's time to read a whole book, maybe more. Local groups experience another side of their lives with the shorter business days. Theatre performances, art exhibits and poetry readings become the focus in the towns and villages on the Outer Banks. Local writers read original works at an art gallery. There's story-telling in a local bookshop. Coming to the beach in winter allows for a mini-safari to take your mind off DC, Philly and other busy places.

Sometimes we have snow. Have you ever seen snow at a beach? Everything is still. The Spanish moss blows listlessly from its thin connections with live oak trees. Looking out over the dunes, tall clumps of pampas grass and sea oats seem to dance in solitude on shorter days and under sometimes-gray skies. Recently, several whales were sighted off-shore, leading marine experts to investigate further this phenomenon of nature. Whales don't usually come this far south. You sight them during long, quiet periods on the beach, when nothing can distract you from keeping your eyes peeled on the horizon.

In winter the salt breezes are as thick as fog. And, there's real fog, too! Stop in at a warm restaurant and talk with the local people. Or, go on and treat yourself to a day-long seige of silence all bundled up on the beach or in a Jacuzzi tub of a cottage or hotel. Take a long drive out to the north beaches or south along the Hatteras shores.

About mid-February, you'll experience the first urge to sun-bathe on the Outer Banks. It might not last long, but catch it and·do it -- the season's first suntan. Try fishing off the beach in the spring or off the piers which open by late March. Trees begin to green-up and replace the brownish-salt burn of winter winds. Flowering camelia trees burst with a splash of color almost overnight. Acres of maritime forest come to life again. The variety of hardy plants in this salty environment is astounding. In March the good news about spring is settled when the osprey return; it's as if the people on ladders fixing and painting

Insiders' Tip

Insiders like:

Spending time chatting and making new friends during the unhurried fall, winter, and spring seasons on the Outer Banks.

cottages or shops and adding new signs are given the signal and the seasons changes.

In late spring and early summer volunteers begin signing up for the turtle watch. Certain areas of the Hatteras seashore are home to sea turtles who lay their eggs on warm sand and return to the sea. Sometimes the eggs are in danger from people or vehicles on portions of the beach. So a "watch" is set up. Later on, baby turtles struggle across the sand to find their ocean home.

If you've vacationed at the beach in summer, a visit to the Outer Banks is a winner. But a visit here in any season will open you to endless possibilities -- of realizing dreams and new adventures.

The discoveries for me are innumerable, and I've recalled a few here to allow a look beyond the housetops, beyond the ordinary trip to the beach. Nature repeats its cycles -- sharing secrets and bringing a sense of order in our lives.

Mary

Photo: Henry Applewhite

The Outer Banks
Fishing Guide

*F*ishing is, beyond any doubt, the number one participant and spectator sport of the Outer Banks. In its various forms — surf fishing, sound fishing, pier fishing, and full-scale Gulf Stream billfishing — it is available for most of the year, with temporary but fierce booms when the season arrives and the big ones begin to bite. It's available right through the Banks, from Corolla down to Portsmouth, and on to Cape Lookout, but Hatteras Island is the true mecca of anglers. Off Cape Point, beyond the lighthouse and Diamond Shoals, is the point where the warm blue waters of the Gulf Stream collide with the cooler, food-rich Virginia Coastal Drift. The combination provides a long fishing season and a variety of species matched by few if any other places in the world. Kitty Hawk and Nags Head have their piers and charter boats, but this special fishing guide will concentrate mainly on Hatteras...because the fish seem to!

The island's heavy dependence and concentration on sport fishing, along with its relative isolation, have made it the testing ground for many of the rigs and ideas that are now common in salt water fishing. Probably 60 to 65% of the terminal gear used in North Carolina has traditionally been made by various small subcontractors on the Outer Banks, who sit around in the off season and manufacture instead of fish. This has, in turn, led to the development of specialized rigs for the different types of fishing found on the Banks.

"We basically get two kinds of fishermen here on the Banks," says Ken Lauer. "The first are the tourists, who like to 'play' on a pier, or in the surf. They're happy with a six or twelve inch fish. We see them between May and Labor Day. After that, the serious fishermen start to arrive."

Though the techniques overlap at places, there are basically three ways to fish on the Banks. These are from the surf (or a pier); from a boat, in the sounds; or from a larger boat, out in the Stream.

SURF AND PIER FISHING

Surf fishing is a sport and an art form all its own. It involves, much of the time, the use of four-wheel-drive vehicles. Armed with specialized gear and up to seven rods apiece, the hard core surf fisherman spends September and December roving the Hatteras beaches at low tide to read the configuration of the sand bars. Where is it shallow? they ask themselves, and every other fisherman they meet. Where are the bars? Where are there offshore holes at high water, where the fish will lurk?

On the Banks, the surf fisherman will find distinct species of fish around at different times of the year. Surf fishing really begins in early to mid-March, for those migratory fish (such as croakers and trout) that 'hibernate' offshore in winter and then move inshore and head north in the spring.

The next class is perhaps the most sought after: the drum family, or channel bass, as the largest are called (to clarify: a *Sciaenops ocellata* weighing, say, one pound, is known on the Banks as a puppy drum. A little older, a little bigger, and it becomes a yearling drum. One from 35 to about 70 lbs. will be called a red drum, or sometimes an old drum. The really big ones, and it takes from forty to sixty *years* out there for them to attain this seniority, are 'channel bass,' for which the world's record is 94 pounds, caught off Avon in 1984). The drum and channel bass have two seasons: mid-March to mid-May, as they move north, and then again mid-October to early December, as they move south again.

Another popular surf and pier fish is the blue, or bluefish, a vicious, toothy little fellow who's found at his best around here from mid-October to late November. There's a spring run for blues, too, but they tend to be emaciated. These, along with flounder, are the most popular fish available to the serious surf or pier fisherman. By the end of May surf fishing begins to taper off. In May to July about all the surf holds is one-pound blues, sea mullet and Spanish mackerel in about the same size range. There are some summer fish, available mainly from the piers, and good for fun; spot, croaker, grey trout — nice pan fish, but nothing to write home about. The pompano, also available then up to four lbs., are very tasty. And then there are the miscellanea: skate, blowfish, dogfish, rays, tarpon in late summer, and assorted sharks — none all that common, but don't be surprised if one shows up on your hook.

Most fishing from piers and in the surf is done with casting lures or rigs using a sinker that will anchor in the sand and one or two hooks arranged to keep the bait away from the bottom. Hooks are usually size 4 to 6 for the smaller species and 6/0 to 9/0 for the larger. Bait is generally cutbait, cut mullet, shrimp, minnows, bloodworms, squid or flounder and shark belly. Trout are commonly caught on a medium to large plastic lure; mackerel and large bluefish on metal casting lures; channel bass on mullet heads, cut menhaden or spot. As far as tide and time, low and incoming tides are often more productive than high water. Trout are best taken near dawn in clear water, while smaller drum are most likely found in the morning or evening in rough, murky water.

To try for the really big fish, you've got to haunt the ends of the piers, with a long rod (most often custom made), live-lining bluefish or spot with a heavy cork float and a four-foot wire leader.

Sounds too complex for you? Novices *can* catch fish on the Banks, if they use their heads. The tackle shops listed at the end of this section are stocked up not only with equipment but with information. All too often the visiting fisherman brings equipment that is too light and not suited to unique Banks conditions. It can make sense to leave your stuff at home and buy equipment here — it will certainly be better suited to conditions, and may (since it's made here) be cheaper as well. There are bait and tackle shops scattered in every village and on every pier. And, believe it or not, fishing gear is also sold in drug stores, department stores and even some gas stations that serve as general stores.

A second option is renting. Most Banks tackle shops and piers rent rod, reel, terminal gear and sometimes even foul weather gear and waders, and most can direct you to a local guide service.

Frank Merillat is a local guide who specializes in surf fishing. He has 26 years of fishing under his belt, the last eleven in Hatteras. Here are his surf fishing tips. "The first thing you have to realize is that all these fish are transitory. It's not like inland fishing where they hang around a tree or a rock. Off Hatteras it changes from tide to tide. This makes for more risky fishing, in terms of getting a predictable catch.

"It also means you have to work a little — study the habits, or patterns, of the fish. The hard part is not catching them, it's finding 'em. Very few surf fish are difficult to catch. They bite readily at a variety of bait. Again, it's not like freshwater fishing, where you have to feed them the proper fly, place it just right, etc. Blues and drum are aggressive eaters and will readily bite.

"To find the fish — the hard part — you've got to learn to read the water. To understand what the bottom looks like; where the bars and sloughs are. The coast here has features something like this:

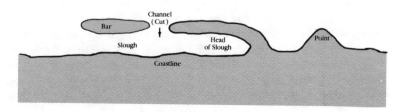

"The point is that this structure is rapidly changing. Day to day. So if you fish at the Point, for example, all the time — just because it's been written about so much — you may not get consistent catches.

"How do you read the water? Look at it. At low tide you can see the distinguishing marks: breaking waves, smooth water where the channels run. So it's very important to do your homework.

"Also, if you want to catch fish at Hatteras you need to spend time actively fishing. Not sitting in your motel room, not watching from your truck. You have to stand out there with a bait in the water. It's no mystery: these fish pass in migratory groups, and if you have a bait in the water when they're there you'll catch one.

"It's also important to vary your methods. If you're not catching anything with mullet you might try a lure or shrimp. Fish are changeable characters! Fish far out; fish close in. Jiggle the bait, vary the speed and motion of your retrieve. Hold your rod, then you can feel a bite. When the rod's in the rod holder you may be missing fish.

"Much of the time you catch nothing. You wait. Then suddenly there's a burst of action. You just got to be ready.

"Don't depend on the tackle shop people for *all* of your information. They talk to hundreds of people a day, so even when they give you a good spot it'll be crowded. A guide obviously can aid a fisherman. If you want to learn about gear, methods, habits, places to fish, then a guide's the way to go. Somebody who knows all this stuff doesn't need one. Or if it's not important to you to catch a fish. It's important to me to catch fish, and I'm a good fisherman. But if I went to Florida, I'd hire a guide. I don't like to waste the money and time. There's no way in the world a guide can guarantee you a fish, but I can guarantee you'll be better prepared to fish on your own afterward.

"Another subject. The time is here that fishermen need to be aware of our impact on the beach. If you drive on the dunes, or leave trash, you're ruining the island. Throw back fish you don't want. And if you do catch a beautiful forty-pound drum, use it! Eat it or give it to some old-timer on the island. There are lots of people who'll take a nice fish off your hands. Don't throw it in the dumpster. If I came to your home town and treated it the way some people treat this island I'd be thrown in jail. If we don't conserve and behave thoughtfully, we'll lose these beaches and our sport with them."

HEAD BOATS

An excellent intermediate choice between pier fishing and chartering a big boat yourself is the head boat, so called because it takes all comers on a regular schedule and charges X dollars "a head" (usually from fifteen to twenty dollars per person for a half-day, morning or afternoon). A lot of experienced fishermen enjoy head boating, but beginners especially love it. There's no pressure to bring home a big one, though certainly you can, and there's lots of fun and camaraderie for a small amount of cash.

Banks head boats generally cruise the sounds and inlets. In the spring and fall, however, they often head out to sea. Croaker, flounder, spot and sea trout are the mainstays, depending of course on the season and your luck. Head boats generally provide fishing tackle, ice, bait, snack facilities, restrooms and soft drinks, and the crew will help you bait your hook and deal with the fish once it's aboard, if you really aren't sure how it's done.

Oregon Inlet Fishing Center, Hatteras Harbor Marina, Pirate's Cove and several other locations on the Banks run head boats, especially during the season.

FRESH WATER FISHING

The fresh water fishing on the Outer Banks isn't nearly as well known as the salt water fishing, but it's there, as Dick Baker told us, and it's good. Kitty Hawk Bay and Currituck Sound offer "super bass fishing," and there are white and yellow perch and some

nice catfish in the brackish sounds, too. Numerous bass clubs fish this area, and the Master's Bass Classic has been held at Kitty Hawk. In early spring, Baker recommends crank and spinner baits, and worms in the summer, of course; go back to spinner and crank baits in the fall. For Kitty Hawk Bay, the public boat ramp west of the bypass opposite Avalon Pier offers the easiest access.

Don't say we didn't warn you, though, that fresh water licenses are required. North Carolina has carefully drawn lines between prominent points, and state fish and wildlife commission patrols will take *you* if you fish inside them or north of the Wright Memorial Bridge. Licenses are available at Tatem's and Tackle Express in Nags Head, Virginia Dare Hardware in Kitty Hawk and Colington Creek Marina on Colington Island, among other agents.

BOAT FISHING: THE SOUNDS

Pamlico, Albemarle, Roanoke Sounds — the small boater excels in these broad, shallow, brackish waters between the Banks and the mainland. The sounds in summer are crammed with fourteen-to- twenty-four footers after the hordes of gray trout, croakers, spot, flounder and tarpon, and at night even channel bass. Another popu-

---

Insiders know:
When the bluefish "blitz" in the spring and fall the water can turn almost white with feeding fish. You never know when blitzes are going to happen, so be prepared.

Insiders' Tip

lar fish in the sounds is cobia, which seems to hit its peak about the third week in May; this is a dramatic fish, a hard fighter, and good eating as well.

But in general, sound fishing is a more relaxed, family type of recreation than either surf or ocean fishing. You can hire a guide and a boat or just set out on your own from a handy ramp in your own rig. A long, carefree day of summer fishing in the calm sound, maybe a case of beer...who needs to fight a marlin?

OCEAN FISHING

The ocean fisherman, that's who. He (and a lot of shes) revels in the Hemingwayesque challenge of a big, fighting billfish. And they're out there...**big** ones; in 1974 the IGFA all-tackle record blue marlin, 1,142 lbs., was taken off Oregon Inlet, and this was no fluke...hundreds are regularly taken off Hatteras during the summer months. Read our interview with Captain Ernal Foster of the *Albatross* who started the Gulf Stream charter business in Hatteras in 1938.

Most of the Gulf Stream charter boats operate out of Oregon and Hatteras Inlets, plus a couple from Ocracoke and Roanoke Island. The Stream lies a couple of hours out, depending on from where you depart, some 25 to 40 miles offshore. This is the closest the Stream comes to the coast north of Florida. Black and white marlin, dolphin, tuna and wahoo are taken primarily by trolling. The blue marlin begin to show in mid-April, and peak in

June; during July and August they taper off, but they're still there. By then the white marlin is getting plentiful, with a normal catch being one per boat per day. August is a good month for sailfish. Just beginning to catch on is the technique of long-lining for swordfish at night. There is a little wreck fishing off the Banks coast, but not as much as elsewhere along the Atlantic coast; skippers seem to prefer trolling to wreck-fishing. Certainly there are enough wrecks.

An excellent introduction to Stream fishing is the annual Sport Fishing School, held every June since 1950. This six-day course takes groups into the Gulf Stream on local boats for some exciting fishing. Most "students" are retirees or professional people, including families, who regard it as a vacation. Cost is about $600, lodging not included. For a brochure write North Carolina State University, Division for Lifelong Education, Box 7401, Raleigh NC, 27695-7401.

AUTUMN AND WINTER FISHING

Most Banks fishermen look forward to autumn. As the water cools in September, the larger fish begin to come inshore once again. The bluefish reappear, in larger sizes; Spanish mackerel show from four up to possibly nine pounds; puppy drum arrive in the surf. In November begins the return of the bluefish, now fat at ten and fifteen pounds. There is generally a terrific run of spot in September and

October, averaging around a pound apiece, but copious, easy to catch and tasty. As autumn goes on, the 'pier jockeys' begin to pull in channel bass again.

November is the most looked-for month in terms of both quality and quantity of fishing, with Thanksgiving traditionally the peak (channel bass, bluefish, loads of two to five-pound flounder, and gray trout). This may continue on into December if the weather is warm. Tournaments are prevalent beginning in June and lasting through November. Pirate's Cove, located just over the bridge on the way to Manteo, has become the base for many of these, but others are held in Nags Head and Hatteras.

The winter is a lull, it's very cold so there is little fishing from mid-December to mid-March. But the fish are there; big trout, croakers and bluefish. As it gets colder they move off-shore, to 80-100 feet of water. The commercial fishermen take them there, and many of the charter captains are commercial fishermen in the winter. Few sport anglers can muster much enthusiasm for the Hatteras winter weather.

All in all, the Banks, especially Hatteras, offer the best year round saltwater fishing to be found for a long way up or down the Atlantic coast.

OFF-ROAD VEHICLES — THE CONTROVERSY

The use of Off-Road Vehicles (ORVs) on the beaches of Hatteras, Ocracoke, and Bodie Island has been limited. A 'zone' concept governs beach driving now, with these zones being opened or closed by National Park Service officials depending on erosion, nesting season, high visitor use areas, etc.

Though no permit is currently required to drive on the beach in the Park area, it is smartest to check with a ranger before you venture out to make sure you understand their guidelines and assure you are not entering a closed zone. Not knowing is no excuse, especially if you've wound up in some ecologically sensitive area.

One tip, there is NO beach driving allowed on the Pea Island National Refuge. Local towns outside the park require ORV permits.

Once you're safely and legally on the beach, having reached it only by using one of the clearly marked and numbered ramps, you should remain on the portion of the beach between the water and the foot of the dunes, in other words, DO NOT drive on the dunes. Access points in the National Seashore Park areas are marked by a light-brown sign with a white jeep icon. An "X" or "/" through a jeep means "no access" by 4-wheel drive vehicle. The same goes for sound side driving: you should stay on the marked routes only. Your speed should be reasonable and prudent. And please pick up your trash — not just to be a nice person, but to avoid the access-limit laws that have closed much of Cape Cod, for example, to any 4WD traffic at all. Vehicles must be state registered and street legal; the driver must also be licensed.

For current information on open zones and guidelines, you may contact the Headquarters, National Park Service, Cape Hatteras Group, 473-2111, any National Park Service visitor contact facility, or you may write to: Cape Hatteras National Seashore, Route 1, Box 675, Manteo, N.C. 27954.

Each township on the Banks has its own requirements for permits to allow beach driving during certain times of the year. To get information or permits, contact the town administrative offices individually.

Citations and Tournaments

The Official North Carolina Saltwater Fishing Tournament is held annually to recognize outstanding angling achievement. The Department of Commerce, Travel and Tourism Division, awards citations for eligible species caught at or over certain minimum weights. Regulations on eligibility and boundaries may be obtained at these locations, which are also weighing stations for fish presented for citation:

Avalon Fishing Pier, Kill Devil Hills

Avon Fishing Pier, Avon

Bob's Bait & Tackle, Duck

Cape Hatteras Fishing Pier, Frisco

Dillon's Corner, Buxton

The Fishin' Hole, Salvo

Frisco Rod & Gun Club, Frisco

Hatteras Fishing Center, Hatteras Village

Hatteras Harbor Marina, Hatteras Village

Hatteras Marlin Club, Hatteras Village

Hatteras Tackle Shop, Hatteras Village

Hatteras Island Fishing Pier, Rodanthe

Island Marina, Manteo

Jennette's Pier, Nags Head

Kitty Hawk Fishing Pier, Kitty Hawk

Nags Head Fishing Pier, Nags Head

Nags Head Ice & Cold Storage, Nags Head

O'Neal's Dockside, Ocracoke

Oregon Inlet Fishing Center, Oregon Inlet

Outer Banks Pier and Fishing Center, South Nags Head]

Pelican's Roost, Hatteras Village

Pirate's Cove, Manteo-Nags Head Causeway

The Red Drum Tackle Shop, Buxton

Salty Dawg Marina, Manteo

TW's Bait & Tackle Shops, Duck and Kitty Hawk

Teach's Lair Marina, Hatteras Village

Tradewinds Tackle Shop, Ocracoke

Village Marina, Hatteras Village

Whalebone Tackle Shop, Nags Head

Willis Boat Landing, Hatteras Village

ELIGIBLE SPECIES AND MINIMUM WEIGHTS FOR CITATIONS, 1991

(Note: new information had not been submitted by the State when we went to press, so this information is current as of 1991. In our experience over the years with this list, it doesn't change much from year to year, but if it's important to you, ask at local tackle shops if the new list is available.)

Amberjack 50 lbs., or 50" with release

Barracuda 20 lbs.

Bass, Black Sea 3 lbs.

Bass, Channel/Red Drum 45 lbs., or 40"
with release

Black Drum 40 lbs.

Bluefish 17 lbs.

Cobia 40 lbs.

Croaker 3 lbs.

Dolphin 35 lbs.

Flounder 5 lbs.

Grouper (any) 20 lbs.

Jack, Crevalle 20 lbs.

Mackerel, King 30 lbs.

Mackerel, Spanish 6 lbs.

Marlin, Blue 300 lbs.*

Marlin, White 50 lbs.*

Sailfish 30 lbs.*

Sea Mullet 1.5 lbs.

Shark (any) 100 lbs.

Sheepshead 10 lbs.

Snapper, Red 10 lbs.

Snapper, Silver (porgy) 4 lbs.

Spot 1 lbs.

Tarpon 30 lbs.*

Tautog 8 lbs.

Triggerfish 7 lbs.

Trout, Gray 6 lbs.

Trout, Speckled 4 lbs.

Tuna, Bigeye 100 lbs.

Tuna, Bluefin 80 lbs.

Tuna, Yellowfin 70 lbs.

Wahoo 40 lbs.

*CITATION FOR RELEASE REGARDLESS OF SIZE

Current All-Tackle N.C. Saltwater Game Fish Records

Fish	Weight	Location	Date
Amberjack	125	Off Cape Lookout	1973
Barracuda	67-7	Off Cape Lookout	1985
Bass,Black Sea	8	Off Oregon Inlet	1979
Bass, Channel	94*-2	Hatteras Island	1984
Bluefish	31-12*	Off Hatteras Island	1972
Cobia	103	Off Emerald Isle	1988
Croaker	5	Oregon Inlet	1981
Dolphin	77	Off Hatteras Island	1973
Drum, Black	84	Cape Fear River	1980
Flounder	20-8	Carolina Beach	1980
Grouper, Warsaw	245	Off Wrightsville Beach	1967
Mackerel, King	79	Cape Lookout	1985
Mackerel, Span.	13*	Off Ocracoke	1987
Marlin, Blue	1142	Off Oregon Inlet	1974
Marlin, White	118-8	Off Oregon Inlet	1976
Pompano	5	Oregon Inlet	1987
Sailfish	100	Off Ocean Isle	1987
Sea Mullet	3-8	Bogue Banks	1971
Shark, Tiger	1150	Yaupon Beach	1966

Sheepshead	18-7	Carolina Beach	1982
Snapper, Red	40	Off Cape Lookout	1970
Snapper, Silver	13	Off Cape Lookout	1987
Spot	1-13	Manns Harbor	1979
Tarpon	164	Indian Beach	1978
Tautog	12-14	Gulf Stream	1987
Triggerfish	10-8	Off Cape Lookout	1987
Trout, Gray	14-14	Nags Head	1980
Trout,Speckled	12-4	Wrightsville Beach	1961
Tuna, Bigeye	282	Off Oregon Inlet	1988
Tuna, Bluefin	732-8	Off Cape Hatteras	1979
Tuna,Yellowfin	237	Off Cape Lookout	1979
Wahoo	127	Off Oregon Inlet	1973

*WORLD ALL-TACKLE RECORD

To make application for all-tackle record recognition, write Suzanne Hill, Coordinator, N.C. Division of Marine Fisheries, P.O. Box 769, Morehead City, N.C. 28557.

Call 1-800-682-2632 for information or to report violations.

Photo: Michael Halminski

The Outer Banks
Windsurfing, Surfing, & Ocean Swimming

*S*urfing has been around on the Banks since Bob Holland first began coming down from Virginia Beach in the late 50s. Word of the good surf here has spread; the East Coast Surfing Championships started here in the late 70s, and in 1978 and 1982 the U.S. Championships were held here.

"The best spot is at the lighthouse," says Scott Busbey, a resident pro and owner of the Natural Art surf shop. "Waves there usually break from the left, and the three jetties they built for erosion control formed a good sand bar."

Local surfers look forward to the hurricane season, from about the first of June to the end of November. This is when they begin to watch weather reports, hoping for the big northern swells. Waves get up to eight feet, and sometimes larger, but over about eight feet it tends to be "victory at sea."

Cape Hatteras (not just the Lighthouse beach) is always a popular spot. It has the advantage of having two beaches, facing in different directions; one faces south, the other east by southeast, so that when wind and swells are unsuitable at one, the other may be surfable. But when the wind comes from the southeast, which it often does in midsummer, be prepared to go swimming; surfing is poor. Two to three feet tends to be summer average. There's no channel at the Cape, which means you've got to muscle your way out there in heavy weather. Beware of the current when the waves come up; it's often two knots or more to the south along the beach, faster than you can swim, though on a board you might fight it. Wet suits a must until about the first of June; after that skin is OK till late October, or even later, depending on the lateness of the summer.

The lighthouse is usually the best, but not the only good break. The sandbars off the Banks are constantly shifting and changing, and there's a continual migration of surfers along them to find the best spots, which are then kept more or less secret. Surf along the Banks is where you find it. Places to check: Ramp 41; Frisco pier (off Billy Mitchell airport stay at least 400 feet from the pier itself); Kitty Hawk Pier, south of Coquina Beach. But you can always find a crowd at the Lighthouse.

LEARNING TO SURF

A lot of people, many of them from far inland, have learned to surf at Hatteras. If you've never done it, but you suspect that riding those big Atlantic waves in to the Cape Point break might be your kind of thrill, here are some tips to help you get started.

First, a bit of traditional surfer lore: the younger you are, the easier it is to start. If you're old enough to swim, and feel confident a hundred yards off the beach, you can surf. Here's how.

You can't surf without a board (body surfing doesn't count). You can rent one, or borrow one if you can convince a surfer to let go of his custom-made. Fortunately, any of the surf shops will rent you one for around ten dollars or so a day, a reasonable price, we think. (There will also be a deposit.) If you rent yours, be sure to ask if it's been waxed; if it hasn't, you'll be sliding all over the wave.

Second, you've got to find a break. We suggest not starting off where all the others are surfing. Get off by yourself, so that you won't be in the way of the more skilled. The break won't be as good, but then, neither are you. Right?

Item number three. To surf, you've got to learn to paddle the board.

Find your balance position. Your chest should go about at the thickest part of the surfboard. This is important, so try paddling about till you feel comfortable. Watch how the others do it, up the beach.

Now paddle out to sea.

To surf, you must realize that the wave is moving toward the beach at some speed, while the shallowing water forces it to crest. You won't be picked up by it unless you're moving in the same direction at almost the same speed (this is why paddling is so important). This is the hardest part of learning, getting your timing down, learning to watch and catch the wave at that exactly correct fraction of a second.

Once the wave has you, you'll know it. You'll be carried forward fast and effortlessly, part of the sea in motion. It's a thrill.

Finally, to get up: just stand up, just as if you were doing a push-up from the speeding board. Don't get to your knees first. Just stand up naturally. Place one or the other foot forward (most people do it left foot forward, but there's no shame in being a "goofy-foot"), about a shoulder-width apart.

If you can stand up, and ride a wave into the beach that way once, you've done pretty well for your first day; don't stay out forever and agonize with sunburn tomorrow. The rest, the turning, and the other advanced maneuvers you see the more experienced people doing, will come with practice.

When you feel more confident, when you want to try the good breaks with the others, remember your manners. Stay out of the way if someone's already on a wave. That's about the only point of etiquette that's really important. You'll find, after hanging around for a while, that most surfers are friendly, and with time you'll fit in with the others just fine.

"Awoo!"

WINDSURFING

Windsurfing, or board sailing, is almost as popular in this area as surfing...some would argue more so, and they could be right. Some days when the wind is up, the sound is so colorful with the sails of windsurfing boards it looks like a floating carnival. It's well-known that the entire Outer Banks and, some think, especially Hatteras, is the best windsurfing location on the Atlantic coast. To be even more specific, the Canadian Hole, located soundside just before you get into Buxton, is considered the best of the best spots. But there are plenty of other great places -- wherever you can get out onto the shallow, wind swept waters.

Ted James came to Hatteras in '72 from Florida to surf and fish,

"Looking for what Florida lost years ago." He runs a commercial fishing boat in the winter, and has been making his Fox boards here and in Florida since 1968. James was one of the first to put sailboards in big surf here, and he was instrumental in improving the boards and rigs to their present state of excellence. He was busy shaping a racing board in his Buxton workshop when we asked him to tell us a little about windsurfing.

"It's real simple why Hatteras is so popular for windsurfers. People have been cussin' the wind here since there was wind. But with sailboards, the more wind the better.

"The equipment you use is a board and a rig. The heart of the system is a `universal' that swivels and pivots in every direction. That allows you to position the mast, boom and sail, and determine the direction you go. Basically, to sail cross wind, the mast is up and down. To sail downwind, tip the mast forward, and that turns the front of the board downwind. Mast back, that turns the board upwind.

"Now, that sounds complicated, and that's why I recommend lessons. What we do is spend two and a half hours — the first lesson — on teaching people to sail short distances. The second lesson we practice, increasing sail area, smaller boards, switching rigs — whatever challenges the individual. We also teach self-rescue and rigging in the second lesson. Self-rescue's important in case the wind dies, or something breaks. People are recreationally proficient after two lessons.

"Now, that's not experienced surfers; that's people who walk in the door. You don't have to be athletic. Though it's easier to teach people who sail, in a way, because they know the wind. Surfing is not as big an advantage. No, you don't have to know how to swim. We put a jacket on them.

"It's not easy — you have to pay attention — but we've had people uncoordinated, overweight, and they catch on. A lot of them, it's the first athletic success they've ever had. And it means a lot to me to help them succeed. Our students range from twelve to sixty. We've taught over 1000 people in the last three years and only had one person who couldn't do it. It's neat — sometimes you get teen aged sons, and Dad outshines them. They kind of laugh a little bit then."

Ralph Buxton, owner of Kitty Hawk Sports, started teaching windsurfing in 1980 in the Nags Head area. He is well-known for his participation in and promotion of the sport. He explains that while the Canadian Hole, as the favorite spot in Hatteras is known, is certainly a great place to sail, windsurfers also enjoy the many upper Banks windsurfing areas be-cause the wind conditions are just as good and there are many other attractions available to them if the wind isn't cooperating. Kitty Hawk Sport's Windmill Point Sailing Site in Nags Head is an ideal place to learn because of the shallow and sheltered water.

The basic sailboarding season is year round. December to March is slow, though, simply because it's cold (there's plenty of wind out there, however, if you want it). James runs competitive events, the Hatteras Wave Classic in October and the Pro-Am in spring. Kitty Hawk Sports runs the Easter Dash for Cash, the August Watermelon Regatta and the Thanksgiving Classic Regatta. They're as much fun to watch as they are to participate in.

Kitty Hawk Sports gives away a 10 page windsurfing publication listing sites, weather, gear and other helpful information. Call 441-6800 to get your copy.

SURF SHOPS

There are plenty of surf shops on the Banks, scattered north and south. For a 24-Hour surf report, call 995-4646.

Windsurfing Hatteras, Avon, 995-4970
Hatteras Island Surf Shop, Waves, 987-2296
Wave Riding Vehicles, Kitty Hawk, 261-7952
Kitty Hawk Sports, Nags Head, 441-6800 and 441-2756; Avon, 995-5000; Duck, 261-8770

Secret Spot Surf Shop, Nags Head, 441-4030

Vitamin Sea Surf Shop, Kill Devil Hills, 441-7512

BW's Surf Shop, Ocracoke, 928-6141

Bert's Surf Shop, Kitty Hawk, 261-7584; Nags Head, 441-1939

Cavalier Surf Shop, Nags Head, 441-7349

Chicamacomico Watersports, Rodanthe, 987-2296

Natural Art Surf Shop, Buxton, 995-5682

New Sun Surf Shop, Nags Head, 441-3994

Resin Craft Surf Shop, Whalebone Junction, 441-6747

Rodanthe Surf Shop, Rodanthe, 987-2412

17th St. Surf Shop, Kill Devil Hills, 441-1797

Sun Bums, Outer Banks Mall, Nags Head, 441-2444

Whalebone Surf Shop, Nags Head, 441-4647 and 441-6747; Kitty Hawk, 261-8737

Fox Water Sports, Buxton, 995-4102

Ride The Wind, Ocracoke, 928-7451

OCEAN SWIMMING

If you've grown up around the sea, sailing as a kid, spending long days on surfboards, you probably know that Mother Ocean can sometimes be dangerous. It's important to know that the Outer Banks surf can, at times, be especially treacherous. We feel it is a good idea, especially if you have children, to only swim in areas that are guarded. And, if the red flags are flying, warning swimmers to stay out of the ocean, please pay attention to them.

Here are a few tips to make you better acquainted with the ocean.

RIPS

Rip currents can carry a child or a wader out into rough water in seconds. They generally move along the shore and then straight out toward sea. They often occur when there's a break in a submerged sandbar. You can see a rip; it's choppy, turbulent, often discolored water that looks deeper than the water around it. If you are caught in a rip, don't panic, and don't try to struggle straight back to shore against its force. Remember that rip currents are narrow. Very few are wider than thirty feet across. So simply swim parallel to the beach until you're out of it, or let it carry you seaward till it peters out. Then move to one side or the other of it and swim back.

UNDERTOW

When a wave comes up on the beach and breaks, the water must run back down to the sea. This is undertow. It sucks at your ankles from small waves, but in heavy surf undertow can knock you off your feet and carry you out. If you're carried out, don't resist. Let the undertow take you out till it stops. It will only be a few yards. The next wave will help push you shoreward again.

LOSING CONTROL IN WAVES

If a wave crashes down on you while you are surfing or swimming, and you find yourself being tumbled in bubbles and sand like a sheet in a washing machine, don't try to struggle to the surface against it. Curl into a ball, or just go limp and float. The wave will take you to the beach or else you can swim to the surface when it passes.

PRECAUTIONS

• Never swim alone.
• Don't go into the water without observing the surf first.

• Look for currents.
• Don't go in unless you can swim.
• Don't stay on the beach during electrical storms.
• Try to swim in guarded areas.
• Observe warning flags near public accesses. If they're red, don't go in.
• Protect yourself from the sun. Sunburns don't turn into tans. They peel off.
• Keep non-swimming children well above the marks of the highest waves.
• Don't swim near fishermen or deployed fishing lines.

Photo: Judy Wilson

The Outer Banks
Scuba Diving

*M*ost people aren't aware that scuba diving on the Outer Banks is an adventure of some importance. While the waters off the Florida Keys, Caribbean islands and south seas are full of colorful fish and vegetation, the Outer Banks has shipwrecks.

These waters are for the serious divers who are tough and willing to brave cold water and little visibility in some cases. The changeable weather off the Outer Banks is another consideration. But the shifting sands uncover new wrecks almost every year and the divers of the area are kept busy discovering them. Check local shops for the latest information on what's being picked up and where. Enjoy the opportunity to explore the sea and its sometimes ancient treasures.

We've listed a few spots you might want to dive into:

LST 471, a ship sunk in 1949. About 1/4 mile north of the Rodanthe Fishing Pier, 100 yards offshore in 15 feet of water.

Oriental (Boiler Wreck) thought to be a Federal Transport that sank in 1862. About 4 miles south of Oregon Inlet. The boiler of the ship is visible in the surf.

Marore Tanker, off Rodanthe. Approximately 22 miles SE of Oregon Inlet, 12 miles offshore. Torpedoed in February 26, 1942. 100 feet deep.

Tug, identification unknown. Kill Devil Hills. Approximately 300 yards south of Avalon Pier, 75 yards offshore, in 20 feet of water.

Metropolis Freighter, Corolla (Horsehead Wreck). Three miles south of Currituck Beach Lighthouse, 100 yards offshore in breakers. About 15 feet deep. Went down in 1878. 85 lives were lost. Was carrying 500 tons of iron rails and 200 tons of stones. Was formerly the Federal Gunboat, *Stars and Stripes*. Good off-season wreck. Accessible by 4-wheel drive only.

Triangle Wrecks. *Josephine* (lost 1915), *Kyzickes* (1927), *Carl Gerhard* (1929). Off 7-milepost at Kill Devil Hills about 100 yards out and 200 yards south of the Sea Ranch. Depth about 20 feet.

USS Huron Federal screw steamer lost off Nags Head in 1877. Now in 26 feet of water. Many artifacts.

Liberty Ship (*Zane Grey*) about one mile south of Oregon Inlet at 80 feet.

U-85 German sub sunk in 1942. Northeast of Oregon Inlet in 100 feet of water. Boat needed. (See Bodie Island Section.)

York, Benson, Buarque Freighters and tankers sunk by the U-boats during Operation Paukenschlag in 1942. They lie offshore, but within dive boat range, in from 100-120 feet of water. Good, challenging dives.

Beach Diving -- There are over 12 wrecks in shallow water between Duck and Hatteras. Great for free diving (without scuba gear) and spear fishing. Ask local divers for locations.

Sound Diving -- If you don't mind shallow, murky water, you may enjoy groping around north and west of Roanoke Island. Old Civil War forts lie submerged and local divers have found cannonballs, bottles and relics with metal detectors.

Numbers to keep handy:
Oregon Inlet USCG Station 987-2311

Ocean Rescue Squad (helicopter available) 911

Diver Alert Network (DAN) (919) 684-8111

SHOPS AND FACILITIES

NAGS HEAD PRO DIVE CENTER
Kitty Hawk Connection, MP 13-1/2
441-7594

The is the oldest dive facility on the Outer Banks offering a full line of services. Located across from Jockey's Ridge, they sell and rent equipment, airfills to 5,000 psi, and PADI instruction. The Nags Head Divers also run their 50' dive board, the *Sea Fox*, out of the Manteo Waterfront to the historic wrecks off the Outer Banks. They're open seven days a week from 10 a.m. to 5 p.m. during the season. Call Phil Nutter or Rob Dubay for information.

HATTERAS DIVERS
Hatteras Village
986-2557

Located just west of Hatteras Harbor Motel on the waterfront, this shop is owned by Donny Lang who plans charter trips to Tarpon, Abrams, Dixie Arrow, Proteus, Box-Car reefs and other popular destinations. From June to October the hours are 9 to 6 Monday-Saturday. They can arrange charters and fill your air tanks and offer rental gear. For information call or write: P.O. Box 213, Hatteras, NC 27943.

Ferry
Connections

HATTERAS INLET
(OCRACOKE) FERRY
Hatteras Village

This free state-run ferry service links Hatteras with Ocracoke Island with an enjoyable 40-minute trip. During this trip you cross the county line — so there's a point that's neither Hyde nor Dare (couldn't resist that one). The ferries accommodate cars and even large camping vehicles and are scheduled often enough during the summer so that your wait will not be long. Reservations are not required, as they are for the Cedar Island and Swan Quarter ferries from Ocracoke Village. Yes, Johnny, there are (small) bathrooms on the ferry. The summer schedule is as follows:

SUMMER SCHEDULE
APRIL 15th thru OCT. 31st

Leave HATTERAS	Leave OCRACOKE
5:00 AM	5:00 AM
6:00 AM	6:00 AM
7:00 AM	7:00 AM
7:30 AM	8:00 AM*
8:00 AM *	8:30 AM
8:30 AM	8:45 AM
Then Every 15 minutes until	
6:00 PM	6:00 PM
6:30 PM	6:30 PM*
8:00 PM	7:00 PM
10:00 PM	7:30 PM
12:00 PM	9:00 PM
11:00 PM	*Priority for commercial vehicles (permit only)

WINTER SCHEDULE NOV. 1st
thru APRIL 14th

Leave Hatteras every hour on the hour from 5:00 AM to 5 PM, and at 7:00 PM, 9:00 PM, and 11:00 PM.

Leave Ocracoke every hour on the hour from 6:00 AM to 6:00 PM; 8:00 PM and 10:00 PM

FROM OCRACOKE:
SWAN QUARTER AND CEDAR
ISLAND RESERVATIONS

To avoid possible delay in boarding the Cedar Island-Ocracoke Ferry and the Swan Quarter-Ocracoke Ferry, reservations are recommended. These may be made in person at the departure terminal or by telephone. For departures from Ocracoke, call (919) 928-3841; for departures from Cedar Island, call (919)225-3551; and for reservations for departures from Swan Quarter, call (919) 926-1111. (Office hours 6 a.m. to 6 p.m., later in summer.)

Reservations may be made up to 30 days in advance of departure date and are not transferable. These reservations must be claimed at least 30 minutes prior to departure time. The name of the driver and the vehicle license number are required when making reservations.

GROSS LOAD LIMITS

All Crossings:
Any axle -- 13,000 lbs.
Two axles (single vehicle) -- 24,000 lbs.
Three or more axles -- 36,000 lbs. (single or combination vehicle)

More information may be obtained from Director, Ferry Division, Morehead City, NC 28557, or by calling (919) 726-6446 or 726-6413.

OCRACOKE-SWAN QUARTER TOLL FERRY

Crossing Time Approx.
2 1/2 hrs.
Capacity Approx. 30 Cars
YEAR ROUND

Leave Ocracoke	Leave Swan Quarter
6:30 AM	9:30 AM
12:30 PM	4:00 PM

FARES AND RATES APPLICABLE (ONE WAY) Same as Cedar Island — Ocracoke Ferry Rates.

CEDAR ISLAND — OCRACOKE TOLL FERRY

Crossing Time Approx.
2 1/2 hrs.
Capacity Approx. 30 Cars

SUMMER SCHEDULE

April 15 thru Oct 31

Leave Cedar Island	Leave Ocracoke
7:00 AM	7:00 AM
8:15 AM	9:30 AM
9:30 AM	10:45 AM
12:00 Noon	12:00 Noon
1:15 PM	3:00 PM
3:00 PM	4:15 PM
6:00 PM	6:00 PM
8:30 PM	8:30 PM

WINTER SCHEDULE

Nov. 1 thru April 14

7:00 AM	10:00 AM
1:00 PM	4:00 PM

FARES AND RATES APPLICABLE (ONE WAY)

A. Pedestrian -- $1.00

B. Bicycle and Rider -- $2.00

C. Single vehicle or combination 20' or less in length and motorcycles (minimum fare for licensed vehicle) -- $10.00

D. Vehicles or combinations from 20' to 40' in length -- $20.00

E. All vehicles or combinations 40' to 55' in length having a maximum width of 8 feet and height of 13'6" -- $30.00

Outer Banks
Medical Care

*S*ince there is no hospital on the Outer Banks, a growing number of emergency care centers have been developed. Along with these centers is the establishment of community health care clinics which have increased their staffs and medical laboratory technicians. The facilities are supported by ambulance and helicopter evacuation to the nearest hospitals in the event such transportation is necessary.

> Emergency service in Dare and Currituck counties: 911
> Ocean-rescue: 911
> Northern and southern regions of the Outer Banks fire and rescue service: 911
> Outer Banks areas Coast Guard (emergency only): 995-6410
> Ocracoke Island Coast Guard: 928-3711

Medical Centers and Clinics

REGIONAL MEDICAL CENTER
Route 158 Bypass, MP 1-1/2
Kitty Hawk   261-9000
This much-needed Outer Banks medical facility opened a year ago. With 35-40 physicians working on rotation it continues to increase the number of medical services available to residents and visitors.

A state-of-the-art facility, family medicine and urgent or emergency care is accommodated with efficiency. Approximately 30 medical specialties and the Roche Biomedical laboratory, where blood tests are handled quickly for complete diagnosis, are located here. There is a radiology and imaging laboratory. In March of 1992 a surgery and procedures center opened to offer a option for outpatient surgical needs.

The communities of the Outer Banks rely on this medical center for convenient and competent health care whether it is routine or specialized. The separate units are thoughtfully arranged in order to provide quick access to the appropriate diagnostic and health care center.

In addition there is an educational and preventive medicine facility, a cardiac rehab center and neurological diagnostic service. Psychological counseling services and an audiologist are available. This important part of the facility is to support the growing need for personal knowledge about healthier lives. If a particular program is not in session, defining an interest and need will bring it closer to reality. Whether it is nutritional counseling, CPR training, smoking cessation, LaMaze classes or fitness management, it's all part of the Regional Medical Center's commitment to the community. Normal hours are from 9:00 a.m. till 9:00 p.m daily. During the summer season, extended hours will be from 8:00 a.m. till 10:30 p.m.

NORTH BEACH MEDICAL CENTER
Juniper Trail
Southern Shores   261-4187

With the opening of the new Regional Medical Center in Kitty Hawk, this facility is primarily a support facility for services prescribed by physicians at the Regional Center.

BEACH MEDICAL CENTER
Route 158, Bypass, MP 10-1/2
Nags Head   441-2174

Open weekdays for medical appointments, this clinic provides general medical care. Walk-in services are available as well.

Hours are from 9 to 5 Monday through Friday.

VIRGINIA DARE WOMEN'S CENTER
Route 158, Bypass, MP 10-1/2
Beach Medical Center
Nags Head   441-2144

Appointments are available for women-centered medical care. Patty Johnson is a certified nurse-midwife and family nurse practitioner. Maternity care, baby care and pap smears are offered along with generalized care. Hours are M,T,TH,FR from 9 a.m. to 1 p.m. and 2 to 5 p.m.

OUTER BANKS MEDICAL AND EMERGENCY CARE CENTER
West of Route 158 Bypass,
MP 10-1/2
W. Barnes Street
Nags Head   441-7111

This is the only 24-hour medical facility on the beach. Walk-ins are welcome and there is an x-ray laboratory on the premises.

MACDOWELL FAMILY HEALTH CENTER
Hwy 64, Main Road
Manteo   473-2500

Dr. Brian MacDowell provides complete family medical care at this office. X-ray is available, as well as psychological counseling services provided by Debra MacDowell, MA, NCC. Call for appointments. Hours are 8:30 to 5:00 Monday, Tuesday, Wednesday and Friday.

DARE MEDICAL ASSOCIATES
Hwy. 64, Main Road
Manteo   473-3478

Dr. Walter Holton provides family service and acute care from this office. Hours are 8 a.m. to 5 p.m. Monday through Friday.

HATTERAS ISLAND
MEDICAL CENTER
Hwy. 12

Buxton   **986-2756**

Dr. Seaborn Blair, III and Katie Williams, FNP have recently combined their knowledge and skills to form a solid medical care and services center on the lower end of Hatteras Island. They maintain 24-hour emergency call coverage and have office hours on weekdays from 8:30 a.m. to 5:00 p.m. except Wednesday and Saturday. Wednesday hours are from 9 to 5 and Saturday hours, 9 to 1.

BUXTON MEDICAL CENTER
Hwy. 12

Buxton   **995-4455**

Dr. J. Whit Dunkle and Katie Williams, FNP offer comprehensive family medical care and operate a 24-hour emergency on-call service. Their hours are M,W,F 1:30 p.m. to 5:30 p.m and Tuesday 8:30 a.m. until 12 noon.

OCRACOKE HEALTH CENTER
Past the firehouse
928-1511

General medical care is offered in this small island clinic. Hours are limited and, if necessary, call the res-

cue squad, 928-4831.

DENTISTS

Though not a complete list of the dentists located on the Outer Banks, the following have indicated they're available for emergency care.

BUDDE & BUEKER, DDS
Route 158, Bypass, MP 5-1/2
Executive Center
Kill Devil Hills   441-5811

FRANK AUSBAND, DDS
Route 158, Bypass, MP 11
Nags Head   441-0437

JEFFREY JACOBSON, DDS
Route 158, Bypass, MP 5-1/2
Executive Center
Kill Devil Hills   441-8882

MICHAEL MORGAN, DDS
Juniper Trail
Southern Shores   261-2358

Chiropractic Care

NORTH BEACH CHIROPRACTIC
The Marketplace
Southern Shores   261-5424

Jan C. VanBeelen, DC offers a full range of chiropractic services and nutrition management.

DARE CHIROPRACTIC
Route 158 Bypass, MP 5

Kitty Hawk   261-8885

Burt Rubin, DC, Allan S. Kroland, DC and B.L. Ackley, DC have the largest full-service chiropractic clinic on the beach. Nutritional counseling and stress management support is available. They have a new location in Kitty Hawk. Holly King, CMT is available for massage. Call for an appointment.

OUTER BANKS CHIROPRACTIC CLINIC
Route 158, Bypass, MP 10
Nags Head   441-1585

Craig Gibson, DC has office hours by appointment.

OTHER SERVICES

Dare Vision Center is located on the beach on the Bypass at MP 9, Kill Devil Hills, 441-4872 and in Manteo on Hwy 64 near McDonalds, 473-2155.

Outer Banks Hotline, 473-3366, north of Oregon Inlet or 995-4555 south of the inlet, is a 24-hour crisis counseling service that also provides shelter to victims of abuse.

Atlantic Counseling Services, 441-1372, Route 158, Bypass in Nags Head is run by Robin Craven, MA, certified professional counselor. He offers individual and family counseling as well as psychotherapy. Call for appointment.

Alcoholics Anonymous: Hatteras, 995-4240 or 995-4283; Northern beaches, 261-1681, 441-6020 and 473-5389.

Photo: Phillip Ruckle

Jogging through Nags Head Woods Ecological Preserve.

Service and Information
Directory

COAST GUARD

Buxton Village	995-5881
Hatteras Island	987-2311
Hatteras Village	986-2175
N. of Oregon Inlet	987-2311
Ocracoke	928-3711 or 995-6452*

*Call goes through Hatteras and is more
reliable according to Coast Guard.

COUNTY SHERIFF

Hatteras Island (Dare County)	986-2144
N. of Oregon Inlet	
(Dare County)	473-3481
Northern Outer Banks (Currituck County)	
232-2216	
Ocracoke Island (Hyde County) 928-3701	

FIRE DEPARTMENT -
For emergencies call 911

Avon Village	995-5021
Buxton Village	986-2500
Corolla	232-2424
Duck	261-3929
Hatteras Village	986-2500
Kill Devil Hills	441-2531
Kitty Hawk	261-3552
Manteo	473-2133
Nags Head	441-5508
Ocracoke	928-4831
Salvo Village	987-2411

Most homes and cottages are
provided with a fire extinguisher. If
you need service, your rental property
manager will take care of this. However, if you own a home, or for any
reason need service, call Fire Defense
Center, 261-1314 or 491-2478. They
will pick up and deliver for refills and
new products.

POLICE DEPARTMENT

(If no listing for a particular
community, call the Sheriff's Department.)

Hatteras Village	986-2144
Kill Devil Hills	441-7491
Kitty Hawk	261-3895
Manteo	473-3481
Nags Head	441-6386
Southern Shores	261-3331

NATIONAL PARK SERVICE
OFFICES

North of Oregon Inlet	473-2111
or 441-6644	
South of Oregon Inlet	995-4474
Ocracoke Island	928-4531

CRISIS HOTLINE

Outer Banks Hotline (confiden-
tial counseling and information for

any crisis, and shelter for battered women and their children).

| North of Oregon Inlet | 473-3366 |
| South of Oregon Inlet | 995-4555 |

VETERINARIANS

Kitty Hawk, Nags Head, Manteo and Hatteras Island all have established veterinary clinics. Check the Yellow Pages under Veterinarians for a complete listing.

Dare County Animal Shelter   473-2143

KENNELS
Water Oak Kennel
Buxton Village   995-5663

Animal Hospital of Nags Head
441-8611

Salty Dog Grooming & Boarding
Colington   441-6501 (cats, too!)

North River Kennel
Powells Point   491-2284

AUTOMOTIVE SERVICES

The Outer Banks's automotive services and parts stores have improved through the years. It's a good idea to get your automobile serviced before vacation time rolls around. However, if you are here and need service, here's a handy listing of some businesses we've had good experiences with.

R.D. Sawyer Ford,
Manteo   473-2141

Coastal (formerly in Manteo)
Chevrolet/Buick
Kitty Hawk   261-5900

Outer Banks Chrysler/Plymouth/
Dodge/Jeep
KDH   441-1146

Other recommended auto services and towing:

Kitty Hawk Exxon
Kitty Hawk   261-2720

Johnny's Towing Service (AAA)
KDH   441-7473 or 441-7283

Bayside Towing
Kill Devil Hills   441-2985

Kill Devil Hills Amoco Auto Repair
Kill Devil Hills   441-7283

Berry Automotive
Manteo   473-6111

Autotech
Nags Head   441-5293

Jackson Auto
Manteo   473-5990

Manteo Wrecker Service (AAA)
Manteo   473-5654

Farrow Brothers Automotive

Avon   995-5944

Ballance Gulf & Oil

Hatteras Village   986-2424

CAR RENTALS

Car rentals are available at the Dare County Airport in Manteo and at a few other places on the Outer Banks.

National Car Rental

(Kill Devil Hills Amoco)   441-5488

B & R Rent-A-Car

(Dare County Airport   473-2600

R.D. Sawyer Ford

Manteo   473-2141

Outer Banks Chrysler/Plymouth
441-1146

CHILD CARE

Better Beginnings

Kitty Hawk   261-2833

This owner-operated, year round service provides day care for families on the Outer Banks. They take children 6-weeks to 12 years old, provide lunch and two snacks daily and are state licensed.

Sun•sational Sitters
441-TOTS

This service sends mature, trained sitters directly to your hotel, motel or cottage, allowing you some free time while on vacation. Sitters are bonded and insured, trained in CPR and first-aid and have passed extensive reference, background and police checks. Service is available 24-hours a day, seven days a week. Early reservations are recommended.

AuPairCare
1-800-288-7786

AuPairCare provides live-in European au pairs on yearly cultural visas, providing affordable, long term, live-in child care. Host families choose from well-qualified, English-speaking applicants between the ages of 18-25. Unlike employees, au pairs function much like family members, sharing meals and social occasions. Local community counselors are close at hand to provide guidance and support. This is a great way to share the world with your children.

FISHING REPORT

WOBR Radio	473-3373
Red Drum Tackle Shop, Hatteras	995-5414
Oregon Inlet Fishing Center (for their boats)	441-6301
Kitty Hawk Fishing Pier	261-2772
Nags Head Fishing Pier	441-5141
Hatteras Island Fishing Pier (Rodanthe)	987-2323
Frisco Pier	986-2533
O'Neals' Dockside, Ocracoke	928-1111

LIQUOR LAWS & ABC STORES

Most restaurants in Duck, Kitty Hawk, Kill Devil Hills and Nags Head

Sharing cultures, enriching lives.

Affordable live-in child care with a special European flair.

AuPairCare

800 - 288 - 7786

serve mixed drinks. Areas where you are allowed to "brown-bag" your own liquor are found in Corolla, Manteo, Wanchese and the beaches south of Oregon Inlet.

Some restaurants serve only beer and wine which can be purchased at most convenience stores and grocery stores. Liquor by the bottle is available only in ABC stores, as follows:

Kitty Hawk, MP 1,	
Route 158 Bypass	261-2477
Duck Village,	
Wee Winks Square	261-6981
Nags Head,	
MP 10, Route 158 Bypass	441-5121
Manteo, Route 64	473-3557
Buxton, NC 12,	
Osprey Shopping Center	995-5532
Ocracoke Island,	
next to Variety Store	928-3281

ABC Store hours are generally 10:00 a.m. till 9:00 p.m. Monday through Saturday. No personal checks or credit cards are accepted. Maximum purchase is one gallon and legal age for admittance to a store is 21 years.

LIBRARIES

The main Dare County Library, 473-2372, is located in Manteo on Hwy.64/264 across from the Manteo Elementary School. Bookmobile service is provided through the county. Call for schedule.

The Kill Devil Hills branch, 441-4331, is located off Bypass 158

between the Baum center and the water treatment center near Colington Road.

The Hatteras branch of the Dare County Library, 986-2385, is located in the county recreation building across from Burrus' Red & White store.

The Ocracoke Library is located behind the Fire hall. The hours are posted on the door.

MEDIA INFORMATION
Newspapers

The Outer Banks has a local paper, *The Coastland Times*, which is published on Sundays, Tuesdays and Thursdays. The offices are located in Manteo (473-2105) and in Kill Devil Hills (441-2223).

The *Daily Advance* is a newspaper published in Elizabeth City and can be obtained at some newsstands on the beach.

Stores throughout the Outer Banks carry a wide range of papers during the week and on Sunday.

The *Carolina Coast*, part of the *Virginian Pilot*, is produced weekly and is available throughout the Outer Banks.

Look for your copy of The *Washington Post*, The *New York Times*, The *Wall Street Journal*, The *Virginian Pilot-Ledger Star*, *Richmond Times Herald*, The *Raleigh News & Observer* and others -- costs are a bit inflated for some papers due to the distribution to this remote area.

A favorite local newspaper with strong appeal is the *North Beach Sun*.

The friendly folks at Gulfstream Publishing have created a popular tabloid, filled with personal and local news on the northern Outer Banks. It is published four times a year and distributed to convenience stores, real estate offices and other businesses along the beach from Kitty Hawk to Corolla.

Television

Outer Banks Cablevision supplies cable connection service for the Outer Banks. Most motels, hotels and cottages have cable connections. Some add other special features such as HBO or the Disney Channel.

When visiting the Outer Banks, Channel 12 features Outer Banks Panorama, an informative program of communities, shopping, restaurants and attractions of the Banks. There is other local programming in between the four or five information segments. Channel 19 provides a continuous preview of all programming carried on channels 2 (PBS) through 43. Most newspaper also carry a listing, however the Channel 19 listings are most convenient.

Radio

The Banks' first native radio station was WOBR, Wanchese, FM 95 stereo, and is still owned by the same person who began it. The station plays Adult contemporary and has a great Sunday morning jazz show from 10 to noon. They stay in tune with what a majority of Outer Bankers want to hear.

WOBR now leases their AM (1530) station to the Outer Banks Wor-

ship Center for Christian programming.

WRSF 106 (FM 105.7 to be exact) is the former WWOK out of Columbia. One of America's most powerful stations, Surf 106 plays popular music. Hunt Thomas' "Hot 9 at 9" evening show is particularly popular with the local teens.

WVOD FM 99.3, "The Voices of Dare," Manteo, is a locally-owned station that began broadcasting in the spring of '86. They offer a lot of different sounds and a varied format centering around adult contemporary. If you're here on Sunday, they have some great programming, starting with Sunday Classics, playing classical music, then, in the evening, Fritz on Jazz. This station is also very community- minded, offering air space and the support of their personnel to local groups with worthy causes

WNHW FM 92, "Carolina 92" is the Outer Banks' newest radio station. They play country music in all aspects, including modern, pop, traditional, folk and rockabilly. Carolina 92 also airs music features like a weekly countdown on Sunday afternoons. They also feature CNN news and sports, local news and weather, and fishing and beach reports.

POSTAL SERVICE
& PACKAGE SHIPMENT

Post Offices:

Corolla -	
Next to Winks Store	453-2552
Kitty Hawk -	
MP 4, Route 158 Bypass	261-2211

Kill Devil Hills -

MP 8, Route 158 Bypass	441-5666
Nags Head -	
MP 13, Route 158 Bypass	441-7387
Manteo -	
Downtown across	
from Tranquil House	473-2534
Wanchese - Route 345	473-3551
Rodanthe -	
NC 12, south of Joe Bob's	987-2273
Avon - NC 12, near	
Avon Shopping Center	995-5991
Buxton - NC 12	
past Buxton Books	995-5755
Hatteras -	
NC 12 , 1 mile before ferry	986-2318
Ocracoke -	
NC 12 in the village	928-4771

Hours vary at these island post offices, so if you have a particular need, call first.

Outer Banks Transit, 441-7090, Route 158, MP 9 in Kill Devil Hills, is centrally-located on the Banks and serves as a UPS and Postal Service pick-up point. They sell packaging materials and will lend a friendly hand to accommodate your needs. Package delivery service to the Norfolk area, Xerox copies, FAX service and money orders are available here.

UPS has a service center on Roanoke Island. They accept packages for shipment weekdays from 3:30 p.m. to 5:45 p.m. There are some size limitations. They offer overnight shipment to many locations in the US. For information, call 1-800-662-7506.

Federal Express has several drop box locations all around the Outer Banks. Large self-service drop boxes are located near Surfside Books at the Seagate North Shopping Center in Kill Devil Hills as well as in Manteo at Chesley Mall and in front of Manteo Booksellers. Call 1-800-238-5355 for information or door pick-up in most areas. (If you're in a rental cottage, make sure you know the house number and street, in order to give exact directions. The villages of the Outer Banks are fairly well-known for their lack of specific street numbers and names!)

RENTAL SERVICES

In the section on Outer Banks Rentals, we've listed a number of equipment rental places to assist you in having everything you need for a pleasant stay at the beach. But, since we know this to be a very valuable service for vacationers, here they are again.

Lifesaver Rent-Alls, open all year in Kill Devil Hills, MP 9 Beach Road. 441-6048. Open in season in Kitty Hawk, MP 1 across from Southern Shores Marketplace, 261-1344. They have a tremendous inventory of things like baby cribs, mattresses, jogging strollers, beach umbrellas, surf boards, fishing rods and tackle, volleyball set and VCRs.

Ocean Atlantic Rentals is spread out all over the Outer Banks with five locations. Corolla Light Shops, 453-2440; Duck, 261-4346;

Kill Devil Hills/Nags Head, 441-7823; Waves, 987-2492; Avon, 995-5868. Call 1-800-635-9559 to reserve from their huge inventory of everything from cottage items to things for the beach.

Metro Rentals, located in Kill Devil Hills just west of the Bypass on Colington Road. 480-3535. They carry everything for the beach, cottage items and can handle banquets or party needs, including tables, chairs, table cloths, glassware, punch bowls and more.

Beach Outfitters, a division of Ocracoke Realty, 928-1711 or 1-800-242-5394, can take care of your needs on the island -- for the cottage or the beach.

SELF-SERVICE LAUNDERETTES

Superette Launderette, Route 158, Bypass, MP 6, Kill Devil Hills

Wash 'N Dry, Meadowlark St., near KDH Post Office, MP 8-1/2

P & G Wash & Dry, Outer Banks Mall, Nags Head, MP 15

Speed Wash, Route 158 Bypass, MP 16-1/2, Nags Head

Mr. Clean Laundromat, Chesley Mall, Manteo

The Wash Basket, off NC 12, Buxton

Frisco Launderette, Route 12, across from Scotch Bonnet, Frisco.

There are no self-service laundry centers in Hatteras Village or on Ocracoke Island.

RECYCLING AT THE BEACH

Dare County has a dedicated population when it comes to recycling. The recycling centers on the Outer Banks are conveniently located in each town. A well-organized group of volunteers stands by to receive your recyclables. The schedules vary from town to village.

Give recycling your attention while you're at the beach. Basically, the items accepted are all kinds of paper, corrugated cardboard, aluminum cans (beverage cans only, flattened to save space), steel cans, glass -- green, brown and clear jars and bottles with lids removed, milk and water jugs with lids removed, plastic bottles and jars with marking on the bottoms with a 1 or 2 in the recycle-logo. Be as organized as possible and have newspapers flat in brown bags or tied. Here's a list of recycling centers:

Locations of Recycling Centers:

Corolla-Whalehead Centers on Currituck County northern Outer Banks are being selected at press time. Rental companies will have current information in all their cottages.

Duck - Duck Fire Station, Friday only from 10:00 a.m. till noon.

Southern Shores - Behind the Fire Station on Dogwood Trail across from Kitty Hawk Elementary School. Tuesday and Saturday from 9:00 a.m. till noon.

Kitty Hawk - Please use Dare County drop-off site in Kill Devil Hills.

Kill Devil Hills, 441-2531, Ext. 249 - Dare County Public Works Complex off Colington Road, behind the Wright Memorial grounds. Monday,

Wednesday, Friday and Saturday 10:00 a.m. till 2:00 p.m.

Nags Head, 441-1122 - Public Works building behind the Food Lion at MP 10. Monday, 7:00 a.m. till 3:30 p.m. and at the Town Hall on Saturday, 9:00 a.m. till noon. Also at each of two public bathhouses, there are large containers divided into sections for cans, plastic and three colors of glass. These are convenient to help keep the beaches clean and free of litter. Please take a few extra minutes to help out.

Manteo, 473-2133 - Behind the Duke of Dare Motel on Fernando Street. Tuesday and Saturday, 8:00 a.m. till noon.

Hatteras Island, 473-1101, Ext. 311 - Behind Centura Bank, Buxton. Tuesday and Thursday, 11:30 a.m. till 3:30 p.m.

Dare County-Manteo, 473-1101, Ext. 311 - The Manteo Transfer Station, Bowsertown Road: Monday - Friday, 1:00 p.m till 4:00 p.m. and Saturday 9:00 a.m. till 11:30 a.m.

Some centers have telephone numbers. Please call as designated to determine any changes in their hours of operation.

STORM AND HURRICANE PROCEDURES

June through November is hurricane season in the Outer Banks. All of the southeastern U.S. is prone to hurricanes but the Banks, due to their low elevation, frontage on the ocean and lack of shelter, are particularly vulnerable. A hurricane strikes the Banks about every nine years; a major one every 42 years; a tropical cyclone about every five years. The Dare County Civil Preparedness Agency promulgates the following Hurricane Safety Rules:

1. Enter each hurricane season prepared. Every June through November, recheck your supply of boards, tools, batteries, nonperishable foods and the other equipment you will need when a hurricane strikes your area.

2. When you hear the first tropical cyclone advisory, listen for future messages; this will prepare you for a hurricane emergency well in advance of the issuance of watches and warnings.

3. When your area is covered by a hurricane watch, continue normal activities, but stay tuned to the local stations (see Media in this Service Directory), or the National Weather Service Station at Buxton for advisories. Remember, a hurricane watch means possible danger within 24 hours; if the danger materializes, a hurricane warning will be issued. Meanwhile, keep alert. Ignore rumors.

4. When your area receives a hurricane warning:

Plan your time before the storm arrives and avoid the last-minute hurry which might leave you marooned, or unprepared.

Keep calm until the emergency has ended.

Leave low lying areas that may be swept by high tides or storm waves.

Photo: Phillip Ruckle

Leave mobile homes for more substantial shelter. They are particularly vulnerable to overturning during strong winds. Damage can be minimized by securing mobile homes with heavy cables anchored in concrete footings. Moor your boat securely before the storm arrives, or evacuate it to a designated safe area. When your boat is moored, leave it, and don't return once the wind and waves are up.

Board up windows or protect them with storm shutters or tape. Danger to small windows is mainly from wind-driven debris. Larger windows may be broken by wind pressure.

Secure outdoor objects that might be blown away or uprooted. Garbage cans, garden tools, toys, signs, porch furniture and a number of other harmless items become missiles of destruction in hurricane winds. Anchor them or store them inside before the storm strikes.

Store drinking water in clean bathtubs, jugs, bottles and cooking utensils; your water supply may be contaminated by flooding or damaged by hurricane floods.

Check your battery-powered equipment. Your radio may be your only link with the world outside the hurricane, and emergency cooking facilities, lights and flashlights will be essential if utilities are interrupted.

Keep your car fueled. Service stations may be inoperable for several days after the storm strikes, due to flooding or interrupted electrical power.

Remain indoors during the hurricane. Travel is extremely dangerous when winds and tides are whipping through your area.

Monitor the storm's position through National Weather Service advisories.

5. When the hurricane has passed:

Seek necessary medical care at the nearest Red Cross disaster station or health center.

Stay out of disaster areas. Unless you are qualified to help, your presence might hamper first-aid and rescue work.

Do not travel until advised by the proper authorities.

If you must drive, do so carefully along debris-filled streets and highways. Roads may be undermined and may collapse under the weight of a car. Slides along cuts are also a hazard.

Avoid loose or dangling wires, and report them immediately to your power company or the nearest law enforcement officer.

Report broken sewer or water mains to the water department.

Prevent fires. Lowered water pressure may make fire-fighting difficult.

Check refrigerated food for spoilage if power has been off during the storm.

Remember that hurricanes moving inland can cause severe flooding. Stay away from river banks and streams.

Tornadoes spawned by hurricanes are among the storm's worst killers. When a hurricane approaches, listen for tornado watches and warnings. A tornado watch means tornadoes are expected to develop. A tornado warning means a tornado has actually been sighted. When your area receives a tornado warning, seek inside shelter immediately, preferably below ground level. If a tornado catches you outside, move away from its path at a right angle. If there is no time to escape, lie flat in the nearest depression, such as a ditch or ravine.

During the summer season visitors may be notified of hurricane watches or hurricane warnings. The hurricane watch means that a hurricane could threaten the area within 24 hours. Evacuation is not necessary at that point, but you should be alert and check on the storm's progress from time to time via radio. If a hurricane warning is promulgated, visitors should leave the Banks and head inland using Rt. 64/264 or U.S. 158, following the recently installed "Hurricane Evacuation Route" signs, which are green and white, as well as heeding the instructions of local authorities.

SURF REPORT

Provided by Wave Riding Vehicles for surfers, 261-3332.

Beach Service, through Nags Head Volunteer Fire Dept., 441-5853.

In the Hatteras area, 995-4646.

TOURS, LIMOS AND TAXI SERVICE

Kitty Hawk Aero Tours, 441-4460, offers light-plane tours over the Outer Banks. This is a good way to become familiar with the geography of these barrier islands. They fly several times a day depending on weather and demand.

Wright Brothers Air Tours, 441-6235, offers flights leaving the airstrip adjacent to the Wright Brothers Memorial. Flights are several times a day, depending on weather conditions and demand, over the ocean and islands.

Burrus Flying Service, 986-2679, takes off from Billy Mitchell Airfield in Frisco, for tours over the lower Hatteras Island, Pamlico Sound and Portsmouth Island.

Pamlico Air Service, 928-1661, take off from Ocracoke for a sight-seeing tour or service to Norfolk. Rates vary.

Historically Speaking offers small group or individual tours in a comfortable van, complete with historical commentary on Roanoke Island and the Outer Banks. Call for your personalized tour reservation, 473-5783.

Island Limo offers shuttle service between Norfolk International Airport and the Outer Banks, Memorial Day through Labor Day, along with morning, evening and weekend shuttle service. They also have a stretch limo for nights-out around the beach. Regular taxi service and 4-wheel drive off-road excursions, to Hatteras, Oregon Inlet or Carova Beach are also offered. Call 441-LIMO (5466) or (800)828-LIMO.

Outer Banks Limousine Service offers 24-hour taxi and limousine service on the Outer Banks and to and from Norfolk International Airport by appointment. Deliveries are also accommodated. Call 261-3133.

Outer Banks Transit provides scheduled trips to Norfolk International Airport and other Norfolk destinations. Package delivery and pick-up are also accommodated. Call for a schedule at 441-7090.

Beach Cab is based at Kill Devil Hills Amoco, MP 6 and offers point to point service, on call. Call 441-2500.

TICKS, CHIGGERS AND OTHER PESTS

Whenever you're in the woods or scrub anywhere on the Outer Banks in warm weather, it's possible to pick up ticks. Ticks are small, hard-shelled black or brown insects endemic to the South. Check yourself all over carefully within 3-4 hours after the walk. The ticks bury their heads beneath the skin and gorge themselves on your blood. They head instinctively for hairy, warm areas.

The Outer Banks Medical Center advises their removal with tweezers, using slow, steady traction to make them release. Or, put a little alcohol on them: that often makes them back out on their own. There are other folk remedies you hear, too. If the head breaks off and is left in the skin, just leave it. It's not alive and the area will gradually heal.

If within 2-14 days after a tick bites you have headaches, flu symptoms and a rash, see a doctor. Some ticks carry Rocky Mountain Spotted Fever. It's treated with antibiotics. A recently identified scourge carried by ticks is Lyme Disease.

Chiggers are tiny reddish insects that live in dirt or fallen pine needles, as on a trail. To avoid them, spray your socks, shoes and pants with a chigger-specific repellant before your walk. Don't sit down. Chiggers, once on you, will migrate to where your clothes are tight and start biting. Locals use clear fingernail polish over the bites. Calamine or Benadryl lotions work for the itching (don't scratch!)

Watch out for poison ivy and poison oak in the Banks woods, as well. For any severe or extensive tick, chigger or poisonous plant symptoms, see a doctor.

WEATHER REPORT

Call 473-5665 (a local call) to hear a recording of the latest weather report, provided by WOBR-FM, 95.3.

WESTERN UNION

You can send cables or telegrams or get information by calling their toll-free number: 800-325-6000. There are three Outer Banks locations where you can pick up or send messages and money: Outer Banks Transit, Rt. 158 Bypass, MP 9, Kill Devil Hills, 441-7090

Island Pharmacy, Highway 64, Manteo, 473-5801

Outer Banks
Places of Worship

*I*t used to be that we could report on all the churches the Banks had to offer. But, as with so many other aspects of life here, the number of worship centers has grown to such a degree that listing them all is impractical. So, we're compromising and giving you information on some of the churches in all the denominations represented here. We'd suggest you pick up a copy of the Sunday edition of the *Coastland Times* where you'll find a comprehensive list of all services available.

ASSEMBLY OF GOD

Worship Center Ark, Rt. 158 Bypass MP 11-1/2, 441-5182
Manteo Assembly of God, 473-3767
Wanchese Assembly of God, 473-5646
Avon Assembly of God, 995-5111

BAPTIST

First Baptist Church, Rt. 158 Bypass MP 4-1/2, Kitty Hawk, 261- 3516
Seashore Baptist, Beach Road MP 15-1/2 (meets at Surfside Motel) 441-2001
Manteo Baptist Church, 473-2840
Cape Hatteras Baptist, Buxton, 995-5159

CATHOLIC

Holy Redeemer, Kill Devil Hills MP 7, 441-7220
Holy Trinity, Whalebone Junction, Nags Head, 441-7650
Our Lady by the Sea, Buxton, 441-7220

CHURCH OF CHRIST

Roanoke Acres, Manteo, 473-5584

EPISCOPAL

St. Andrews by the Sea, Beach Road MP 13, Nags Head, 441-5382

FULL GOSPEL

Liberty Christian Fellowship, Colington, 441-6592
Rock Church, Rt. 158 Bypass MP 4, Kitty Hawk, 261-3500

LUTHERAN

Grace Lutheran, Rt. 158 Bypass MP 13, 441-1530

METHODIST

Duck United Methodist, Duck, 261-3813
Colington United Methodist, Colington, 261-3813
Kitty Hawk United Methodist, 803

Kitty Hawk Village Rd., Kitty Hawk, 261-2062

Bethany United Methodist, Wanchese, 473-5254

Mt. Olivet United Methodist, Manteo, 473- 2089

Buxton United Methodist, Buxton, 995-4306

PRESBYTERIAN

Outer Banks Presbyterian Church, Rt. 158 Bypass MP 8-1/2, Kill Devil Hills, 441-5897

Roanoke Island Presbyterian Fellowship, Hwy. 64, Manteo, 473-6356

UNITARIAN

Unitarian Universalist Congregation of the Outer Banks, located at the intersection of W. Kitty Hawk and Herbert Perry roads, 1/2 mile from intersection of Bypass and Kitty Hawk Rd. Services held 1st and 3rd Sundays at 11 a.m., 261-2801

Fourth of July pyrotechnics on the Manteo waterfront.

Outer Banks
Annual Events

Early January - Old Christmas celebration at Rodanthe. Dancing, oyster roast, appearance of Old Buck the Christmas bull.

February - Frank Stick Memorial Art Show at Glenn Eure's Ghost Fleet Gallery in Nags Head, 441-6584, and Dare County Arts Council Writers' Group Original Readings at Ghost Fleet Gallery, call 473-1699. (February is dedicated to the visual, literary and performing arts in Dare County. Several activities occur throughout the month.)

Easter Weekend - Easter Windsurfing Regatta at Windmill Point in Nags Head, 441-6800.

April - SpringFest, with German oompah band and folk dancers at the Weeping Radish in Manteo, 473-1157.

Blues Festival in Rodanthe. Fishing contest, festivals, crafts and children's activities, 987-2201.

Late April - Wilbur Wright Fly-In, Wright Brothers Memorial, Kill Devil Hills and Dare County Airport,

Manteo, 473-2600.

Early May - Ocracoke Surf Fishing Invitational Tournament, Ocracoke Harbor Days. Festivals and fun, 928-6711.

Hang Gliding Spectacular, Jockey's Ridge in Nags Head, 441-4124.

Duck Village Fair, held Saturday before Mothers' Day. Treasure hunt, food, games, arts and crafts and live music, 261-3901.

British Cemetery Ceremony in Ocracoke, 928-6711.

Mid-May - Nags Head Woods 5K Run, 441-2525.

Memorial Day Weekend - Arts & Crafts Fair at Ramada Inn, 441-2151.

June - Dare Days Street Festival in Manteo, first Saturday in month, 473-1101.

Rogallo Kite Festival, Jockey's Ridge, 441-4124.

Pirate's Cove Inshore-Offshore Shootout, register June 12, fish June 13, 473-3906.

Mid-June - The Lost Colony Outdoor Drama. Roanoke Island, 473-3414 or 1-800-488-5012.

Living history aboard the *Elizabeth II*, downtown Manteo, 473-1144.

Hatteras Marlin Fishing Tournament, Box 155, Hatteras, NC 27943.

Annual Outer Banks Celebrity Offshore Fishing and Golf Tournament, Pirate's Cove, June 16-18, 473-3906.

Summer Art Celebration '92, Ramada Inn, 261-4964.

Late June - Boogie Board Contest, Bonnet Street Beach, Nags Head, 441-6800.

Third Annual Nags Head Invitational Volleyball Tournament, Village Beach Club, June 20-21. Rain date June 27, 28. Contact Tom Hall, 480-2222.

Annual Seafood Festival in Wanchese, Blessing of the Fleet, 473-5501.

Annual Blue Water Open Billfish Tournament, Hatteras, 986-2166.

Wil-Bear's Festival of Fun, Kitty Hawk Connection, Nags Head, 441-4124.

Tuna-Dolphin Six-Weeks Rodeo begins June 20 - July 31 at Pirate's Cove Yacht Club, 473-3906.

July - Fireworks displays at several locations on the Outer Banks

Independence Day Parade in Ocracoke, 928-6711.

Oscar Mayer/Seamark Children's Tournament at Pirate's Cove Yacht Club. Special Olympics kids invited, 473-3906.

Sand Sculpture Contest, National Park Service Beach in Ocracoke at lifeguard station, 473-2111.

Mid-July - Annual Youth Fishing Tournament, Kill Devil Hills, 441-7251.

Wright Kite Festival, Wright Memorial, 441-4124. Cosponsored by Kitty Hawk Kites and the National Park Service.

August - 19th Annual Senior Adults Craft Fair at Thomas A. Baum Center, Kill Devil Hills, 261-5388.

Virginia Duck Unlimited Billfish Release Tournament, 473-3906.

Wacky Watermelon Weekend and Windsurfing Regatta, 441-6800.

Mid-August - Pirate's Cove Yacht Club Alice Kelly Memorial "Lady Angler" Billfish Tournament, 473-3906.

Pirate's Cove Yacht Club Billfish Tournament, 473-3906.

Observance of National Aviation Day, Wright Memorial, 441-3761.

New World Festival of the Arts, Manteo, 261-3165.

Late August - Carolina/Virginia Offshore Invitational Tournament, Pirate's Cove Yacht Club, 473-3906.

September - Annual Labor Day Arts & Crafts Fair, Ramada Inn, 261-5388.

Eastern Surfing Championships, Buxton, 995-5785.

Pirate's Cove White Marlin Open, 473-3906.

Fall Classic Fishing Tournament, Manns Harbor, 473-5150.

Mid-September - Annual Outer Banks Triathalon, Roanoke Island, 473-2400.

Oregon Inlet Billfish Release Tournament, 441-6301.

Flying Wheels Rollerblade Spectacular at Monteray Shores on the northern Banks, 441-4124.

North Beach Sun Trash Festival, Operation Beach Sweep and afternoon festival in Duck, 441-8288.

October - Wildfoods Weekend, Manteo (N.C. Aquarium), 473-3494.

Nags Head Surf Fishing Club Invitational Tournament, 441-7251.

Outer Banks Stunt Kite Competition, Jockey's Ridge, 441-4124.

Pirate's Cove King Mackerel & Bluefish Tournament, Pirate's Cove Yacht Club, 473-3906.

Early November - Cape Hatteras Anglers Club Invitational Surf Fishing, 995-4253.

Rock Fish Tournament, Manns Harbor, 473-5150.

Late November - Annual Christmas Arts & Crafts Fair, Ramada Inn. 261-5388.

Thanksgiving Windsurfing Regatta, Windmill Point in Nags Head, 441-6800.

December - Christmas Parade & Christmas on The Waterfront, Manteo, 473-2774.

Outer Banks Hotline's Annual Festival of Trees, at the Ramada Inn.

NC Aquarium/Roanoke Island Christmas Open House, 473-3494.

Elizabeth II Christmas Open House, tours by costumed guides, 441-1144.

"Man Will Never Fly Memorial Society" Seminar, 441-7482.

First Flight Commemoration at Wright Memorial, 441-3761.

PERFORMING ARTS

Within the past year the performing arts have provided a series of events for cultural appreciation. Two groups, Outer Banks Forum and The Dare Players, have presented plays and musicals using local talent and outside performers and troupes. Cultural events are held monthly during the off season. Interest continues to grow and events are planned in cooperation with the Dare County Arts Council.

DARE COUNTY ARTS COUNCIL
Manteo, 473-2774

This ever-expanding organization recognizes the importance of artists and their work all over the Outer

Banks. Although based in Manteo, the Arts Council has regular events throughout the year in various locations such as Nags Head and Kitty Hawk. This year, the annual Frank Stick Memorial Art Show was held and drew record crowds. It has become the social and cultural event of the year for residents of the Outer Banks, held each year in February.

This year marked the initial start-up of the Dare County Arts Council Writers' Group. Member of the Group held a evening of reading, in conjunction with the Frank Stick Memorial Art Show. Both were February events, held at Glenn Eure's Ghost Fleet Gallery in Nags Head.

OUTER BANKS FORUM

Based in Kitty Hawk, 261-2064, the organization promotes several events during the year and others in conjunction with the Dare County Arts Council.

THEATRE OF DARE

A new group of performing artists whose two performances this year serve notice to those looking for cultural pursuits either as spectators or performers. Call Pay Clayton, 441-6124 for information.

THE LOST COLONY
Manteo, 473-3414

A continuing outdoor drama, written by Paul Green and performed during the summer only, at an outdoor theatre, Waterside Theatre, on the grounds adjacent to the Fort Raleigh National Historic Site on Roanoke Island. The Lost Colony was reviewed in the section on Attractions, Roanoke Island.

ART GALLERIES
OF THE OUTER BANKS

John de la Vega Gallery, Corolla Village, 261-4964

Duck Blind Ltd., Duck Village, 261-2009

Marine Model Gallery, Duck Waterfront Shops, 261-5977

Morales Art Gallery, Scarborough Faire, 261-7190

Wooden Feather, Seagate North, Kill Devil Hills, 480-3066

Port O'Call Res. & Gallery, Kill Devil Hills, Beach Rd. 441-8001

Glenn Eure's Ghost Fleet Gallery, Driftwood St., Nags Head, 441-6584

Morales Art Gallery, Gallery Row, Nags Head, 441-6484

Terra Cotta Gallery, Driftwood St., Nags Head, 480-2323

Jewelry by Gail, Driftwood St., Nags Head, 441-5387

Greenleaf Gallery, Bypass, Nags Head, 480-3555

Seaside Art Gallery, Beach Rd., Nags Head, 441-5418

Island Art Gallery, Christmas Shop, Main Rd., Manteo, 473-2838

Island Trading Co., Waterfront, Manteo, 473-3365

Brownings Artworks, NC 12, Buxton, 995-5538

Village Craftsmen, Howard St., Ocracoke, 928-5541

Inside
Portsmouth Island

*S*outhwest of Ocracoke

It's deserted now, except for its "ghosts" in Park Service uniforms. Empty. If you've never had that eerie feeling...then maybe you'll want to take the trip that most Banks visitors never make, to quiet, roadless, unpopulated Portsmouth Island.

It wasn't always that way. Portsmouth, which was a "planned community" authorized by the Colonial Assembly in 1753, was for many years the largest (actually, the only) town on the Banks. The slow changes of geology and economics have left it behind, however, and now it is no more. Will New York go the same way?

There is no bridge to Portsmouth from Ocracoke. There isn't even a vehicle ferry. The only way to get there, unless you brought a boat with you, is to make an arrangement with one of the authorized licensed operators in Ocracoke. They are: Dave McLawhorn (928-5921) and Rudy and Junius Austin, 928-4361/4281. You can contact them or the NPS for rate and schedule information; you'll probably pay between ten and forty dollars depending on how many are in your party.

As you cross the inlet, if you decide to go, reflect on the fact that this was once the channel for much of the trade of Virginia and North Carolina. You see, throughout the 1700s and up to the mid-nineteenth century, Ocracoke channel was deeper than it is now. And of course ships were of shallower draft then, too. Seagoing ships could enter the inlet, moor or anchor near the southwest side, and offload their cargo into smaller coasters. Then these took it up the sound to such early ports as New Bern and Bath. Portsmouth Village was established to facilitate this trade by providing piers, warehouses, other port facilities and labor.

The new town grew rapidly. The British raided Portsmouth during the Revolutionary War; a steady flow of supplies moved through it to General Washington's embattled armies. The British captured the town again during the War of 1812, but this again was only a temporary interruption and the town continued to grow. At its peak, just before the Civil War, it handled over 1,400 ships a year and had a total population of almost 600 — no Boston, but definitely the largest town on the outer islands.

Two things doomed Portsmouth: war and weather. In September of 1846, a terrific storm had opened two new inlets (named Hatteras and Oregon), and these gradually deepened as Ocracoke Inlet began to shoal. The Federals didn't help matters by sinking several ships laden with rock in Ocracoke channel, but war merely hastened Portsmouth's end. Such seagoing traffic as was left to the Banks shifted to Hatteras Inlet, and the backcountry trade was carried more and more by the new railroads. After that it was a question only of time. Few villagers returned after the war ended, even when a fish-processing plant was built, and the population steadily declined. Its last male resident, Henry Piggott, died in 1971, and with that Portsmouth's last two residents, Elma Dixon and Marian Babb, finally left.

Except for a single family National Park Service volunteer caretakers who spend much of the year there, only mosquitoes inhabit the village. Portsmouth Island now belongs to the Cape Lookout National Seashore, and stabilization and preservation of the town is underway.

As you debark, at a newly-built dock at Haulover Point, you'll be able to look over the harbor from whence wharves, warehouses and lighters once served the merchant ships anchored inside the Inlet. For a short tour, proceed southeast down the road. The first house on the right is the Salter-Dixon House, built around 1900. Part of this house is open as a visitor center, regularly in the summer months and

intermittently in the spring and fall. Displays and more information, as well as restrooms and drinking water, are available inside. Down the main road you'll see a fence on the right and then a collapsed house. This is the Henry Babb house, built before 1875.

The small white building south of the Salter-Dixon house is the former Post Office. This was more or less the center of the village in its day. About forty yards west of it is the community cemetery, the largest in the village, with about 40 graves.

From the crossroads, follow the footpath south across the marsh to the former schoolhouse. Miss Mary Dixon taught classes in this one-room building until 1947. Now go back to the Post Office and proceed down the main road eastward. If you stop on the first little bridge and look to the north across the creek you will see a (now) yellow-painted cottage formerly owned by Henry Piggott, mentioned above. Continue across the second little bridge. To your left you will now see the Methodist Church. You may go in. (There used to be a collection plate for the public to leave donations to aid the Park Service in the upkeep of the church, but the plate was removed because its use conflicts with Federal regulations regarding the safeguarding of public funds.) The rope operating the church bell, formerly functional, has been disconnected due to excessive use. Do not try to play the organ either. Behind the church is the Babb, Dixon plot where Mr. Piggott is buried.

Continuing east from the church, beyond the last houses you'll enter a stretch of open road. Beyond this lies the landing strip, the old Coast Guard station, watch tower and out-buildings. Surf rescue boats were kept in the large building, as at Chicamacomico. The station was closed in 1937, though it was briefly reactivated for WWII.

About a hundred meters south of the station is the cistern of the old marine hospital, which was built in 1846 to serve sick and/or quarantined seamen. The Park Service has cut back the vegetation that threatened at one point to overwhelm it. The hospital proper burned down in 1894 and was not replaced.

To get to the Atlantic beach and the Wallace Channel Dock, walk on past the station; it's about another mile. If a northerly wind is blowing, there may be a few inches of water to wade through on the way.

A few notes of caution are in order. Prepare for mosquitoes in the summer. There's no mosquito control any more on the island and they get fierce. (Imagine what it was like living here before window screens and insect repellant were invented.) Wear sun-screen, too. Don't go inside any of the buildings other than the Salter-Dixon house and the church. They belong to the Park Service and are off-limits.

A note to fishermen: Portsmouth Island has great surf fishing, and you don't have to share it with a million other people. Don Morris, in Atlantic, N.C., has a car ferry that can take a limited number of four wheel drive vehicles over. He's at (919)225-4261. NPS permits are required for all vehicles on Cape Lookout and Portsmouth Island; as of this writing they are free and available from the concessionaire and from any Cape Lookout Ranger Station.

Nearby
Attractions

MERCHANTS MILLPOND
STATE PARK

Gatesville, NC 357-1191

Located off Route 158, NC 32 and NC 37, this state park is approximately 30 miles from Elizabeth City and Suffolk, Virginia. It is one of North Carolina's rarest ecological communities. Overnight tent camping is available and campsites contain a picnic table and grill. Drinking water and washhouse facilities are available. Primitive camping facilities include a canoe-in campground for fishermen. Reserve in advance during the spring, summer and fall. Canoes can be rented for use in the millpond and Lassiter Swamp.

Fishing is a popular activity and the millpond has largemouth bass, blue-gill, chain pickerel and black crappie just waiting to bite your hook. A NC fishing license is required. Hiking, photography, picnicking and nature study are popular activities as well.

We discovered the beautiful 2700-acre state park on a side trip to the Dismal Swamp. Actually, the Dismal Swamp we observed from Highway 17 is a minor natural wonder compared to Merchants Millpond State Park. The Dismal Swamp canals along the road are picturesque and provide shaded picnic areas. On the other side, off Hwy. 32, there are no signs directing one to the Great Dismal Swamp. Only when we stopped in Sunbury were we told that the Dismal Swamp is all but dried up -- the same as the Florida Everglades -- and that the Millpond State Park canoe area provides a more in-depth study of a swamp. We discovered helpful, friendly people on our day-long "safari," but that's another story in itself. North Carolinians are easy-going and hospitable wherever we meet!

Towering bald cypress and tu-pelo gum trees draped in Spanish moss dominate the 760-acre millpond. At its upper end is Lassiter Swamp, an ecological wonderland containing remnants of an ancient bald cypress forest and the eerie "enchanted forest" of tupelo gum whose trunks and branches have been distorted into fantastic shapes by mistletoe.

Over 190 species of birds have been recorded in the park. Spring and fall bring migrations of warblers and other species. In winter, a variety of waterfowl stop by on their journey south. Reptiles, amphibians and mammals such as beaver, mink and river otter make their homes in the park. We observed a great blue heron standing in the shallow water near the dock. Later a beautiful mallard duck glided over to observe us enjoying a picnic.

There is sufficient warning about

ticks and other pests that infest the woods. Proper clothing and hats are recommended, in addition to careful inspection after a trek through this beautiful habitat. On a breezy spring day, we observed several people launch their canoes and kayaks loaded with camping gear and supplies for a weekend of camping in one of the canoe-in camp sites.

An outstanding state park close to the Outer Banks, it is worth the almost 2-hour drive to reach, especially for veteran campers, boaters and anglers who enjoy getting away from everything man-made to a truly beautiful environment.

MUSEUM OF THE ALBEMARLE
Elizabeth City, NC   335-1453

This museum is a part of the North Carolina Archives and History and reflects the story of the people who have lived in the Albemarle region, from the native American tribes to early English-speaking colonists, adventurers, farmers and fishermen. The interpretive exhibits change occasionally, but a variety of handmade quilts and other crafts, carved waterfowl, early farming equipment and English porcelain figurines allows a look-back in time to the days when early Virginia settlers began making their way to the Carolinas.

The geography of the region is displayed by maps. The history of the people and their livelihoods is depicted in the array of tools and equipment used in early times. There are guided tours, lectures and audiovisual programs available for groups or individuals. There is also a small gift shop on the premises.

Admission is free, is accessible for the handicapped and is open Tuesday through Saturday, 9:00 a.m. till 5:00 p.m. and Sunday, 2:00 p.m. till 5:00 p.m. Closed Mondays and holidays. Call for program reservations or inquiries.

To reach the Museum of the Albemarle drive north from Kitty Hawk on Route 158 through Camden, across the Pasquotank River and through Elizabeth City to Route 17 south. It's located a few miles west of the city on the right side of the road. Distance from Kitty Hawk is about 47 miles.

THE NEWBOLD-WHITE HOUSE
Hertford, NC   **426-7567**

As you leave Elizabeth City and drive southwest towards Hertford and Edenton, on Route 17, follow the signs to the Newbold-White House. You'll turn left at a large intersection in Hertford (State Route 1336). The distance from Kitty Hawk is about 60 miles.

The Newbold-White House sits back off the road about one mile and on the left. This late 17-century house was built by Joseph and Mary Scott who were Quakers. He became a magistrate and legislator. In colonial times, permanent settlers came from Virginia by way of the Perquimans River to a territory which became known as the Carolinas. This house is the first one in North Carolina.

Scott patented over 600 acres on the river banks and was believed to have built this house about 1685. (The Newbold-White family later owned it.) Tobacco farming was the primary work here. The use of tobacco as a form of payment (cash) was prevalent during the late years of the 17th century. Many years later cotton and peanuts were farmed.

A tour of the restored home is worth your while. It features large fireplaces with great wooden lintels, pine woodwork and a winding corner staircase. The leaded casement windows with diamond-shaped glass panes were restored with authentic glass made in Germany, copying a piece of glass found on the premises before the start of restoration several years ago. The bricks were handmade and laid in original English bond on the lower portion of the house and Flemish bond higher up. The history behind the use of the house as a public meeting place represents the formative years of the proprietary government and courts of North Carolina. The Visitor Center offers an audio-visual journey to those times and a look at how life was lived. The house is open March 1 till December 22, 10:00 a.m. till 4:30 p.m. Admission is $2.00.

HISTORIC HERTFORD

The older part of Hertford lies to the right of the intersection of Route 17 and State Route 1336. Hertford is one of the oldest towns in North Carolina and was incorporated in 1758, primarily to serve as the county seat and commercial center for Perquimans County.

About fifty 19th-century buildings stand on the tree-lined streets of the downtown. These magnificent homes and yards recreate a sense of the early life of people who lived by farming, fishing, lumbering and later cloth manufacturing. Drive time from Kitty Hawk is about an hour.

ALBEMARLE PLANTATION
Hertford, North Carolina
426-5555 or 1-800-535-0704

Albemarle Plantation is not the name of an 18th- or 19th-century home or plantation but is a golfing and boating community whose golf course is open to the public. A marina and clubhouse are under construction. For now, however, the Dan Maples golf links which opened several years ago, is the sporting challenge here. It's our understanding that the course is in great shape and offers an option to those who enjoy the sport while they're on vacation. While we're not advertising the real estate sales, the golf course is close enough to the Outer Banks to mention. For tee-times call the toll-free number. Follow Route 17 from Elizabeth City to Hertford. Drive time from Kitty Hawk is just over an hour.

HISTORIC EDENTON

One of the oldest towns in America, Edenton was settled about 1660 along the shores of Edenton Bay and Albemarle Sound. To reach Edenton, continue on Route 17 from Hertford. Edenton is in Chowan County, one of the first four counties of North Carolina (Perquimans, Pasquotank, and Currituck are the other three).

Edenton had its own Tea Party in 1774 and fifty-one women gathered at the home of Mrs. Elizabeth King and vowed to support the American cause. The town is quaint and steeped in history. The aforementioned discovery about the Edenton Tea Party encouraged a closer look!

A journey through the history of the town reveals the restored homes of several prominent North Carolinians. James Iredell served as Attorney General during the Revolution and was a Justice of the Supreme Court from 1790-1799. Samuel Johnston was a government leader and Senator during Revolutionary times. Dr. Hugh Williamson signed the Constitution; Joseph Hewed signed the Declaration of Independence. Thomas Barker was a North Carolina agent to England and a reputed leader of the Edenton Tea Party.

The Chowan County Courthouse, the Barker House, St. Paul's Episcopal Church and Iredell House are just a few of the area's 18th-century buildings, representing the finest in colonial architecture. A walk along King Street will reveal a remarkable collection of Georgian, Federal and Greek revival homes nestled among gardens and trees.

Edenton was a prosperous port town, and between 1771 and 1776 over 800 ships served business and commerce with links to Europe and the West Indies. Blackbeard the pirate sailed into Edenton Bay on numerous occasions.

Barker House serves as a Visitor Center. Guided tours of the town begin at Barker House on Edenton Bay. An audio-visual presentation is available here as well. Hours are Monday through Saturday from 10:00 a.m. till 4:30 p.m. November through May; from 9:00 a.m. till 4:30 p.m. June through October. On Sundays from 2:00 p.m. till 5:00 p.m. all year. For group tour reservations and further information, call 482-2637.

There are a number of fine restaurants and bed and breakfast accommodations in Edenton.

Caroline's opens early with homemade breads, pastries and rolls in addition to traditional breakfast. Boswell's is known for its fine seafood and ethnic creations. Bob and Sharon's Bar-be-que on Route 32 is an attractive cafe with good eats.

The Lords Proprietors' Inn, 482-3641, Granville Queen Inn, 482-5296 and The Governor Eden Inn, 482-2072 are very good choices for accommodations. All are beautifully-restored and maintained older homes that operate as bed-and-breakfast type inns. Call for rates and reservations.

Edenton can be reached from Roanoke Island and Manteo via Route 64/264 by driving 40 miles west until you come to Route 32 which will take you, after a right turn, toward Edenton just follow the signs from there.

MULBERRY HILL PLANTATION

Edenton   **482-8077**

Mulberry Hill Plantation is off Route 32, approximately 8 miles from Edenton. Tom and Janie Wood have restored the house, which was built around 1800, and welcome guests who appreciate the simplicity of a bed and breakfast. Most of the acreage of the original plantation is being developed

as golf course-homesites, but when you drive through the small gate to this grand old home, the spacious lawn and mature trees take you back in time. The view of Albemarle Sound is magnificent. There are four guest rooms and three baths. A plantation breakfast is served. Golf and tennis privileges are available to guests. If you're looking for a place away from it all, try Mulberry Hill Plantation. Weddings and other social occasions are sometimes held here. Call for rates and reservations.

HOPE PLANTATION

Windsor, NC   **794-3140**

Hope Plantation depicts the rural domestic life in the 18th and 19th centuries in northeastern North Carolina. Both the King-Bazemore House (1763) and Hope Plantation (c. 1803) are prime examples of a style of architecture combining the details of medieval English and Georgian periods.

The furnishings are from the inventories of the original estates. Some date from the first quarter of the 18th-century.

David Stone, an outstanding North Carolina citizen during the Federal period, owned over 5,000 acres here, many of them devoted to farming. There was a grist mill, saw mill, blacksmith shop and a spinning and weaving room, making the plantation self-sufficient. In his day, Stone was a delegate to the 1789 Constitutional Convention, an attorney, a Superior Court justice and a trustee of the University of North Carolina. He was elected seven times to the North Carolina House of Commons and twice to the House of Representatives of the US Congress. He served two terms as Governor of the State and two terms as a US Senator.

The 1763 King-Bazemore House was built on this site by William King. It was purchased by the Reverend Stephen Bazemore in 1840. His descendants donated it to the Historic Hope Foundation, Inc. in 1974.

Additional reconstruction continues at Hope Plantation to restore out-buildings and gardens. Research continues to reveal important information about this period and this plantation.

SOMERSET PLACE

Pettigrew State Park   797-4560

We don't know who wrote the site press release, but its opening paragraph is worth quoting: "Passion, splendor and grim reality are all found in the epic story of Lake Phelps and the vast plantations carved from the haunting and mysterious coastal swamps on its banks by two extraordinary families. Here among majestic cypress and sycamore trees stands the elegant early nineteenth century home of Josiah Collins, III that once hosted the cultivated elite of North Carolina's planter aristocracy. Nearby, beneath sheltering limbs of great oaks, Charles Pettigrew, the state's first Episcopal bishop-elect, his congressman son and Confederate brigadier general grandson lie in eternal slumber beside rich, fertile farmland wrested from primeval nature by that potent combination of African slave labor and English immigrant ambition that has become the most enduring symbol of the `Old

South.'"

That's a hard act to follow, but let's try. The plantation was one of the four biggest in North Carolina, with over 300 slaves growing corn and rice. The mansion, a 2 1/2-story frame building with fourteen rooms, was built in Greek Revival style circa 1830. It has been fully restored, with period furnishings. Six original outbuildings remain. The lawns and gardens alongside nearby Phelps Lake are especially beautiful in summer. A historically important collection of the plantations's slave records is open for genealogical research. A state historic site now, Somerset Place is open on the following schedule. April to October, Monday through Saturday 9 to 5 and Sunday 1 to 5. November to March, Tuesday through Saturday 10 to 4, Sunday 1 to 4, closed Mondays. Admission is free, but groups planning to visit should write Box 215, Creswell, NC, 27928 to make reservations. To reach it take Rt. 64/264 west across the Croatan Sound from Manteo and follow it west for about 40 miles. Turn left at the little town of Creswell and another five miles will bring you to Pettigrew State Park and Somerset Place.

CAPE LOOKOUT NATIONAL SEASHORE

Low, unpopulated, almost forgotten even by North Carolinians, more barrier islands stretch southwestward for 55 miles from Ocracoke Inlet. North Core Banks with Portsmouth Village, South Core Banks and Cape Lookout, and Shackleford Banks were incorporated into the Cape Lookout National Seashore in 1966.

These low, sandy islands have been untouched by either development or by stabilization. (Remember that the Outer Banks were stabilized by the CCC in the 1930s with dunes and plantings.) As a relatively recent NPS acquisition, and a remote one, there are relatively few facilities available for the visitor. But if you don't mind roughing it a little bit (deer ticks, chiggers, deerflies, mosquitoes, gnats, squalls, hurricanes, rip currents, sharks, and jellyfish), these islands are a great place for primitive camping, fishing, boating and bird watching. A no-kidder: gnats may annoy you, but really stay alert for storms, as there is little shelter on most of these islands. You can call Coast Guard weather at 726-7550 for a forecast before you leave the mainland. Here's some helpful information for you "naturalists":

1) Two concessions operate out of Davis and Atlantic, NC, offering primitive cabins for overnight lodging.

2) There are no established campgrounds but primitive (back pack style) camping is allowed.

3) There are no paved roads but 4-wheel drive vehicles can operate on the beach front.

4) Water is available from pitcher pumps in the Cape Point area.

At Cape Lookout itself are located the lighthouse, erected in 1859, and a small Coast Guard Station, no longer active.

Access: if you have your own boat, you will find launching ramps at marinas throughout Carteret County, though the easiest access to Cape Point is from Shell Point on Harkers Island. Concession ferry services (privately

run, federally overseen) are available from Harkers Island to the Cape Lookout Light area, from Davis to Shingle Point, from Atlantic to an area north of Drum Inlet, and from Ocracoke to Portsmouth Village. For current rates and more information, write or call the Park Service, Cape Lookout National Seashore, 3601 Bridges Street, Suite F, Morehead City, NC 28557-2913; (919) 240-1409 or Harkers Island Station, (919) 728-2250.

For complete information about the Cape Lookout area, get a copy of *The Insiders' Guide to the Crystal Coast and New Bern*, available through bookstores or through our handy order form in the back of this book.

HOPE PLANTATION
Windsor, NC   794-3140

Hope Plantation began as a grant from the Lord Proprietors of the Carolina Colony to the Hobson family in the 1720s. David Stone, a delegate to the North Carolina Constitutional Convention of 1789 and later judge, representative, senator, and governor (1808 - 1810), built an impressive home on the site circa 1800. The Hope Mansion is an outstanding Federal Period residence and is reminiscent in some ways of Monticello and in other ways of Scarlett O'Hara's Tara. Historic Hope Foundation acquired the mansion and land in 1966. Now restored, it and two smaller houses (the King-Bazemore and the Samuel Cox Houses) are open to the public as a furnished house-museum. There are also restored 18th century gardens. Hope is on the National Register of Historic Places.

Hope Plantation is outside of

the town of Windsor, roughly a two hour drive west of Manteo. Take 64 out of Roanoke Island west to its intersection with 13; go north on 13; Hope is on NC 308 four miles west of US 13 bypass. Open March 1 through December 23, Mondays through Saturdays; holiday Mondays 10 a.m. to 4 p.m.; Sundays 2 p.m. to 5 p.m. Closed January and February. Adult admission is $5 for all three houses. Picnic facilities are available.✍

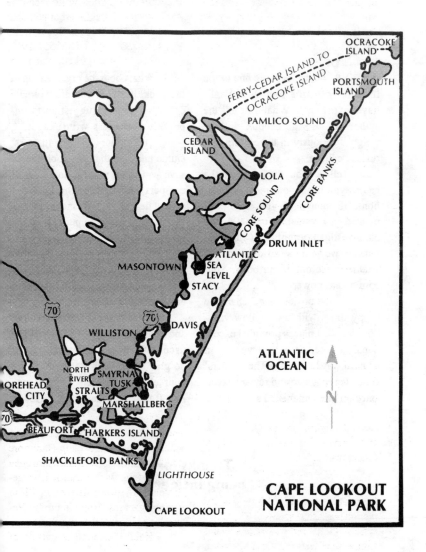

Be An Insider!

You can become one of the Insiders by sharing your Outer Banks travel experience. What you tell the authors of this guidebook will be weighed seriously in the editing of a revised edition.

Tell us about the good and the bad as you follow our recommendations. If enough of you are disappointed in a restaurant or motel, and our investigation confirms your experiences, we promise to drop the offending place out of our book. Your opinion has power.

On the positive side, share the happy times with your fellow vacationers. What places provided exceptional service, or helped you in an unusual way? Let's use The Insiders' Guide to recognize and reward excellence on The Outer Banks.

What about the organization of the book, itself? If you discovered a defect, or have a suggestion to improve its usefulness, write us about it.

The authors of The Insiders' Guide intended that this book should save you time, money, and a lot of exasperation and frustration. We travel a great deal ourselves, and in making this book, we tried to put in it all the things that we would want to know if we came to your city or town. Now that you've used our book, help us to refine it and make it serve you better on your return visit.

Share your experiences with us and become one of the Insiders. Write us collectively, or as individuals. We'll be grateful to hear from you. Send your letters to: Insiders' Guides, Inc., P.O. Box 2057, Manteo, NC 27954.

Thanks for
being Insiders!

The Insiders' Guides Collection

The Insiders' Guide
to Greater Orlando

Written by
Cynthia Gross & Catharine Coward

Orlando, Florida, is the vacation capital of the South as well as one of the fastest growing areas in the country. This indispensable 702-page guide will tell you everything you'll want to know about the sunny city and its surrounding neighbors. There's plenty of information on the major attractions, plus facts and insights into other enjoyable sites and activities the area has to offer. Newcomers will feel as if they know the quickly-changing region better with the Insiders' Guide in hand. $12.95

The Insiders' Guide
To North Carolina's
Crystal Coast and New Bern

Written by
Tabbie Nance & Joan Greene

For years, the Crystal Coast area -- Morehead City, Atlantic Beach, Emerald Isle, Beaufort, Salter Path, Down East and other small communities -- have drawn loyal visitors. Now there's a guide book to make those visits even better. The quaint, historical town of New Bern is also included in this 740-page book, as is the town of Havelock, where one of the largest Marine air bases in the country is located. You'll find it an indispensable guide to all the brightest and best this beautiful area has to offer. $12.95.

The Insiders' Guide
to South Hampton Roads

Written by
Nancy Carothers & Sam Martinette

Anyone who has ever been to the Hampton Roads area of Virginia for business, travel, or as a new resident knows that a good guide is not only helpful, it's almost necessary! This guide to Norfolk, Virginia Beach, Suffolk, Portsmouth, and Chesapeake will answer your questions ranging from what the best child care is in the area to where you'll find a great nightspot. You'll also get authoritative information on relocating, the arts, universities, neighborhoods, the media, hospitals, the Chesapeake Bay, sports and recreation, the Military, history of the area, and much, much more. $9.95

The Insiders' Guide
to Williamsburg

Written by
Michael Bruno & Annette McPeters

Another great Insiders' book that helps visitors to this colonial capital city get the most out of their stay.

Written by two insiders, it gives information on accommodations, restaurants, attractions, campgrounds, shopping and more on Williamsburg, Jamestown, and Yorktown. It has been totally rewritten for the 1992 edition. $12.95

The Insiders' Guide to the Triangle

Written by
Katherine Kopp & J. Barlow Herget

Whether you are planning a vacation, a business trip, or to relocate to the Triangle area of North Carolina — Raleigh, Cary, Durham, Chapel Hill, Carrboro, or the Research Triangle Park — this book will be an invaluable companion. It contains over 750 pages, over 80 pages of detailed maps and informative sections on topics such as neighborhoods, schools and child care, shopping, restaurants, accommodations, recreation, arts, colleges and universities, sports, worship, and much more. There's also a major relocation section with information on Realtors and builders, buying a home, and renting. $12.95

The Insiders' Guide To Charlotte

Written by
Robin A. Smith & M.S. Van Hecke

Here's a complete newcomer/ business/visitor's guide to North Carolina's largest city, filled with information on accommodations, neighborhoods, restaurants, shopping, schools, surrounding smaller towns, places of worship, attractions, homes, and more. Informative maps, too. It's the only guide you'll need to get the most out of Charlotte. $12.95

Coming in 1992 & 1993

The Insiders' Guide to Charleston, The Insiders' Guide to Myrtle Beach, and The Insiders' Guide to Virginia's Blue Ridge.

Use our convenient order form on the previous page to add to your collection of Insiders' Guides.✒

ORDER FORM

Use this convenient form to place your order for any of the Insiders' Guides books.

Fast and Simple!

Mail to:
Insiders' Guides, Inc.
P.O. Box 2057
Manteo, NC 27954

or

for VISA or Mastercard orders call
1-800-765-BOOK

Name _____

Address _____

City/State/Zip _____

Quantity	Title/Price	Shipping	Title/Price
	Insiders' Guide to the Triangle, $12.95	$2.50	
	Insiders' Guide to Charlotte, $12.95	$2.50	
	Insiders' Guide to Virginia Beach / Norfolk, $12.95	$2.50	
	Insiders' Guide to the Outer Banks, $12.95	$2.50	
	Insiders' Guide to Williamsburg, $12.95	$2.50	
	Insiders' Guide to Richmond, $12.95	$2.50	
	Insiders' Guide to Orlando, $12.95	$2.50	
	Insiders' Guide to Virginia's Blue Ridge, $12.95	$2.50	
	Insiders' Guide to The Crystal Coast of NC, $12.95	$2.50	
	Insiders' Guide to Myrtle Beach, $12.95 (Summer '93)	$2.50	
	Insiders' Guide to Charleston, $12.95	$2.50	

N.C. residents add 6% sales tax.

GRAND TOTAL

Payment in full (check, cash or money order) must accompany order form. Please allow 2 weeks for delivery

Novels by David Poyer

*I*f you enjoyed *The Insiders' Guide to the Outer Banks*, be warned: Dave Poyer, author of the historical and recreational sections, has almost two million copies of his best sellers in print. Look for:

THE MED

This huge novel of the Navy and Marine Corps in action in the Mediterranean was compared by Publisher's Weekly to *From Here to Eternity*. Poyer's first official best seller, it follows five major characters through a hostage rescue in Cyprus, Syria, and at sea. Stephen Coonts, author of *Flight of the Intruder,* says "David Poyer pulls no punches. *The Med* is an honest, gritty tale of the real Navy. I loved it." Now in paperback from St. Martin's Press.

HATTERAS BLUE

A rubber raft with the bones of three people is unearthed from a sand dune at Cape Hatteras. Shortly thereafter, Lyle "Tiller" Galloway — a salvage diver with a criminal record, the black sheep of a distinguished Coast Guard family — is approached with a lucrative deal. An enigmatic man named Keyes wants to explore the wreck of a U-boat sunk in 1945, two days after the end of WWII. The boat contains a hoard that may make both of them rich. But there's a greater secret still at large after forty years, a plot as treacherous as the currents off the coast of Hatteras. Available from St. Martin's Press, at bookstores on the Banks and everywhere.

THE GULF

Another bestseller in 1990 and in paperback since 1991. The second novel in Poyer's epic cycle of the modern Navy follows Dan Lenson as the executive officer of *USS Turner Van Zandt,* a frigate on convoy duty in the war-torn Persian Gulf. Library Journal: "It is obvious Poyer is an assured and gifted storyteller... He has a talent for the exact descriptive phrase, the telling episode. This is a sure-fire winner, certain to be of lasting interest and importance."

BAHAMAS BLUE

This novel continues the tale of Lyle "Tiller" Galloway of Hatteras, North Carolina. He and Shad Aydlett are trying to go straight. But when their dive shop in Buxton Village is blown up, and *Miss Anna* is sunk at her anchor (with them trapped inside), they decide to find out what kind of job Señor Juan Sebastiano Nunez has for them in the Bahamas. First-rate diving adventure. From St. Martin's Press, July, 1991.

THE CIRCLE

In this, David's latest bestseller, we meet a cast of characters aboard USS *Reynolds Ryan*, an aging destroyer sent to test an experimental sonar in the world's most dangerous seas. Her mission: head north of Iceland, find the worst storms she can -- and stay in them until something gives way.

The dreams and demons that drive her crew, the codes of conduct they keep or violate, the bonds and betrayals that shape their lives and the shared fate of their ship -- Poyer knows these men and traces out their joined destinies.

David has combined these elements into, arguably, the most ambitious sea novel of a generation. From St. Martin's Press, June, 1992. Available in bookstores everywhere.

Index of Advertisers

Index

E

F

TO THE OUTER BANKS
13th EDITION

TO THE OUTER BANKS
13th EDITION

TO THE OUTER BANKS
13th EDITION

$1 OFF

THE INSIDERS' GUIDE

TO
WILLIAMSBURG
(Normally $12.95)

Mail in this coupon to Insiders' Guides, Inc. along with a check or money order for $15.17 ($11.95+$0.72 NC state tax + $2.50 shipping). <u>Be sure to include a return mailing address.</u>

Mail to:
Insiders' Guides, Inc.
P.O. Box 2057
Manteo, NC 27954

$1 OFF

THE INSIDERS' GUIDE

TO
THE OUTER BANKS
(Normally $12.95)

Mail in this coupon to Insiders' Guides, Inc. along with a check or money order for $15.17 ($11.95+$0.72 NC state tax + $2.50 shipping). <u>Be sure to include a return mailing address.</u>

Mail to:
Insiders' Guides, Inc.
P.O. Box 2057
Manteo, NC 27954

$1 OFF

THE INSIDERS' GUIDE

TO
RICHMOND
(Normally $12.95)

Mail in this coupon to Insiders' Guides, Inc. along with a check or money order for $15.17 ($11.95+$0.72 NC state tax + $2.50 shipping). <u>Be sure to include a return mailing address.</u>

Mail to:
Insiders' Guides, Inc.
P.O. Box 2057
Manteo, NC 27954

TO THE OUTER BANKS
13th EDITION

Offer subject to modification by supplier without notice. Exp. 7/4/93

TO THE OUTER BANKS
13th EDITION

Offer subject to modification by supplier without notice. Exp. 7/4/93

TO THE OUTER BANKS
13th EDITION

Offer subject to modification by supplier without notice. Exp. 7/4/93